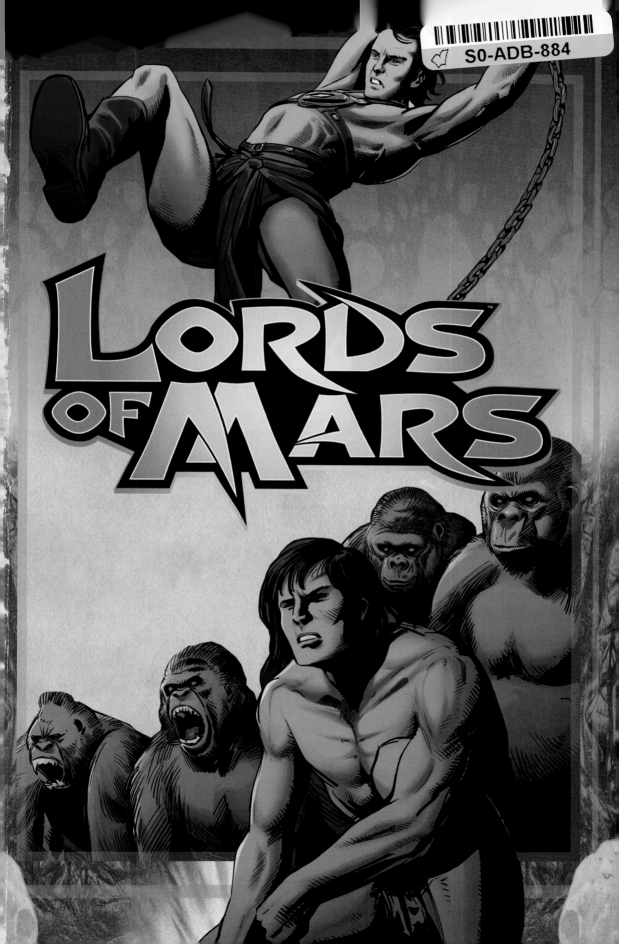

LORDS OF MARS

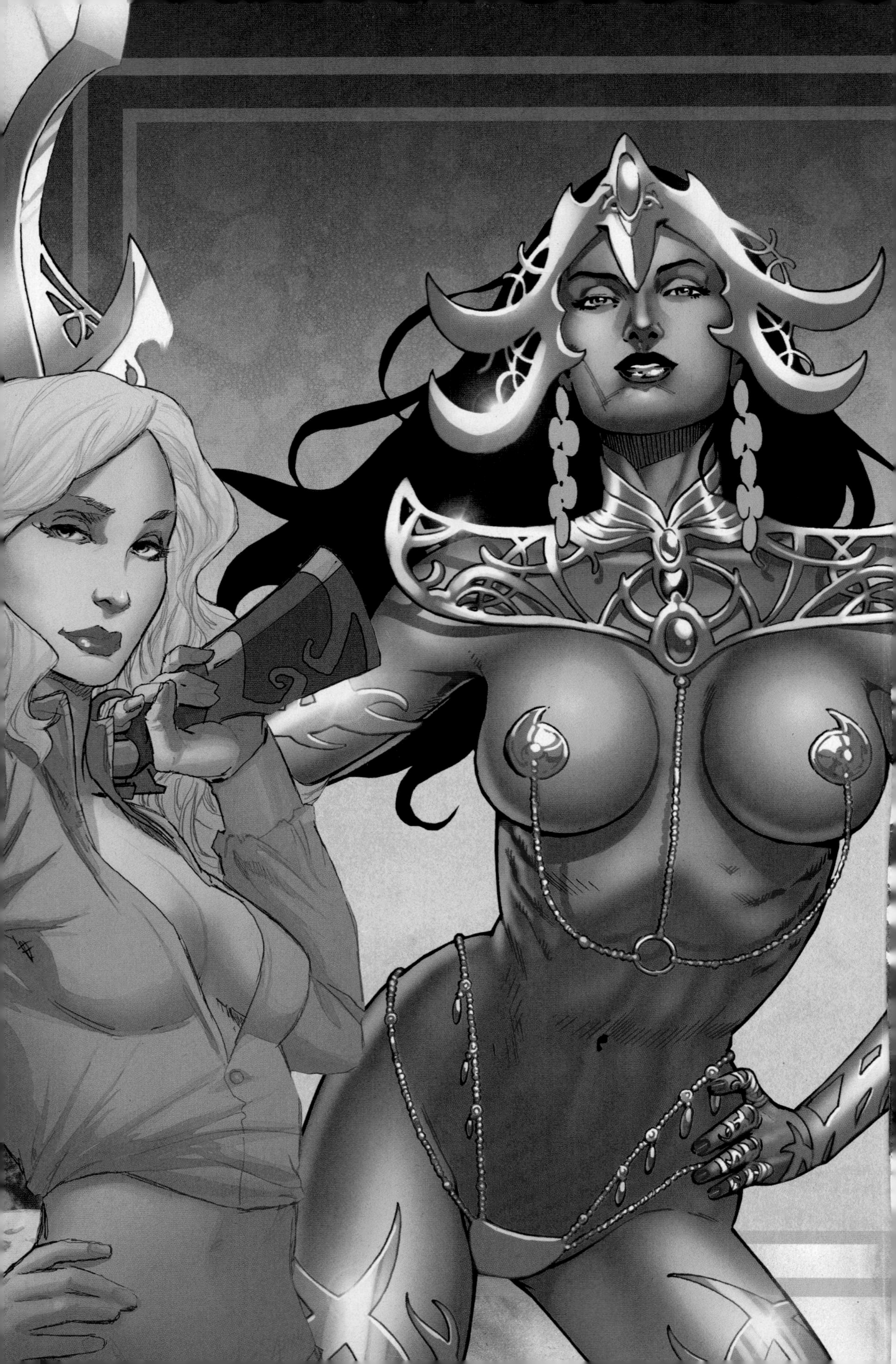

LORDS OF MARS™

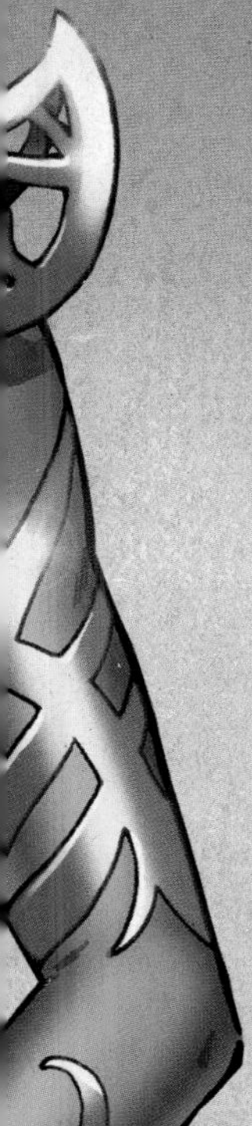

volume one
THE EYE OF THE GODDESS

written by **ARVID NELSON**
illustrated by **ROBERTO CASTRO**
colored by **ALEX GUIMARÃES**
lettered by **MARSHALL DILLON**
collection cover by **ALEX ROSS**
collection design by **KATIE HIDALGO**

based on characters created by
Edgar Rice Burroughs

This volume collects issues 1-6 of
Lords of Mars by Dynamite Entertainment.

DYNAMITE®

Nick Barrucci, CEO / Publisher
Juan Collado, President / COO
Rich Young, Director Business Development
Keith Davidsen, Marketing Manager

Joe Rybandt, Senior Editor
Hannah Gorfinkel, Associate Editor
Josh Green, Traffic Coordinator
Molly Mahan, Assistant Editor

Josh Johnson, Art Director
Jason Ullmeyer, Senior Graphic Designer
Katie Hidalgo, Graphic Designer
Chris Caniano, Production Assistant

Visit us online at **www.DYNAMITE.com**
Follow us on Twitter **@dynamitecomics**
Like us on Facebook **/Dynamitecomics**
Watch us on YouTube **/Dynamitecomics**

This book is not authorized
by Edgar Rice Burroughs, Inc.

ISBN-10: 1-60690-467-1 ISBN-13: 978-1-60690-467-1 First Printing 10 9 8 7 6 5 4 3 2 1

LORDS OF MARS™ VOL. 1: THE EYE OF THE GODDESS. This volume collects material originally published in Lords of Mars #1-6. Published by Dynamite Entertainment. 113 Gaither Dr., STE 205, Mt. Laurel, NJ 08054. **Printed in Canada**

For information regarding press, media rights, foreign rights, licensing, promotions, and advertising e-mail:
marketing@dynamite.com

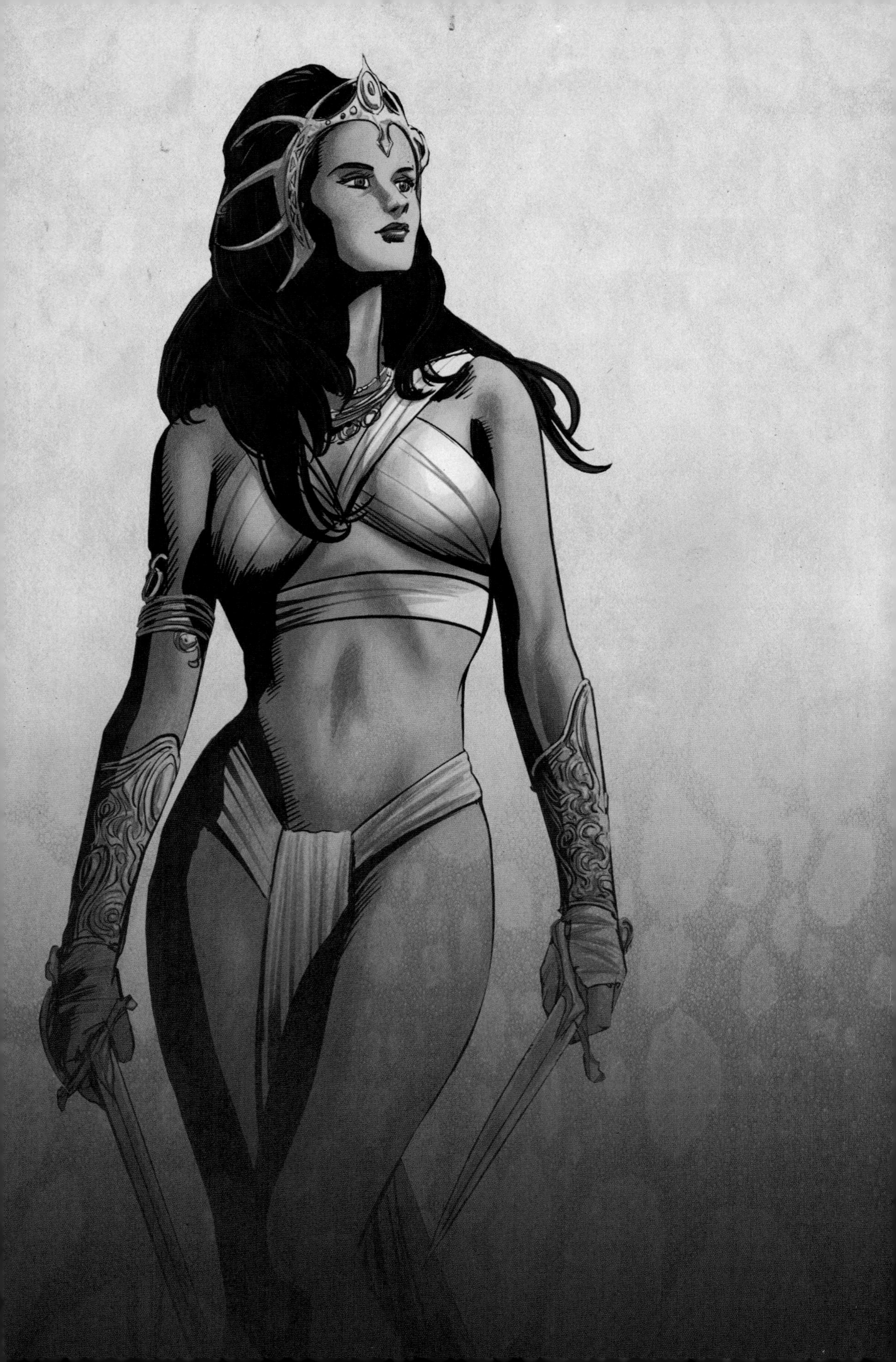

To the Reader of this Work:

In submitting the following tale to you in serialized graphic form, I believe a few words relative to the previous exploits of Captain John Carter, or "Uncle Jack", as I called him, and John Clayton, Viscount of Greystoke, better known as "Tarzan", will be of interest.

John Carter found himself mysteriously transported to Mars while prospecting for gold in Arizona. He has since risen to become the sole monarch, or "Warlord" of the Red Planet, but doing so has earned him many enemies, none so bitter as the white-skinned therns, whose false religion he exposed.

Savage apes raised Tarzan as one of their own in the African jungle. Tarzan developed super-human strength and agility as a matter of pure survival, little knowing he was the heir of the English viscountcy of Greystoke until a group of castaways washed up on the shore of his jungle home. After many travails, Tarzan has claimed his title as Lord Greystoke, and the woman he loves, Jane Porter, now Jane Clayton, his wife.

In retrospect, it seems inevitable that the paths of these remarkable personalities should have crossed, but the circumstances of their meeting, when it finally occurred, were more extraordinary than either man could possibly have predicted, as the reader will soon discover.

Yours very sincerely,
E. R. Burroughs
Croton-on-Hudson, New York
June 6th, 1911

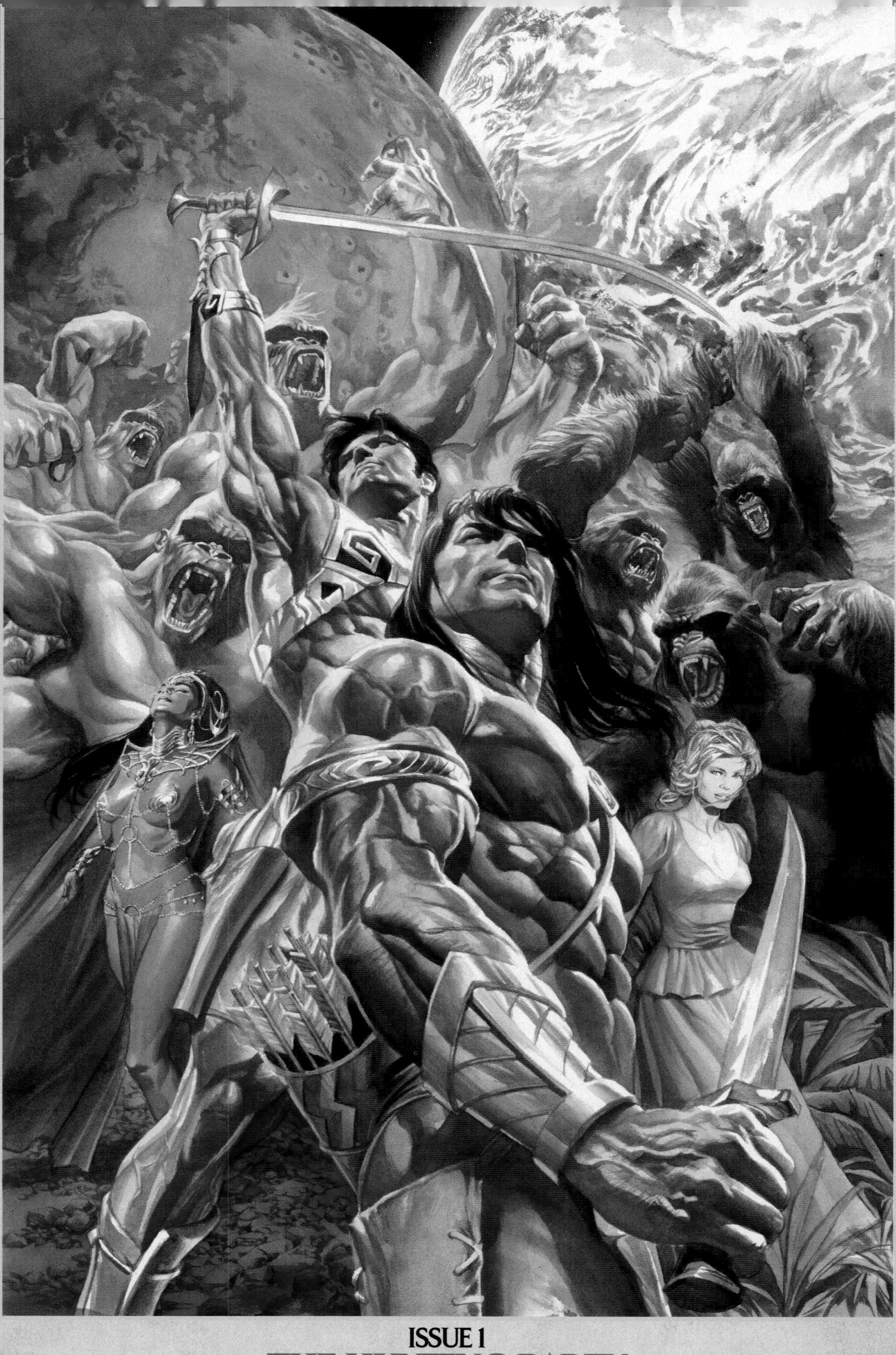

ISSUE 1
THE HUNTING PARTY

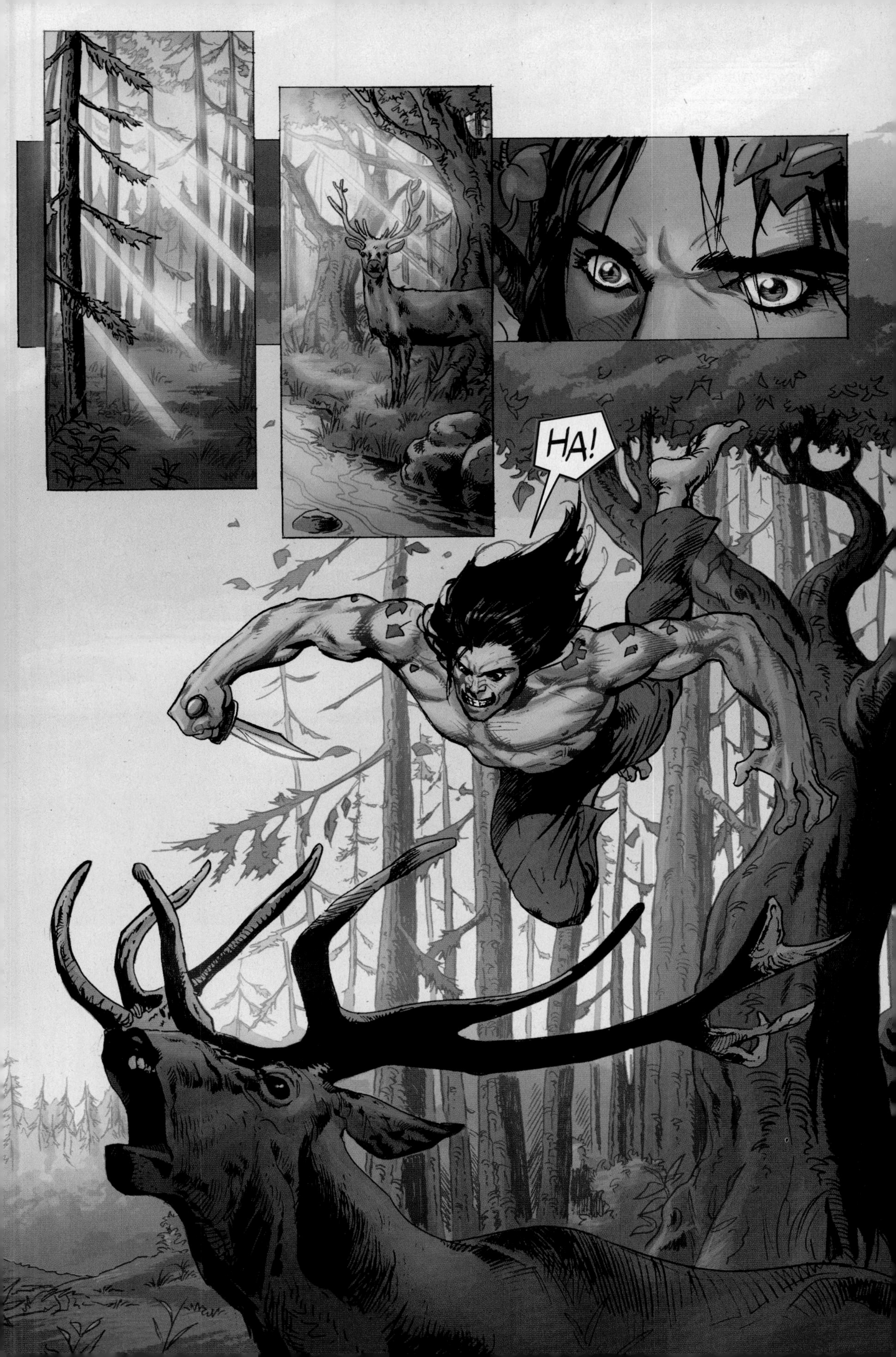
HA!

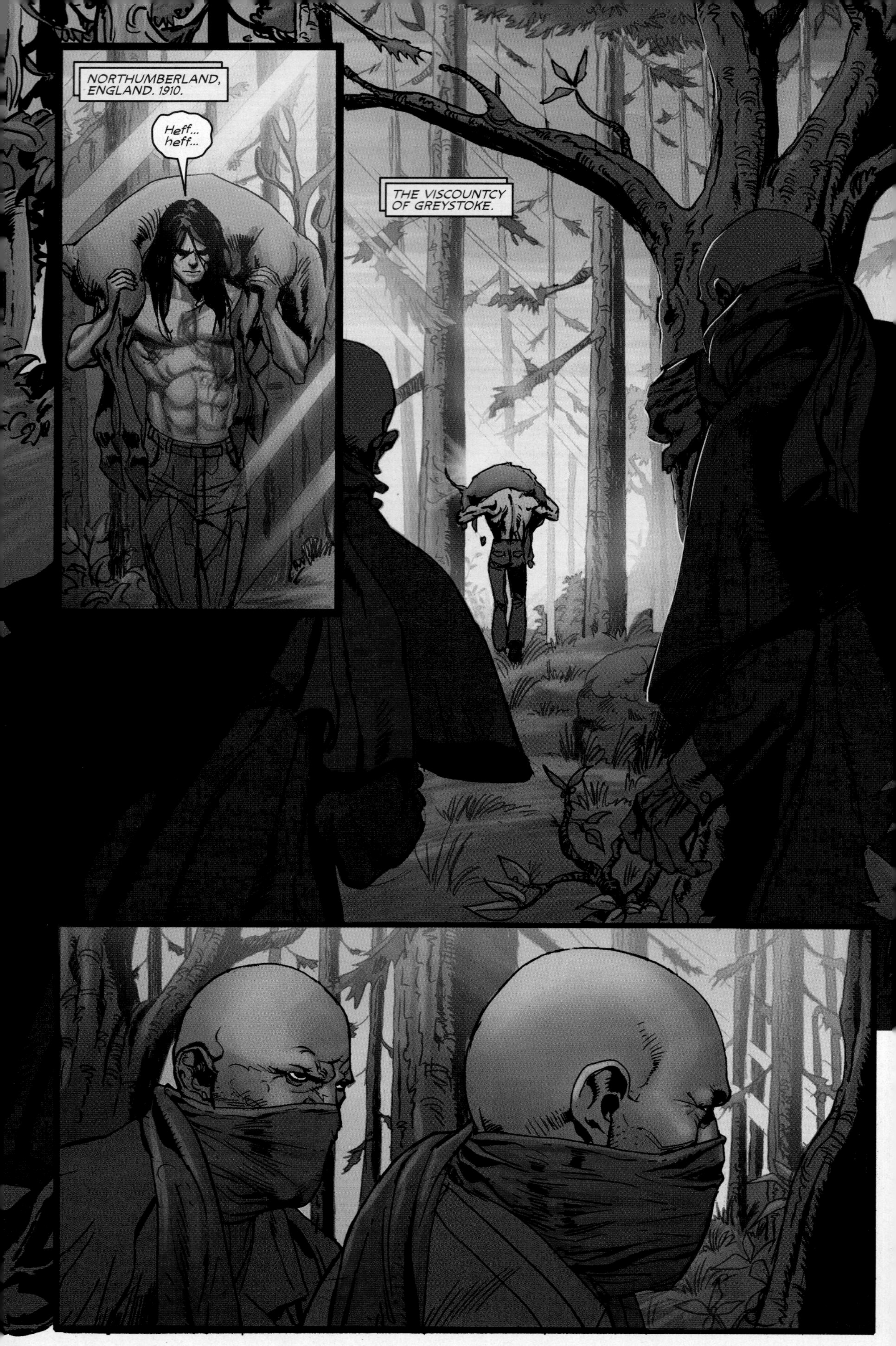
NORTHUMBERLAND, ENGLAND. 1910.
Heff... heff...
THE VISCOUNTCY OF GREYSTOKE.

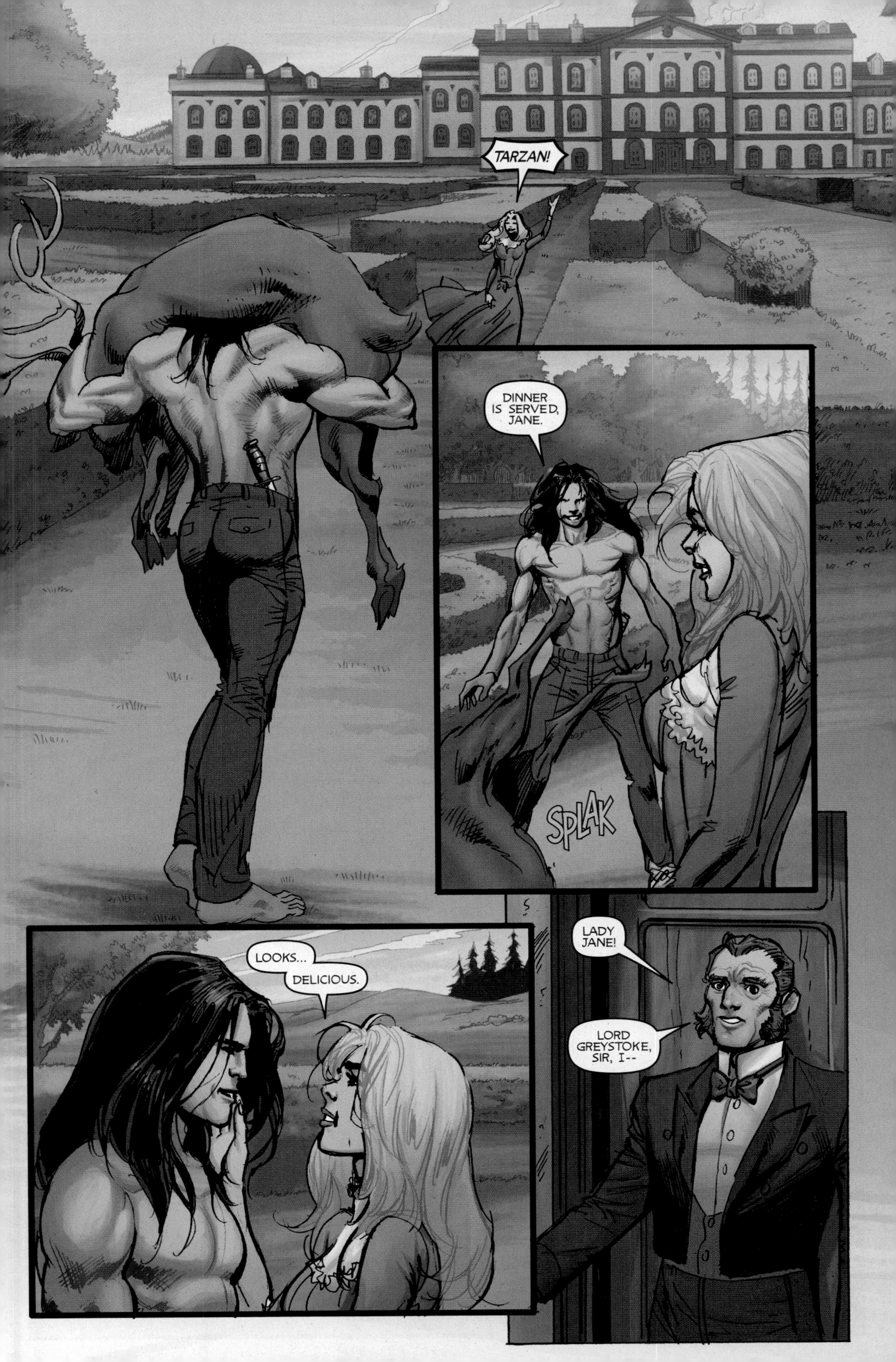
TARZAN!
DINNER IS SERVED, JANE.
SPLAK
LOOKS...
DELICIOUS.
LADY JANE!
LORD GREYSTOKE, SIR, I--

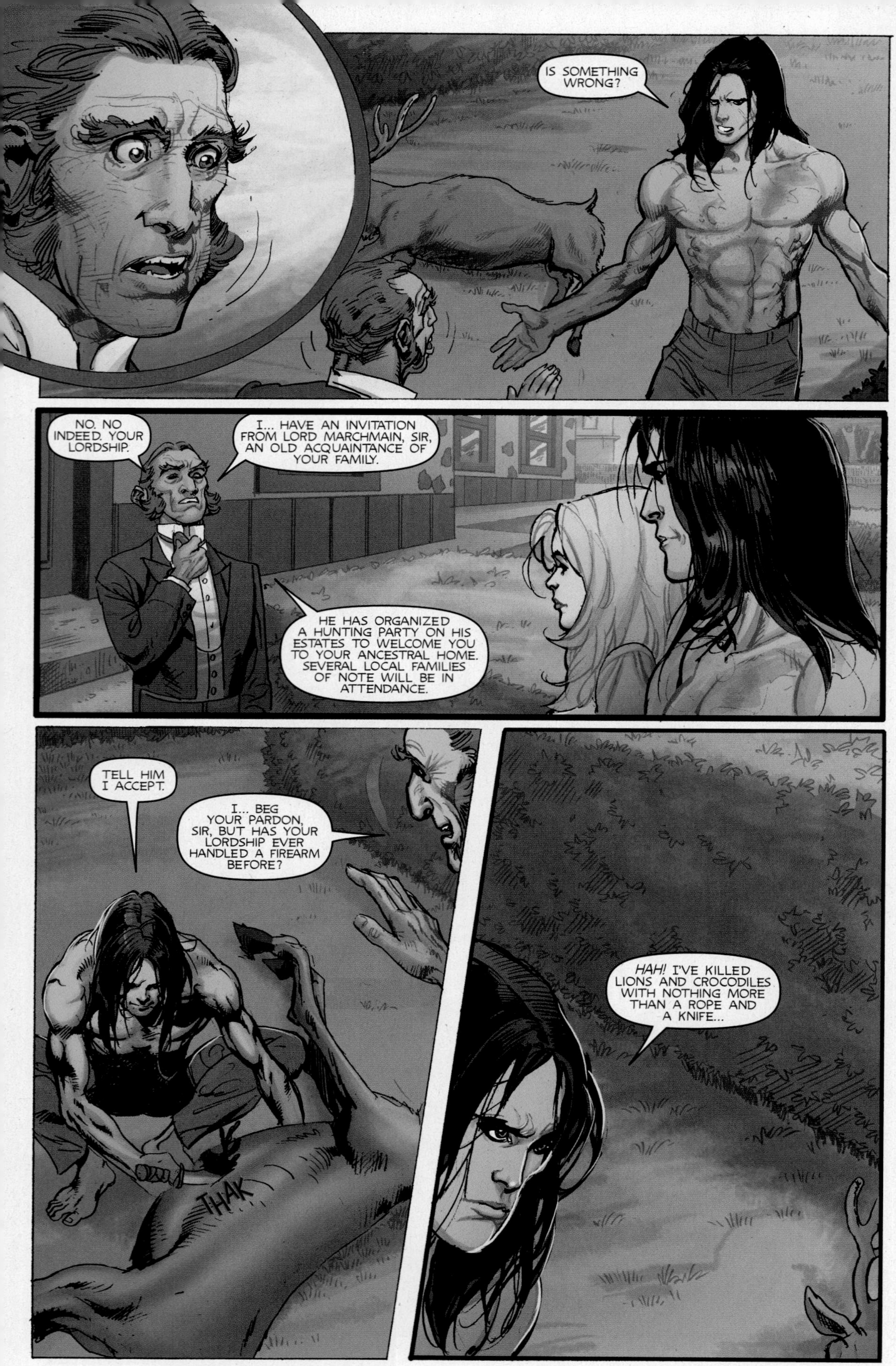
IS SOMETHING WRONG?
NO. NO INDEED. YOUR LORDSHIP.
I... HAVE AN INVITATION FROM LORD MARCHMAIN, SIR, AN OLD ACQUAINTANCE OF YOUR FAMILY.
HE HAS ORGANIZED A HUNTING PARTY ON HIS ESTATES TO WELCOME YOU TO YOUR ANCESTRAL HOME. SEVERAL LOCAL FAMILIES OF NOTE WILL BE IN ATTENDANCE.
TELL HIM I ACCEPT.
I... BEG YOUR PARDON, SIR, BUT HAS YOUR LORDSHIP EVER HANDLED A FIREARM BEFORE?
THAK
HAH! I'VE KILLED LIONS AND CROCODILES WITH NOTHING MORE THAN A ROPE AND A KNIFE...

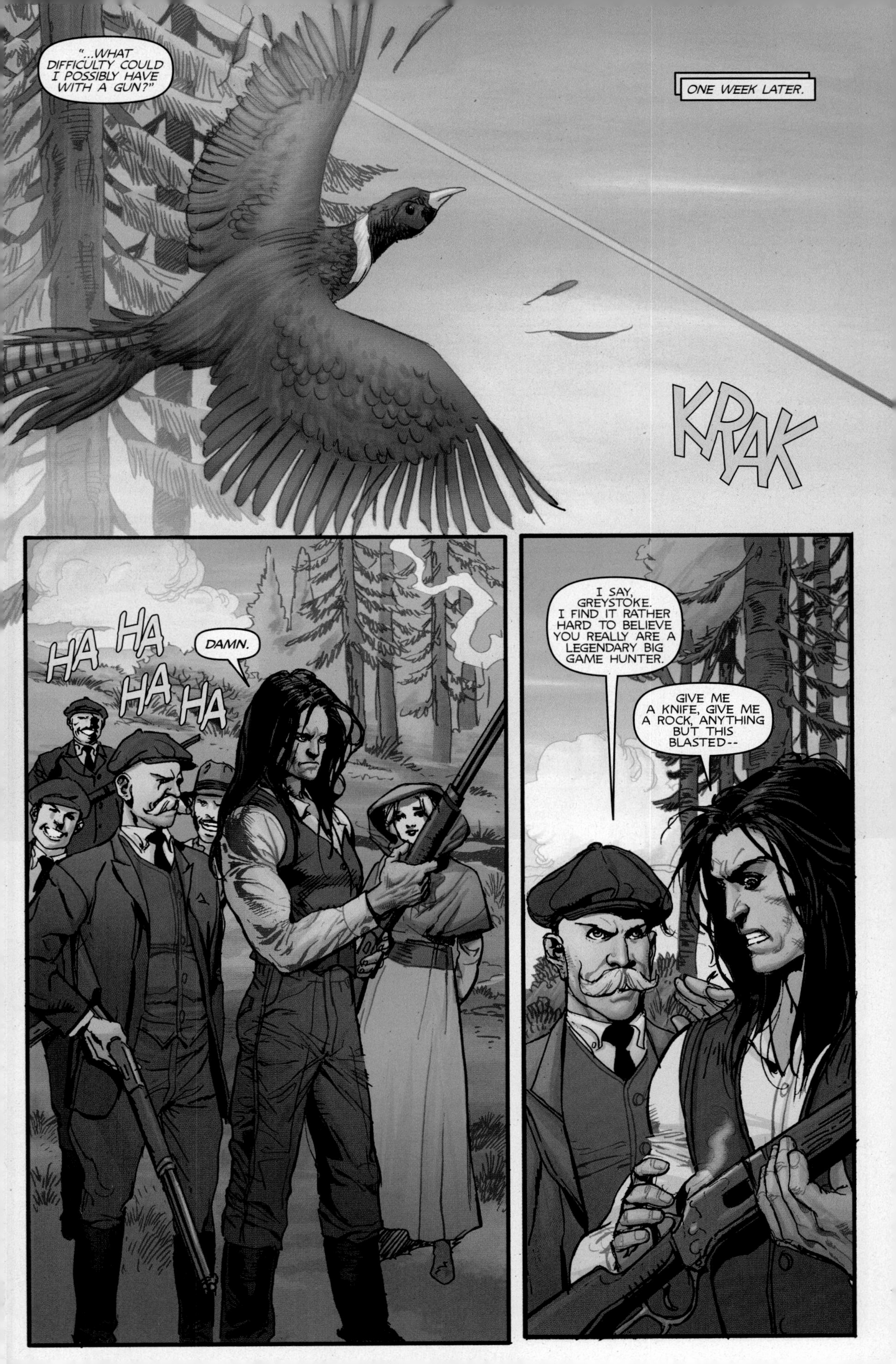
"...WHAT DIFFICULTY COULD I POSSIBLY HAVE WITH A GUN?"
ONE WEEK LATER.
KRAK
HA HA HA HA
DAMN.
I SAY, GREYSTOKE. I FIND IT RATHER HARD TO BELIEVE YOU REALLY ARE A LEGENDARY BIG GAME HUNTER.
GIVE ME A KNIFE, GIVE ME A ROCK, ANYTHING BUT THIS BLASTED--

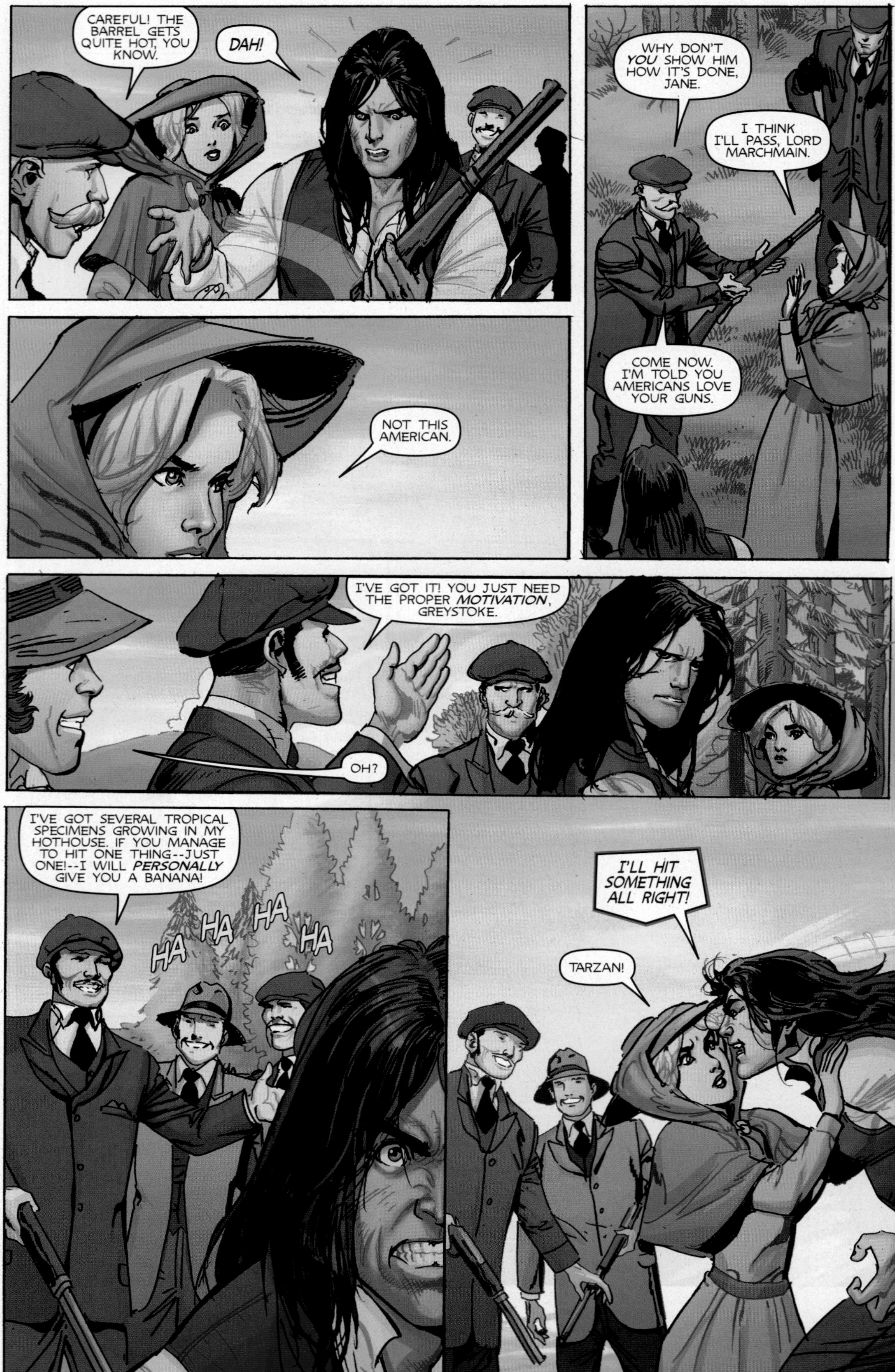
CAREFUL! THE BARREL GETS QUITE HOT, YOU KNOW.
DAH!
WHY DON'T YOU SHOW HIM HOW IT'S DONE, JANE.
I THINK I'LL PASS, LORD MARCHMAIN.
COME NOW. I'M TOLD YOU AMERICANS LOVE YOUR GUNS.
NOT THIS AMERICAN.
I'VE GOT IT! YOU JUST NEED THE PROPER MOTIVATION, GREYSTOKE.
OH?
I'VE GOT SEVERAL TROPICAL SPECIMENS GROWING IN MY HOTHOUSE. IF YOU MANAGE TO HIT ONE THING--JUST ONE!--I WILL PERSONALLY GIVE YOU A BANANA!
HA HA HA HA
I'LL HIT SOMETHING ALL RIGHT!
TARZAN!

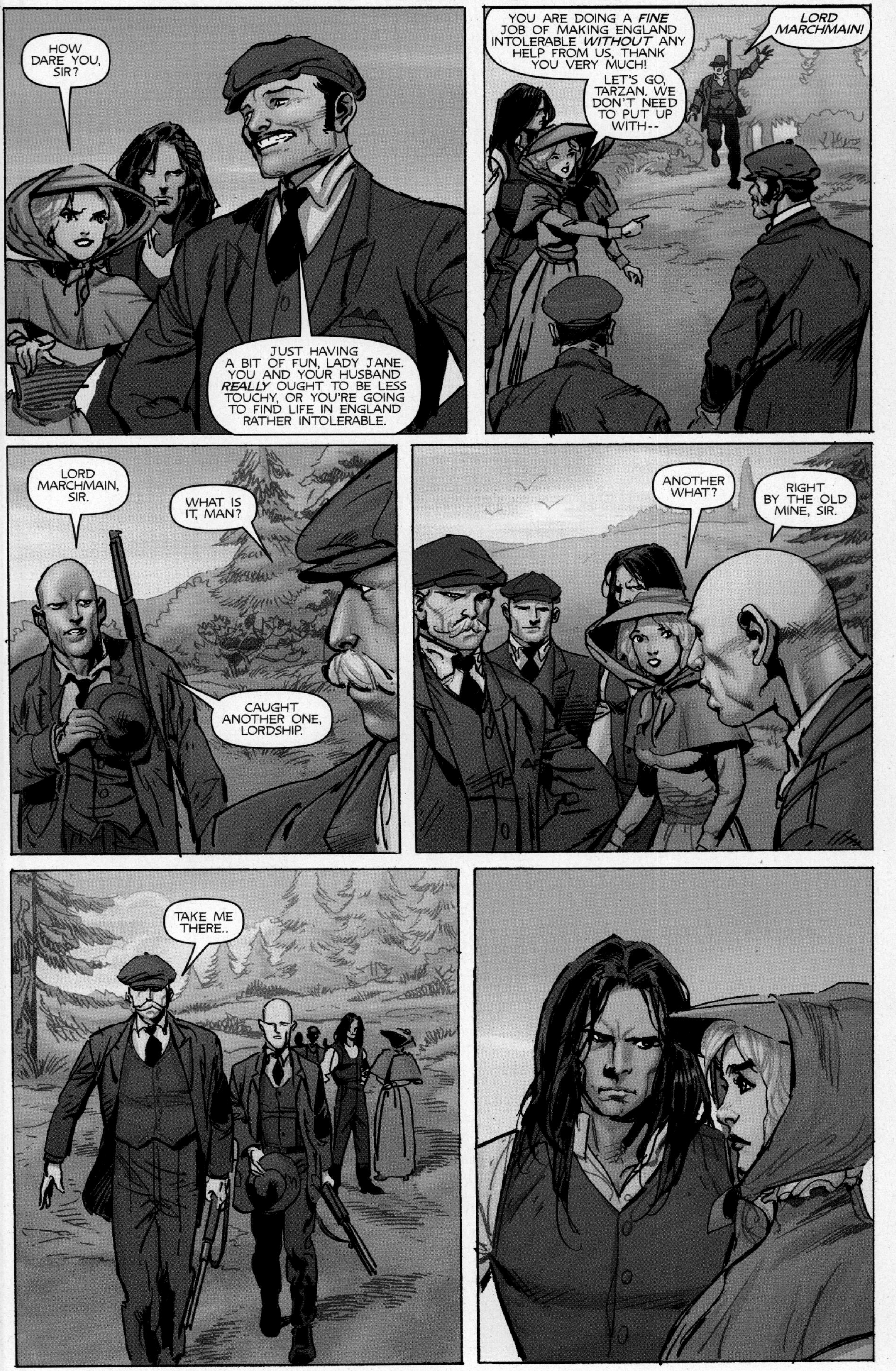
HOW DARE YOU, SIR?
JUST HAVING A BIT OF FUN, LADY JANE. YOU AND YOUR HUSBAND *REALLY* OUGHT TO BE LESS TOUCHY, OR YOU'RE GOING TO FIND LIFE IN ENGLAND RATHER INTOLERABLE.
YOU ARE DOING A *FINE* JOB OF MAKING ENGLAND INTOLERABLE *WITHOUT* ANY HELP FROM US, THANK YOU VERY MUCH!
LET'S GO, TARZAN. WE DON'T NEED TO PUT UP WITH--
LORD MARCHMAIN!
LORD MARCHMAIN, SIR.
WHAT IS IT, MAN?
CAUGHT ANOTHER ONE, LORDSHIP.
ANOTHER WHAT?
RIGHT BY THE OLD MINE, SIR.
TAKE ME THERE..

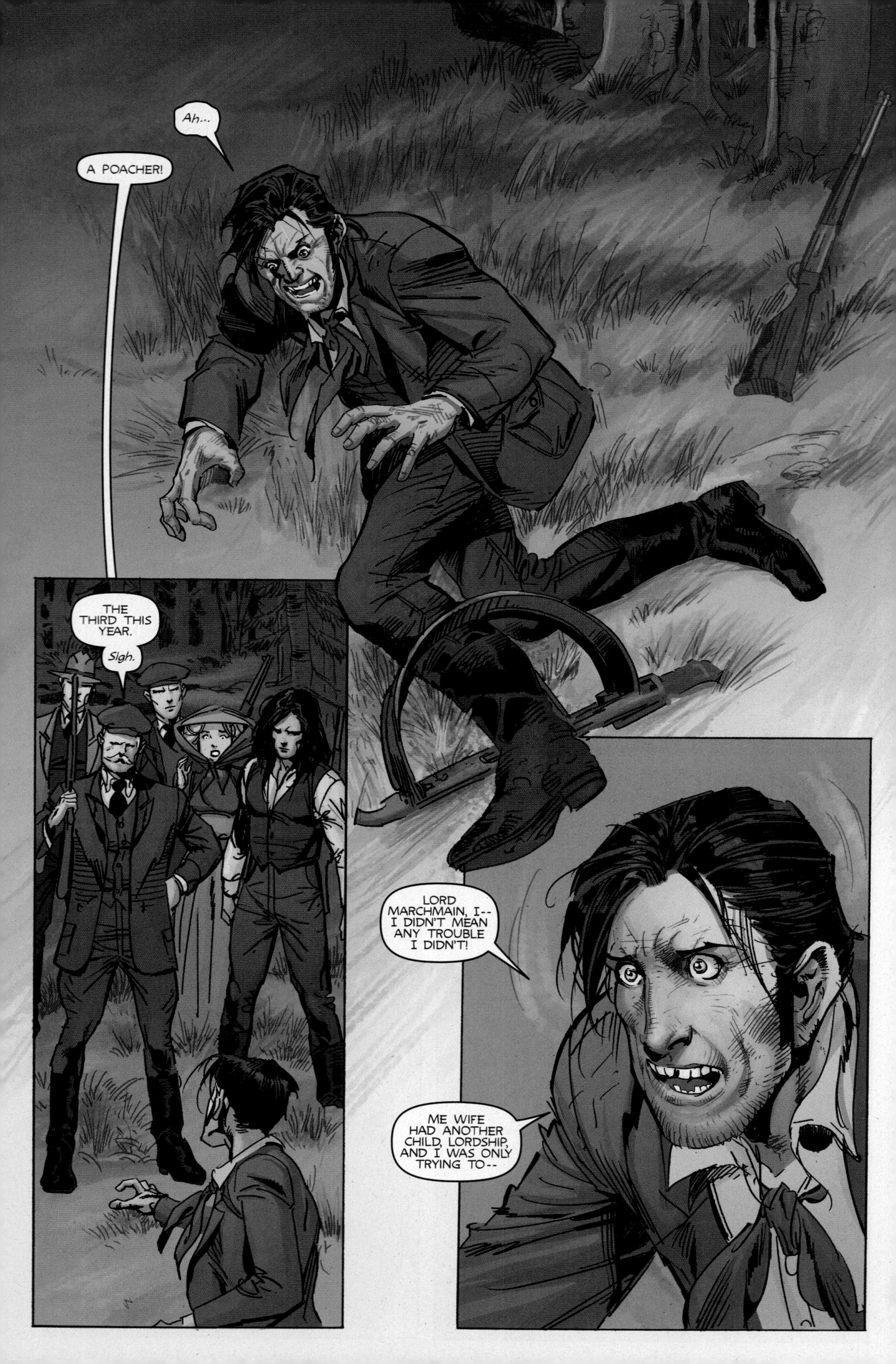
A POACHER!
Ah...
THE THIRD THIS YEAR.
Sigh.
LORD MARCHMAIN, I-- I DIDN'T MEAN ANY TROUBLE I DIDN'T!
ME WIFE HAD ANOTHER CHILD, LORDSHIP, AND I WAS ONLY TRYING TO--

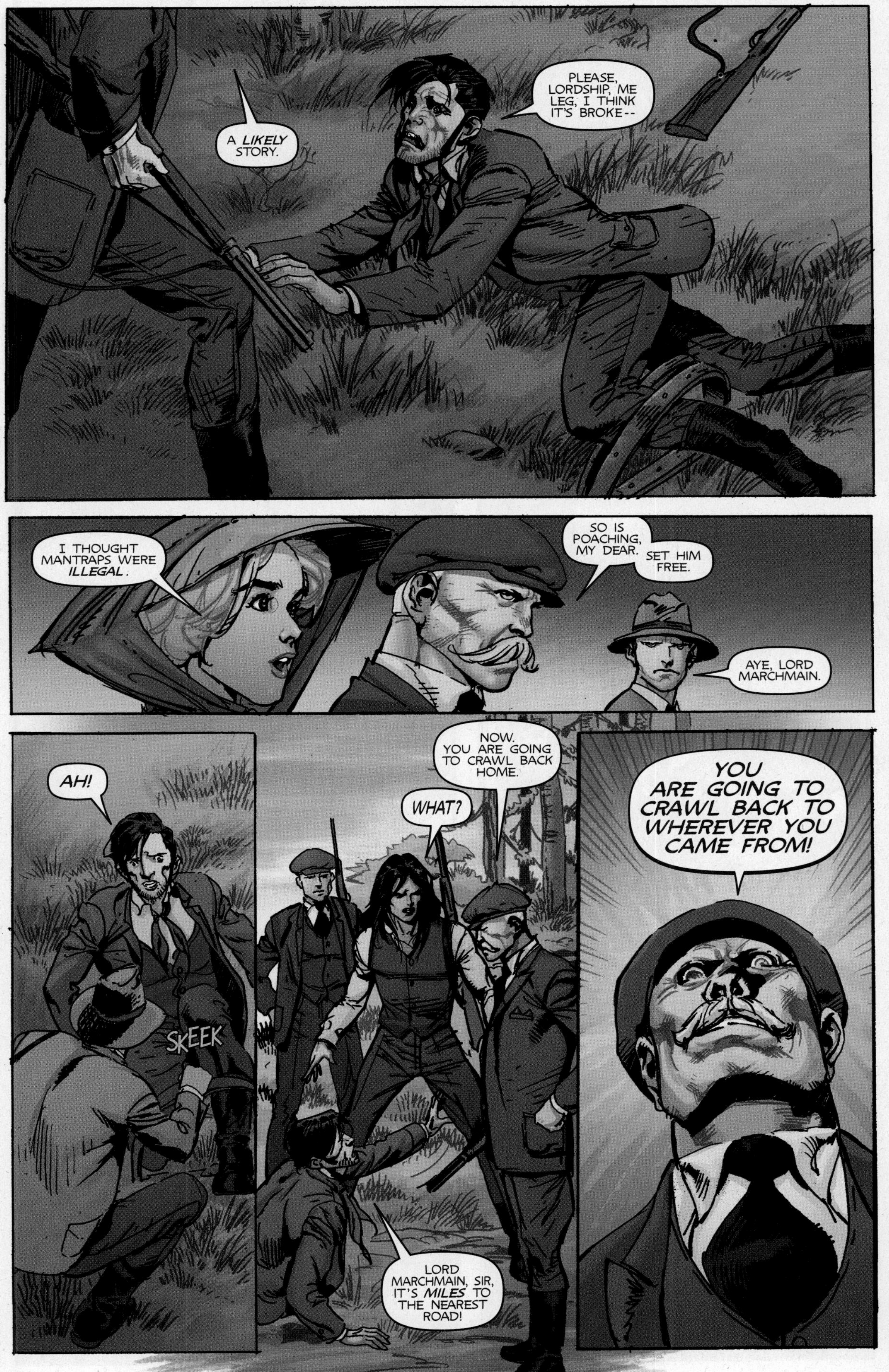
PLEASE, LORDSHIP, ME LEG, I THINK IT'S BROKE--
A *LIKELY* STORY.
I THOUGHT MANTRAPS WERE *ILLEGAL*.
SO IS POACHING, MY DEAR.
SET HIM FREE.
AYE, LORD MARCHMAIN.
AH!
SKEEK
NOW. YOU ARE GOING TO CRAWL BACK HOME.
WHAT?
LORD MARCHMAIN, SIR, IT'S *MILES* TO THE NEAREST ROAD!
YOU ARE GOING TO CRAWL BACK TO WHEREVER YOU CAME FROM!

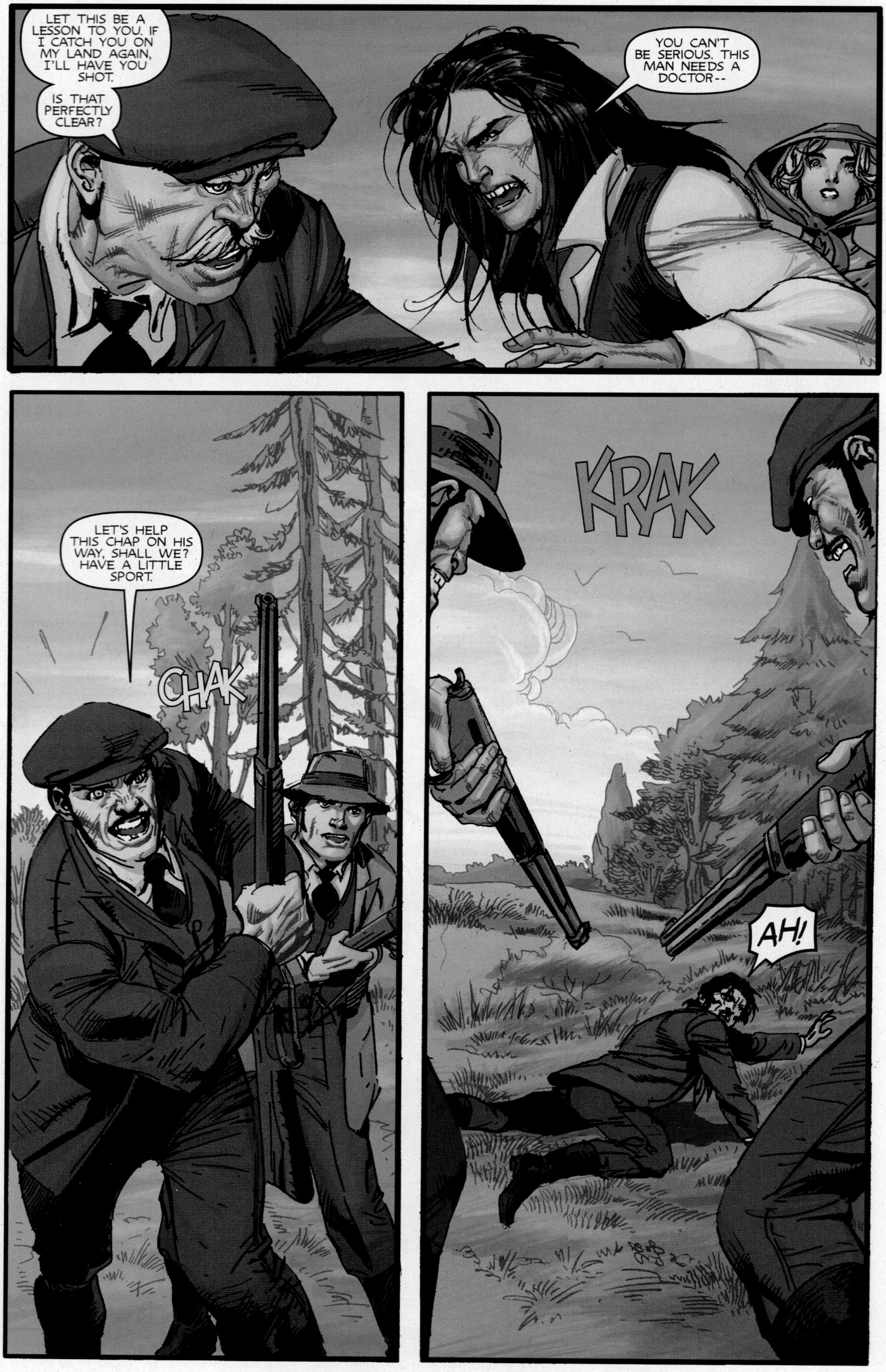
LET THIS BE A LESSON TO YOU. IF I CATCH YOU ON MY LAND AGAIN, I'LL HAVE YOU SHOT.
IS THAT PERFECTLY CLEAR?
YOU CAN'T BE SERIOUS. THIS MAN NEEDS A DOCTOR--
LET'S HELP THIS CHAP ON HIS WAY, SHALL WE? HAVE A LITTLE SPORT.
CHAK
KRAK
AH!

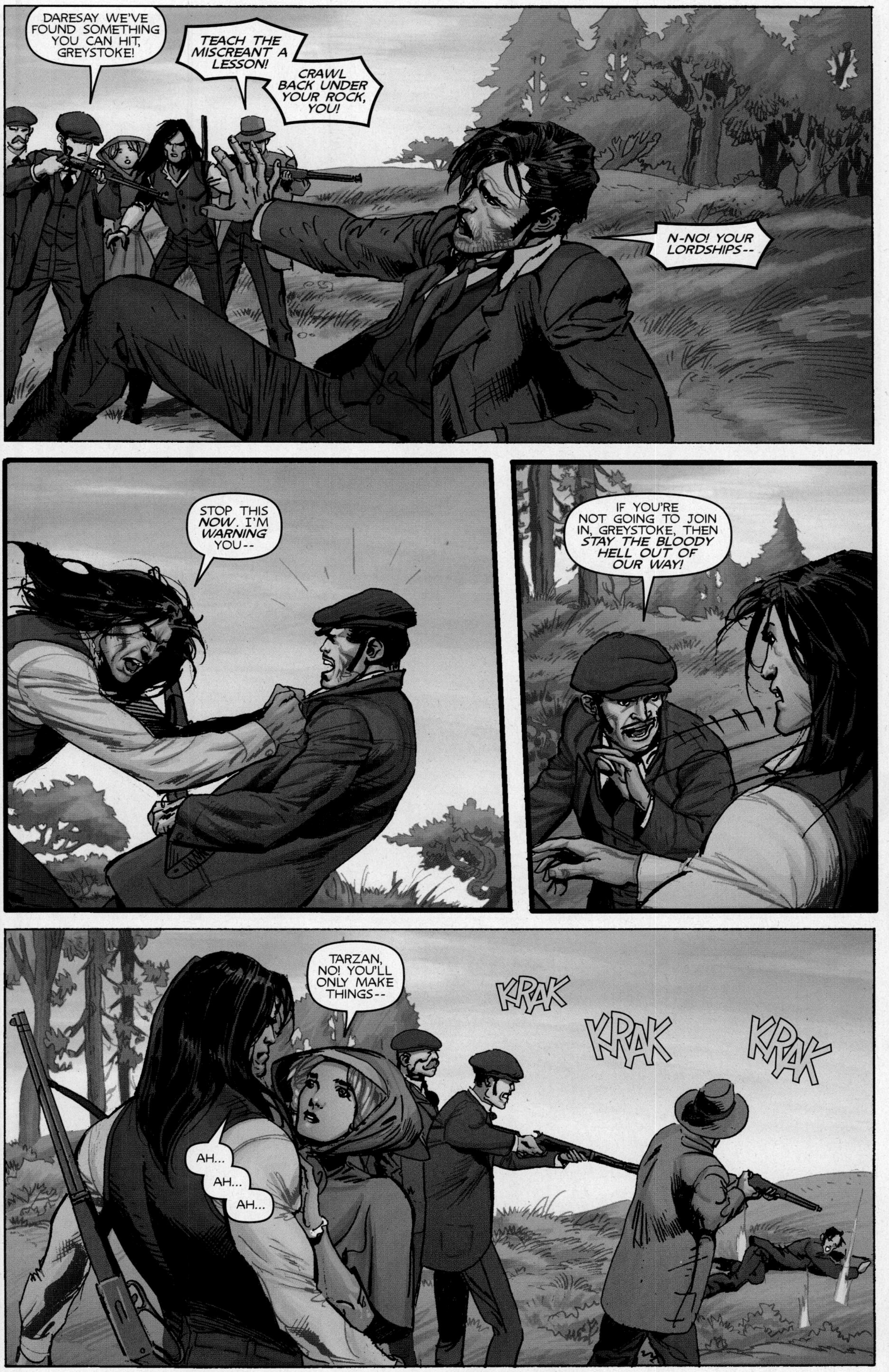
DARESAY WE'VE FOUND SOMETHING YOU CAN HIT, GREYSTOKE!
TEACH THE MISCREANT A LESSON!
CRAWL BACK UNDER YOUR ROCK, YOU!
N-NO! YOUR LORDSHIPS--
STOP THIS NOW. I'M WARNING YOU--
IF YOU'RE NOT GOING TO JOIN IN, GREYSTOKE, THEN STAY THE BLOODY HELL OUT OF OUR WAY!
TARZAN, NO! YOU'LL ONLY MAKE THINGS--
KRAK
KRAK
KRAK
AH...
AH...
AH...

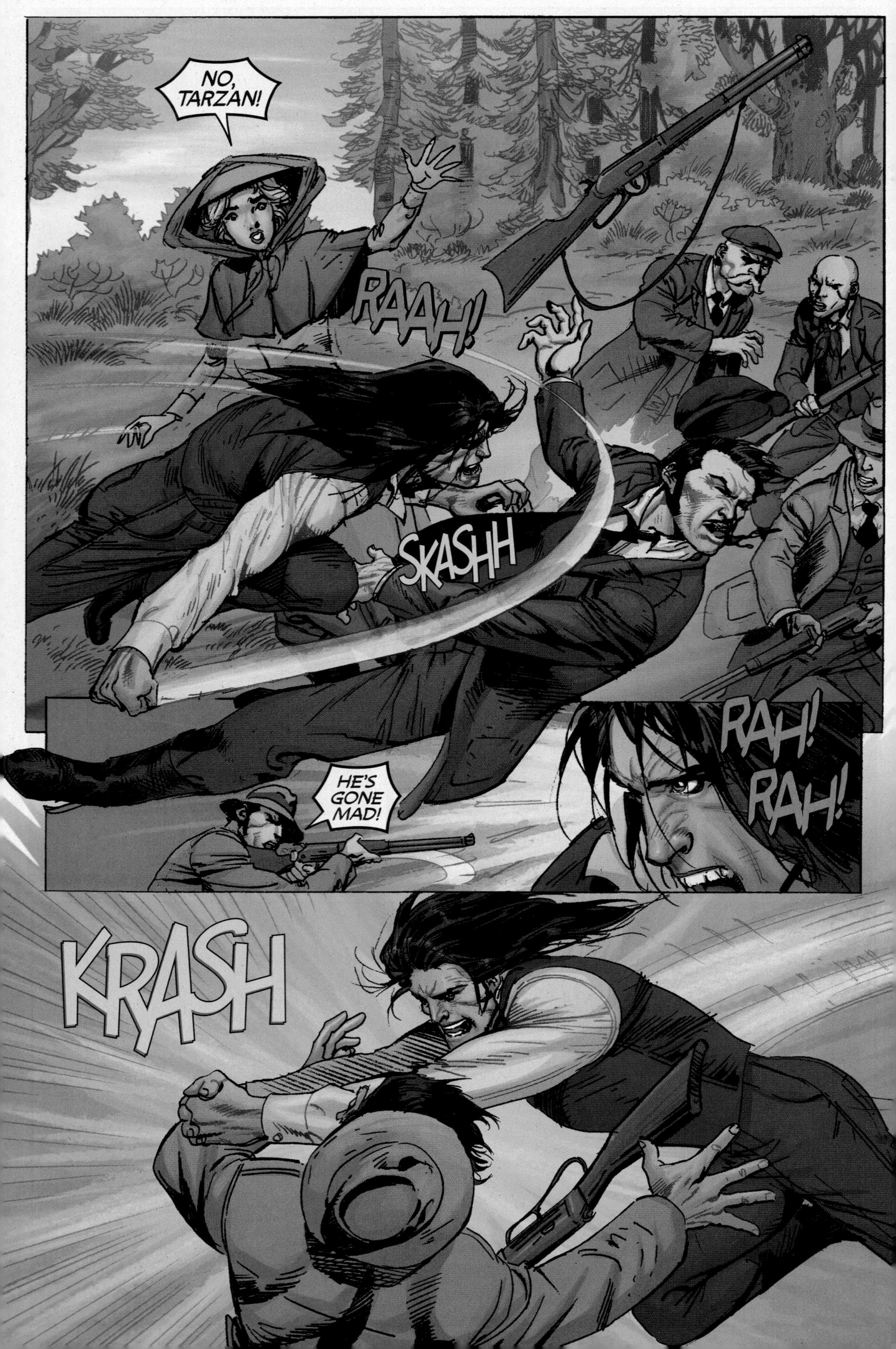
NO, TARZAN!
RAAAH!
SKASHH
RAH! RAH!
HE'S GONE MAD!
KRASH

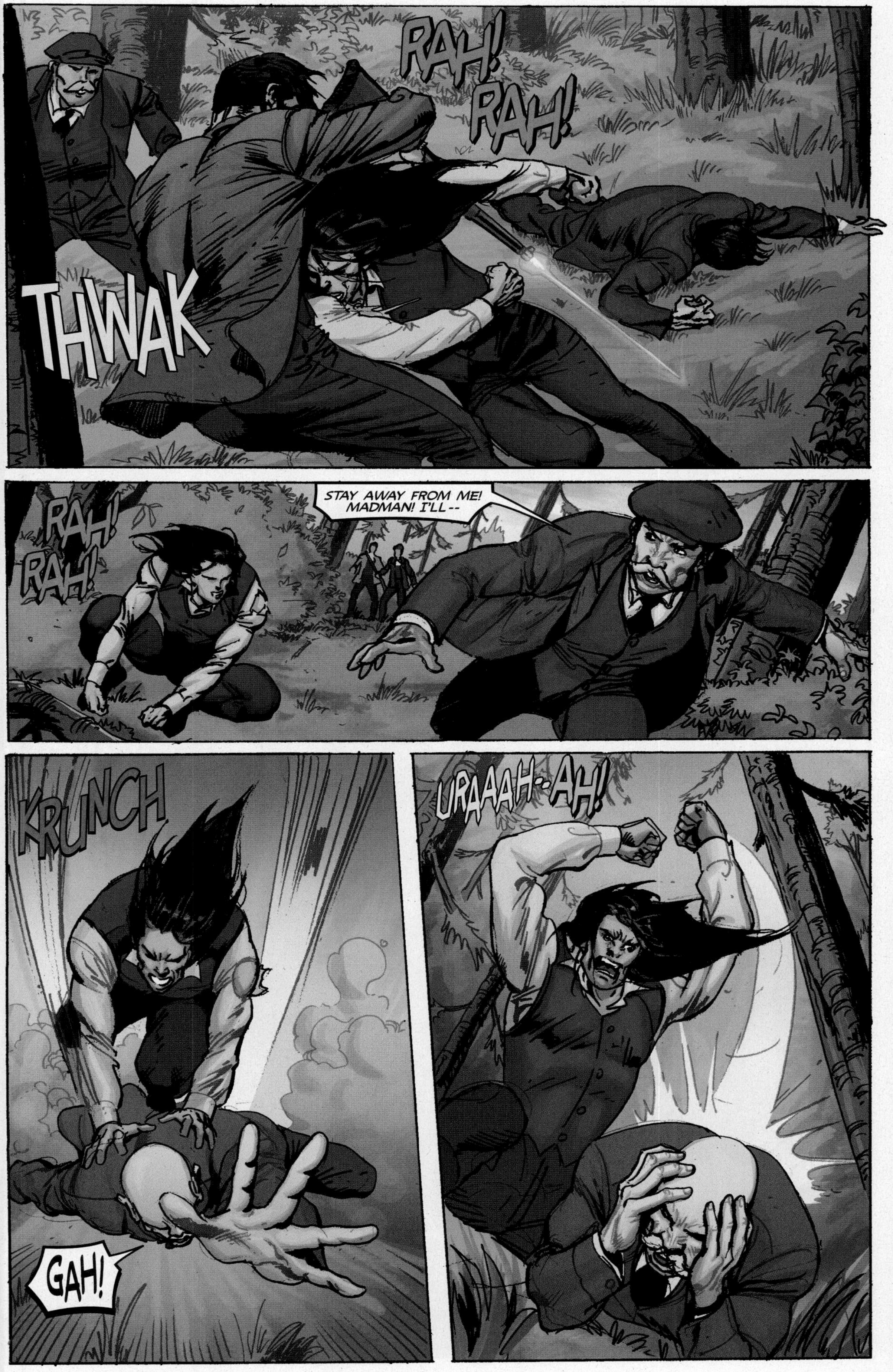
RAH! RAH!
THWAK
RAH! RAH!
STAY AWAY FROM ME! MADMAN! I'LL--
KRUNCH
GAH!
URAAAH-AH!

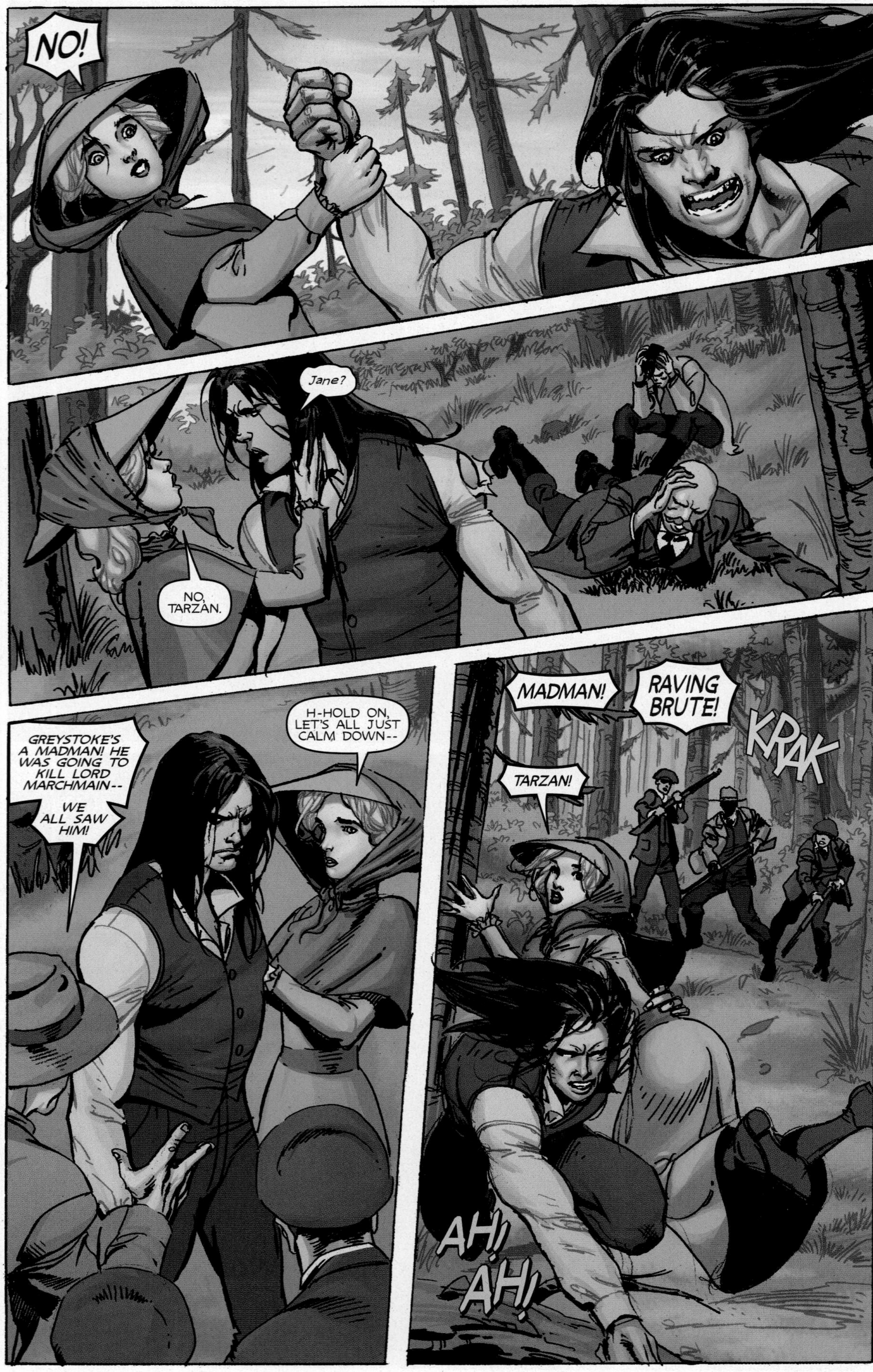
NO!
Jane?
NO, TARZAN.
GREYSTOKE'S A MADMAN! HE WAS GOING TO KILL LORD MARCHMAIN--
WE ALL SAW HIM!
H-HOLD ON, LET'S ALL JUST CALM DOWN--
MADMAN!
RAVING BRUTE!
KRAK
TARZAN!
AH! AH!

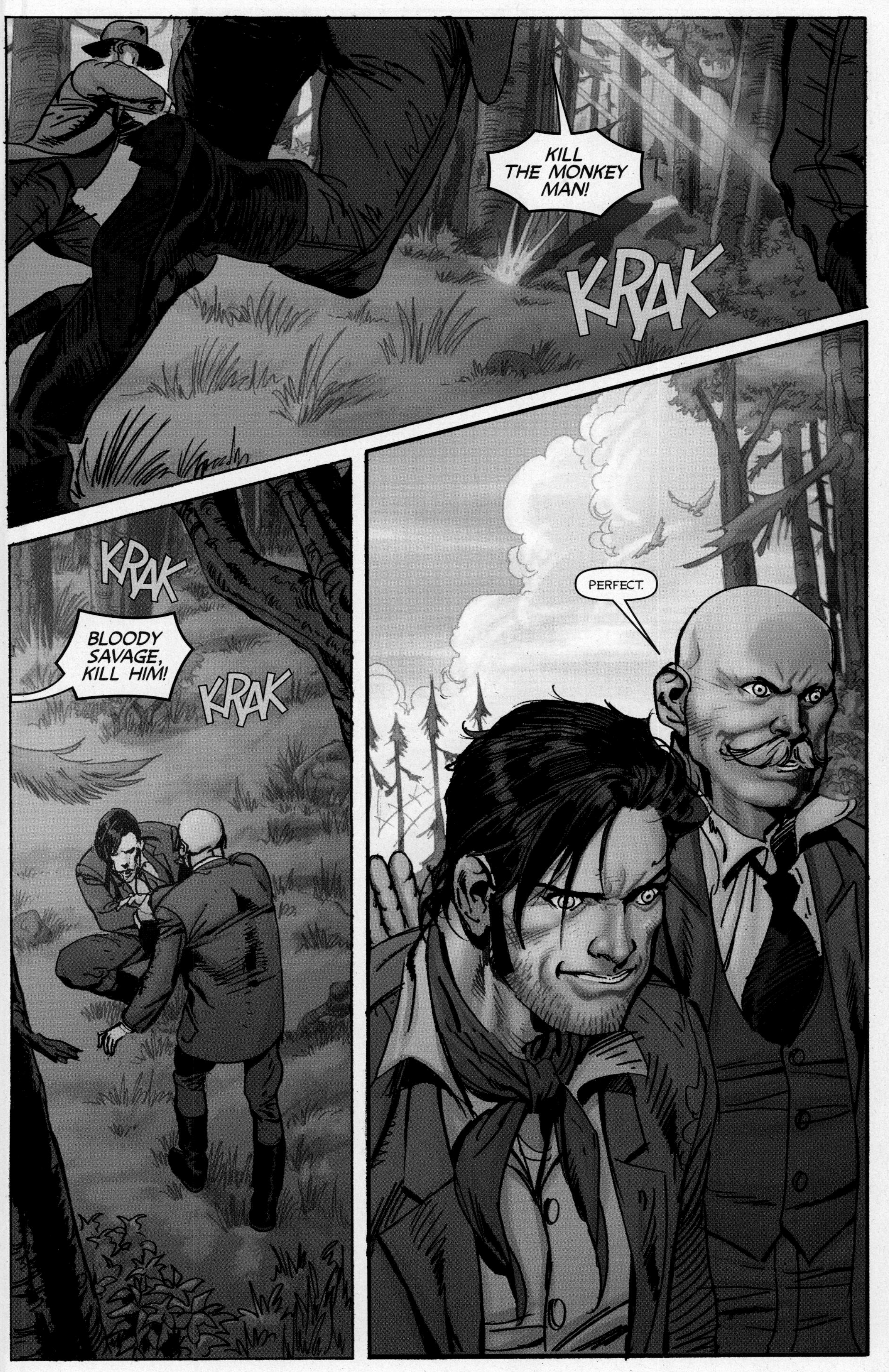
KILL THE MONKEY MAN!
KRAK
KRAK
BLOODY SAVAGE, KILL HIM!
KRAK
PERFECT.

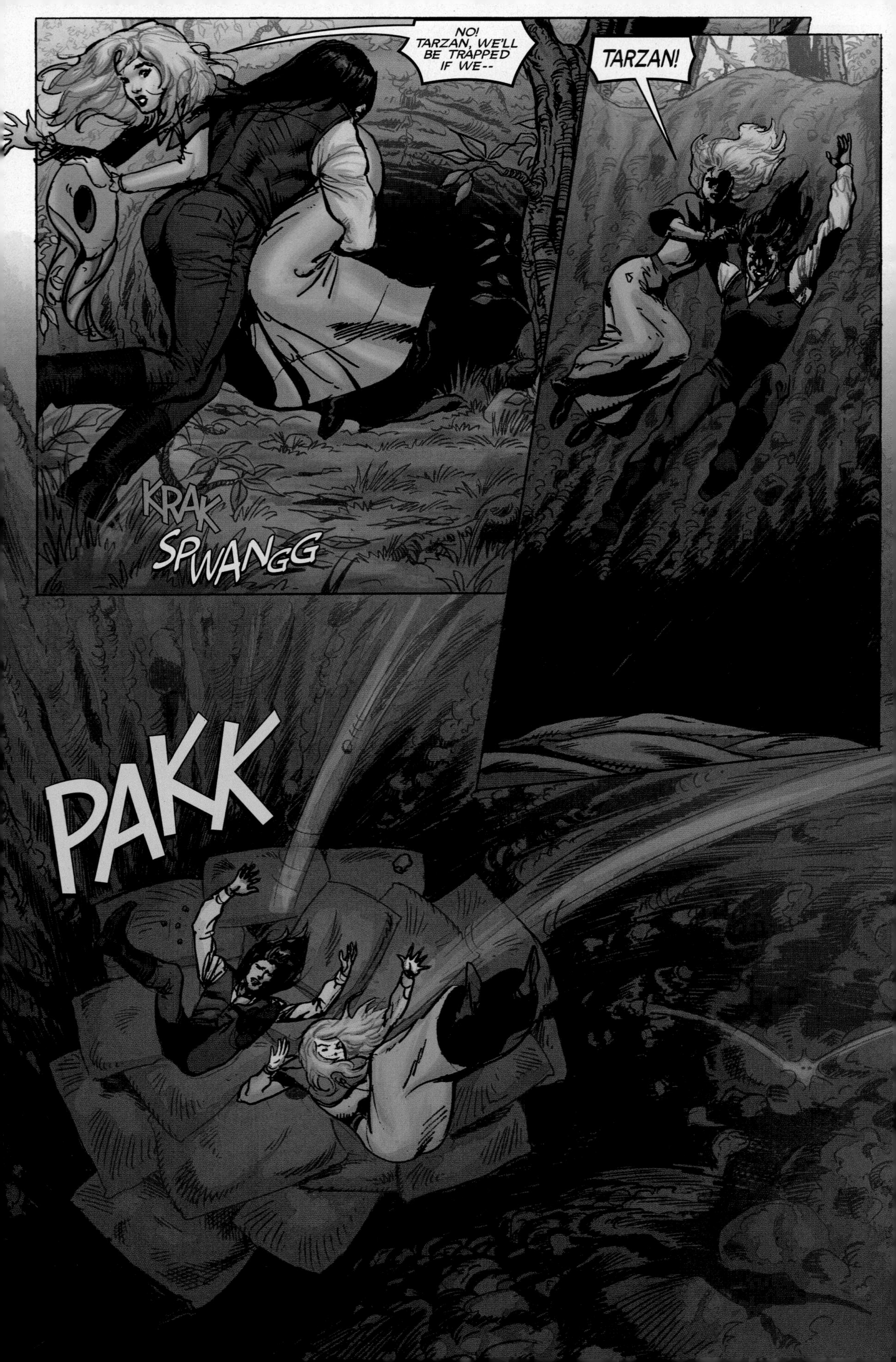
NO! TARZAN, WE'LL BE TRAPPED IF WE--
KRAK
SPWANGG
TARZAN!
PAKK

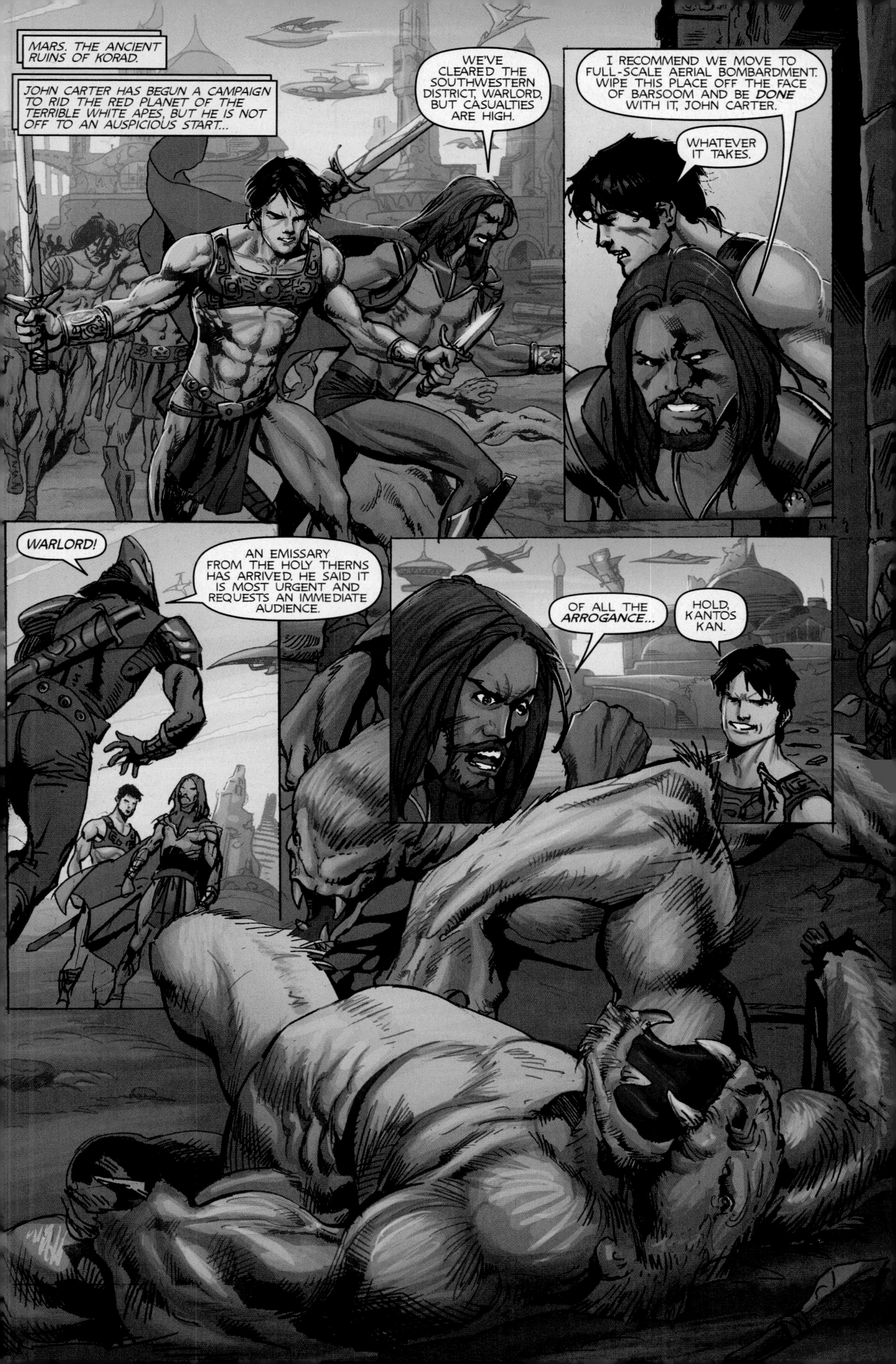
MARS. THE ANCIENT RUINS OF KORAD.
JOHN CARTER HAS BEGUN A CAMPAIGN TO RID THE RED PLANET OF THE TERRIBLE WHITE APES, BUT HE IS NOT OFF TO AN AUSPICIOUS START...
WE'VE CLEARED THE SOUTHWESTERN DISTRICT, WARLORD, BUT CASUALTIES ARE HIGH.
I RECOMMEND WE MOVE TO FULL-SCALE AERIAL BOMBARDMENT. WIPE THIS PLACE OFF THE FACE OF BARSOOM AND BE DONE WITH IT, JOHN CARTER.
WHATEVER IT TAKES.
WARLORD!
AN EMISSARY FROM THE HOLY THERNS HAS ARRIVED. HE SAID IT IS MOST URGENT AND REQUESTS AN IMMEDIATE AUDIENCE.
OF ALL THE ARROGANCE...
HOLD, KANTOS KAN.

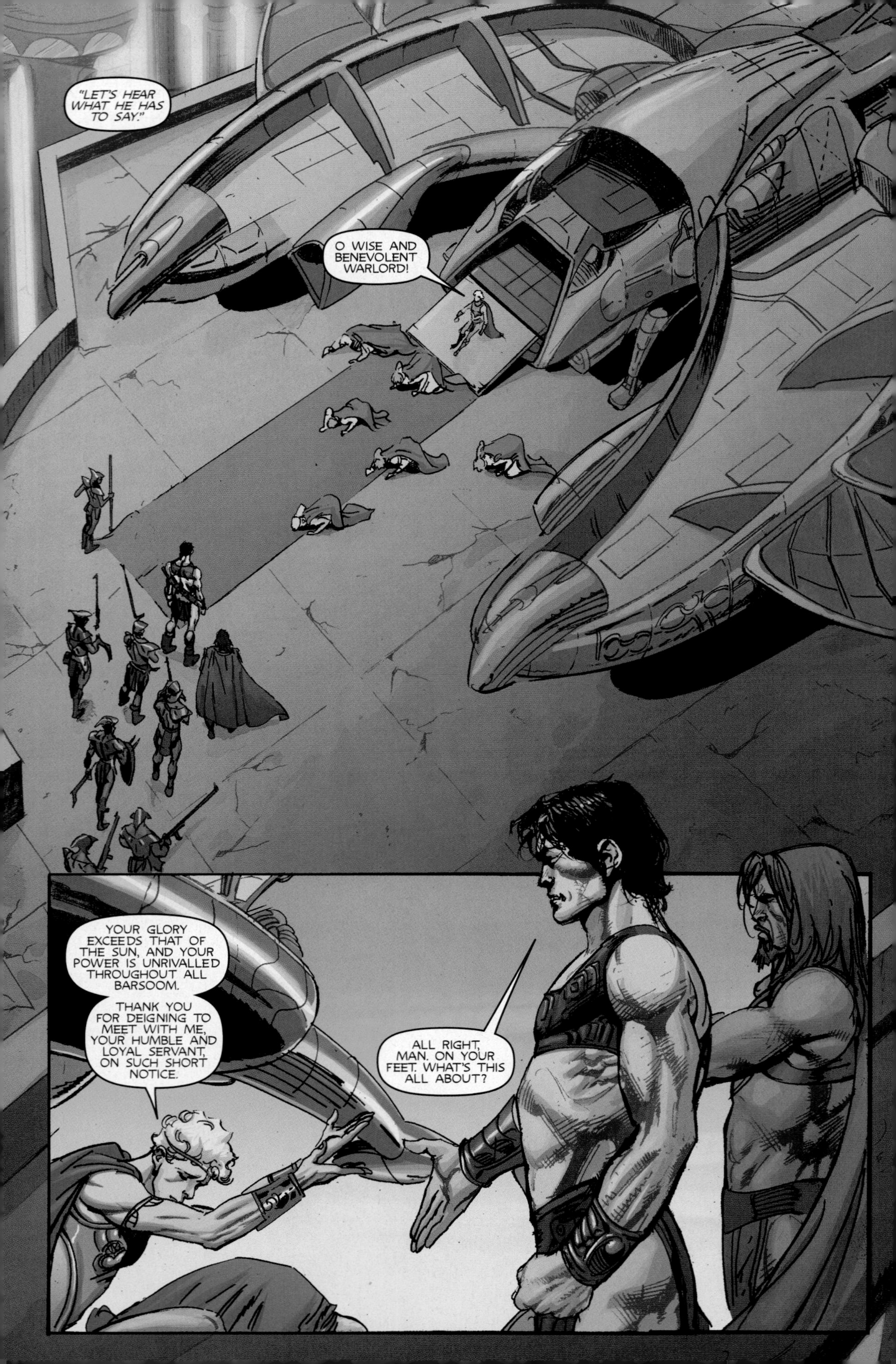
"LET'S HEAR WHAT HE HAS TO SAY."
O WISE AND BENEVOLENT WARLORD!
YOUR GLORY EXCEEDS THAT OF THE SUN, AND YOUR POWER IS UNRIVALLED THROUGHOUT ALL BARSOOM.
THANK YOU FOR DEIGNING TO MEET WITH ME, YOUR HUMBLE AND LOYAL SERVANT, ON SUCH SHORT NOTICE.
ALL RIGHT, MAN. ON YOUR FEET. WHAT'S THIS ALL ABOUT?

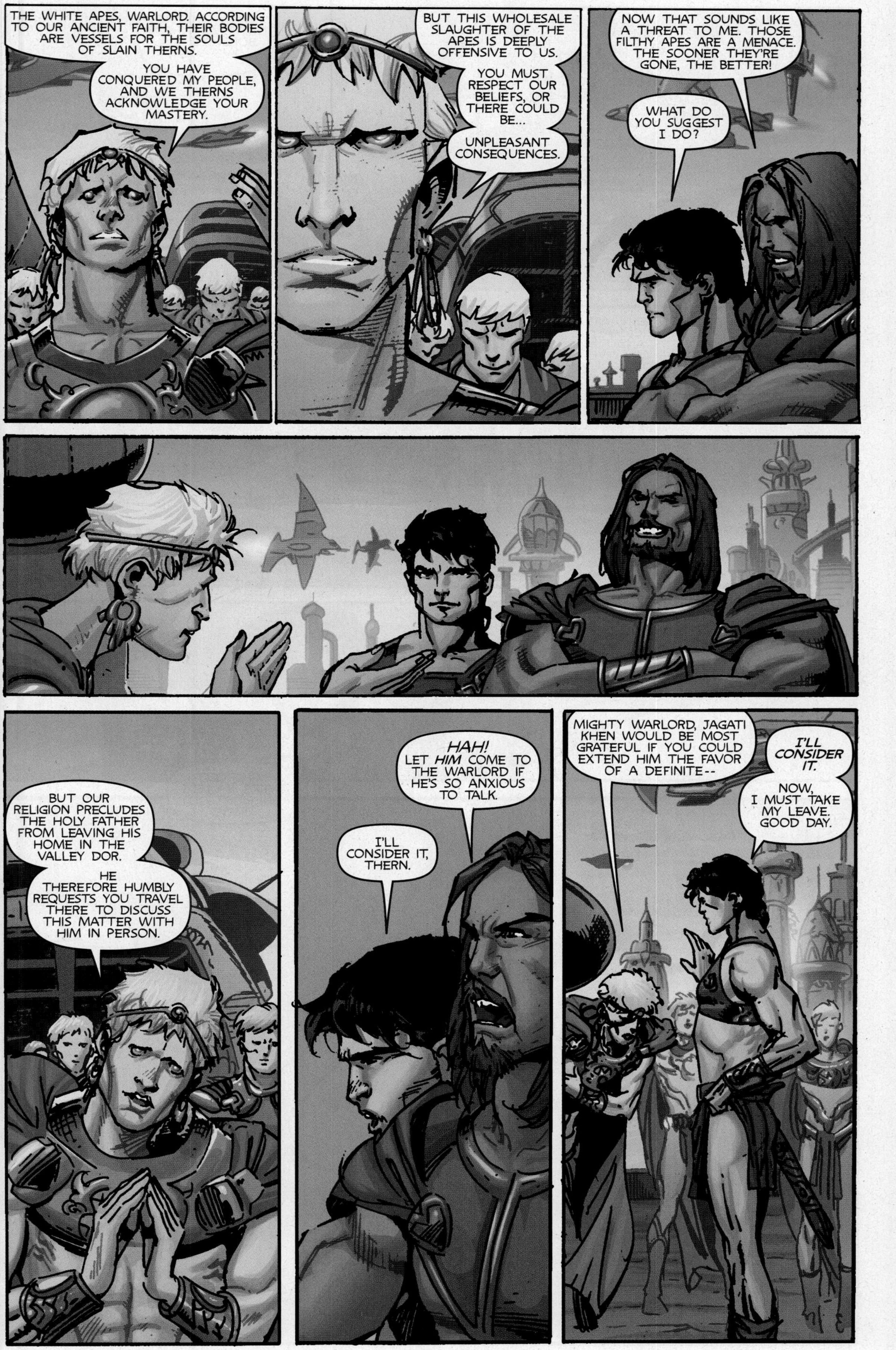
THE WHITE APES, WARLORD. ACCORDING TO OUR ANCIENT FAITH, THEIR BODIES ARE VESSELS FOR THE SOULS OF SLAIN THERNS.
YOU HAVE CONQUERED MY PEOPLE, AND WE THERNS ACKNOWLEDGE YOUR MASTERY.
BUT THIS WHOLESALE SLAUGHTER OF THE APES IS DEEPLY OFFENSIVE TO US.
YOU MUST RESPECT OUR BELIEFS, OR THERE COULD BE...
UNPLEASANT CONSEQUENCES.
NOW THAT SOUNDS LIKE A THREAT TO ME. THOSE FILTHY APES ARE A MENACE. THE SOONER THEY'RE GONE, THE BETTER!
WHAT DO YOU SUGGEST I DO?
BUT OUR RELIGION PRECLUDES THE HOLY FATHER FROM LEAVING HIS HOME IN THE VALLEY DOR.
HE THEREFORE HUMBLY REQUESTS YOU TRAVEL THERE TO DISCUSS THIS MATTER WITH HIM IN PERSON.
HAH! LET HIM COME TO THE WARLORD IF HE'S SO ANXIOUS TO TALK.
I'LL CONSIDER IT, THERN.
MIGHTY WARLORD, JAGATI KHEN WOULD BE MOST GRATEFUL IF YOU COULD EXTEND HIM THE FAVOR OF A DEFINITE--
I'LL CONSIDER IT.
NOW, I MUST TAKE MY LEAVE. GOOD DAY.

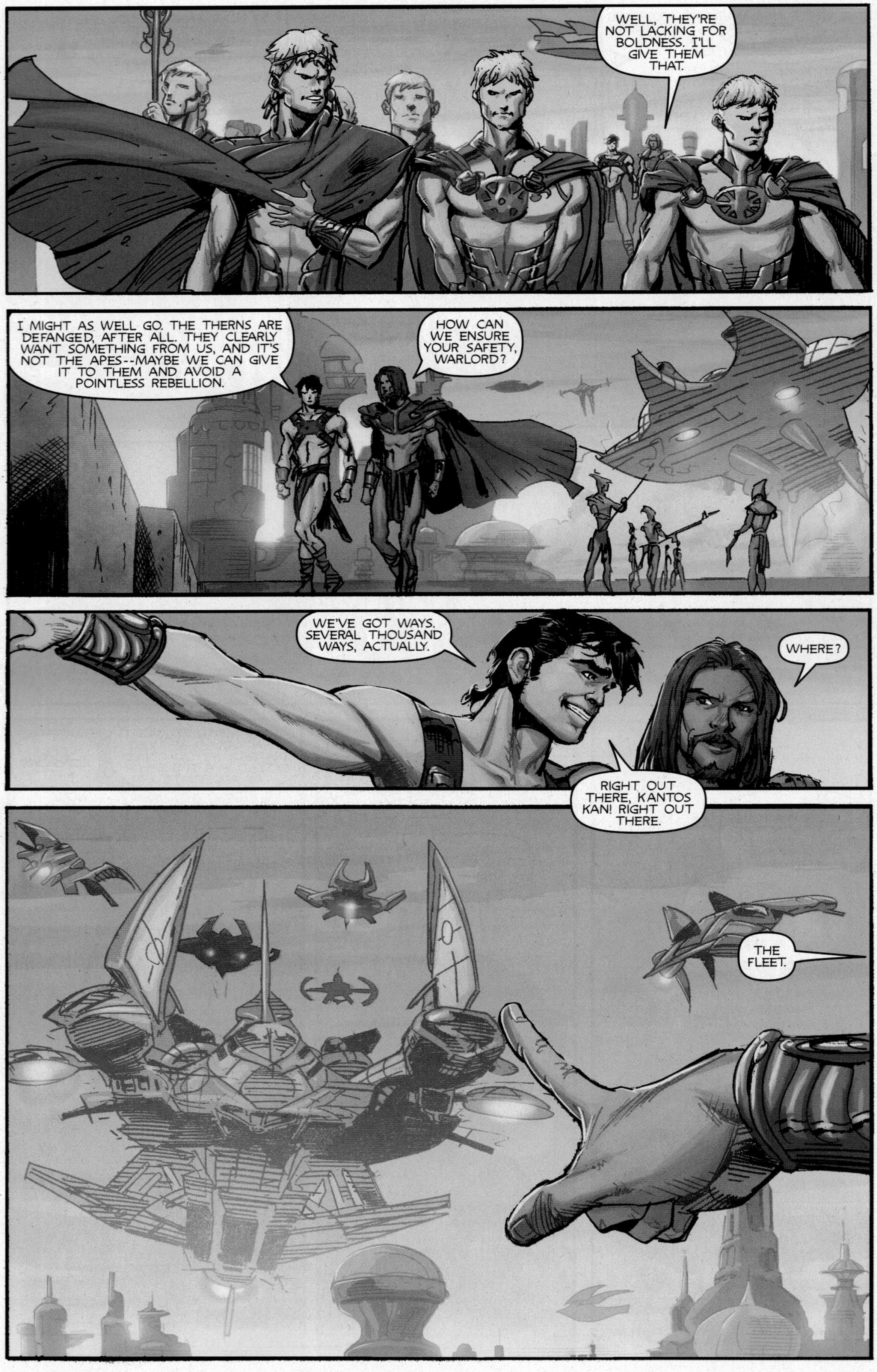
WELL, THEY'RE NOT LACKING FOR BOLDNESS. I'LL GIVE THEM THAT.
I MIGHT AS WELL GO. THE THERNS ARE DEFANGED, AFTER ALL. THEY CLEARLY WANT SOMETHING FROM US, AND IT'S NOT THE APES--MAYBE WE CAN GIVE IT TO THEM AND AVOID A POINTLESS REBELLION.
HOW CAN WE ENSURE YOUR SAFETY, WARLORD?
WE'VE GOT WAYS. SEVERAL THOUSAND WAYS, ACTUALLY.
WHERE?
RIGHT OUT THERE, KANTOS KAN! RIGHT OUT THERE.
THE FLEET.

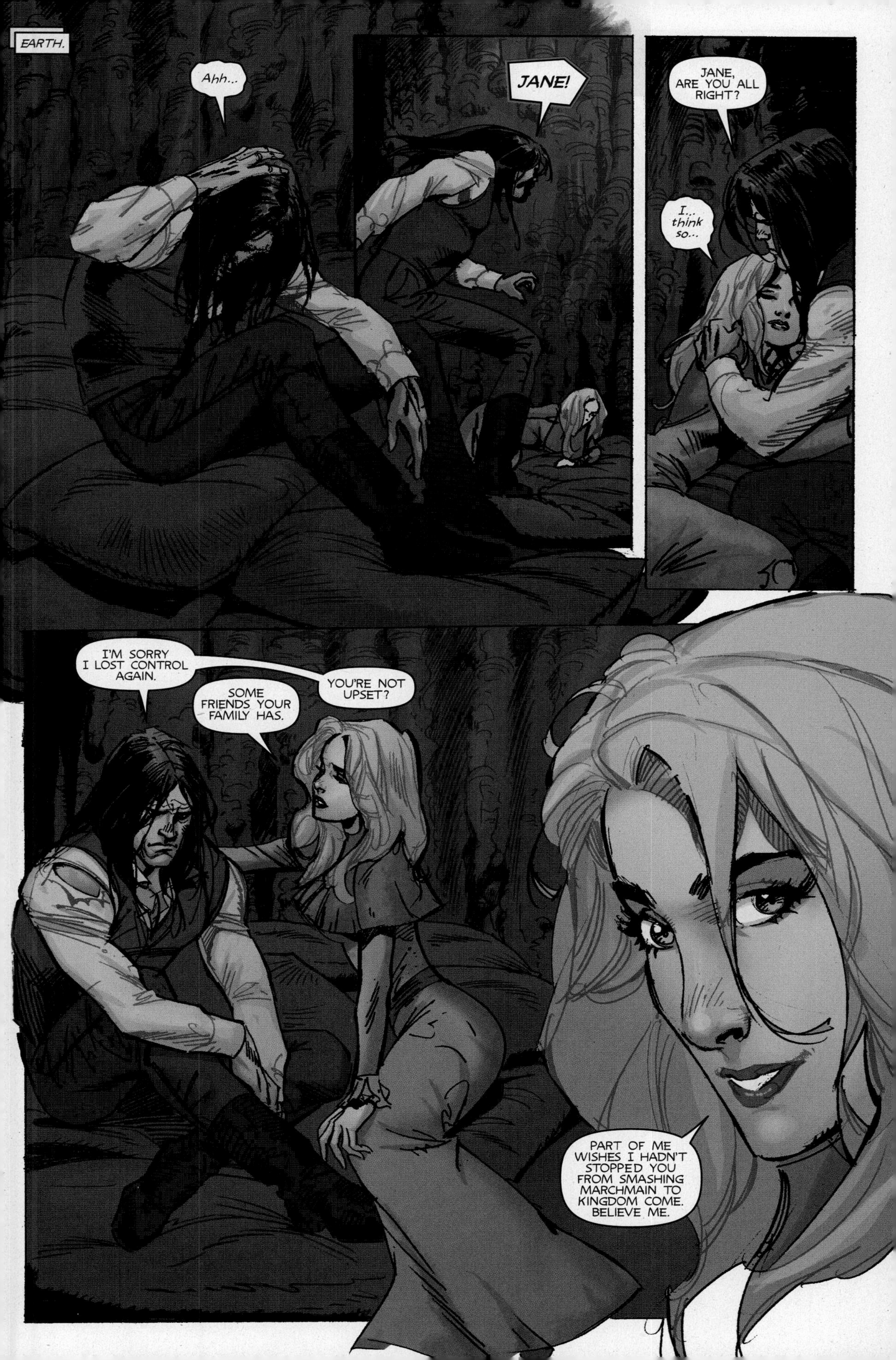
EARTH.
Ahh...
JANE!
JANE, ARE YOU ALL RIGHT?
I... think so...
I'M SORRY I LOST CONTROL AGAIN.
SOME FRIENDS YOUR FAMILY HAS.
YOU'RE NOT UPSET?
PART OF ME WISHES I HADN'T STOPPED YOU FROM SMASHING MARCHMAIN TO KINGDOM COME. BELIEVE ME.

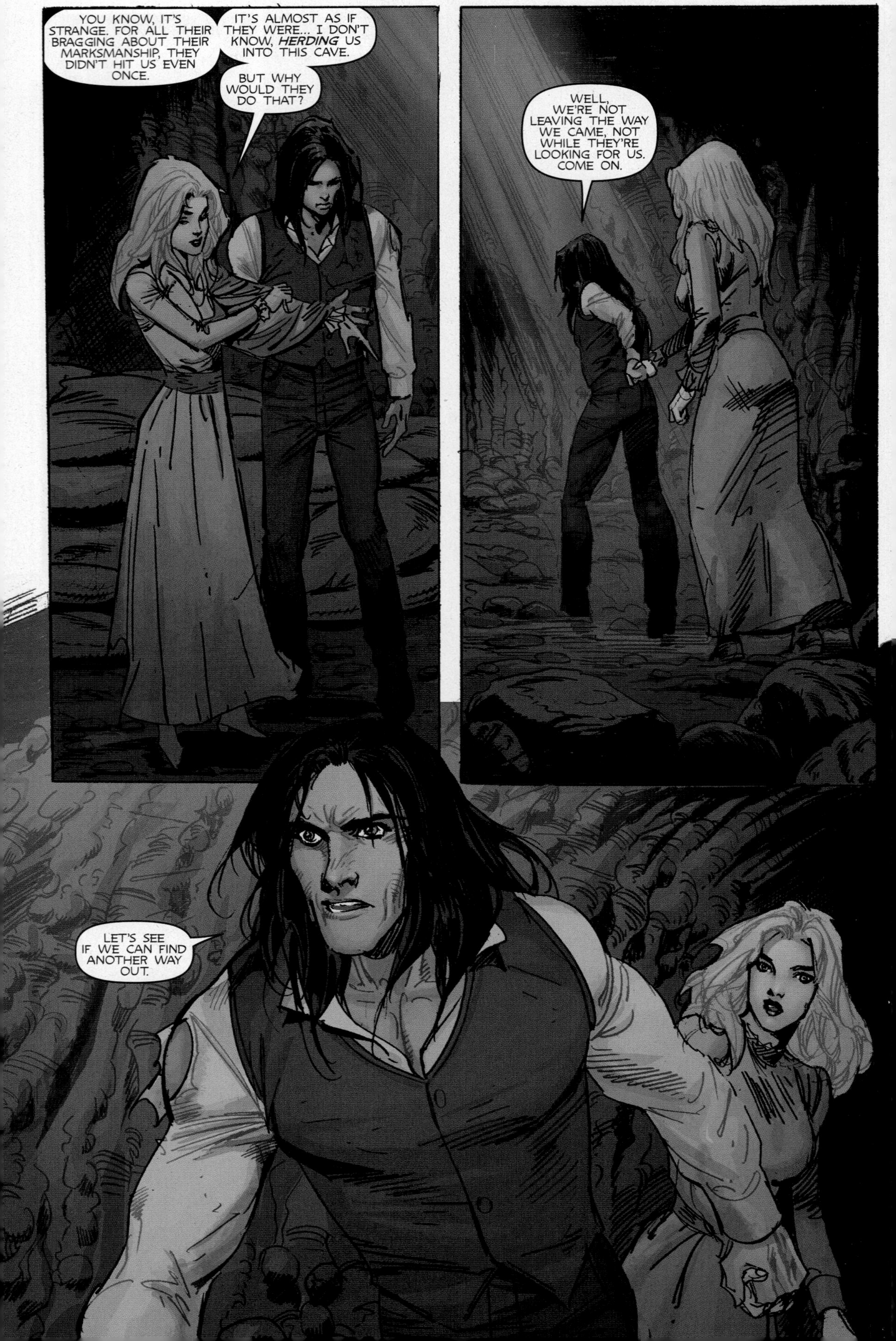
YOU KNOW, IT'S STRANGE. FOR ALL THEIR BRAGGING ABOUT THEIR MARKSMANSHIP, THEY DIDN'T HIT US EVEN ONCE.
IT'S ALMOST AS IF THEY WERE... I DON'T KNOW, *HERDING* US INTO THIS CAVE.
BUT WHY WOULD THEY DO THAT?
WELL, WE'RE NOT LEAVING THE WAY WE CAME, NOT WHILE THEY'RE LOOKING FOR US. COME ON.
LET'S SEE IF WE CAN FIND ANOTHER WAY OUT.

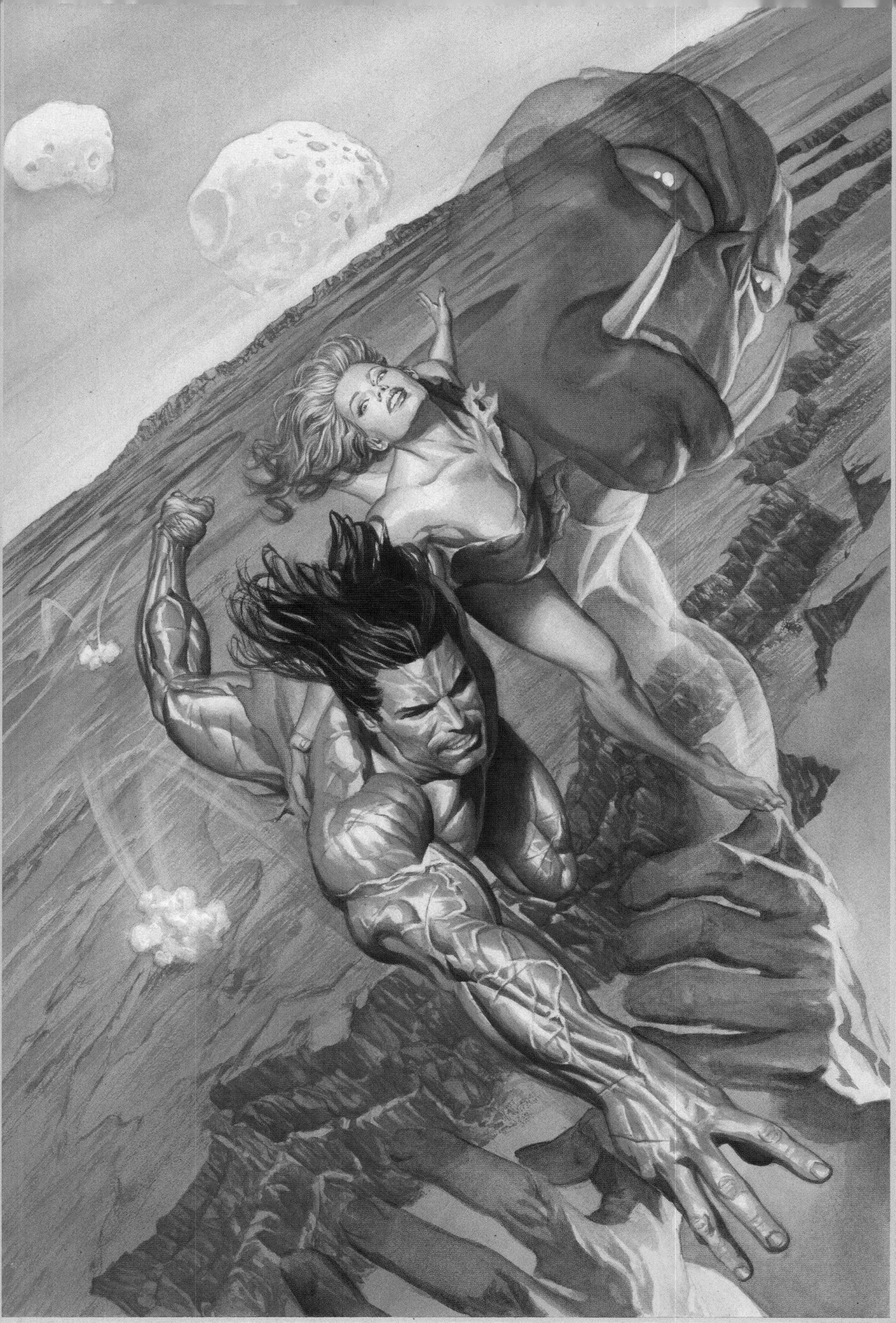

ISSUE 2
A VOICE IN THE WILDERNESS

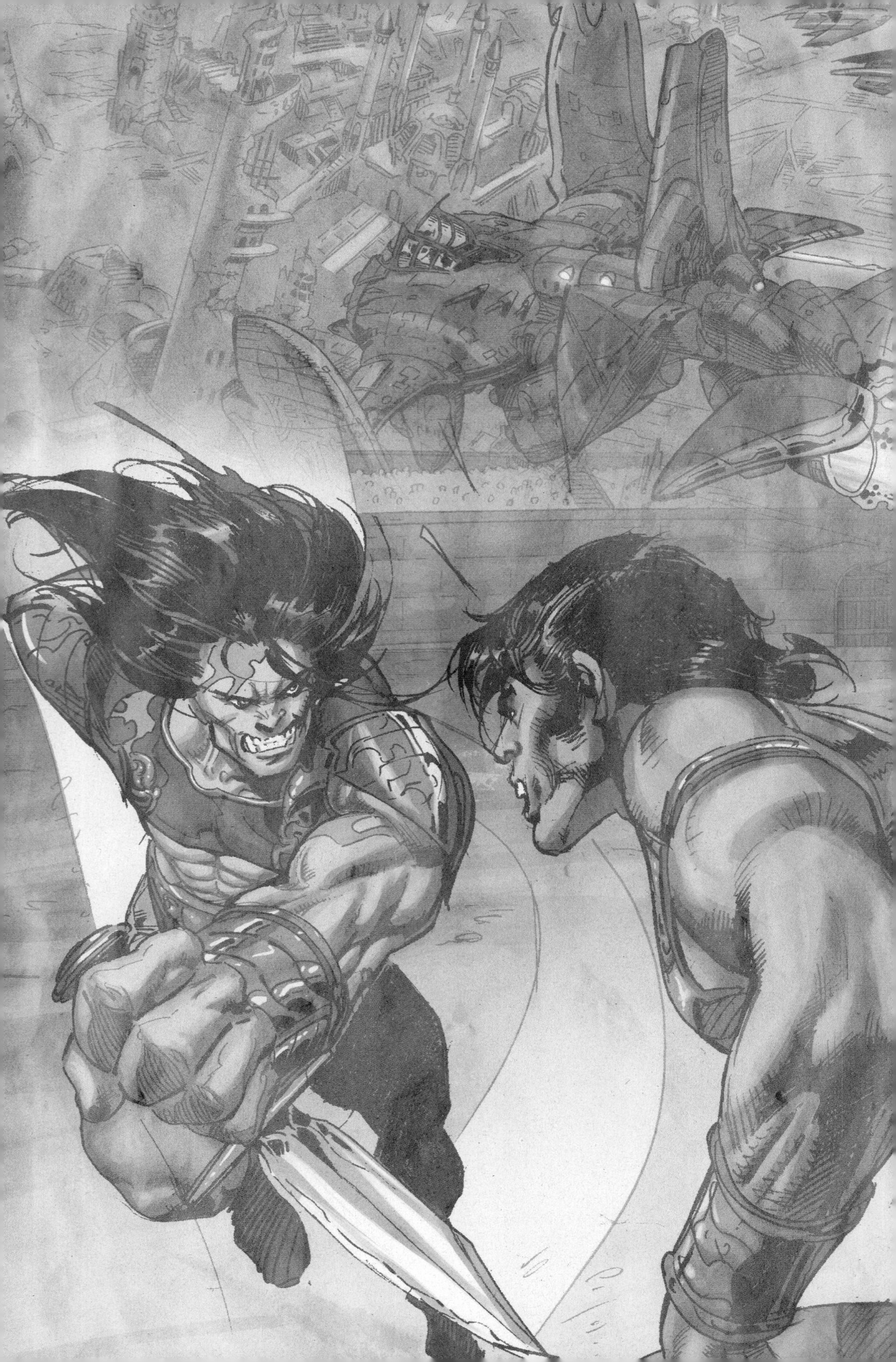

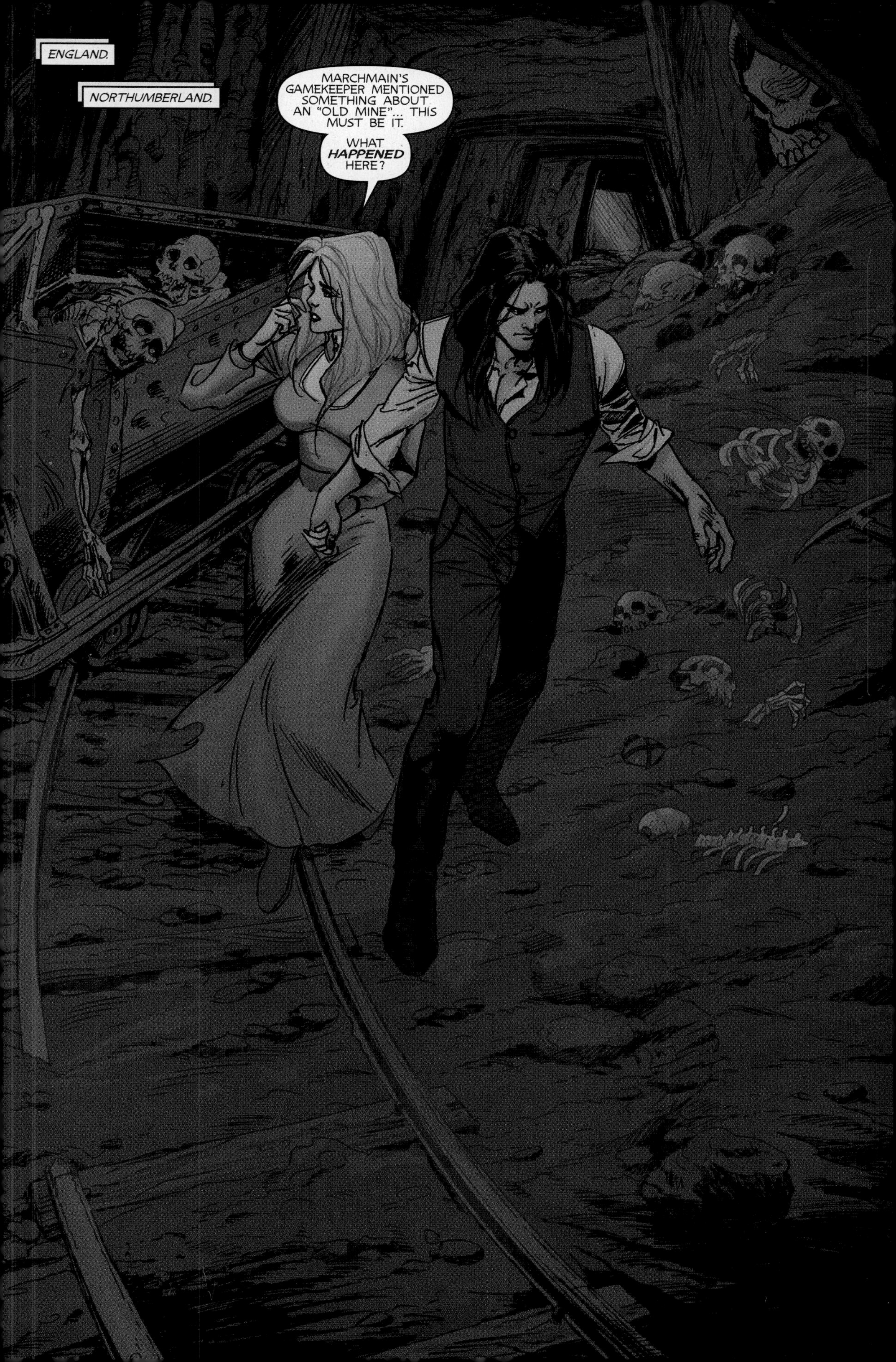
ENGLAND.
NORTHUMBERLAND.
MARCHMAIN'S GAMEKEEPER MENTIONED SOMETHING ABOUT AN "OLD MINE"... THIS MUST BE IT.
WHAT HAPPENED HERE?

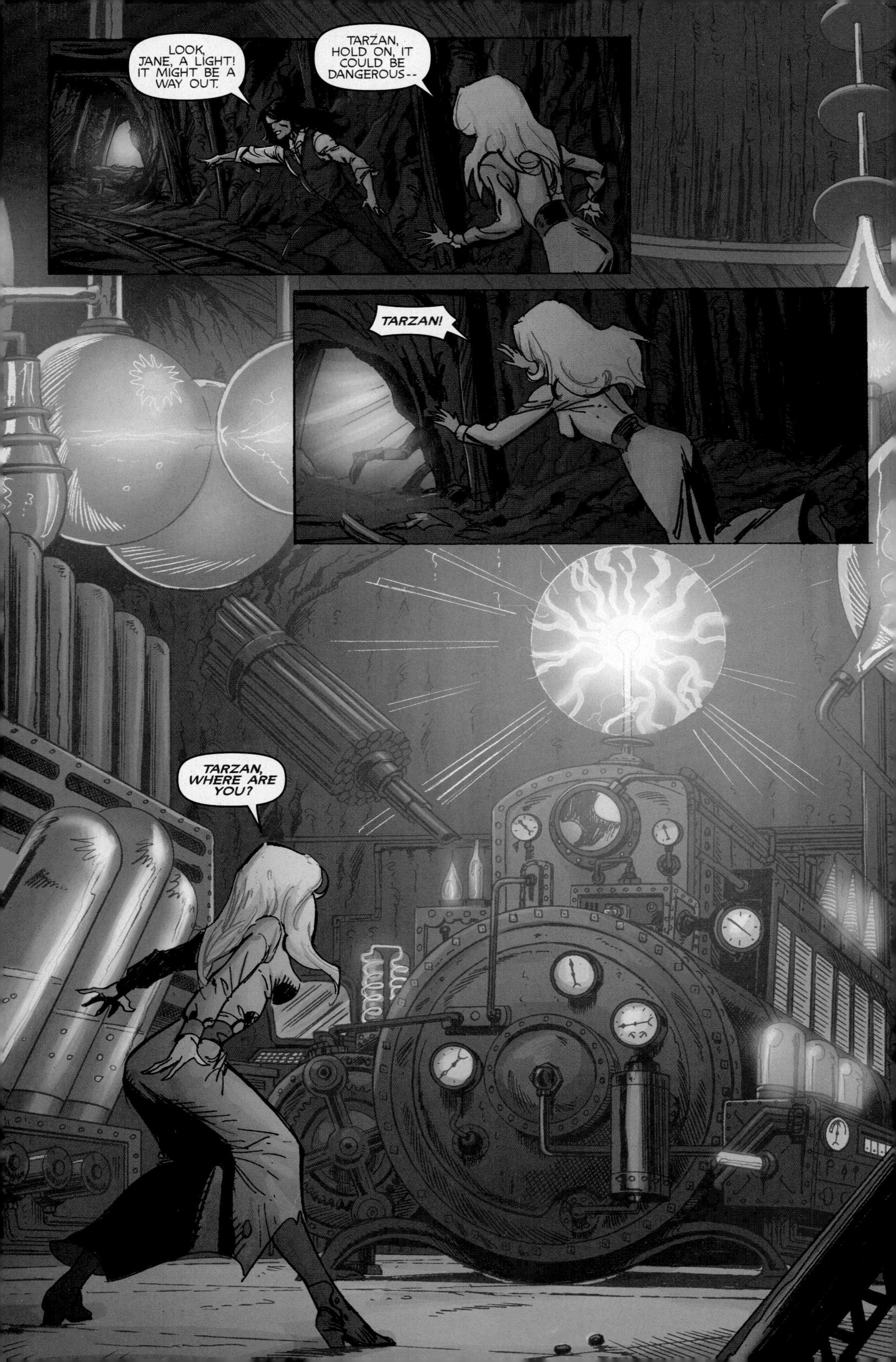
LOOK, JANE, A LIGHT! IT MIGHT BE A WAY OUT.
TARZAN, HOLD ON, IT COULD BE DANGEROUS--
TARZAN!
TARZAN, WHERE ARE YOU?

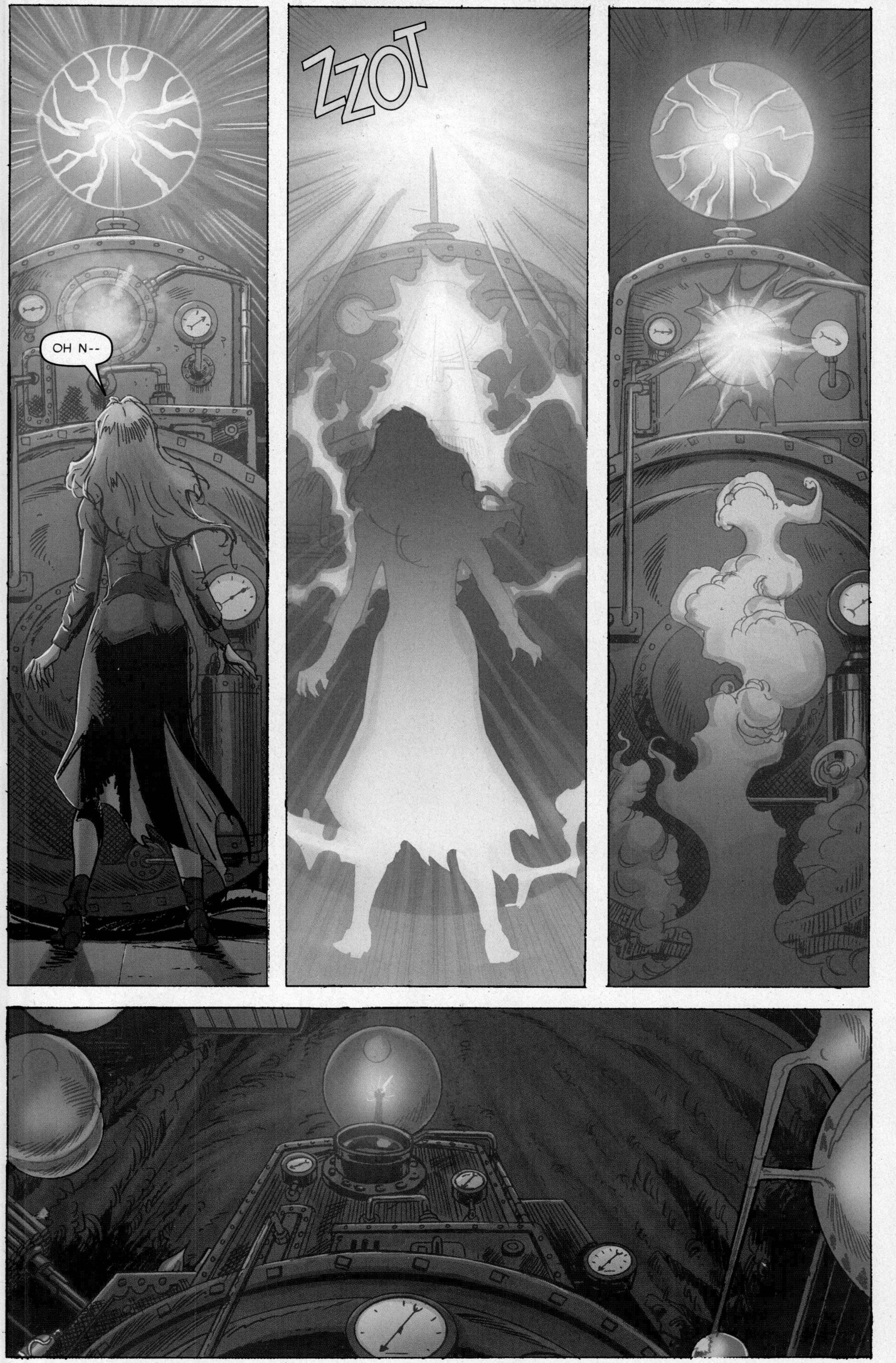
OH N--
ZZOT

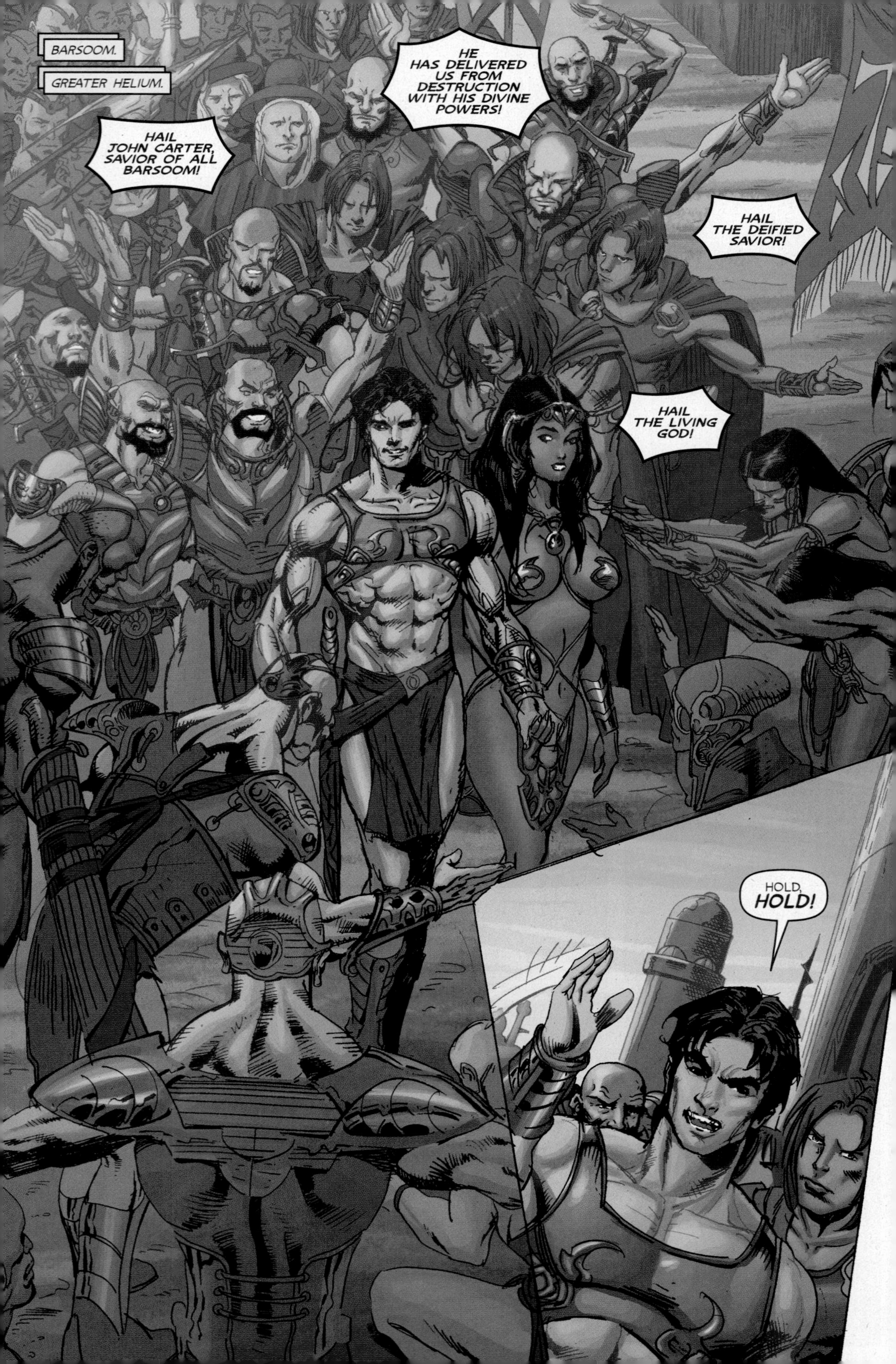
BARSOOM.
GREATER HELIUM.
HAIL JOHN CARTER, SAVIOR OF ALL BARSOOM!
HE HAS DELIVERED US FROM DESTRUCTION WITH HIS DIVINE POWERS!
HAIL THE DEIFIED SAVIOR!
HAIL THE LIVING GOD!
HOLD, HOLD!

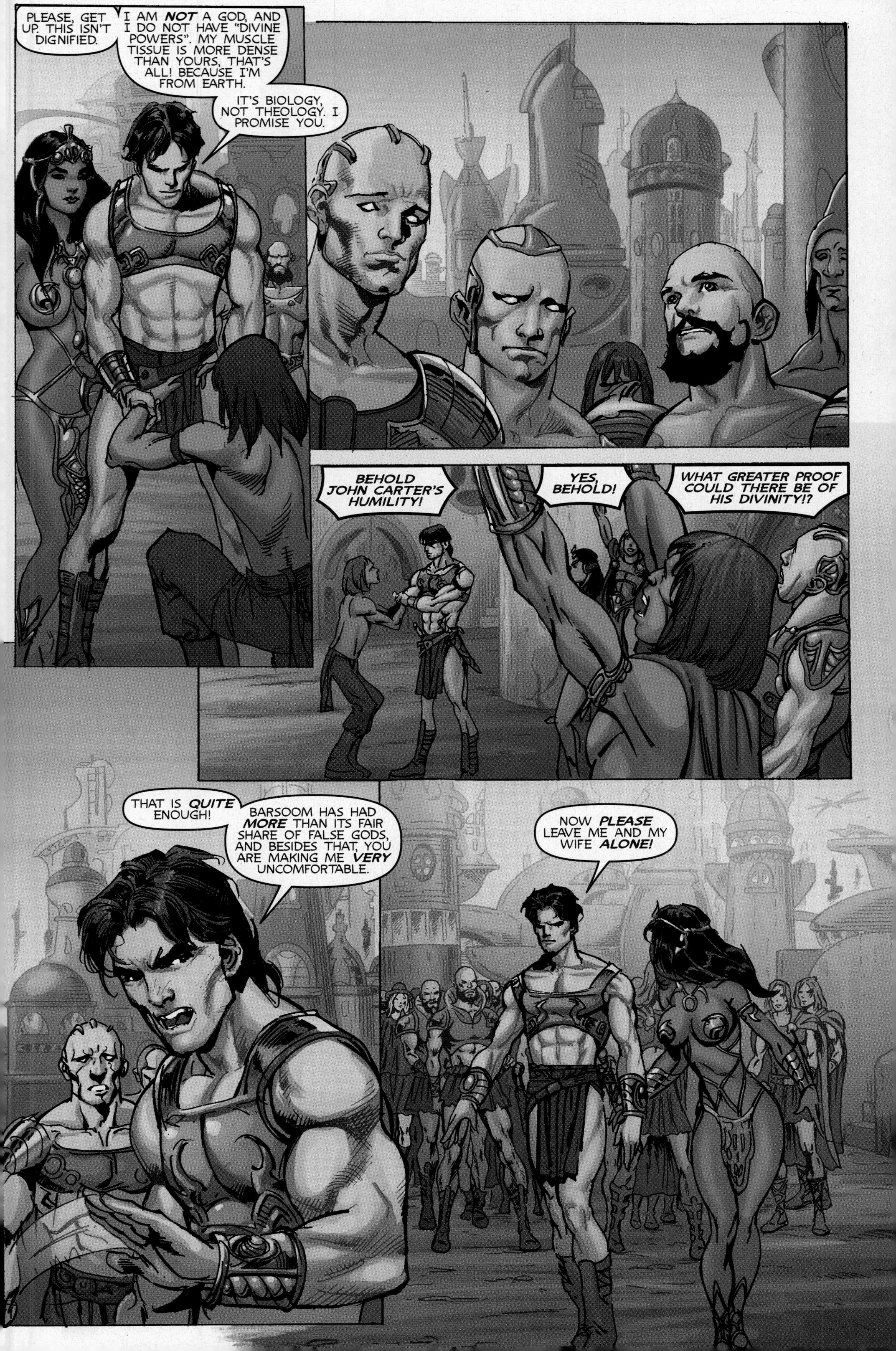
PLEASE, GET UP. THIS ISN'T DIGNIFIED.
I AM **NOT** A GOD, AND I DO NOT HAVE "DIVINE POWERS". MY MUSCLE TISSUE IS MORE DENSE THAN YOURS, THAT'S ALL! BECAUSE I'M FROM EARTH.
IT'S BIOLOGY, NOT THEOLOGY. I PROMISE YOU.
BEHOLD JOHN CARTER'S HUMILITY!
YES, BEHOLD!
WHAT GREATER PROOF COULD THERE BE OF HIS DIVINITY!?
THAT IS **QUITE** ENOUGH!
BARSOOM HAS HAD **MORE** THAN ITS FAIR SHARE OF FALSE GODS, AND BESIDES THAT, YOU ARE MAKING ME **VERY** UNCOMFORTABLE.
NOW **PLEASE** LEAVE ME AND MY WIFE **ALONE!**

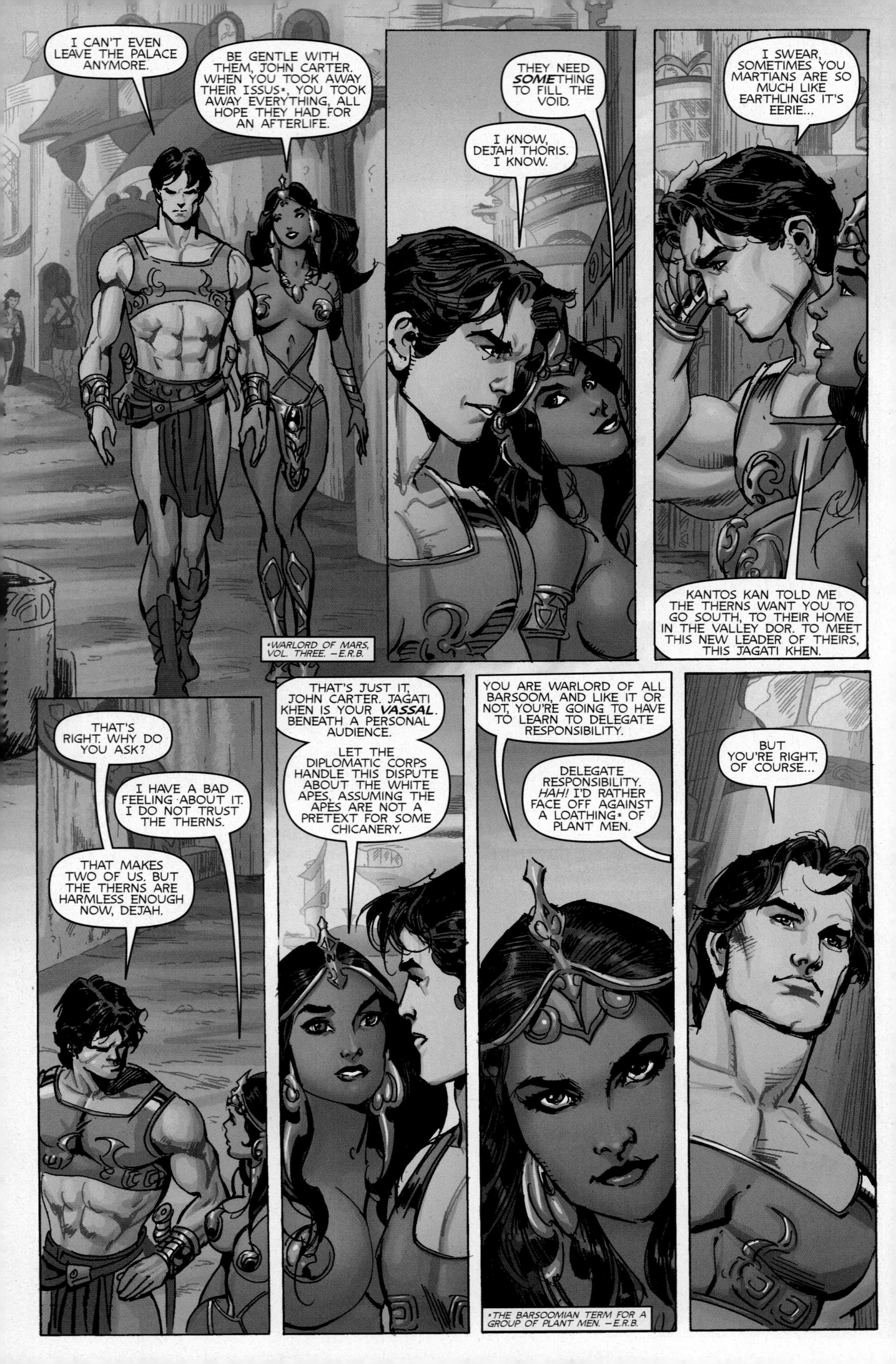
I CAN'T EVEN LEAVE THE PALACE ANYMORE.
BE GENTLE WITH THEM, JOHN CARTER. WHEN YOU TOOK AWAY THEIR ISSUS*, YOU TOOK AWAY EVERYTHING, ALL HOPE THEY HAD FOR AN AFTERLIFE.
*WARLORD OF MARS, VOL. THREE. —E.R.B.
THEY NEED SOMETHING TO FILL THE VOID.
I KNOW, DEJAH THORIS. I KNOW.
I SWEAR, SOMETIMES YOU MARTIANS ARE SO MUCH LIKE EARTHLINGS IT'S EERIE...
KANTOS KAN TOLD ME THE THERNS WANT YOU TO GO SOUTH, TO THEIR HOME IN THE VALLEY DOR. TO MEET THIS NEW LEADER OF THEIRS, THIS JAGATI KHEN.
THAT'S RIGHT. WHY DO YOU ASK?
I HAVE A BAD FEELING ABOUT IT. I DO NOT TRUST THE THERNS.
THAT MAKES TWO OF US. BUT THE THERNS ARE HARMLESS ENOUGH NOW, DEJAH.
THAT'S JUST IT, JOHN CARTER. JAGATI KHEN IS YOUR VASSAL. BENEATH A PERSONAL AUDIENCE.
LET THE DIPLOMATIC CORPS HANDLE THIS DISPUTE ABOUT THE WHITE APES, ASSUMING THE APES ARE NOT A PRETEXT FOR SOME CHICANERY.
YOU ARE WARLORD OF ALL BARSOOM, AND LIKE IT OR NOT, YOU'RE GOING TO HAVE TO LEARN TO DELEGATE RESPONSIBILITY.
DELEGATE RESPONSIBILITY. HAH! I'D RATHER FACE OFF AGAINST A LOATHING* OF PLANT MEN.
*THE BARSOOMIAN TERM FOR A GROUP OF PLANT MEN. —E.R.B.
BUT YOU'RE RIGHT, OF COURSE...

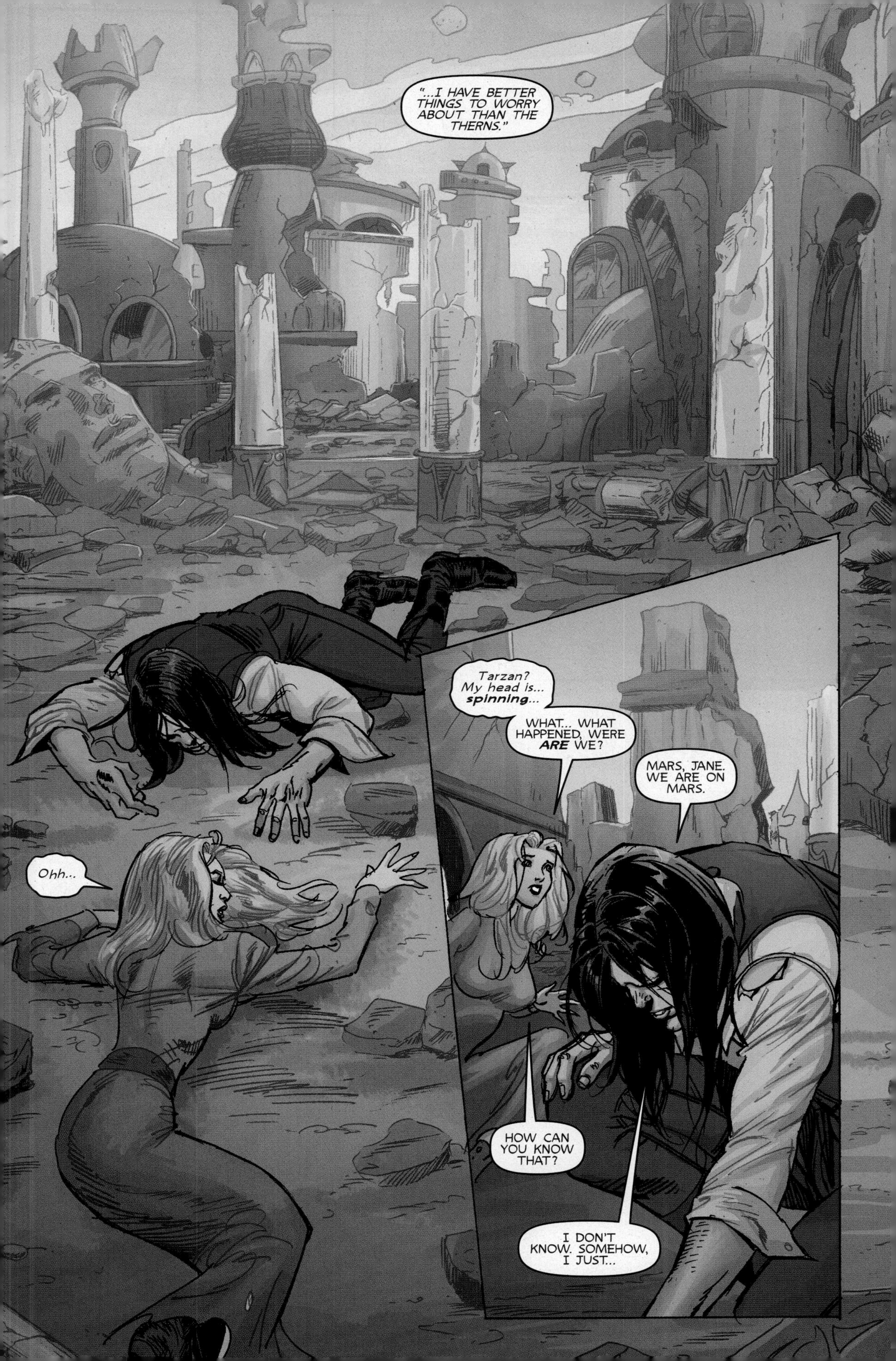
"...I HAVE BETTER THINGS TO WORRY ABOUT THAN THE THERNS."
Ohh...
Tarzan? My head is... **spinning**...
WHAT... WHAT HAPPENED, WERE **ARE** WE?
MARS, JANE. WE ARE ON MARS.
HOW CAN YOU KNOW THAT?
I DON'T KNOW. SOMEHOW, I JUST...

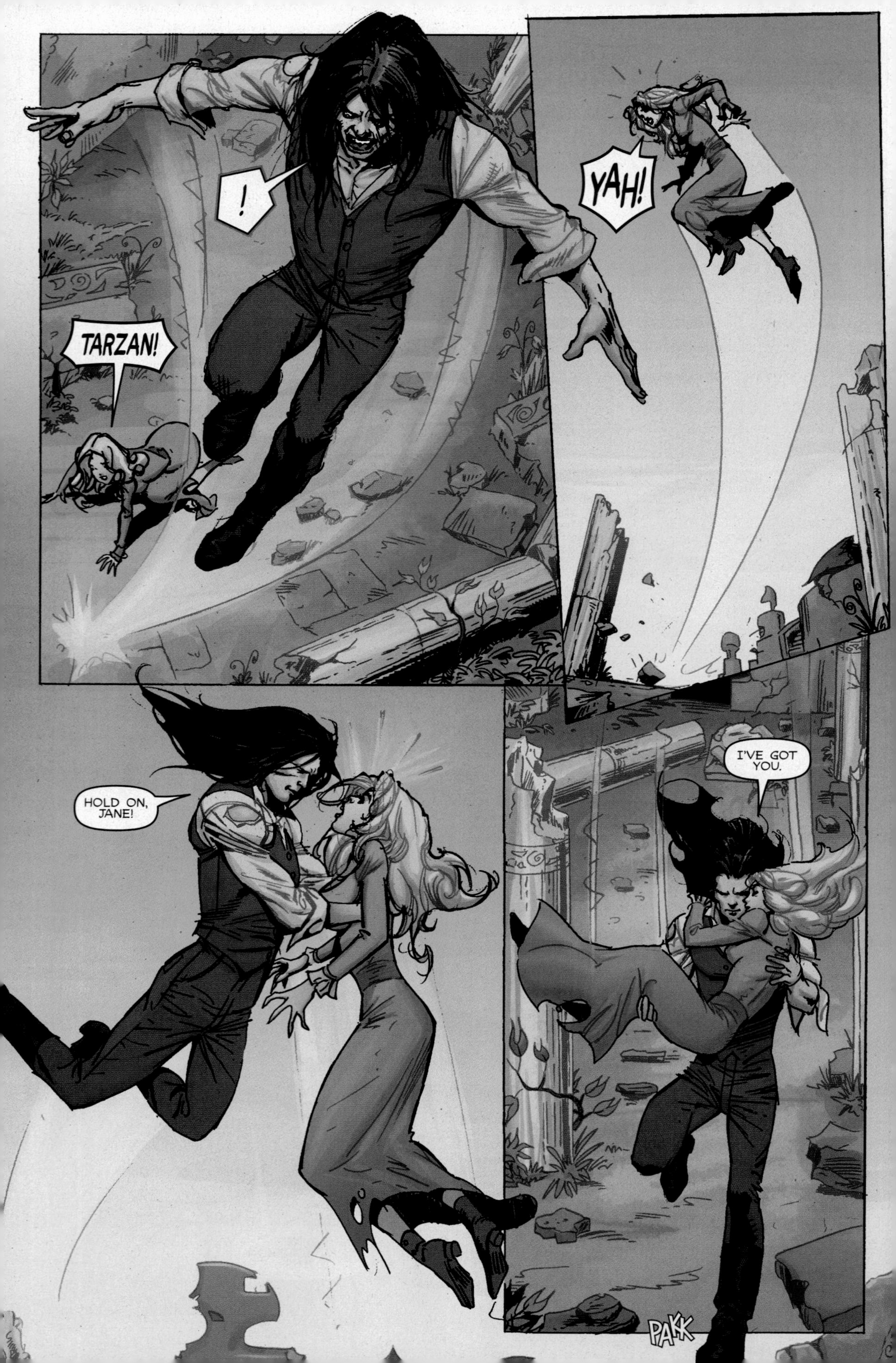
!
TARZAN!
YAH!
HOLD ON, JANE!
I'VE GOT YOU.
PAKK

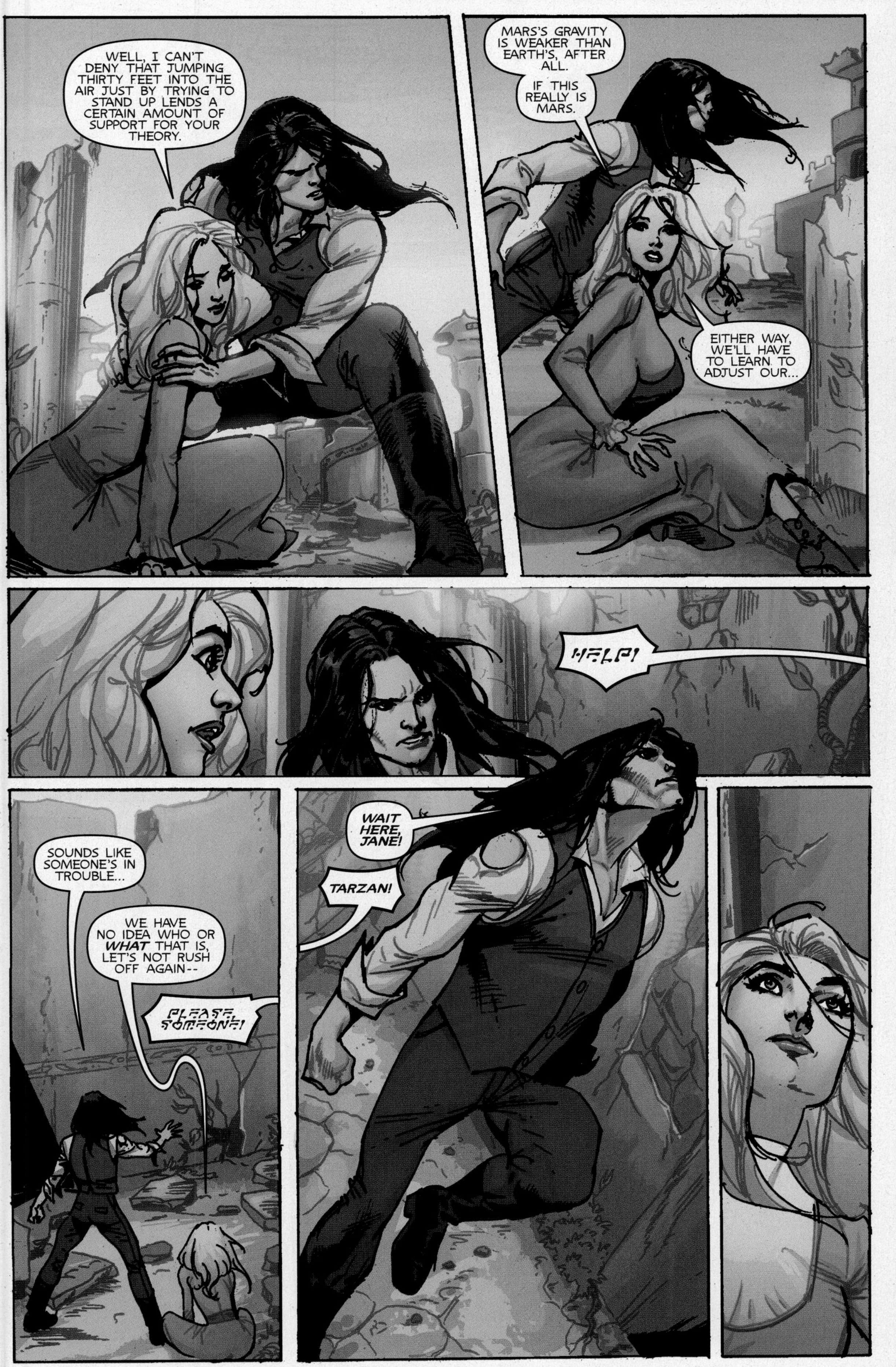

WELL, I CAN'T DENY THAT JUMPING THIRTY FEET INTO THE AIR JUST BY TRYING TO STAND UP LENDS A CERTAIN AMOUNT OF SUPPORT FOR YOUR THEORY.
MARS'S GRAVITY IS WEAKER THAN EARTH'S, AFTER ALL.
IF THIS REALLY IS MARS.
EITHER WAY, WE'LL HAVE TO LEARN TO ADJUST OUR...
HELP!
SOUNDS LIKE SOMEONE'S IN TROUBLE...
WE HAVE NO IDEA WHO OR *WHAT* THAT IS, LET'S NOT RUSH OFF AGAIN--
PLEASE SOMEONE!
WAIT HERE, JANE!
TARZAN!

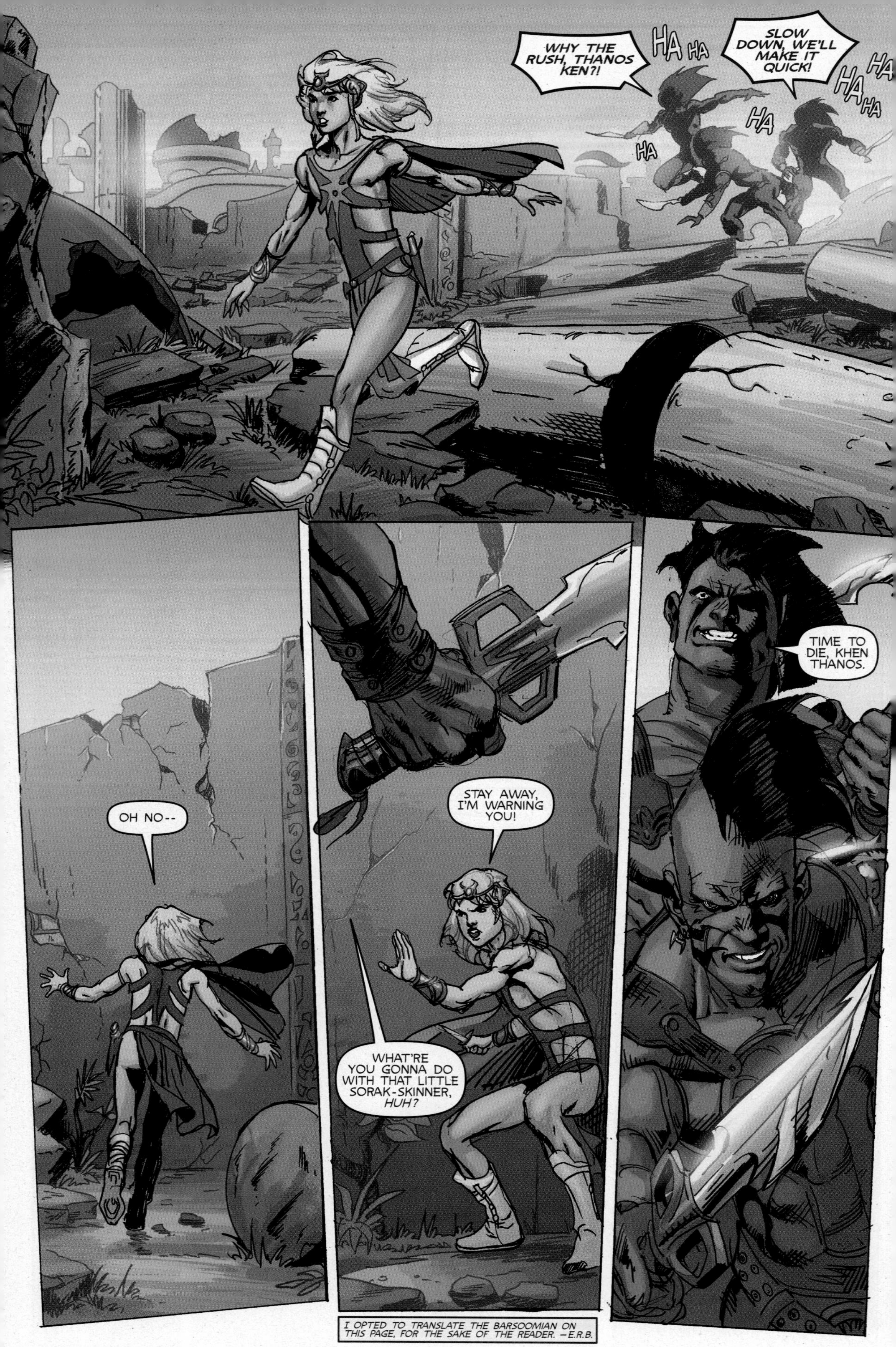
WHY THE RUSH, THANOS KEN?!
HA HA
SLOW DOWN, WE'LL MAKE IT QUICK!
HA HA HA HA HA
OH NO--
STAY AWAY, I'M WARNING YOU!
WHAT'RE YOU GONNA DO WITH THAT LITTLE SORAK-SKINNER, HUH?
TIME TO DIE, KHEN THANOS.
I OPTED TO TRANSLATE THE BARSOOMIAN ON THIS PAGE, FOR THE SAKE OF THE READER. –E.R.B.

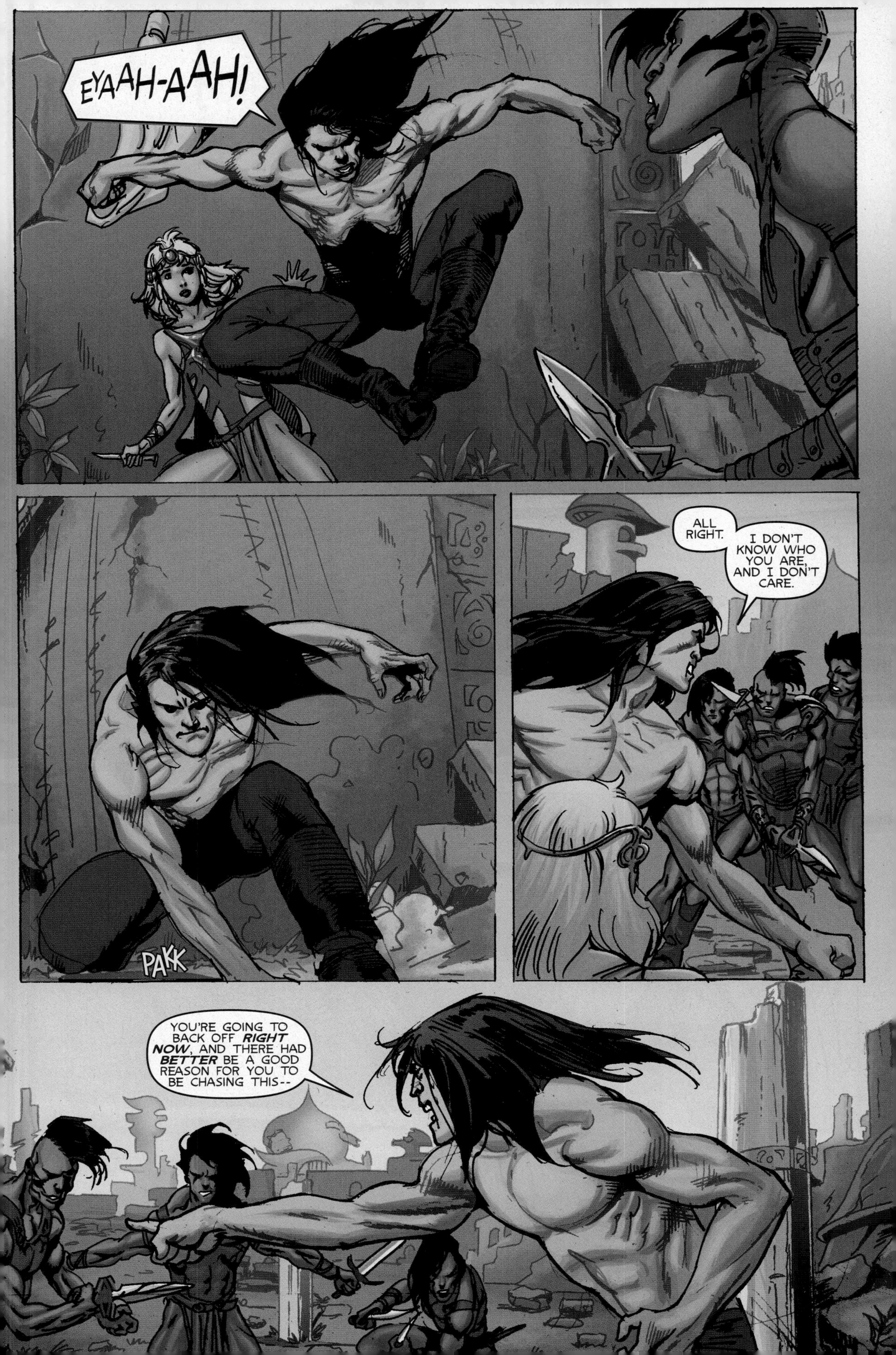
EYAAH-AAH!
PAKK
ALL RIGHT.
I DON'T KNOW WHO YOU ARE, AND I DON'T CARE.
YOU'RE GOING TO BACK OFF RIGHT NOW, AND THERE HAD BETTER BE A GOOD REASON FOR YOU TO BE CHASING THIS--

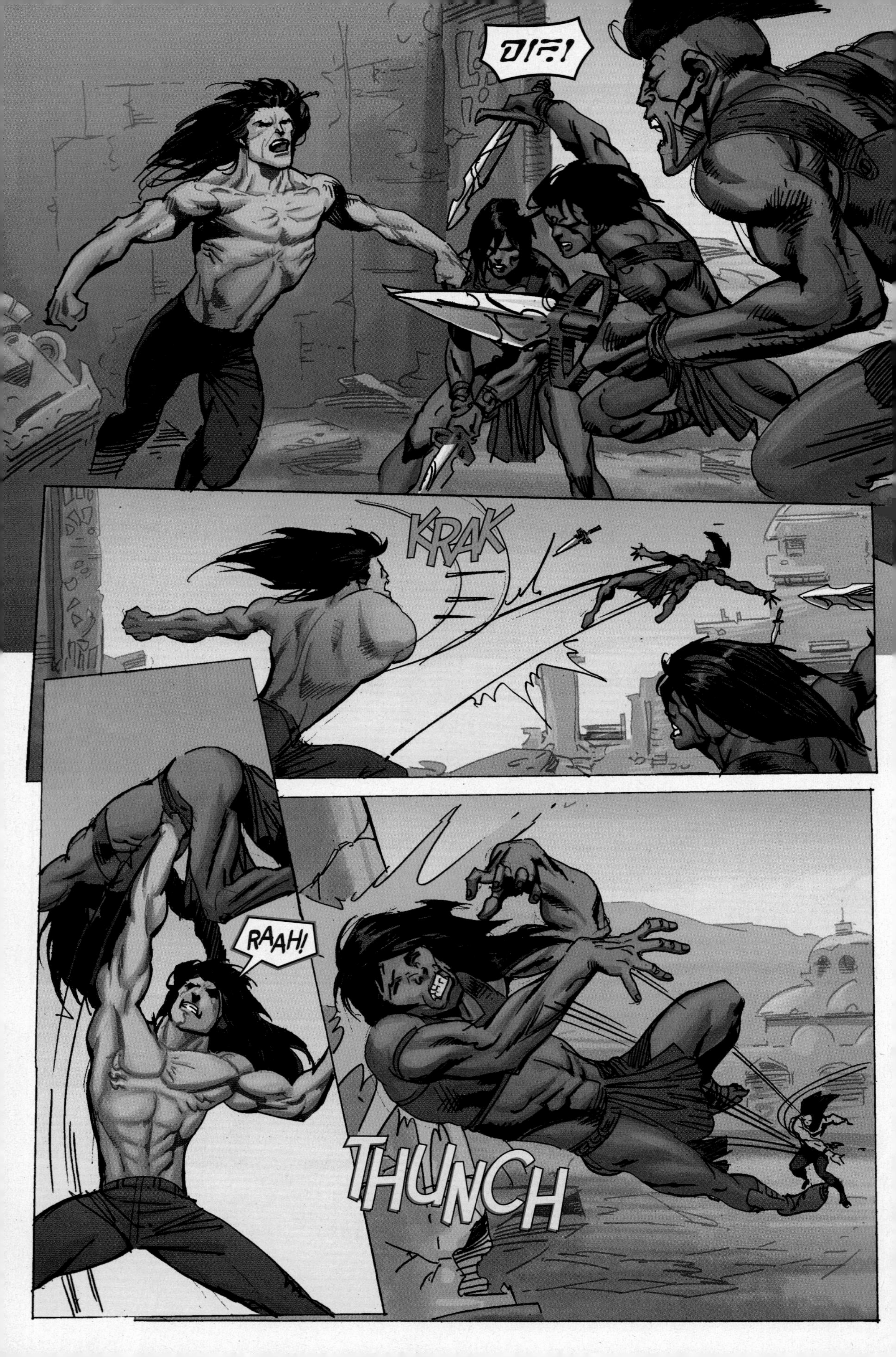
OIF!
KRAK
RAAH!
THUNCH

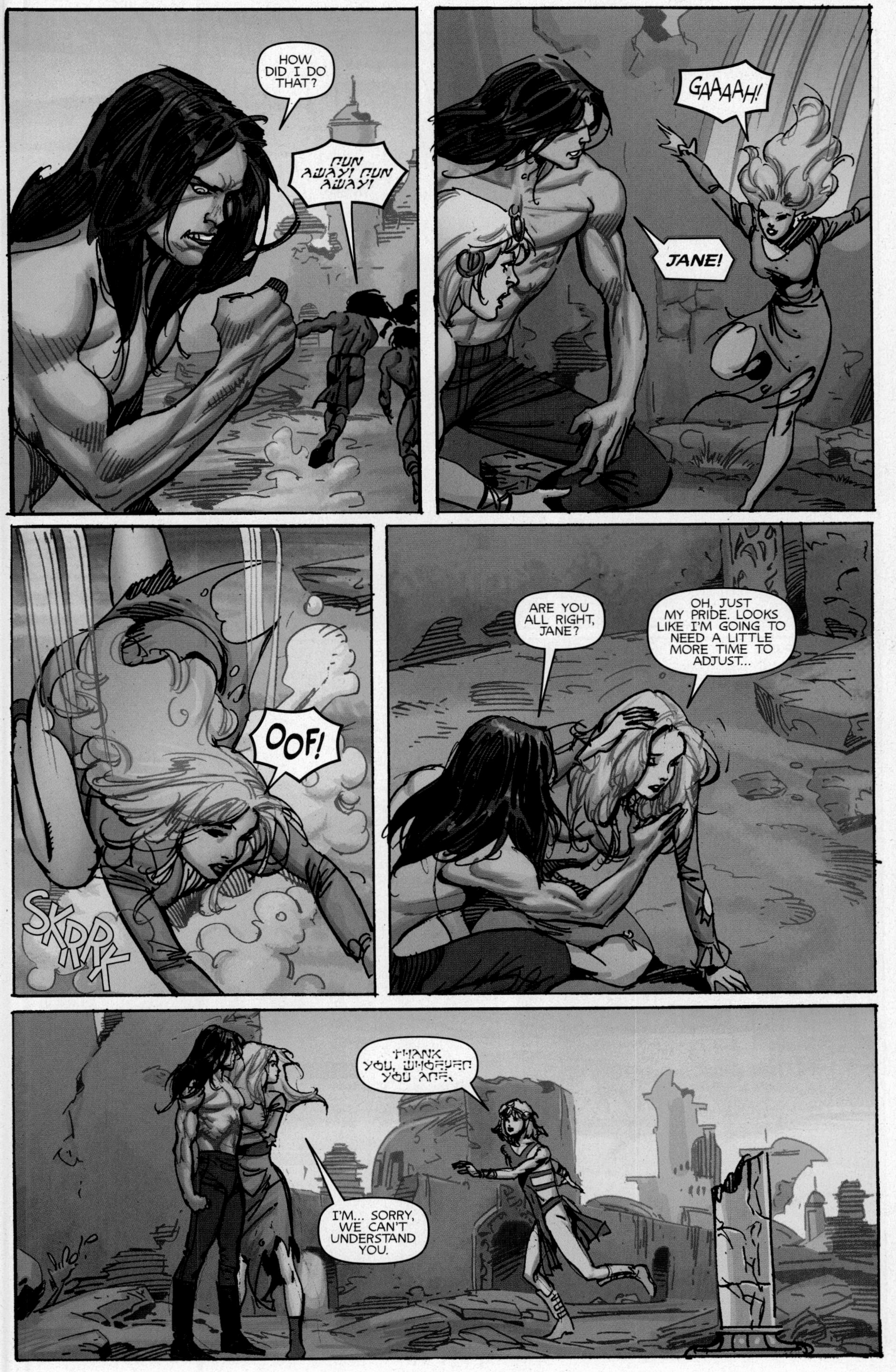
HOW DID I DO THAT?
RUN AWAY! RUN AWAY!
GAAAAH!
JANE!
OOF!
SKRRK
ARE YOU ALL RIGHT, JANE?
OH, JUST MY PRIDE. LOOKS LIKE I'M GOING TO NEED A LITTLE MORE TIME TO ADJUST...
THANK YOU, WHOEVER YOU ARE.
I'M... SORRY, WE CAN'T UNDERSTAND YOU.

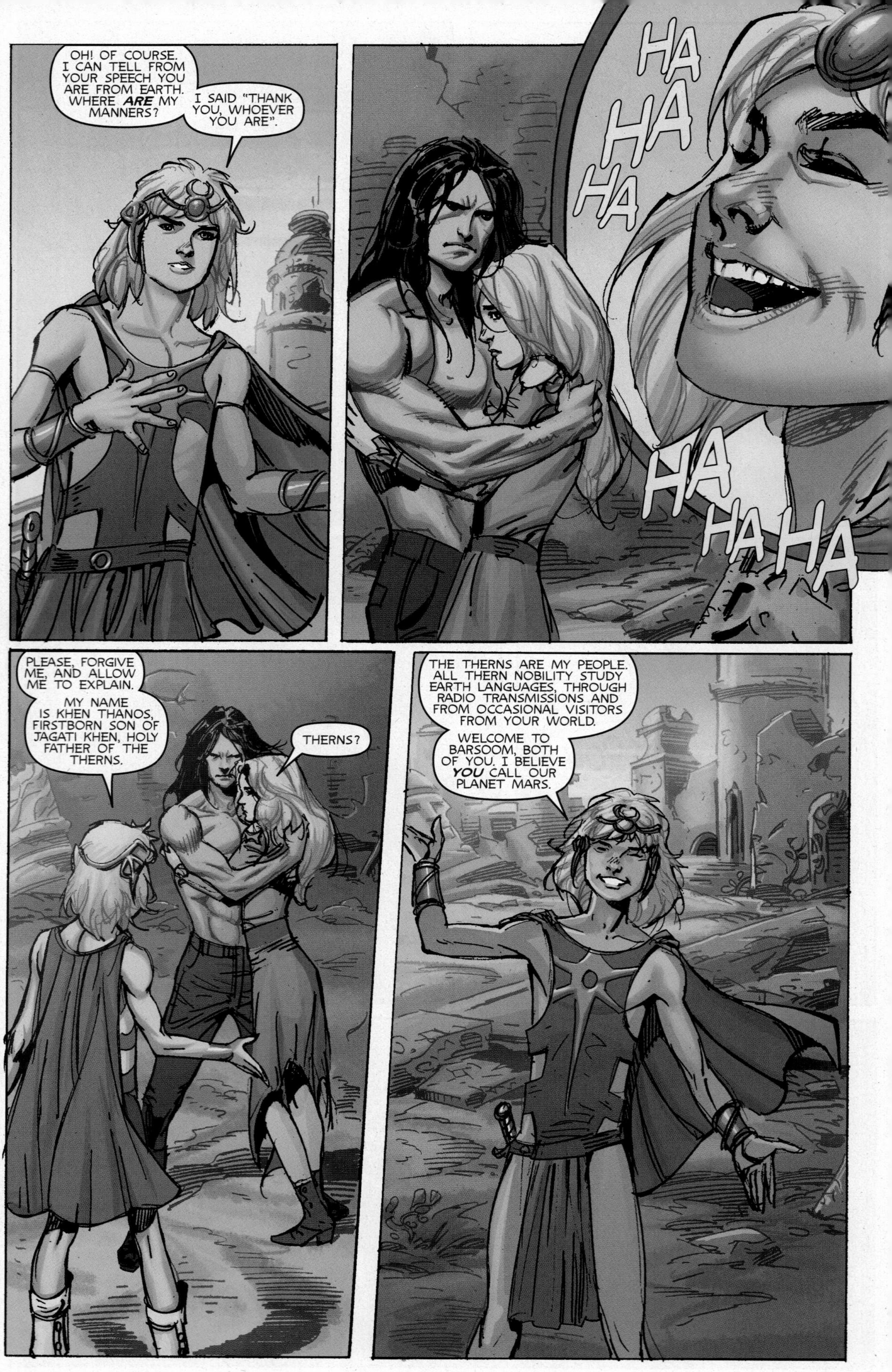
OH! OF COURSE. I CAN TELL FROM YOUR SPEECH YOU ARE FROM EARTH. WHERE ARE MY MANNERS?
I SAID "THANK YOU, WHOEVER YOU ARE".
HA HA HA
HA HA HA
PLEASE, FORGIVE ME, AND ALLOW ME TO EXPLAIN.
MY NAME IS KHEN THANOS, FIRSTBORN SON OF JAGATI KHEN, HOLY FATHER OF THE THERNS.
THERNS?
THE THERNS ARE MY PEOPLE. ALL THERN NOBILITY STUDY EARTH LANGUAGES, THROUGH RADIO TRANSMISSIONS AND FROM OCCASIONAL VISITORS FROM YOUR WORLD.
WELCOME TO BARSOOM, BOTH OF YOU. I BELIEVE YOU CALL OUR PLANET MARS.

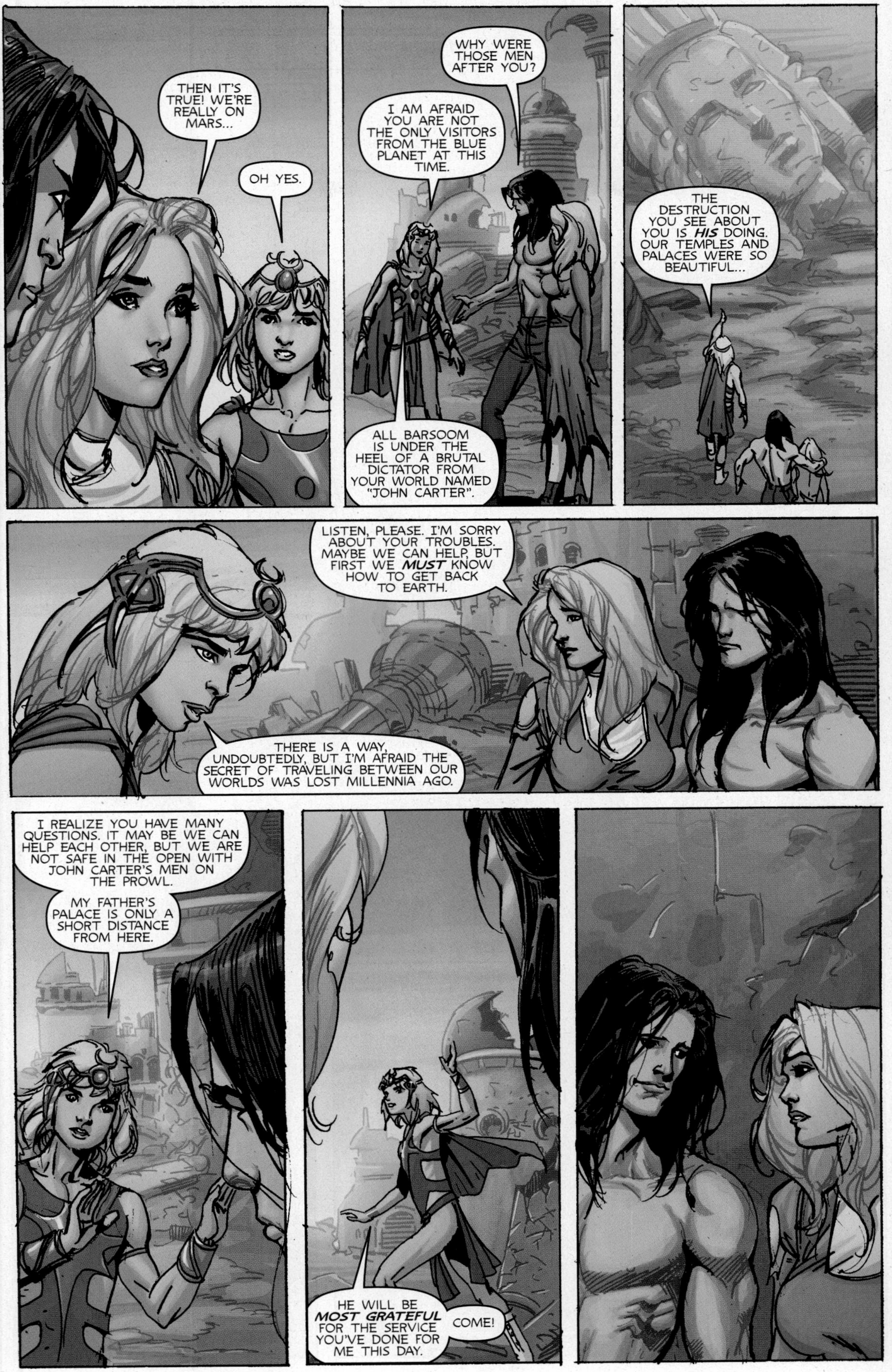
THEN IT'S TRUE! WE'RE REALLY ON MARS...
OH YES.
WHY WERE THOSE MEN AFTER YOU?
I AM AFRAID YOU ARE NOT THE ONLY VISITORS FROM THE BLUE PLANET AT THIS TIME.
ALL BARSOOM IS UNDER THE HEEL OF A BRUTAL DICTATOR FROM YOUR WORLD NAMED "JOHN CARTER".
THE DESTRUCTION YOU SEE ABOUT YOU IS *HIS* DOING. OUR TEMPLES AND PALACES WERE SO BEAUTIFUL...
LISTEN, PLEASE. I'M SORRY ABOUT YOUR TROUBLES. MAYBE WE CAN HELP, BUT FIRST WE *MUST* KNOW HOW TO GET BACK TO EARTH.
THERE IS A WAY, UNDOUBTEDLY, BUT I'M AFRAID THE SECRET OF TRAVELING BETWEEN OUR WORLDS WAS LOST MILLENNIA AGO.
I REALIZE YOU HAVE MANY QUESTIONS. IT MAY BE WE CAN HELP EACH OTHER, BUT WE ARE NOT SAFE IN THE OPEN WITH JOHN CARTER'S MEN ON THE PROWL.
MY FATHER'S PALACE IS ONLY A SHORT DISTANCE FROM HERE.
HE WILL BE *MOST GRATEFUL* FOR THE SERVICE YOU'VE DONE FOR ME THIS DAY.
COME!

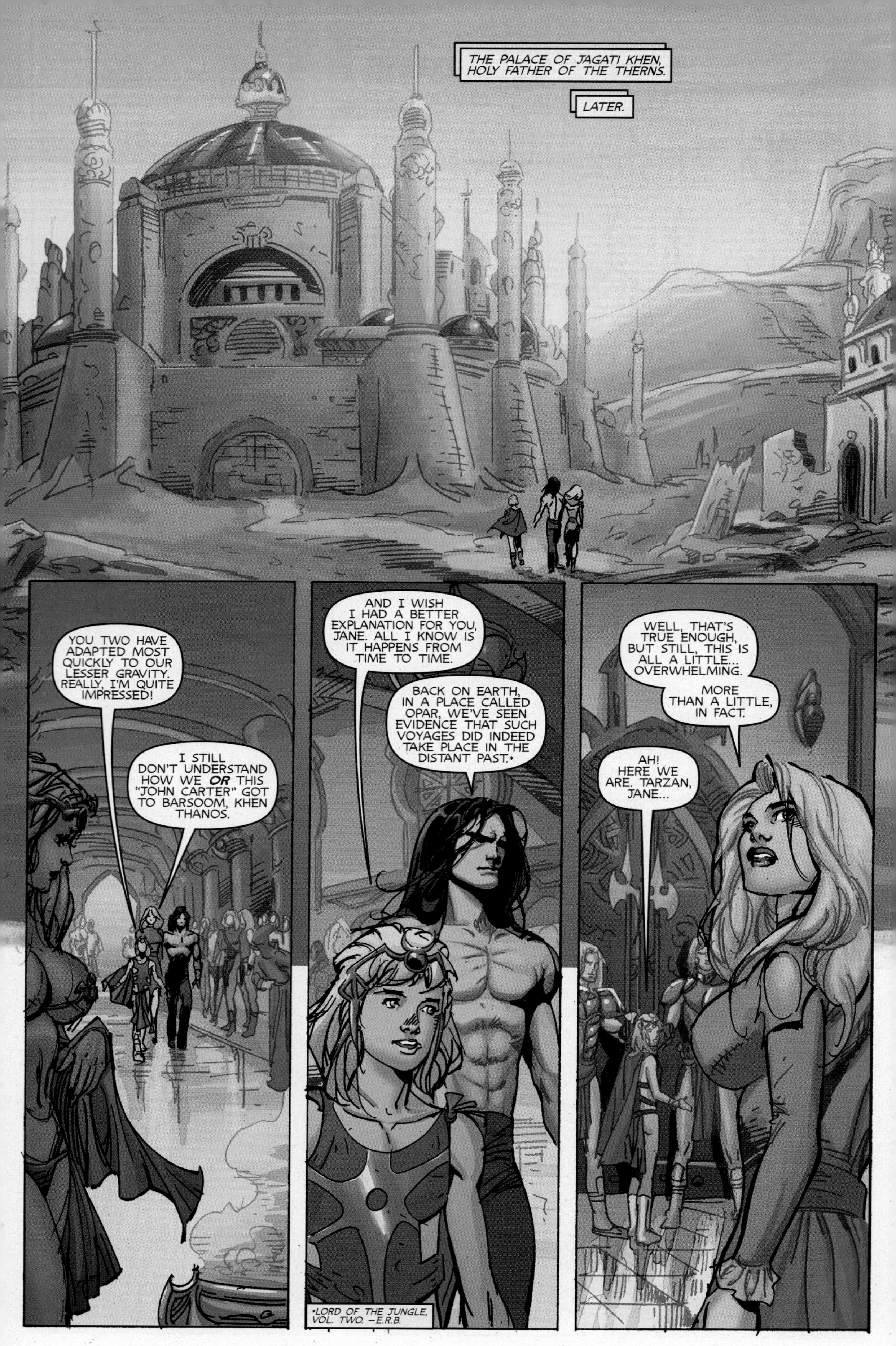
THE PALACE OF JAGATI KHEN, HOLY FATHER OF THE THERNS.
LATER.
YOU TWO HAVE ADAPTED MOST QUICKLY TO OUR LESSER GRAVITY. REALLY, I'M QUITE IMPRESSED!
I STILL DON'T UNDERSTAND HOW WE OR THIS "JOHN CARTER" GOT TO BARSOOM, KHEN THANOS.
AND I WISH I HAD A BETTER EXPLANATION FOR YOU, JANE. ALL I KNOW IS IT HAPPENS FROM TIME TO TIME.
BACK ON EARTH, IN A PLACE CALLED OPAR, WE'VE SEEN EVIDENCE THAT SUCH VOYAGES DID INDEED TAKE PLACE IN THE DISTANT PAST.*
*LORD OF THE JUNGLE, VOL. TWO. —E.R.B.
WELL, THAT'S TRUE ENOUGH, BUT STILL, THIS IS ALL A LITTLE... OVERWHELMING.
MORE THAN A LITTLE, IN FACT.
AH! HERE WE ARE. TARZAN, JANE...

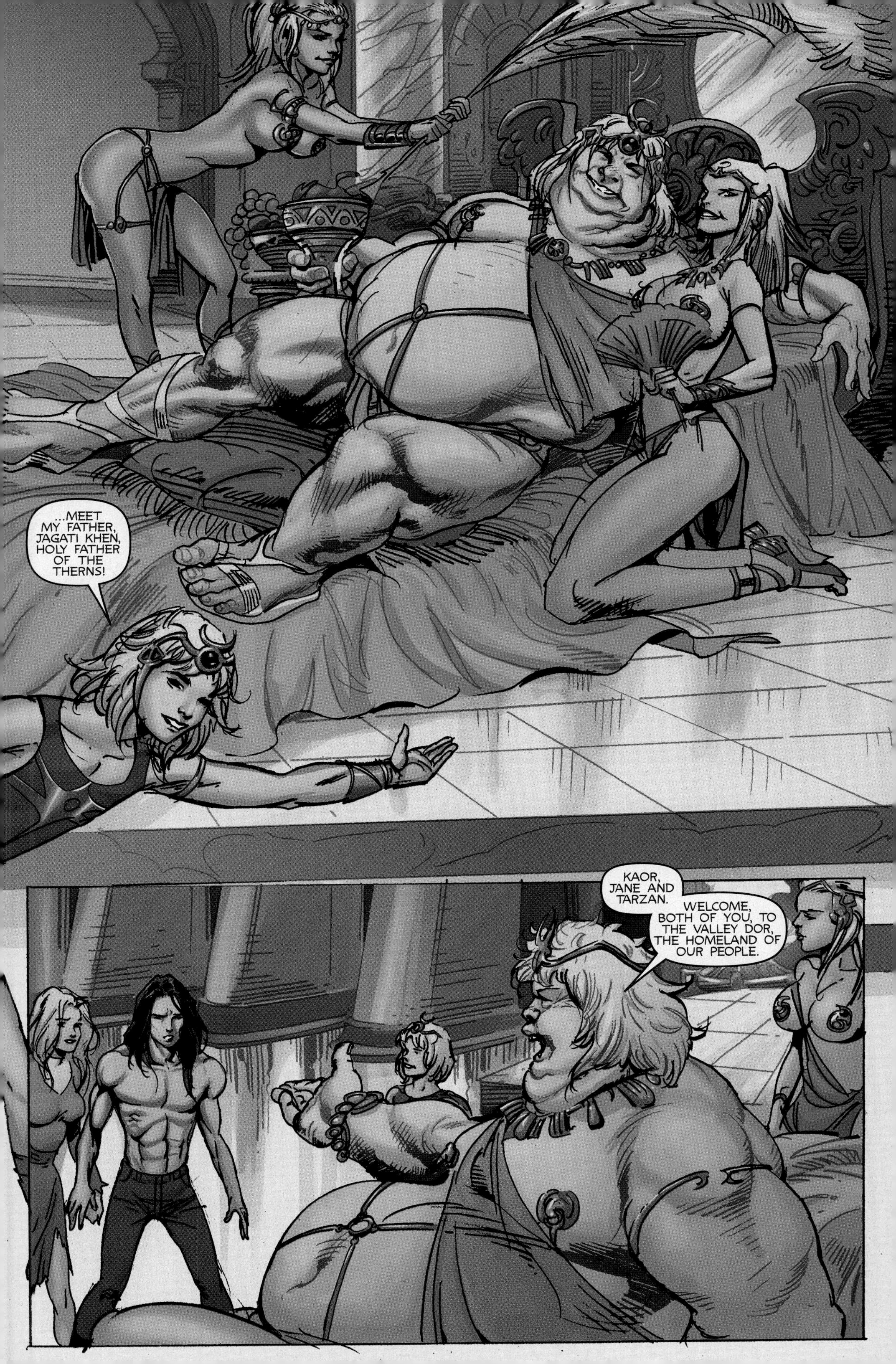
...MEET MY FATHER, JAGATI KHEN, HOLY FATHER OF THE THERNS!
KAOR, JANE AND TARZAN.
WELCOME, BOTH OF YOU, TO THE VALLEY DOR, THE HOMELAND OF OUR PEOPLE.

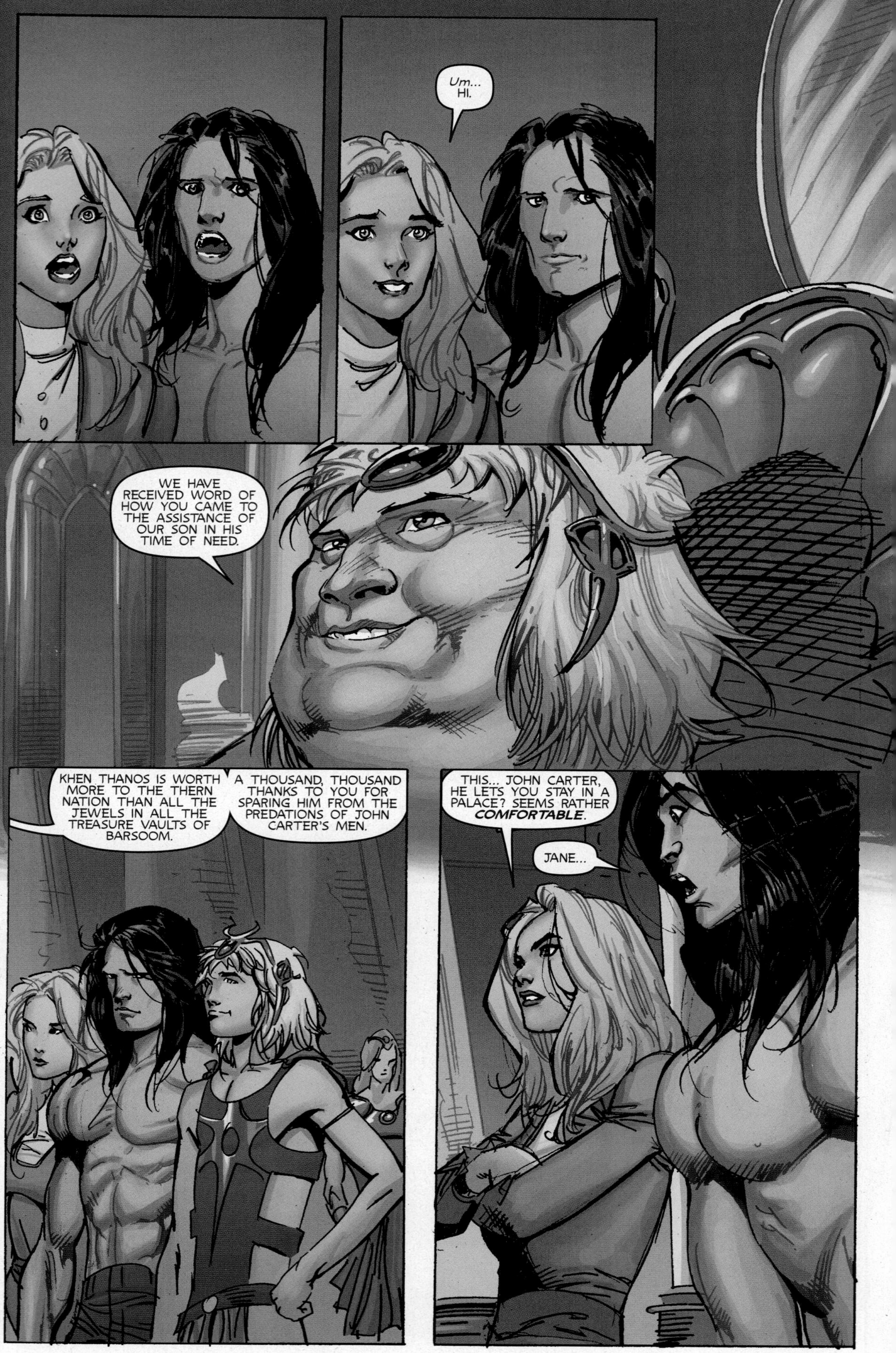
Um... HI.
WE HAVE RECEIVED WORD OF HOW YOU CAME TO THE ASSISTANCE OF OUR SON IN HIS TIME OF NEED.
KHEN THANOS IS WORTH MORE TO THE THERN NATION THAN ALL THE JEWELS IN ALL THE TREASURE VAULTS OF BARSOOM.
A THOUSAND, THOUSAND THANKS TO YOU FOR SPARING HIM FROM THE PREDATIONS OF JOHN CARTER'S MEN.
THIS... JOHN CARTER, HE LETS YOU STAY IN A PALACE? SEEMS RATHER *COMFORTABLE*.
JANE...

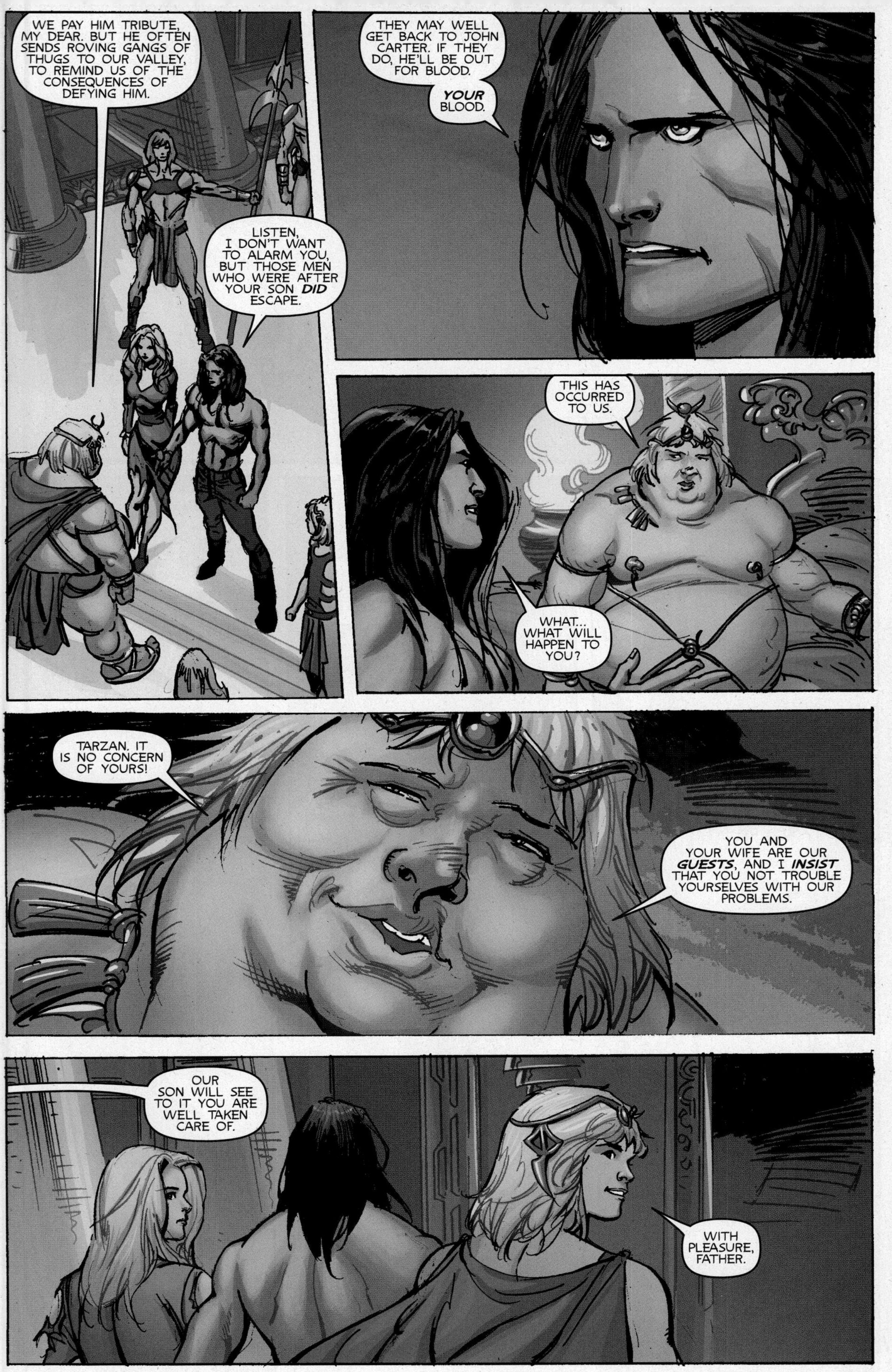
WE PAY HIM TRIBUTE, MY DEAR. BUT HE OFTEN SENDS ROVING GANGS OF THUGS TO OUR VALLEY, TO REMIND US OF THE CONSEQUENCES OF DEFYING HIM.
LISTEN, I DON'T WANT TO ALARM YOU, BUT THOSE MEN WHO WERE AFTER YOUR SON *DID* ESCAPE.
THEY MAY WELL GET BACK TO JOHN CARTER. IF THEY DO, HE'LL BE OUT FOR BLOOD.
YOUR BLOOD.
THIS HAS OCCURRED TO US.
WHAT... WHAT WILL HAPPEN TO YOU?
TARZAN. IT IS NO CONCERN OF YOURS!
YOU AND YOUR WIFE ARE OUR *GUESTS*, AND I *INSIST* THAT YOU NOT TROUBLE YOURSELVES WITH OUR PROBLEMS.
OUR SON WILL SEE TO IT YOU ARE WELL TAKEN CARE OF.
WITH PLEASURE, FATHER.

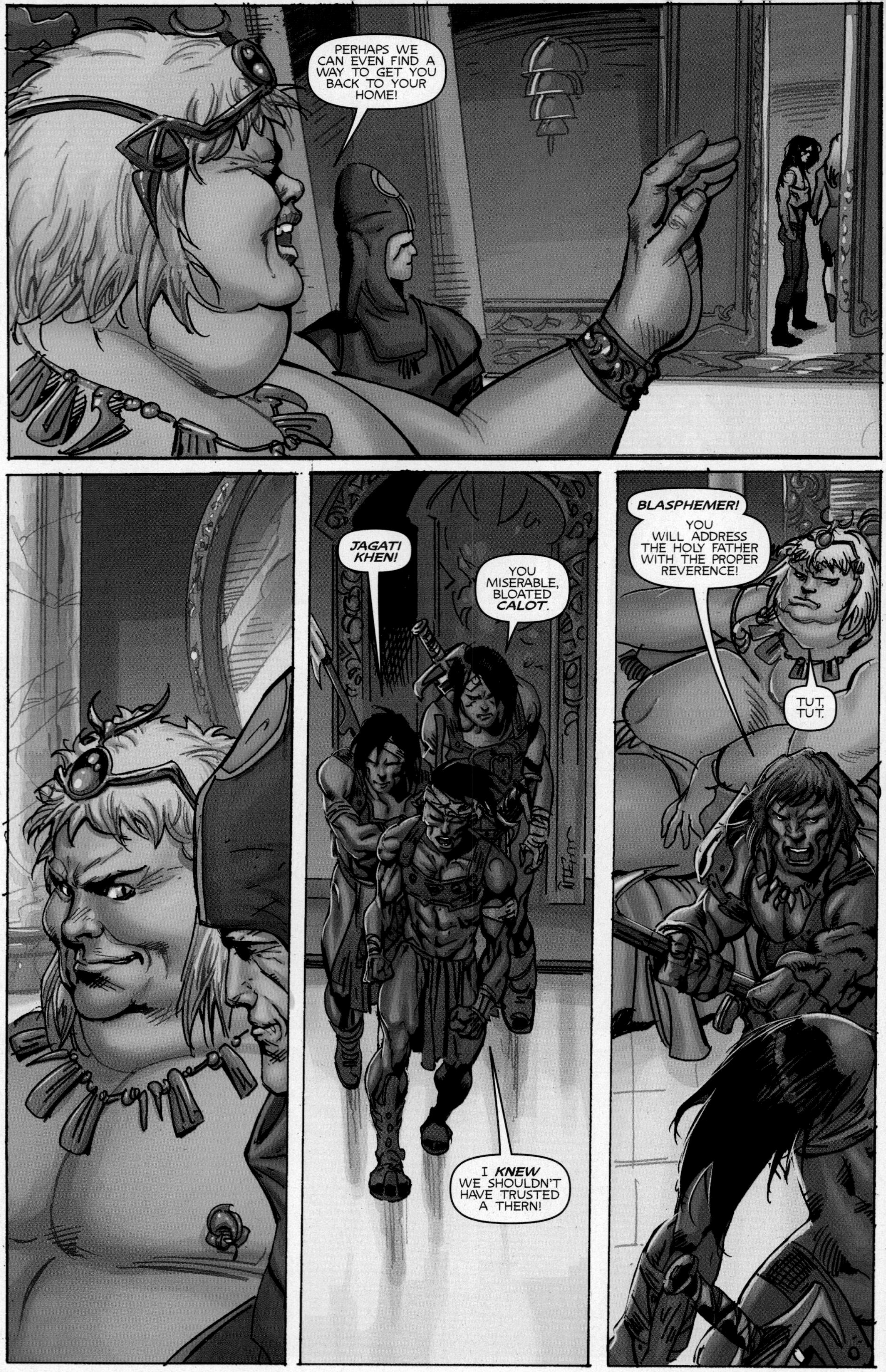
PERHAPS WE CAN EVEN FIND A WAY TO GET YOU BACK TO YOUR HOME!
JAGATI KHEN!
YOU MISERABLE, BLOATED *CALOT*.
I *KNEW* WE SHOULDN'T HAVE TRUSTED A THERN!
BLASPHEMER!
YOU WILL ADDRESS THE HOLY FATHER WITH THE PROPER REVERENCE!
TUT, TUT.

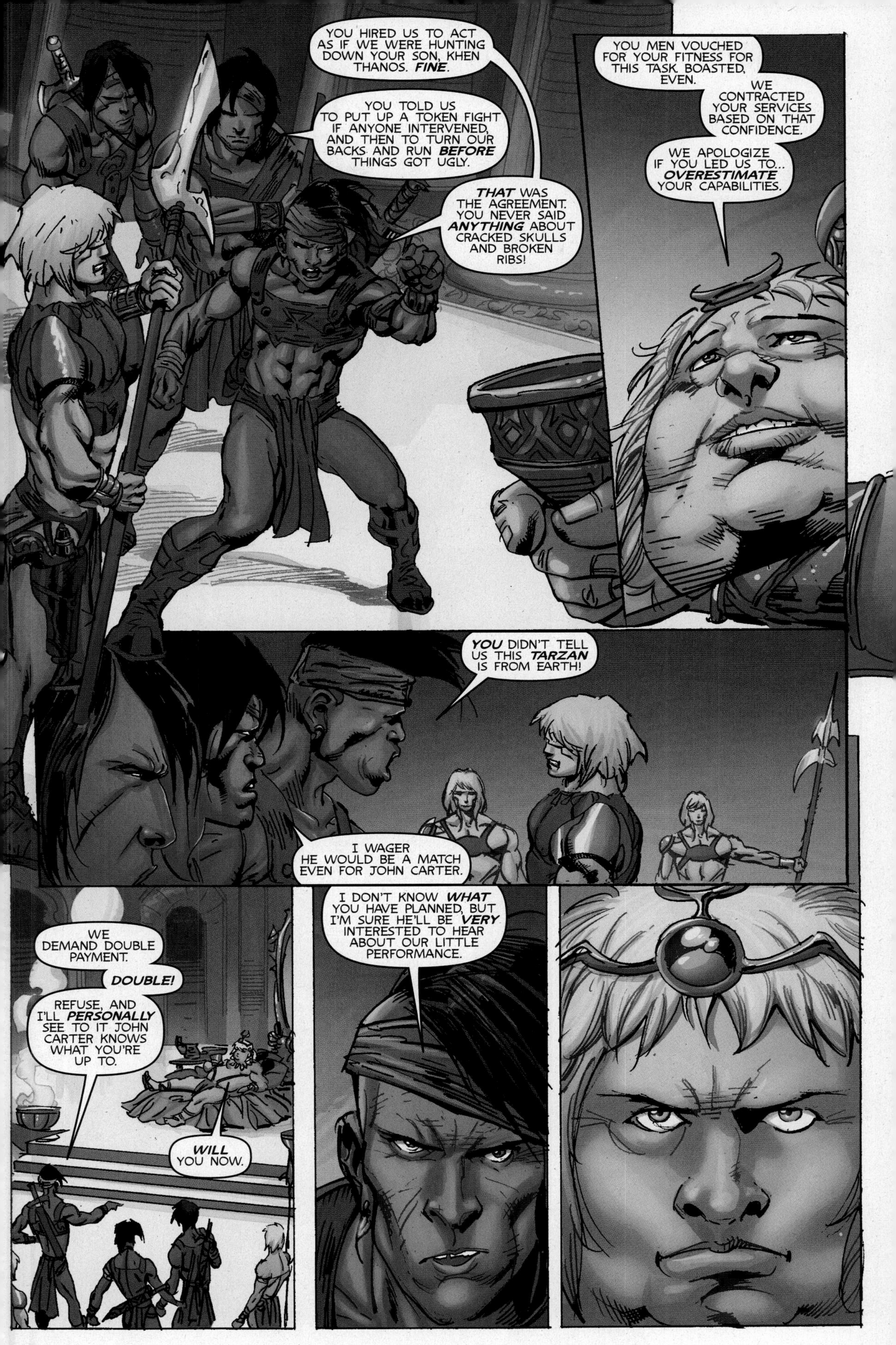
YOU HIRED US TO ACT AS IF WE WERE HUNTING DOWN YOUR SON, KHEN THANOS. FINE.
YOU TOLD US TO PUT UP A TOKEN FIGHT IF ANYONE INTERVENED, AND THEN TO TURN OUR BACKS AND RUN BEFORE THINGS GOT UGLY.
THAT WAS THE AGREEMENT. YOU NEVER SAID ANYTHING ABOUT CRACKED SKULLS AND BROKEN RIBS!
YOU MEN VOUCHED FOR YOUR FITNESS FOR THIS TASK. BOASTED, EVEN.
WE CONTRACTED YOUR SERVICES BASED ON THAT CONFIDENCE.
WE APOLOGIZE IF YOU LED US TO... OVERESTIMATE YOUR CAPABILITIES.
YOU DIDN'T TELL US THIS TARZAN IS FROM EARTH!
I WAGER HE WOULD BE A MATCH EVEN FOR JOHN CARTER.
WE DEMAND DOUBLE PAYMENT.
DOUBLE!
REFUSE, AND I'LL PERSONALLY SEE TO IT JOHN CARTER KNOWS WHAT YOU'RE UP TO.
WILL YOU NOW.
I DON'T KNOW WHAT YOU HAVE PLANNED, BUT I'M SURE HE'LL BE VERY INTERESTED TO HEAR ABOUT OUR LITTLE PERFORMANCE.

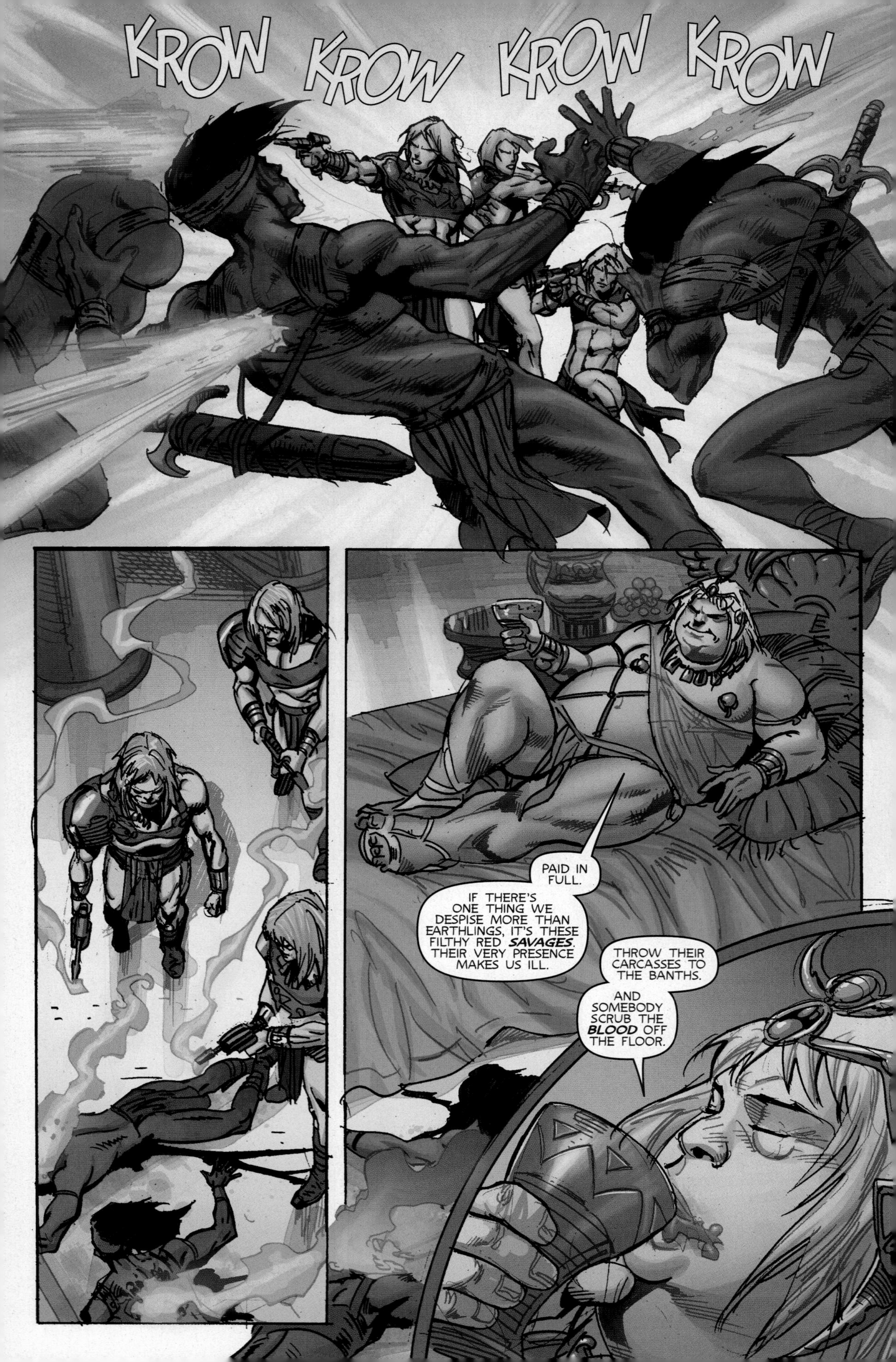
KROW KROW KROW KROW
PAID IN FULL.
IF THERE'S ONE THING WE DESPISE MORE THAN EARTHLINGS, IT'S THESE FILTHY RED *SAVAGES*. THEIR VERY PRESENCE MAKES US ILL.
THROW THEIR CARCASSES TO THE BANTHS.
AND SOMEBODY SCRUB THE *BLOOD* OFF THE FLOOR.

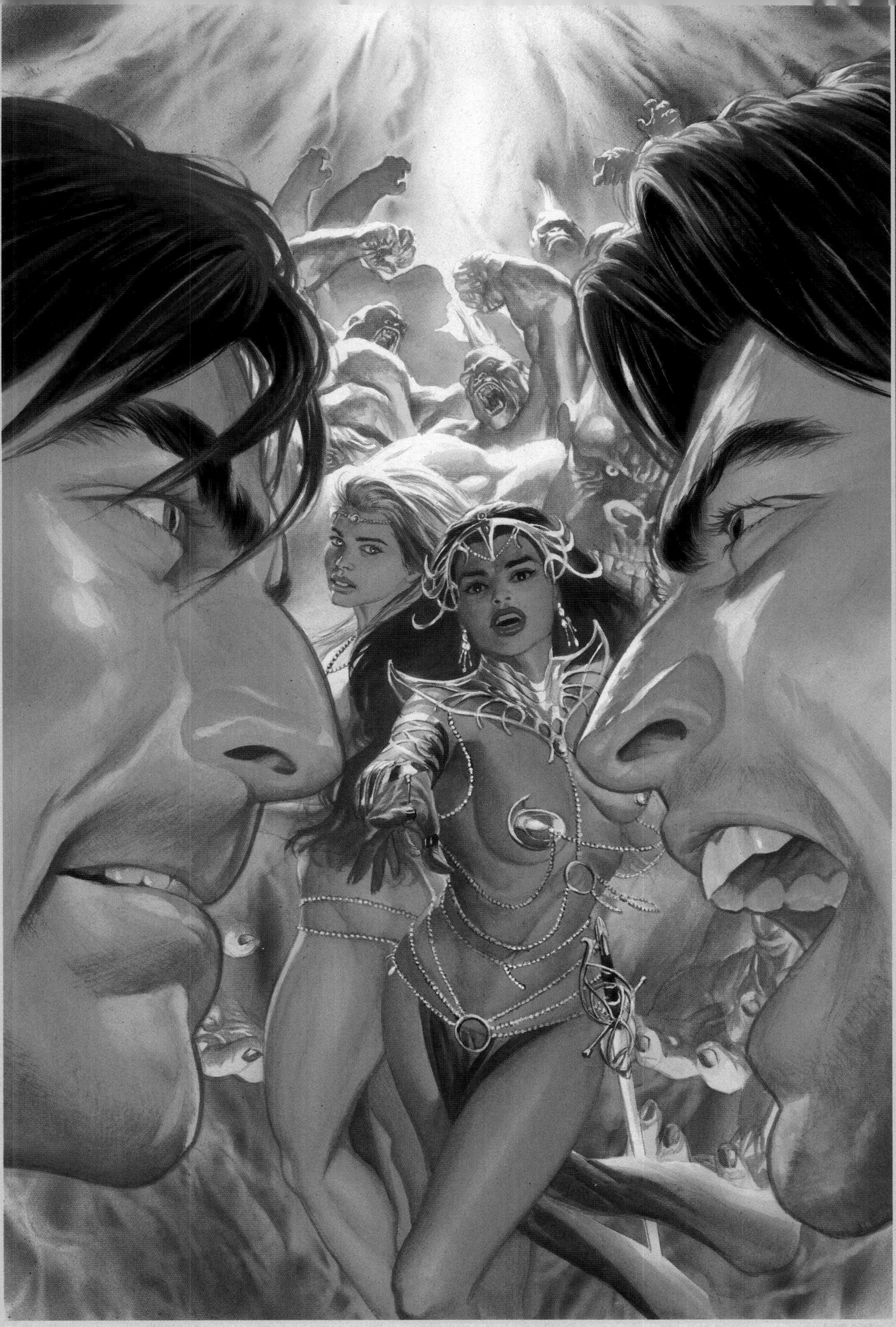

ISSUE 3
TO KILL A GOD

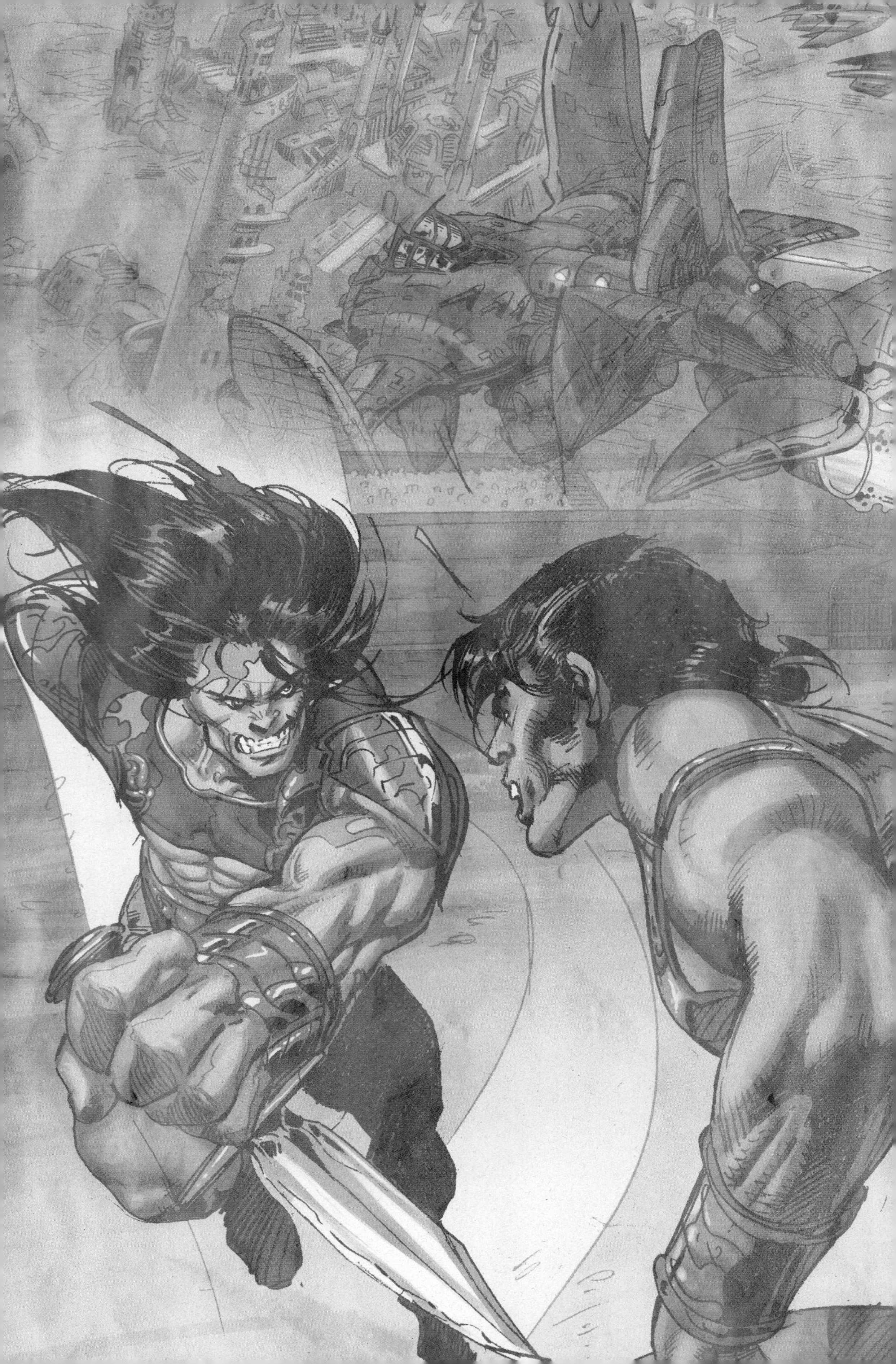

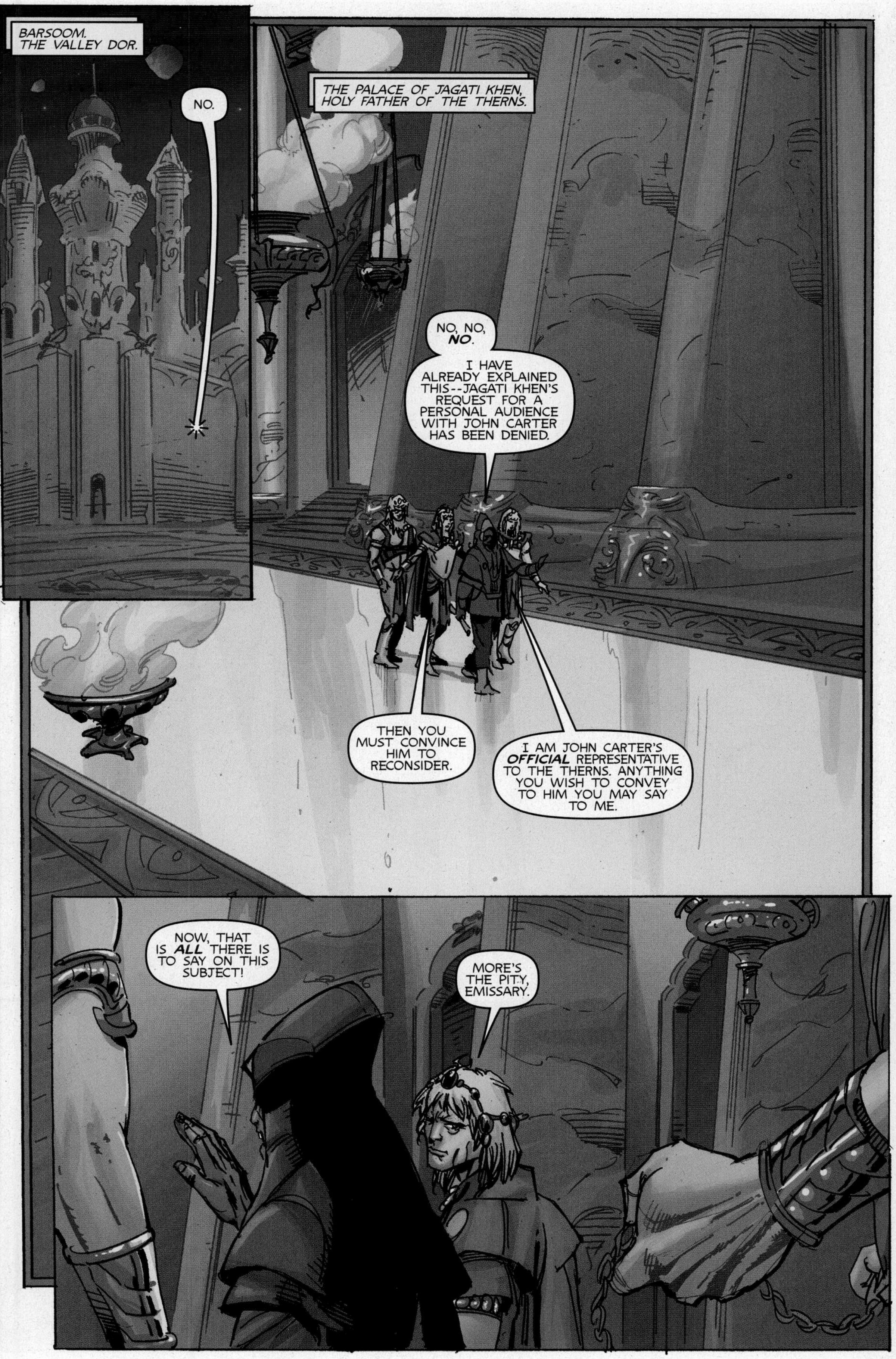

BARSOOM.
THE VALLEY DOR.
NO.
THE PALACE OF JAGATI KHEN, HOLY FATHER OF THE THERNS.
NO, NO, NO.
I HAVE ALREADY EXPLAINED THIS--JAGATI KHEN'S REQUEST FOR A PERSONAL AUDIENCE WITH JOHN CARTER HAS BEEN DENIED.
THEN YOU MUST CONVINCE HIM TO RECONSIDER.
I AM JOHN CARTER'S OFFICIAL REPRESENTATIVE TO THE THERNS. ANYTHING YOU WISH TO CONVEY TO HIM YOU MAY SAY TO ME.
NOW, THAT IS ALL THERE IS TO SAY ON THIS SUBJECT!
MORE'S THE PITY, EMISSARY.

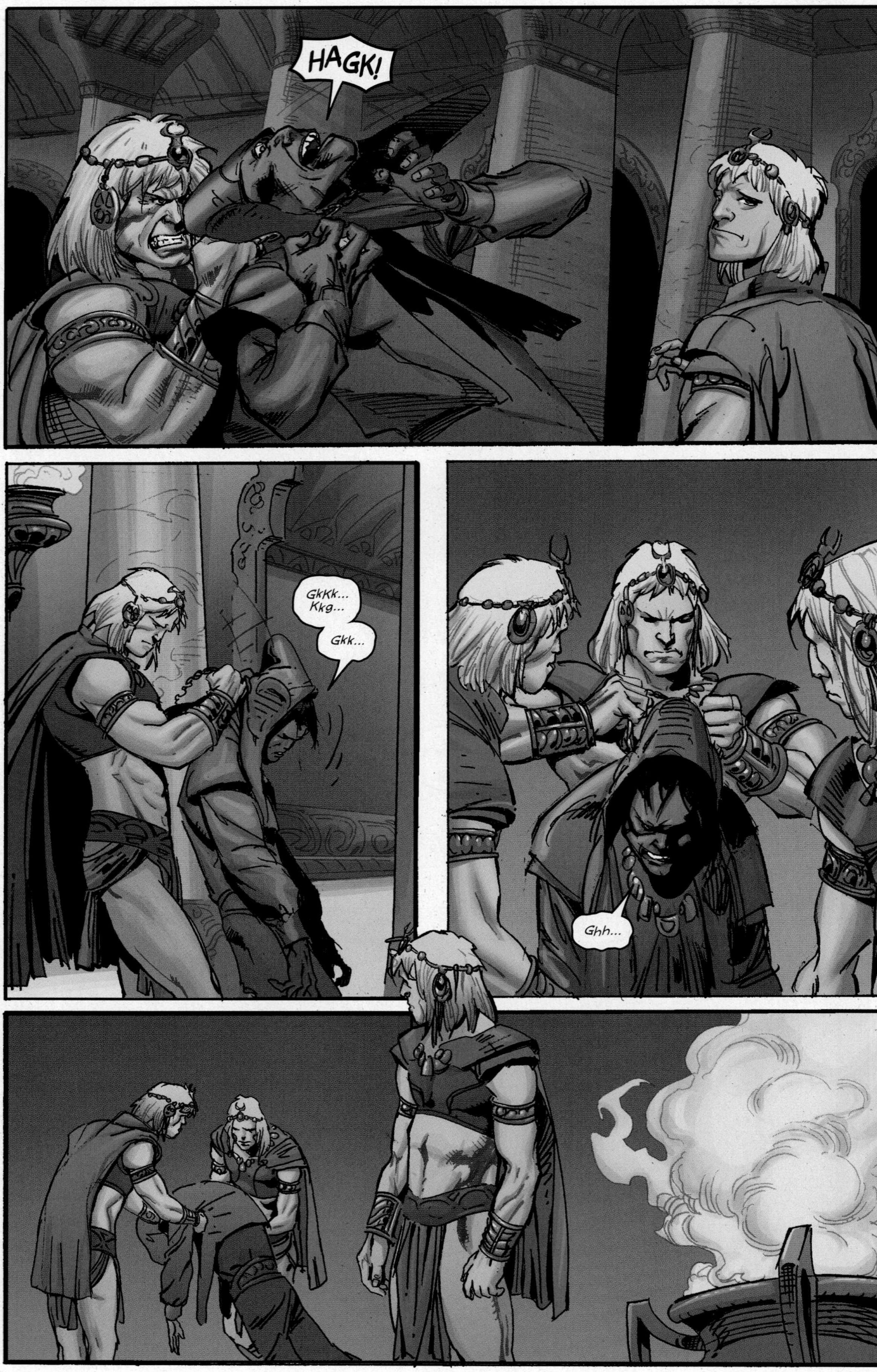
HAGK!
GkKk...
Kkg...
Gkk...
Ghh...

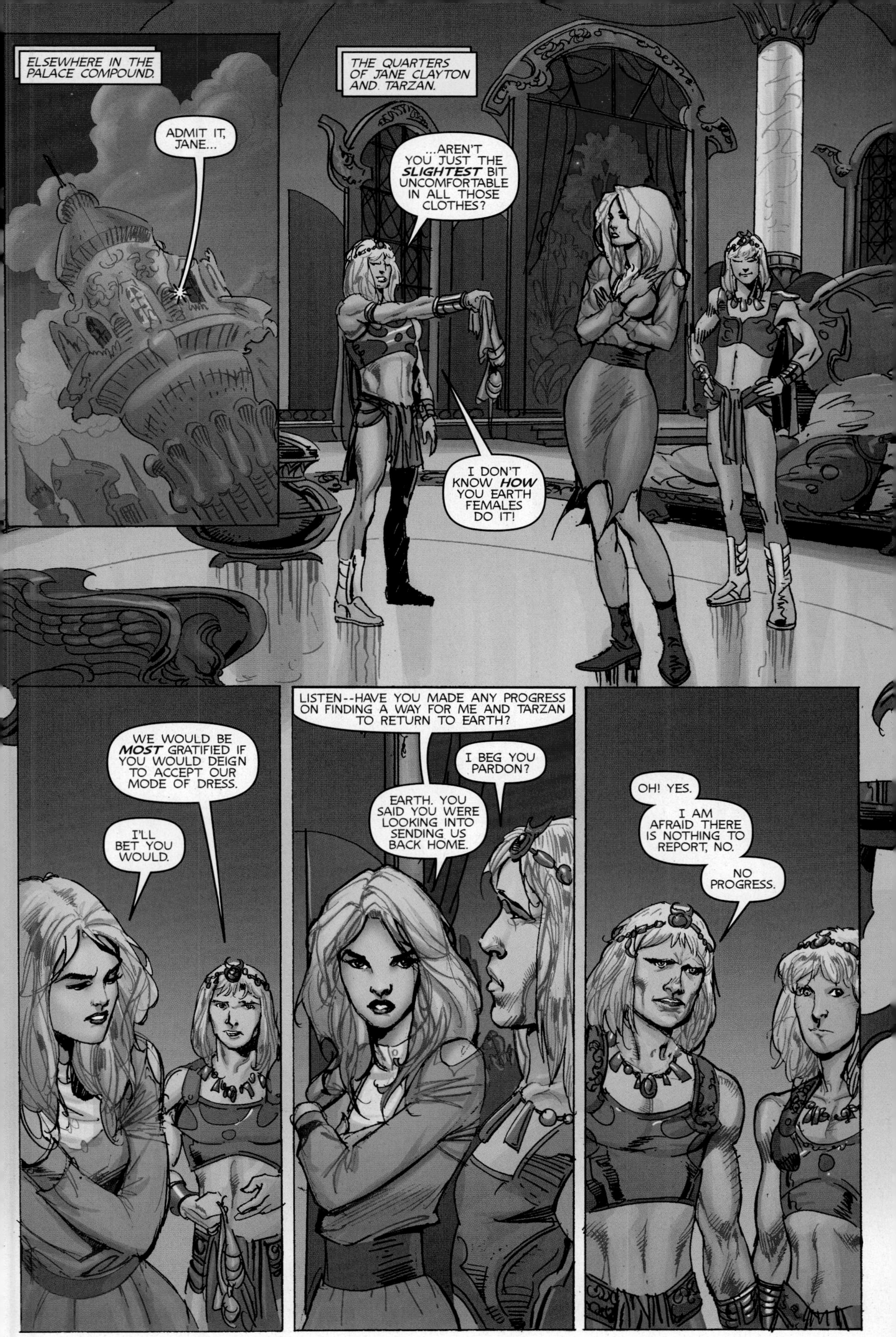
ELSEWHERE IN THE PALACE COMPOUND.
ADMIT IT, JANE...
THE QUARTERS OF JANE CLAYTON AND TARZAN.
...AREN'T YOU JUST THE SLIGHTEST BIT UNCOMFORTABLE IN ALL THOSE CLOTHES?
I DON'T KNOW HOW YOU EARTH FEMALES DO IT!
WE WOULD BE MOST GRATIFIED IF YOU WOULD DEIGN TO ACCEPT OUR MODE OF DRESS.
I'LL BET YOU WOULD.
LISTEN--HAVE YOU MADE ANY PROGRESS ON FINDING A WAY FOR ME AND TARZAN TO RETURN TO EARTH?
I BEG YOU PARDON?
EARTH. YOU SAID YOU WERE LOOKING INTO SENDING US BACK HOME.
OH! YES.
I AM AFRAID THERE IS NOTHING TO REPORT, NO.
NO PROGRESS.

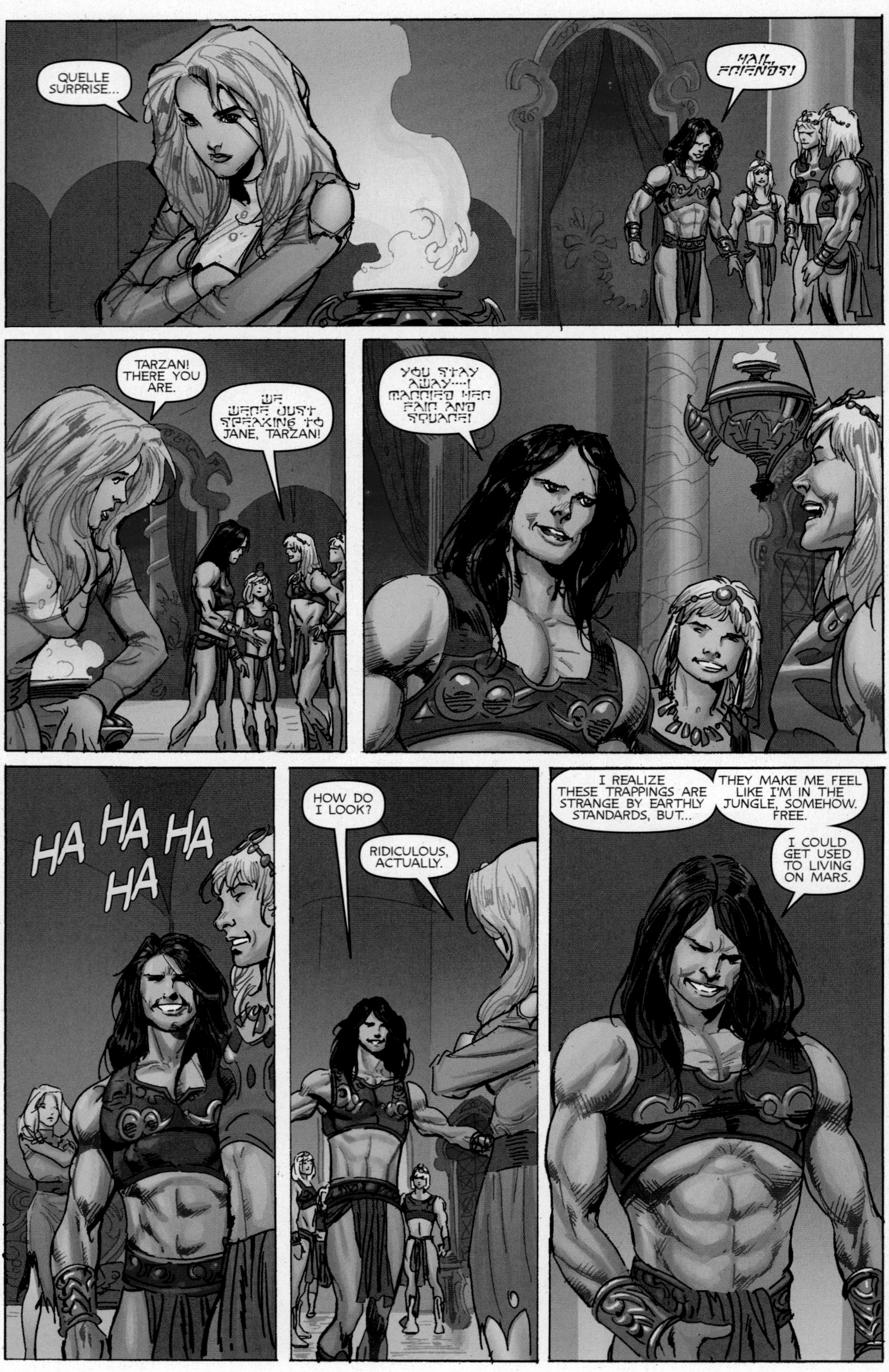
QUELLE SURPRISE...
HAIL, FRIENDS!
TARZAN! THERE YOU ARE.
WE WERE JUST SPEAKING TO JANE, TARZAN!
YOU STAY AWAY... I MARRIED HER FAIR AND SQUARE!
HA HA HA HA
HOW DO I LOOK?
RIDICULOUS, ACTUALLY.
I REALIZE THESE TRAPPINGS ARE STRANGE BY EARTHLY STANDARDS, BUT...
THEY MAKE ME FEEL LIKE I'M IN THE JUNGLE, SOMEHOW. FREE.
I COULD GET USED TO LIVING ON MARS.

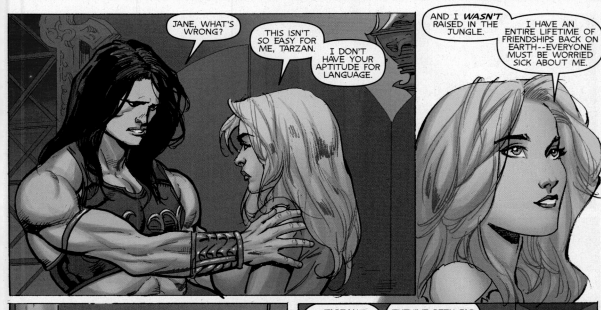

JANE, WHAT'S WRONG?

THIS ISN'T SO EASY FOR ME, TARZAN.

I DON'T HAVE YOUR APTITUDE FOR LANGUAGE.

AND I *WASN'T* RAISED IN THE JUNGLE.

I HAVE AN ENTIRE LIFETIME OF FRIENDSHIPS BACK ON EARTH--EVERYONE MUST BE WORRIED SICK ABOUT ME.

BESIDES...

TARZAN, DO YOU REALLY TRUST THESE PEOPLE?

THEY'VE BEEN FAR MORE WELCOMING THAN ANYONE IN ENGLAND.

A LITTLE *TOO* WELCOMING.

WHAT ARE YOU SAYING?

HOW MUCH DO WE REALLY KNOW ABOUT THESE "THERNS," TARZAN? WE'RE *TRAPPED* IN THIS PALACE...

JANE, I THINK THESE SUSPICIONS ARE A *LITTLE* FAR-FETCHED.

FAR-FETCHED? WE ARE ON *MARS*, TARZAN.

MARS.

HOW COULD *ANY*THING POSSIBLY BE "FAR-FETCHED"?

WE'RE JUST SO... *ALONE* HERE. SO VULNERABLE...

I KNOW. I KNOW WHAT YOU NEED.

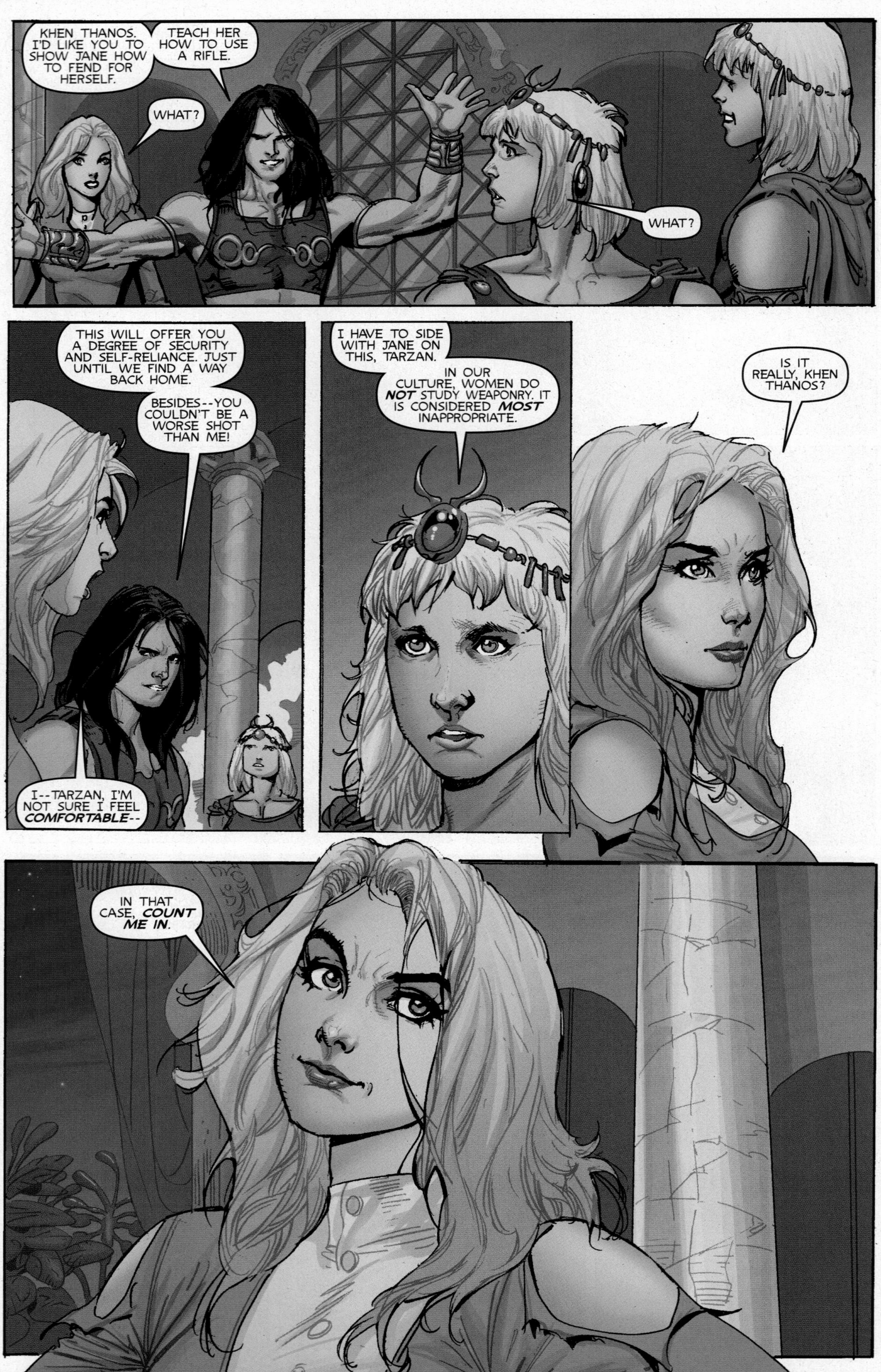
KHEN THANOS. I'D LIKE YOU TO SHOW JANE HOW TO FEND FOR HERSELF.
TEACH HER HOW TO USE A RIFLE.
WHAT?
WHAT?
THIS WILL OFFER YOU A DEGREE OF SECURITY AND SELF-RELIANCE. JUST UNTIL WE FIND A WAY BACK HOME.
BESIDES--YOU COULDN'T BE A WORSE SHOT THAN ME!
I--TARZAN, I'M NOT SURE I FEEL *COMFORTABLE*--
I HAVE TO SIDE WITH JANE ON THIS, TARZAN.
IN OUR CULTURE, WOMEN DO *NOT* STUDY WEAPONRY. IT IS CONSIDERED *MOST* INAPPROPRIATE.
IS IT REALLY, KHEN THANOS?
IN THAT CASE, *COUNT ME IN*.

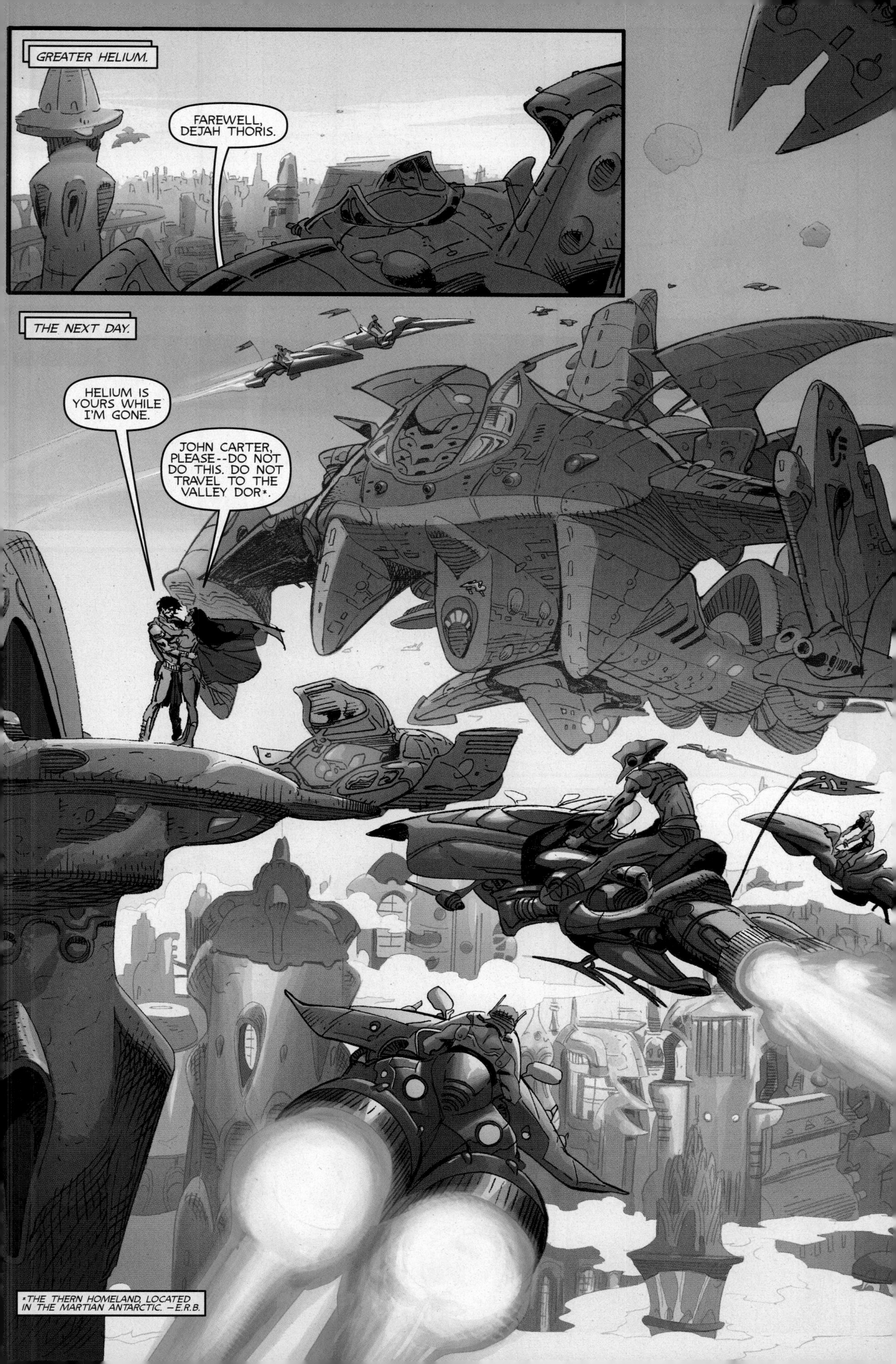
GREATER HELIUM.
FAREWELL, DEJAH THORIS.
THE NEXT DAY.
HELIUM IS YOURS WHILE I'M GONE.
JOHN CARTER, PLEASE--DO NOT DO THIS. DO NOT TRAVEL TO THE VALLEY DOR*.
*THE THERN HOMELAND, LOCATED IN THE MARTIAN ANTARCTIC. —E.R.B.

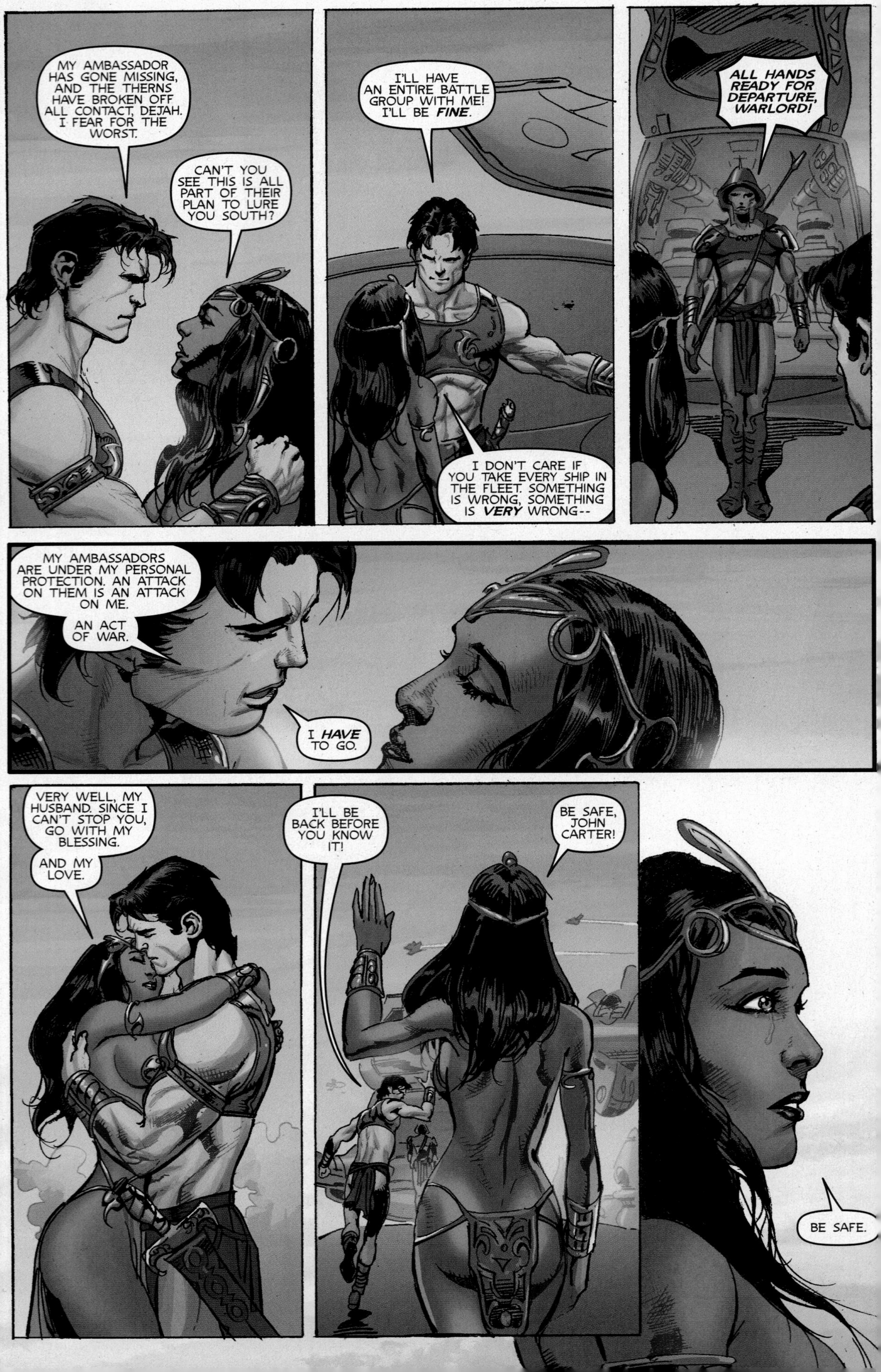
MY AMBASSADOR HAS GONE MISSING, AND THE THERNS HAVE BROKEN OFF ALL CONTACT, DEJAH. I FEAR FOR THE WORST.
CAN'T YOU SEE THIS IS ALL PART OF THEIR PLAN TO LURE YOU SOUTH?
I'LL HAVE AN ENTIRE BATTLE GROUP WITH ME! I'LL BE *FINE*.
I DON'T CARE IF YOU TAKE EVERY SHIP IN THE FLEET. SOMETHING IS WRONG, SOMETHING IS *VERY* WRONG--
ALL HANDS READY FOR DEPARTURE, WARLORD!
MY AMBASSADORS ARE UNDER MY PERSONAL PROTECTION. AN ATTACK ON THEM IS AN ATTACK ON ME.
AN ACT OF WAR.
I *HAVE* TO GO.
VERY WELL, MY HUSBAND. SINCE I CAN'T STOP YOU, GO WITH MY BLESSING.
AND MY LOVE.
I'LL BE BACK BEFORE YOU KNOW IT!
BE SAFE, JOHN CARTER!
BE SAFE.

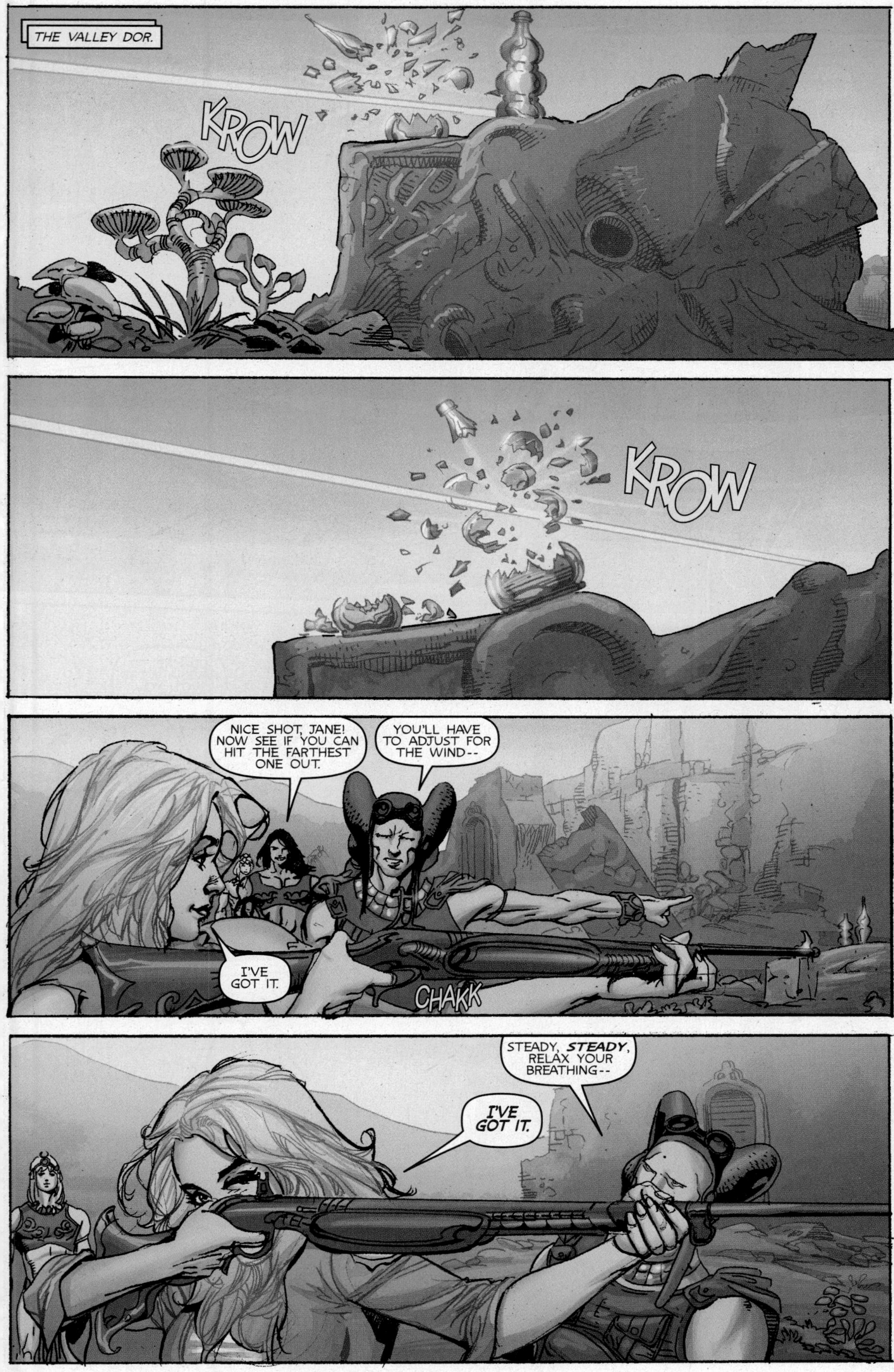
THE VALLEY DOR.
KROW
KROW
NICE SHOT, JANE! NOW SEE IF YOU CAN HIT THE FARTHEST ONE OUT.
YOU'LL HAVE TO ADJUST FOR THE WIND--
I'VE GOT IT.
CHAKK
STEADY, STEADY, RELAX YOUR BREATHING--
I'VE GOT IT.

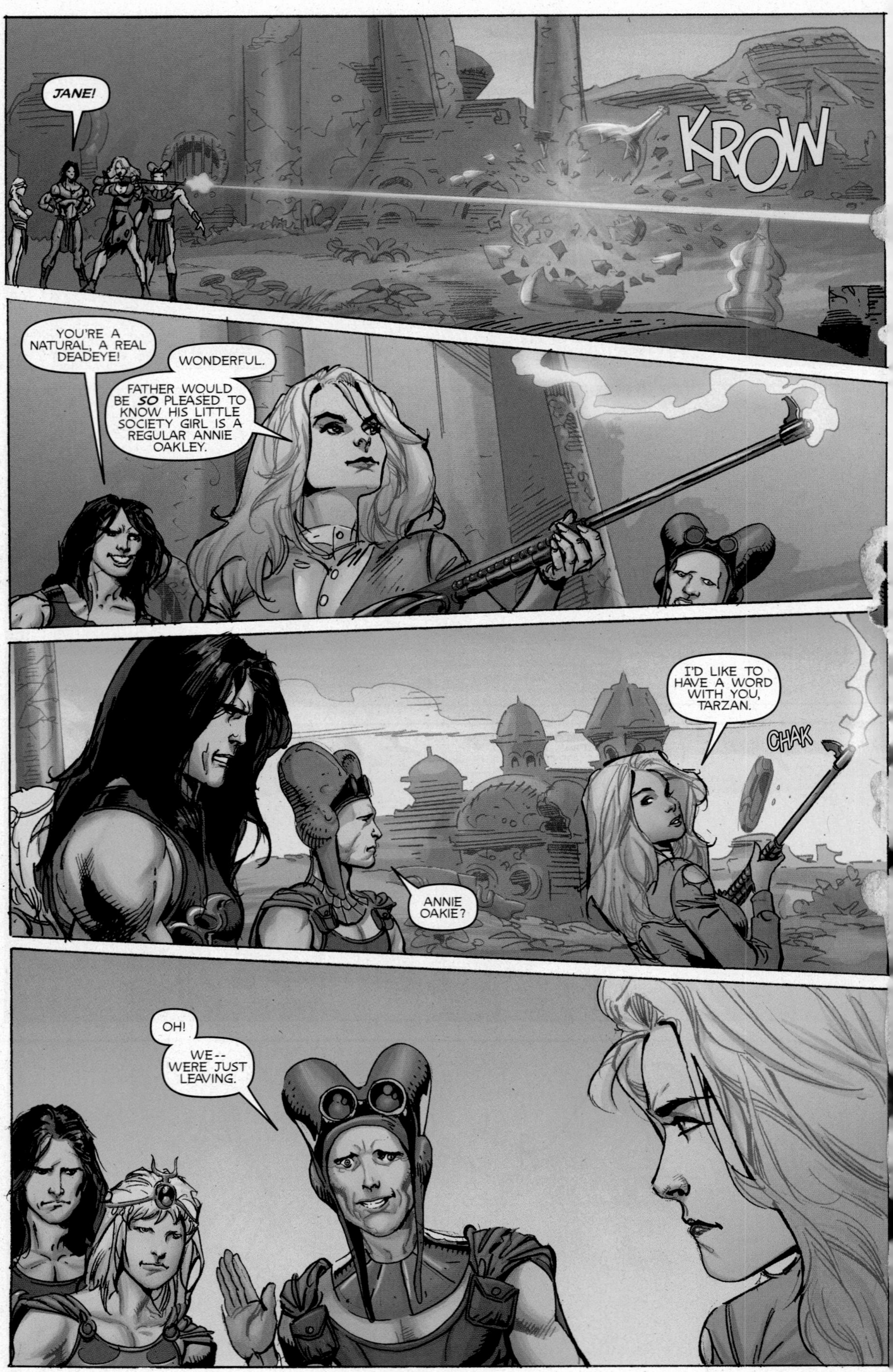
JANE!
KROW
YOU'RE A NATURAL, A REAL DEADEYE!
WONDERFUL.
FATHER WOULD BE *SO* PLEASED TO KNOW HIS LITTLE SOCIETY GIRL IS A REGULAR ANNIE OAKLEY.
I'D LIKE TO HAVE A WORD WITH YOU, TARZAN.
CHAK
ANNIE OAKIE?
OH!
WE-- WERE JUST LEAVING.

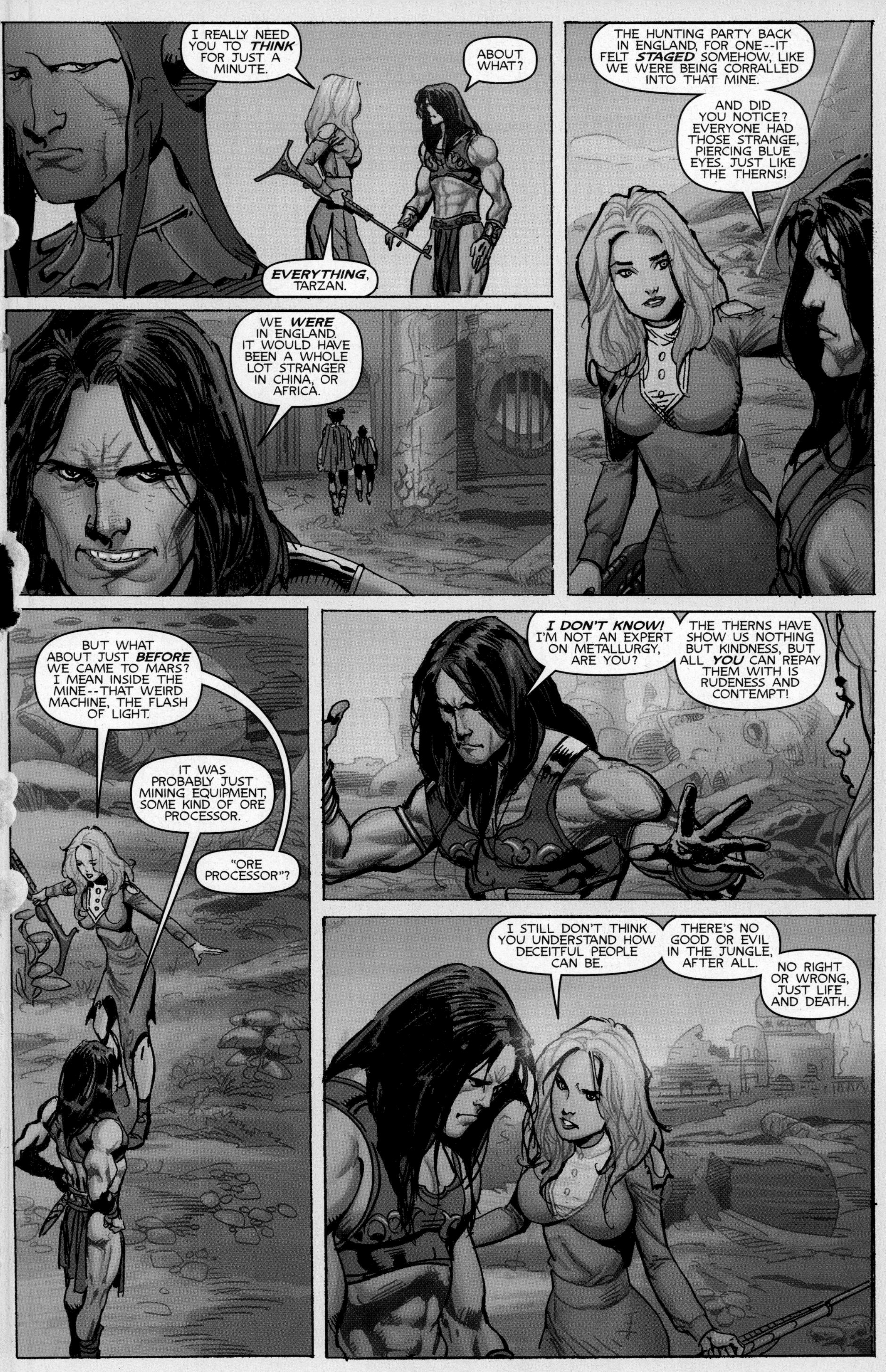
I REALLY NEED YOU TO *THINK* FOR JUST A MINUTE.
ABOUT WHAT?
EVERYTHING, TARZAN.
THE HUNTING PARTY BACK IN ENGLAND, FOR ONE--IT FELT *STAGED* SOMEHOW, LIKE WE WERE BEING CORRALLED INTO THAT MINE.
AND DID YOU NOTICE? EVERYONE HAD THOSE STRANGE, PIERCING BLUE EYES. JUST LIKE THE THERNS!
WE *WERE* IN ENGLAND. IT WOULD HAVE BEEN A WHOLE LOT STRANGER IN CHINA, OR AFRICA.
BUT WHAT ABOUT JUST *BEFORE* WE CAME TO MARS? I MEAN INSIDE THE MINE--THAT WEIRD MACHINE, THE FLASH OF LIGHT.
IT WAS PROBABLY JUST MINING EQUIPMENT, SOME KIND OF ORE PROCESSOR.
"ORE PROCESSOR"?
I DON'T KNOW! I'M NOT AN EXPERT ON METALLURGY, ARE YOU?
THE THERNS HAVE SHOW US NOTHING BUT KINDNESS, BUT ALL *YOU* CAN REPAY THEM WITH IS RUDENESS AND CONTEMPT!
I STILL DON'T THINK YOU UNDERSTAND HOW DECEITFUL PEOPLE CAN BE.
THERE'S NO GOOD OR EVIL IN THE JUNGLE, AFTER ALL.
NO RIGHT OR WRONG, JUST LIFE AND DEATH.

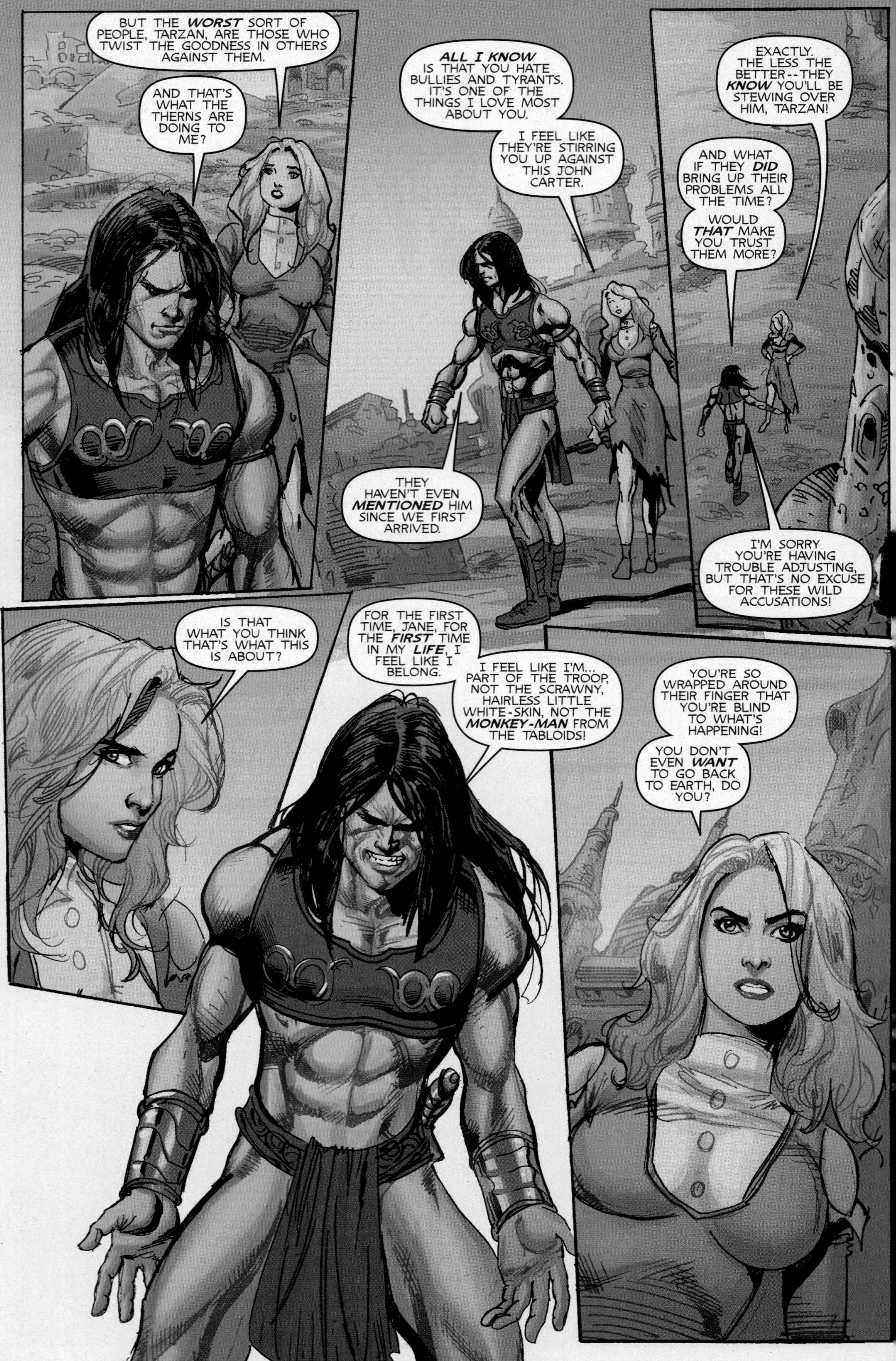

BUT THE WORST SORT OF PEOPLE, TARZAN, ARE THOSE WHO TWIST THE GOODNESS IN OTHERS AGAINST THEM.
AND THAT'S WHAT THE THERNS ARE DOING TO ME?
ALL I KNOW IS THAT YOU HATE BULLIES AND TYRANTS. IT'S ONE OF THE THINGS I LOVE MOST ABOUT YOU.
I FEEL LIKE THEY'RE STIRRING YOU UP AGAINST THIS JOHN CARTER.
THEY HAVEN'T EVEN MENTIONED HIM SINCE WE FIRST ARRIVED.
EXACTLY. THE LESS THE BETTER--THEY KNOW YOU'LL BE STEWING OVER HIM, TARZAN!
AND WHAT IF THEY DID BRING UP THEIR PROBLEMS ALL THE TIME?
WOULD THAT MAKE YOU TRUST THEM MORE?
I'M SORRY YOU'RE HAVING TROUBLE ADJUSTING, BUT THAT'S NO EXCUSE FOR THESE WILD ACCUSATIONS!
IS THAT WHAT YOU THINK THAT'S WHAT THIS IS ABOUT?
FOR THE FIRST TIME, JANE, FOR THE FIRST TIME IN MY LIFE, I FEEL LIKE I BELONG.
I FEEL LIKE I'M... PART OF THE TROOP, NOT THE SCRAWNY, HAIRLESS LITTLE WHITE-SKIN, NOT THE MONKEY-MAN FROM THE TABLOIDS!
YOU'RE SO WRAPPED AROUND THEIR FINGER THAT YOU'RE BLIND TO WHAT'S HAPPENING!
YOU DON'T EVEN WANT TO GO BACK TO EARTH, DO YOU?

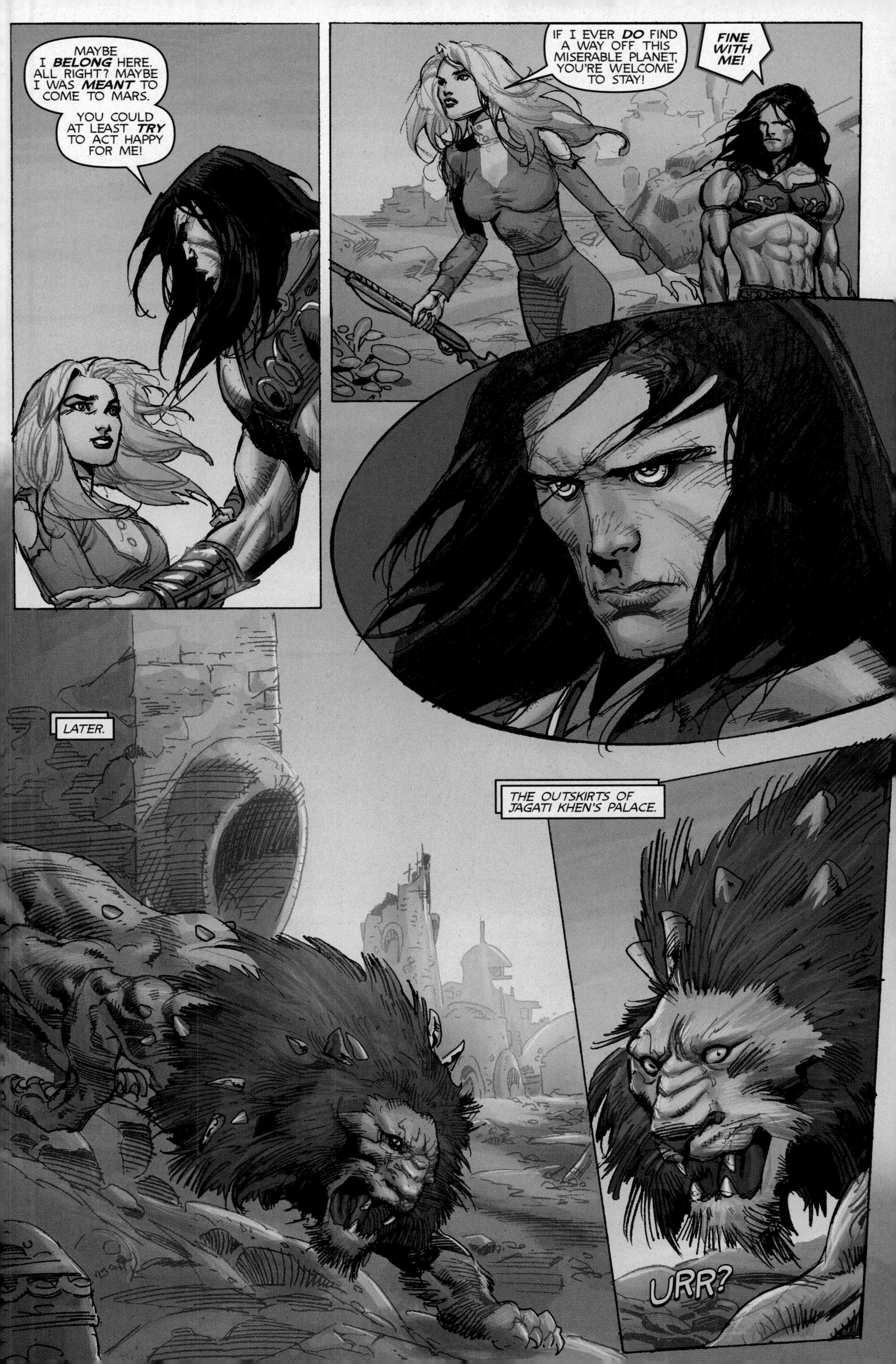

MAYBE I **BELONG** HERE. ALL RIGHT? MAYBE I WAS **MEANT** TO COME TO MARS.
YOU COULD AT LEAST **TRY** TO ACT HAPPY FOR ME!
IF I EVER **DO** FIND A WAY OFF THIS MISERABLE PLANET, YOU'RE WELCOME TO STAY!
FINE WITH ME!
LATER.
THE OUTSKIRTS OF JAGATI KHEN'S PALACE.
URR?

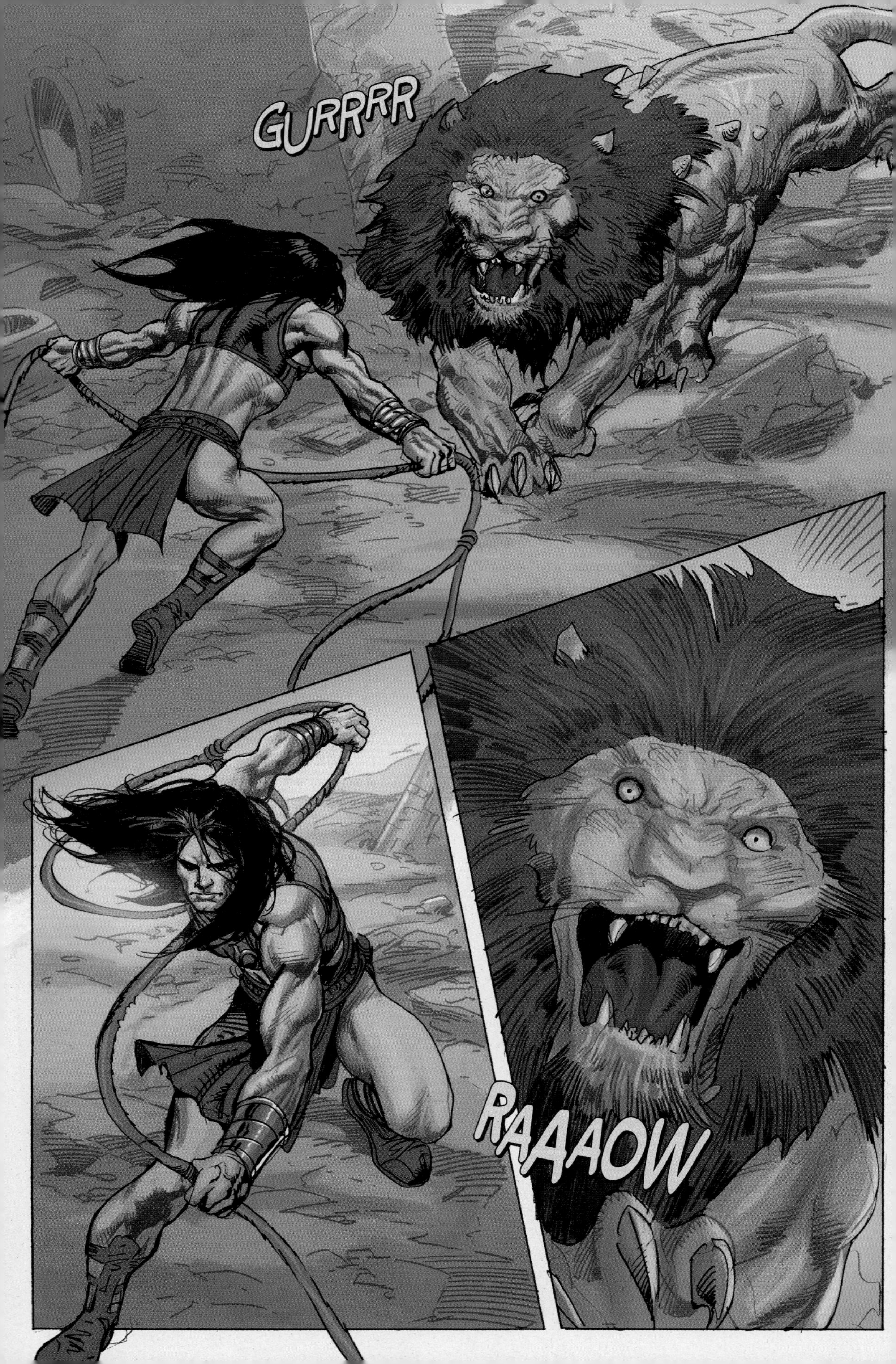
GURRRR
RAAAOW

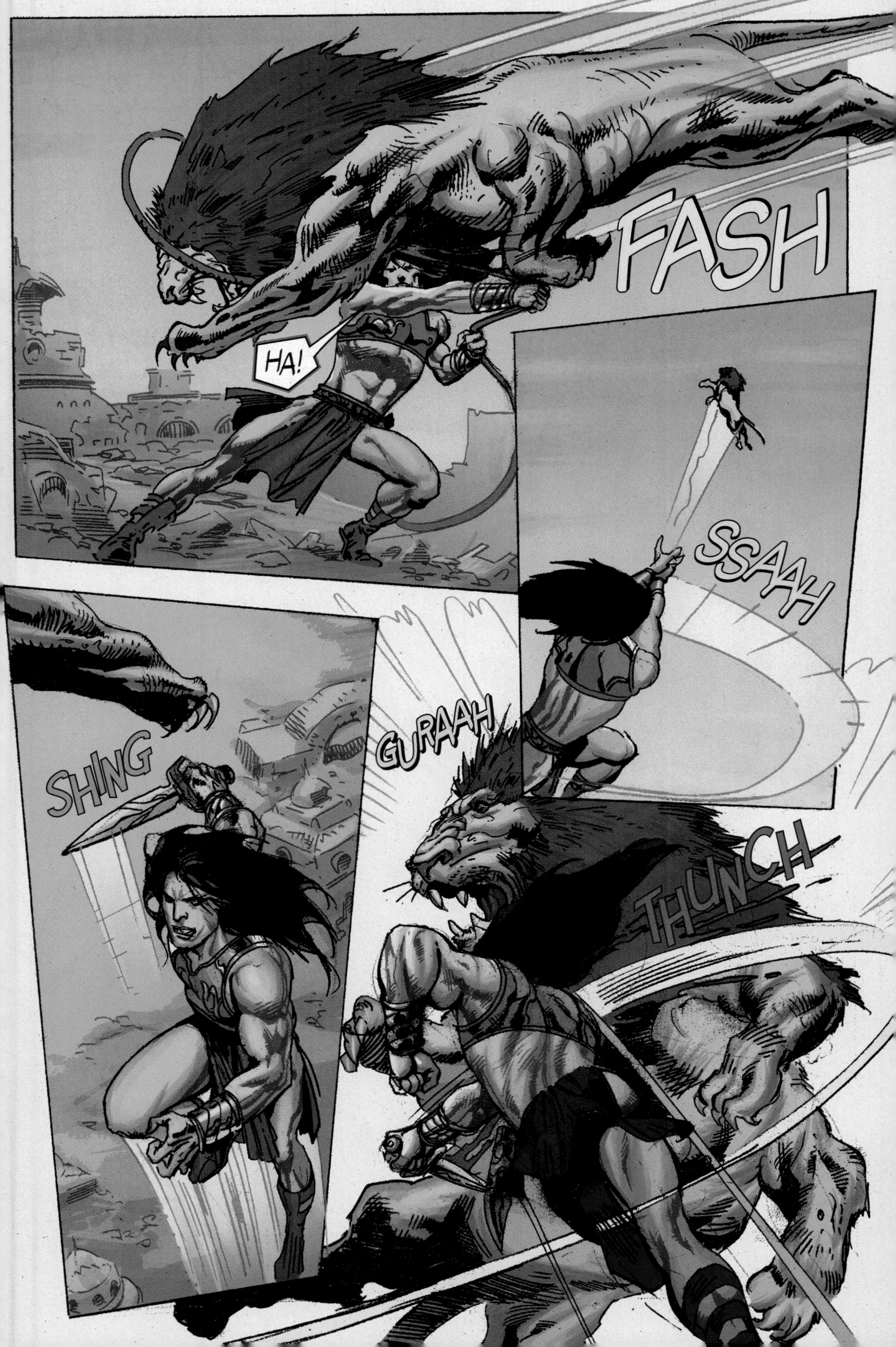
FASH
HA!
SSAAH
SHING
GURAAH
THUNCH

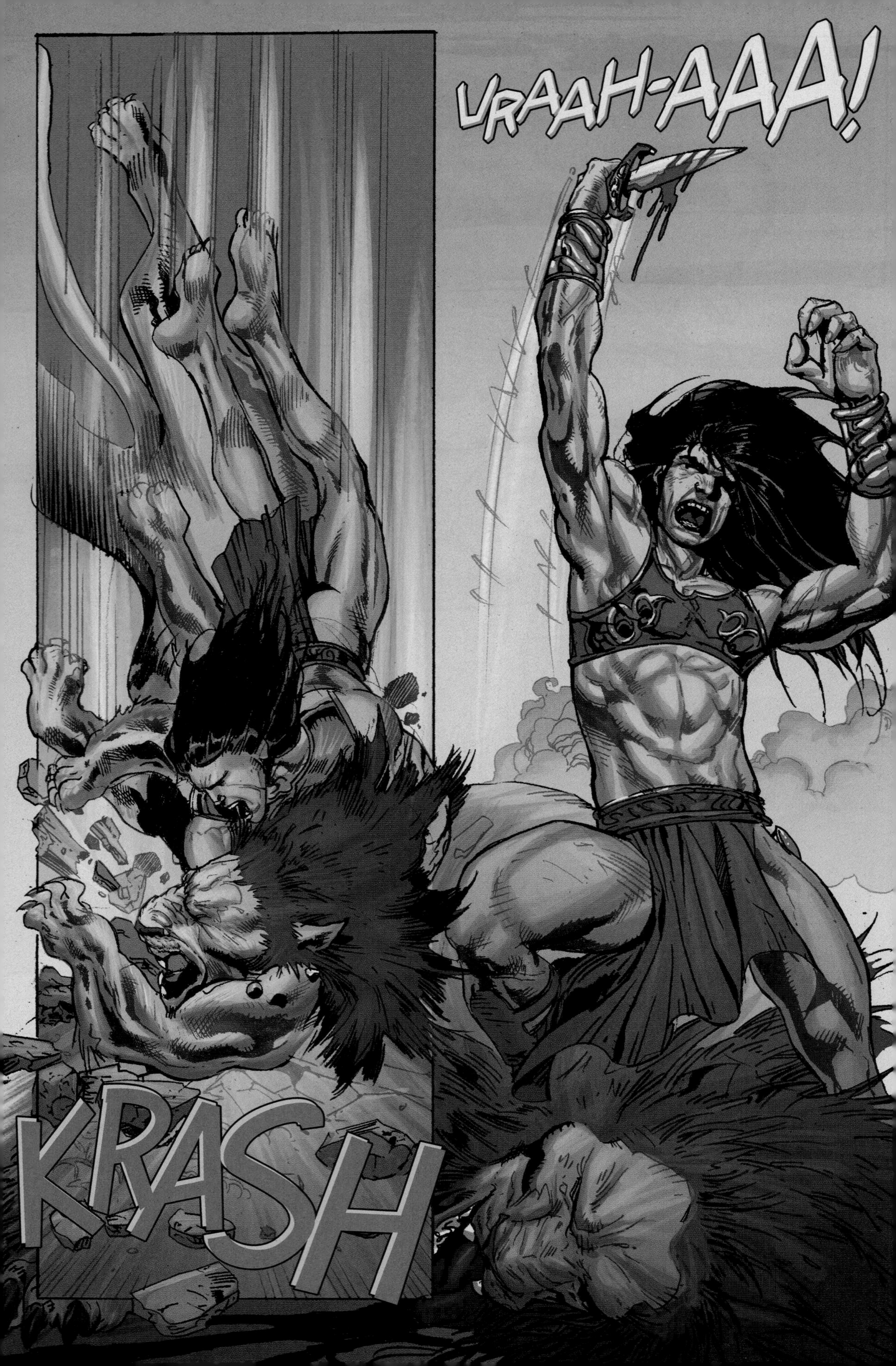
URAAH-AAAA!
KRASH

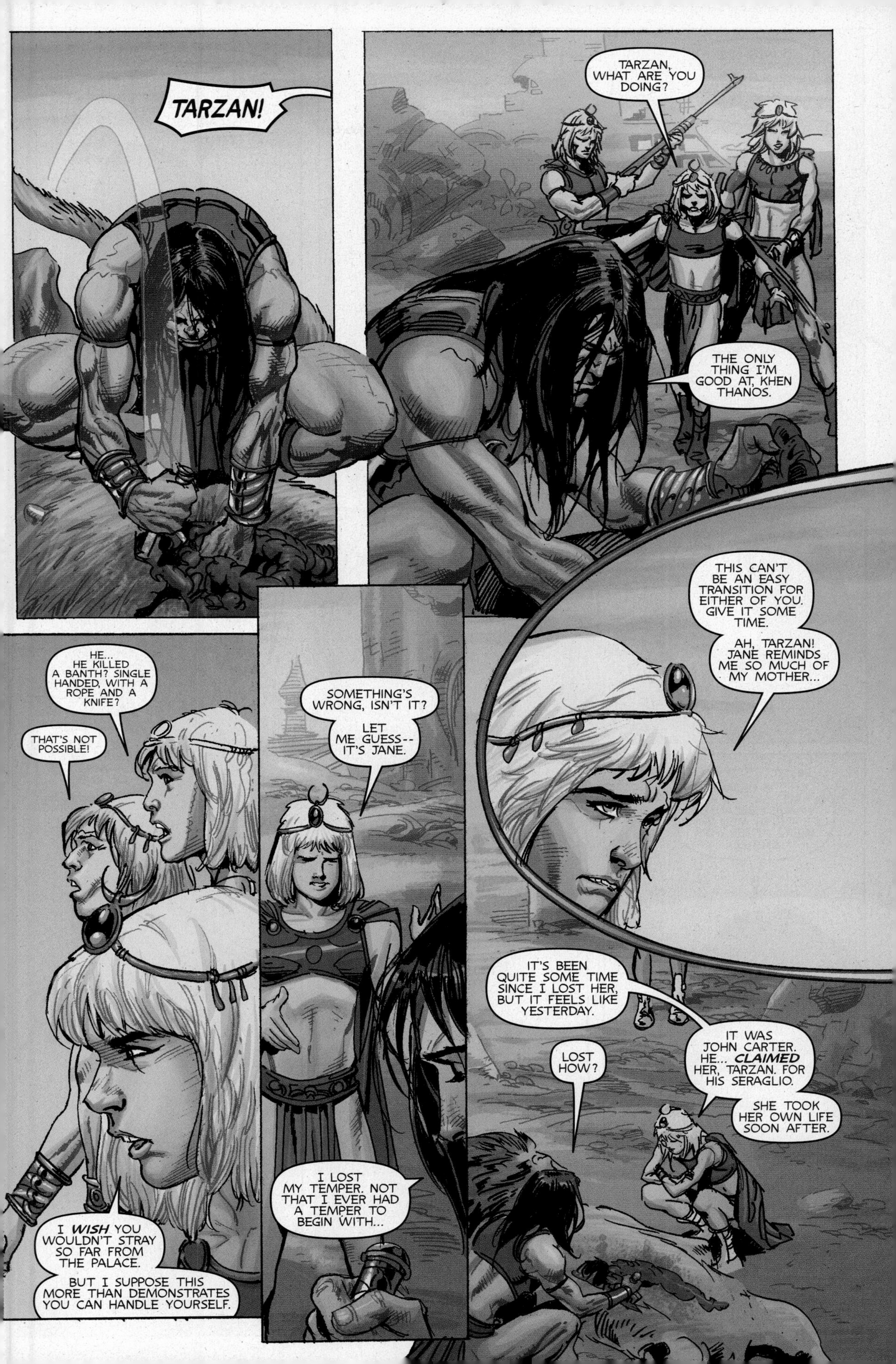
TARZAN!
TARZAN, WHAT ARE YOU DOING?
THE ONLY THING I'M GOOD AT, KHEN THANOS.
HE... HE KILLED A BANTH? SINGLE HANDED, WITH A ROPE AND A KNIFE?
THAT'S NOT POSSIBLE!
I WISH YOU WOULDN'T STRAY SO FAR FROM THE PALACE.
BUT I SUPPOSE THIS MORE THAN DEMONSTRATES YOU CAN HANDLE YOURSELF.
SOMETHING'S WRONG, ISN'T IT?
LET ME GUESS-- IT'S JANE.
I LOST MY TEMPER. NOT THAT I EVER HAD A TEMPER TO BEGIN WITH...
THIS CAN'T BE AN EASY TRANSITION FOR EITHER OF YOU. GIVE IT SOME TIME.
AH, TARZAN! JANE REMINDS ME SO MUCH OF MY MOTHER...
IT'S BEEN QUITE SOME TIME SINCE I LOST HER, BUT IT FEELS LIKE YESTERDAY.
LOST HOW?
IT WAS JOHN CARTER. HE... CLAIMED HER, TARZAN. FOR HIS SERAGLIO.
SHE TOOK HER OWN LIFE SOON AFTER.

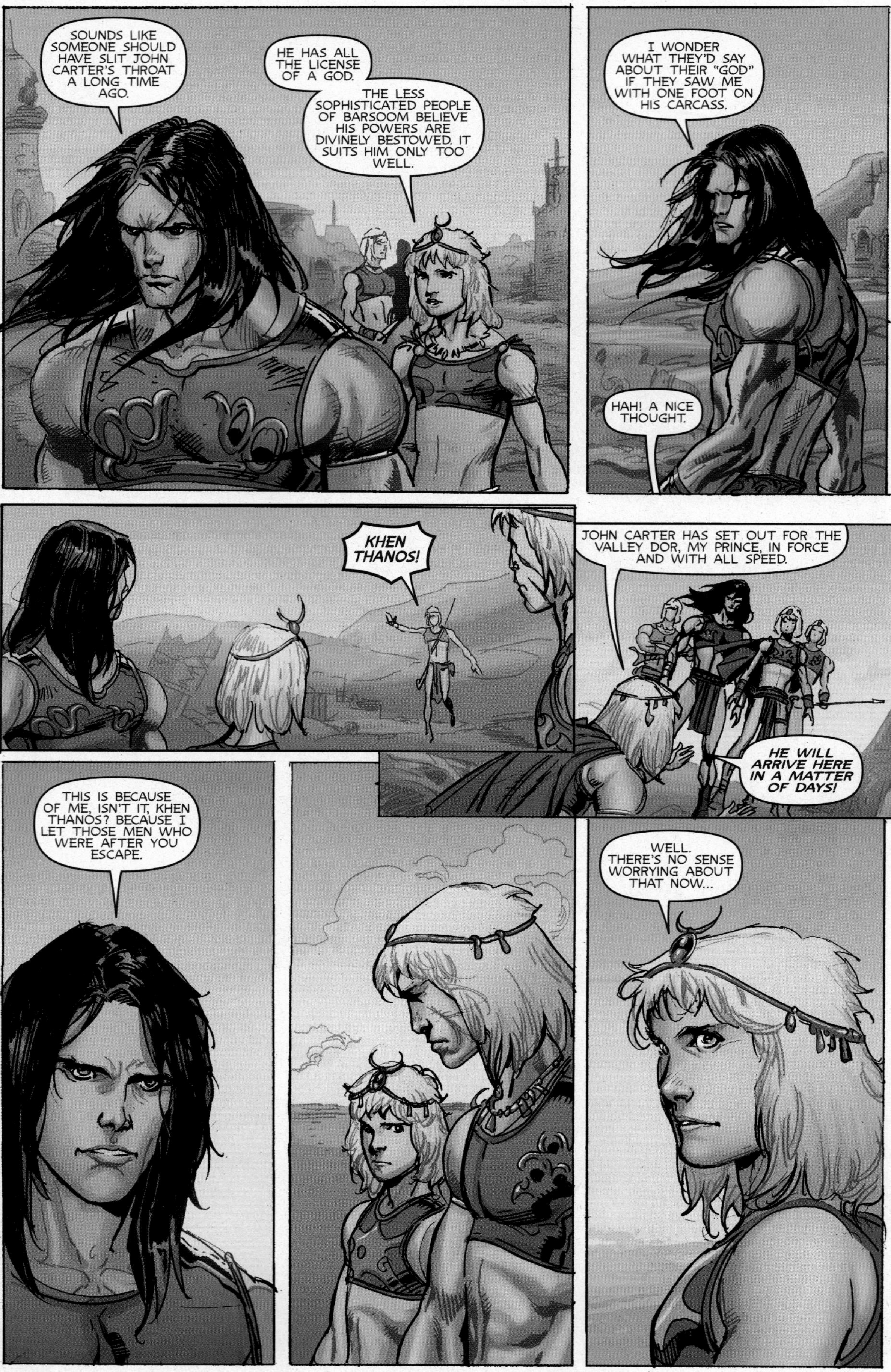
SOUNDS LIKE SOMEONE SHOULD HAVE SLIT JOHN CARTER'S THROAT A LONG TIME AGO.
HE HAS ALL THE LICENSE OF A GOD.
THE LESS SOPHISTICATED PEOPLE OF BARSOOM BELIEVE HIS POWERS ARE DIVINELY BESTOWED. IT SUITS HIM ONLY TOO WELL.
I WONDER WHAT THEY'D SAY ABOUT THEIR "GOD" IF THEY SAW ME WITH ONE FOOT ON HIS CARCASS.
HAH! A NICE THOUGHT.
KHEN THANOS!
JOHN CARTER HAS SET OUT FOR THE VALLEY DOR, MY PRINCE, IN FORCE AND WITH ALL SPEED.
HE WILL ARRIVE HERE IN A MATTER OF DAYS!
THIS IS BECAUSE OF ME, ISN'T IT, KHEN THANOS? BECAUSE I LET THOSE MEN WHO WERE AFTER YOU ESCAPE.
WELL. THERE'S NO SENSE WORRYING ABOUT THAT NOW...

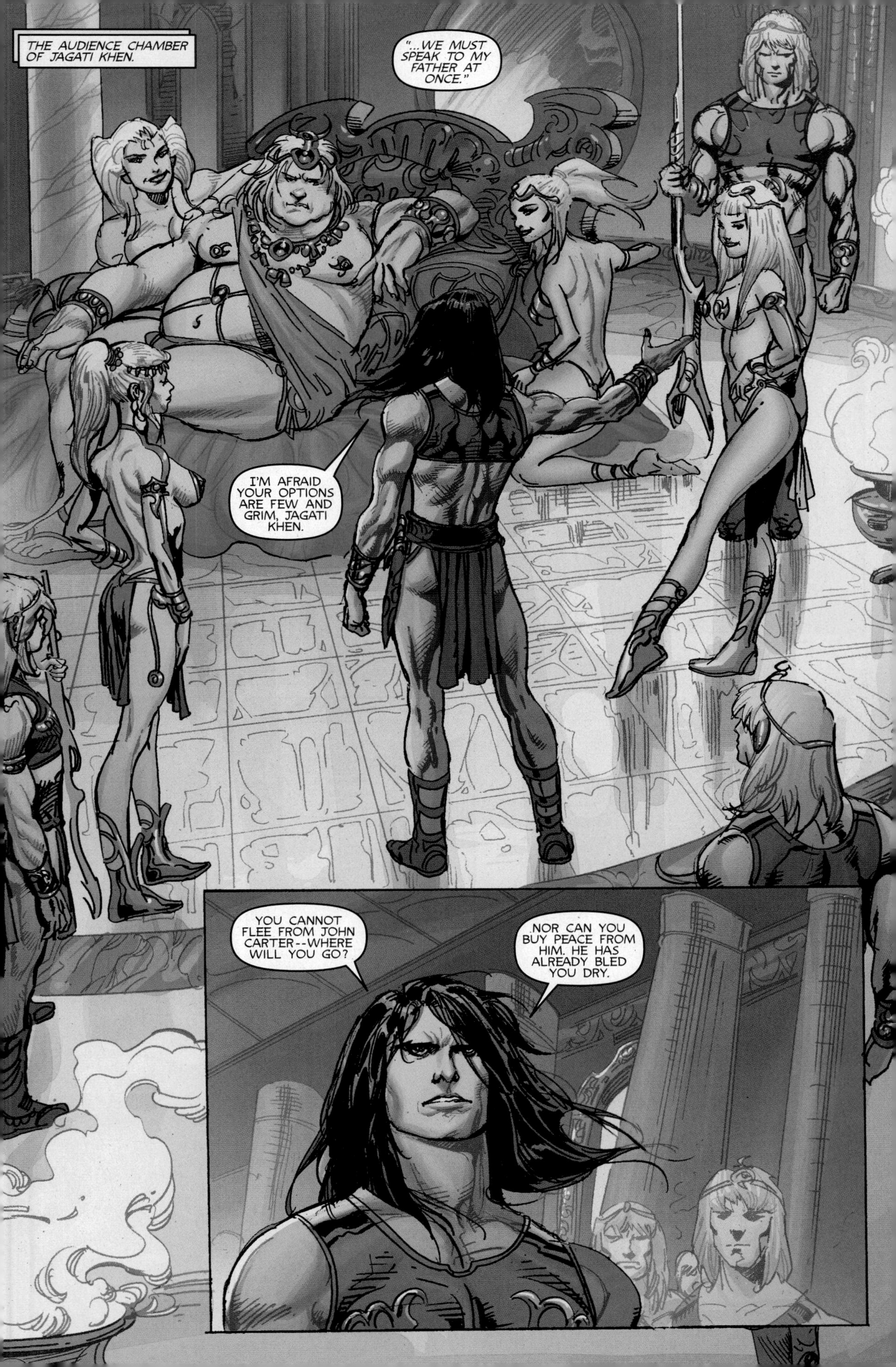
THE AUDIENCE CHAMBER OF JAGATI KHEN.
"...WE MUST SPEAK TO MY FATHER AT ONCE."
I'M AFRAID YOUR OPTIONS ARE FEW AND GRIM, JAGATI KHEN.
YOU CANNOT FLEE FROM JOHN CARTER--WHERE WILL YOU GO?
NOR CAN YOU BUY PEACE FROM HIM. HE HAS ALREADY BLED YOU DRY.

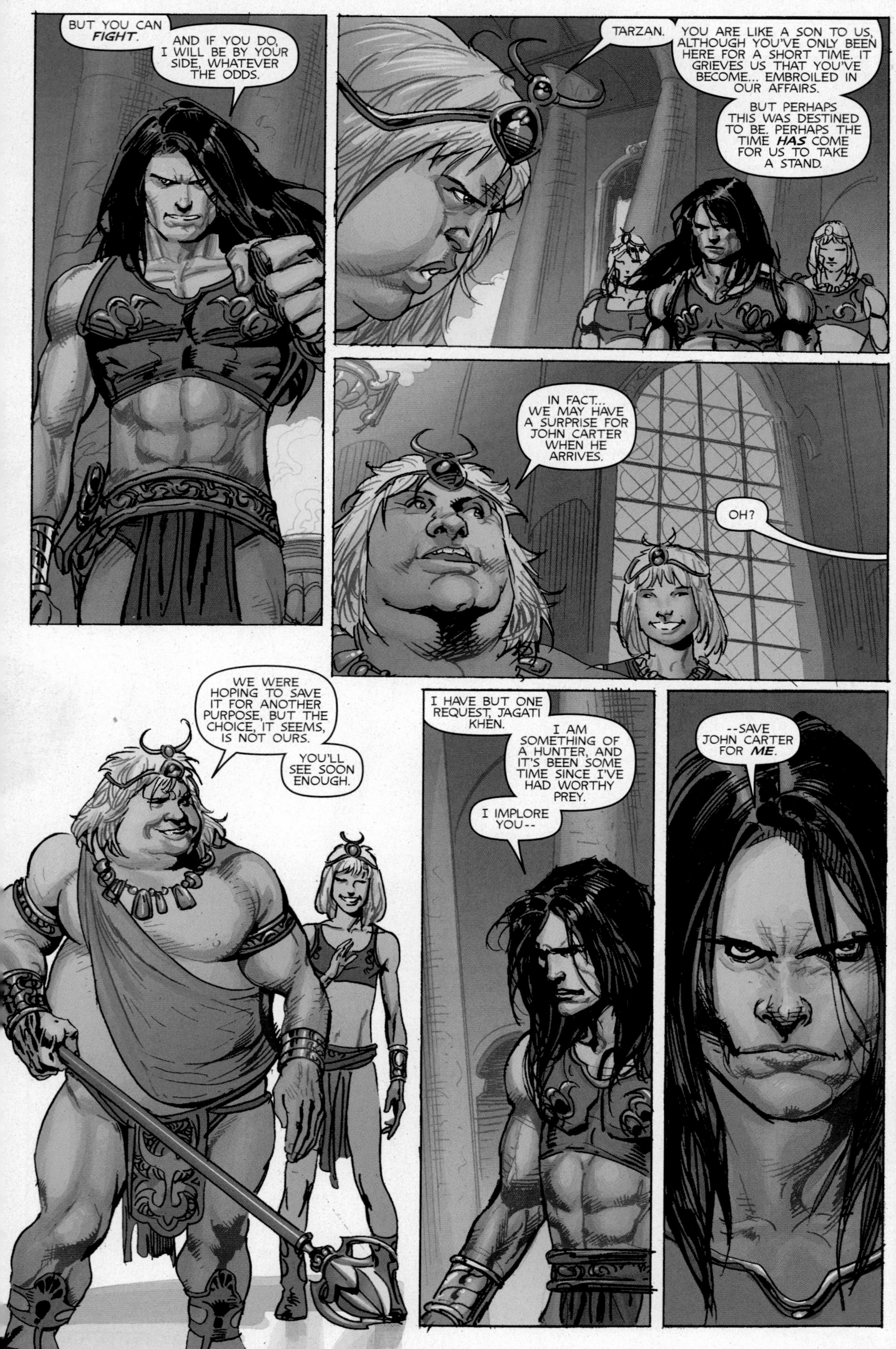
BUT YOU CAN **FIGHT**.
AND IF YOU DO, I WILL BE BY YOUR SIDE, WHATEVER THE ODDS.
TARZAN.
YOU ARE LIKE A SON TO US, ALTHOUGH YOU'VE ONLY BEEN HERE FOR A SHORT TIME. IT GRIEVES US THAT YOU'VE BECOME... EMBROILED IN OUR AFFAIRS.
BUT PERHAPS THIS WAS DESTINED TO BE. PERHAPS THE TIME **HAS** COME FOR US TO TAKE A STAND.
IN FACT... WE MAY HAVE A SURPRISE FOR JOHN CARTER WHEN HE ARRIVES.
OH?
WE WERE HOPING TO SAVE IT FOR ANOTHER PURPOSE, BUT THE CHOICE, IT SEEMS, IS NOT OURS.
YOU'LL SEE SOON ENOUGH.
I HAVE BUT ONE REQUEST, JAGATI KHEN.
I AM SOMETHING OF A HUNTER, AND IT'S BEEN SOME TIME SINCE I'VE HAD WORTHY PREY.
I IMPLORE YOU--
--SAVE JOHN CARTER FOR **ME**.

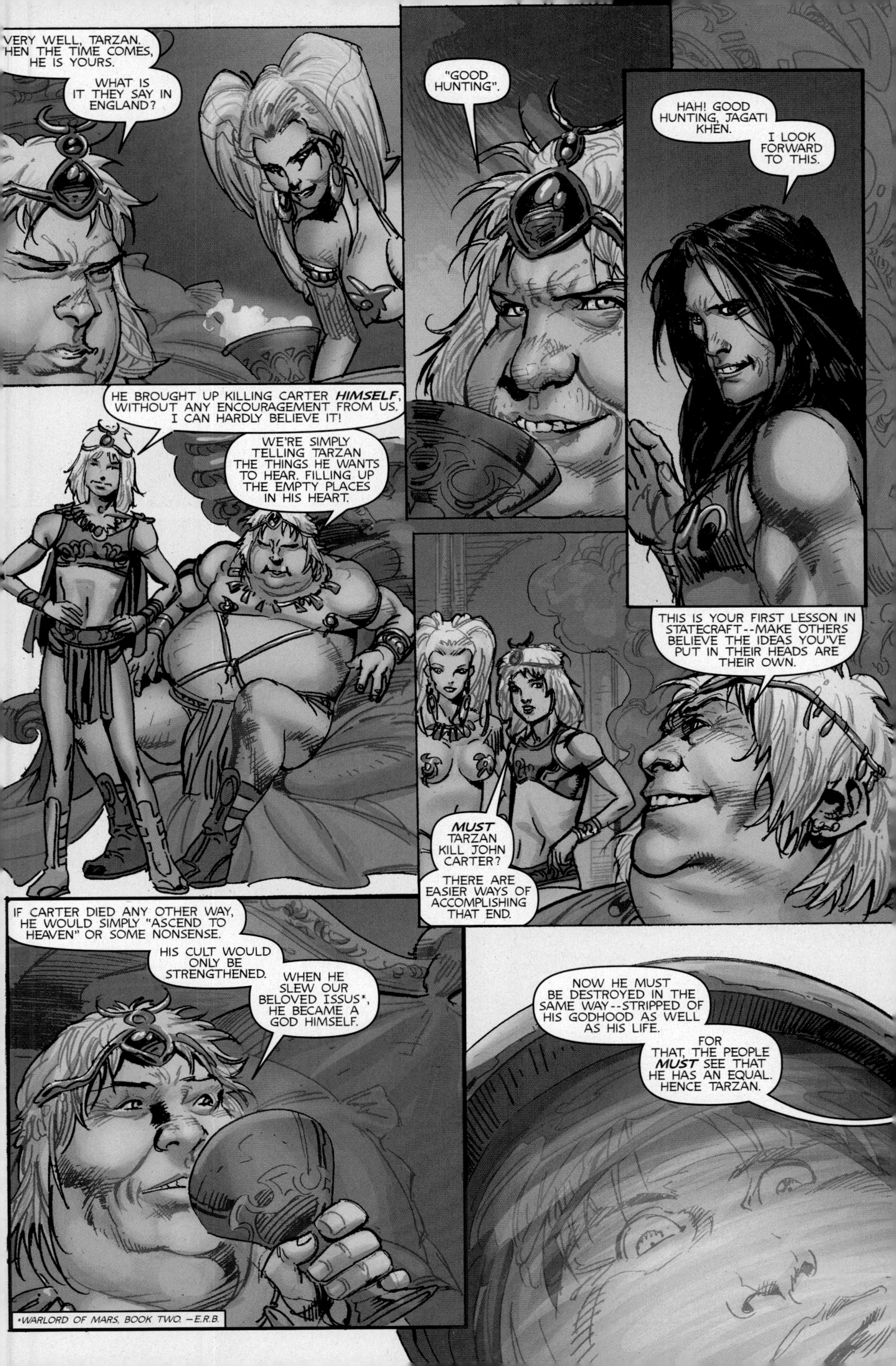
VERY WELL, TARZAN. WHEN THE TIME COMES, HE IS YOURS.
WHAT IS IT THEY SAY IN ENGLAND?
"GOOD HUNTING".
HAH! GOOD HUNTING, JAGATI KHEN.
I LOOK FORWARD TO THIS.
HE BROUGHT UP KILLING CARTER HIMSELF, WITHOUT ANY ENCOURAGEMENT FROM US. I CAN HARDLY BELIEVE IT!
WE'RE SIMPLY TELLING TARZAN THE THINGS HE WANTS TO HEAR. FILLING UP THE EMPTY PLACES IN HIS HEART.
THIS IS YOUR FIRST LESSON IN STATECRAFT--MAKE OTHERS BELIEVE THE IDEAS YOU'VE PUT IN THEIR HEADS ARE THEIR OWN.
MUST TARZAN KILL JOHN CARTER?
THERE ARE EASIER WAYS OF ACCOMPLISHING THAT END.
IF CARTER DIED ANY OTHER WAY, HE WOULD SIMPLY "ASCEND TO HEAVEN" OR SOME NONSENSE.
HIS CULT WOULD ONLY BE STRENGTHENED.
WHEN HE SLEW OUR BELOVED ISSUS*, HE BECAME A GOD HIMSELF.
NOW HE MUST BE DESTROYED IN THE SAME WAY--STRIPPED OF HIS GODHOOD AS WELL AS HIS LIFE.
FOR THAT, THE PEOPLE MUST SEE THAT HE HAS AN EQUAL. HENCE TARZAN.
*WARLORD OF MARS, BOOK TWO. —E.R.B.

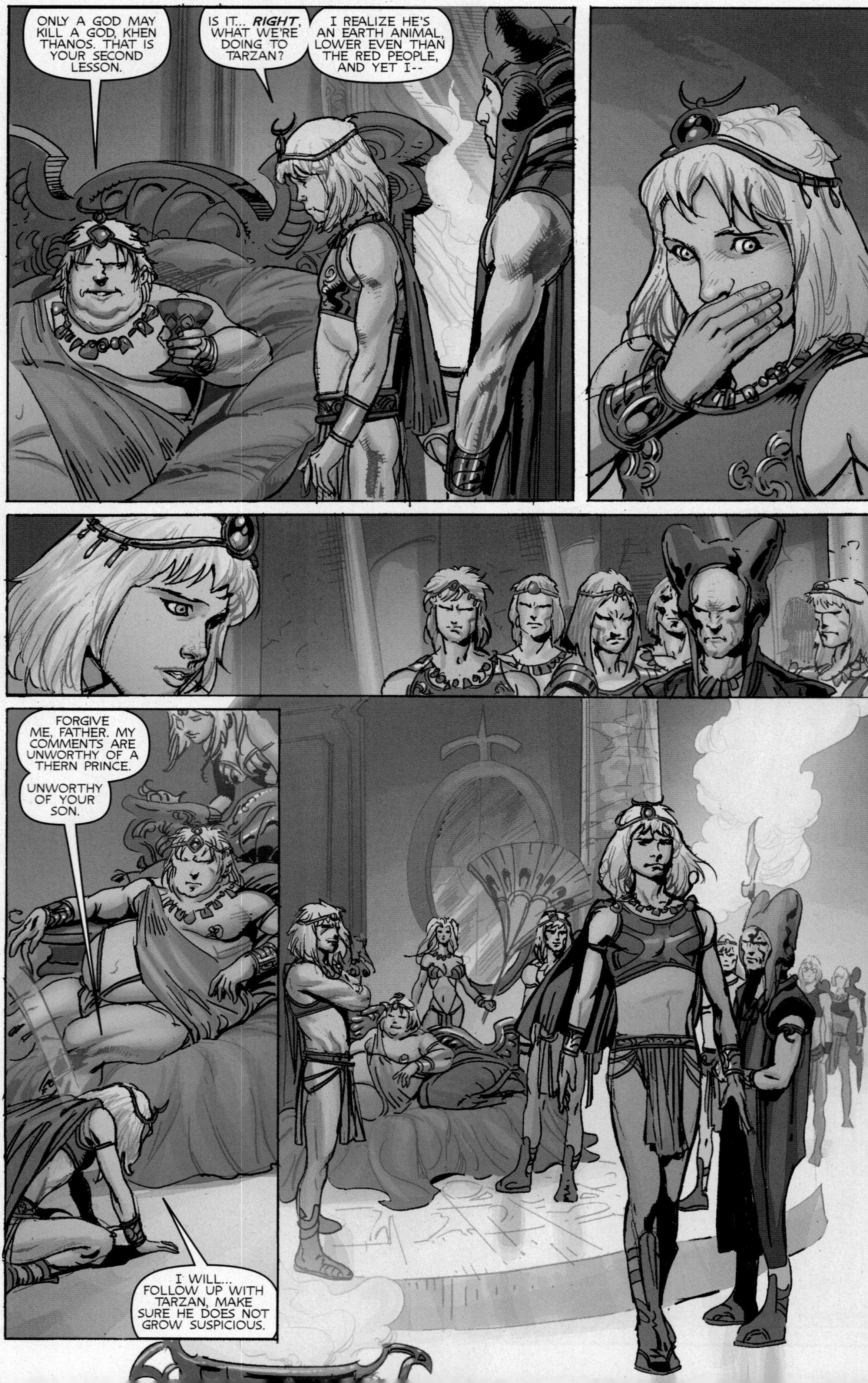
ONLY A GOD MAY KILL A GOD, KHEN THANOS. THAT IS YOUR SECOND LESSON.
IS IT... RIGHT, WHAT WE'RE DOING TO TARZAN?
I REALIZE HE'S AN EARTH ANIMAL, LOWER EVEN THAN THE RED PEOPLE, AND YET I--
FORGIVE ME, FATHER. MY COMMENTS ARE UNWORTHY OF A THERN PRINCE.
UNWORTHY OF YOUR SON.
I WILL... FOLLOW UP WITH TARZAN, MAKE SURE HE DOES NOT GROW SUSPICIOUS.

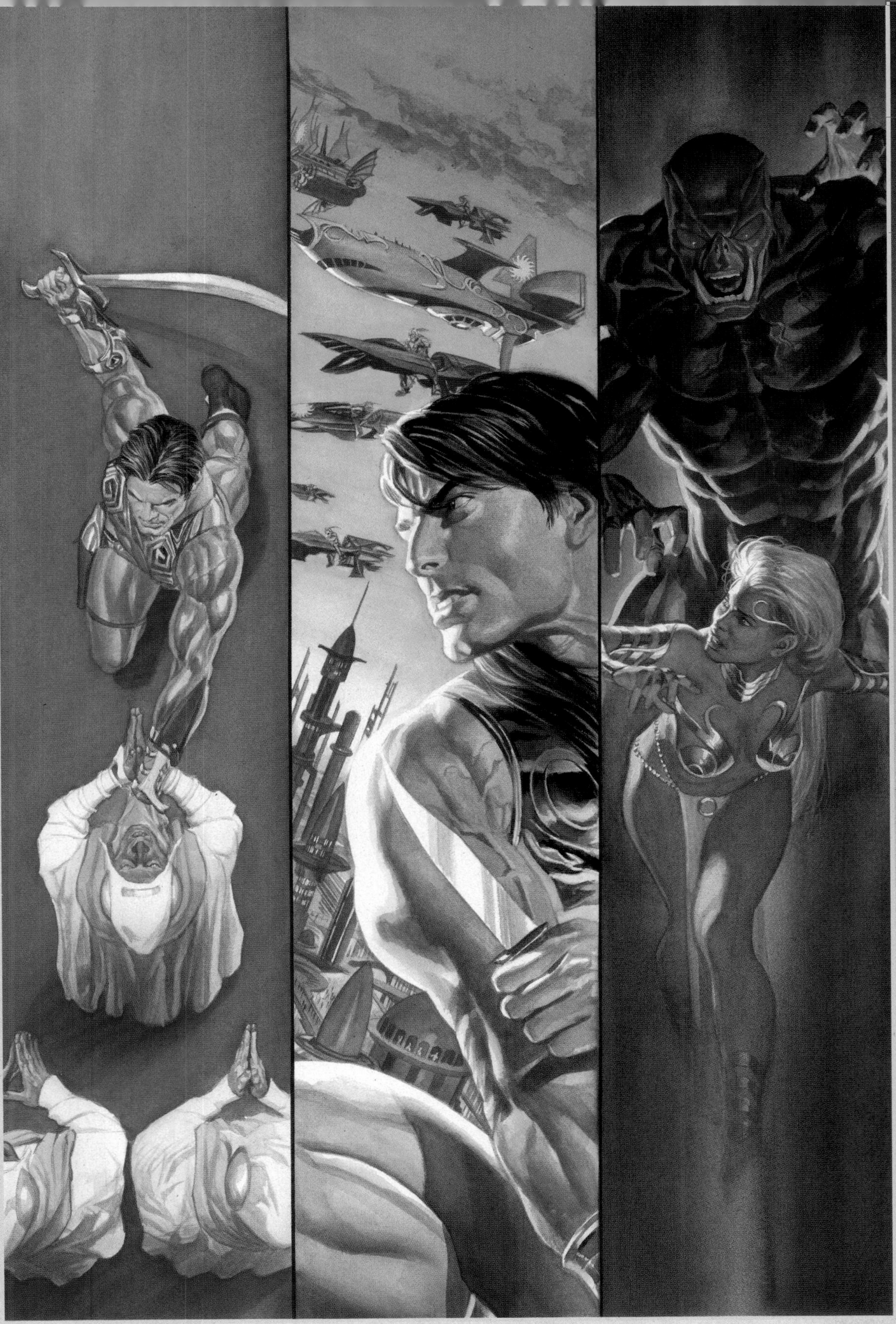

ISSUE 4
WAR IN HEAVEN

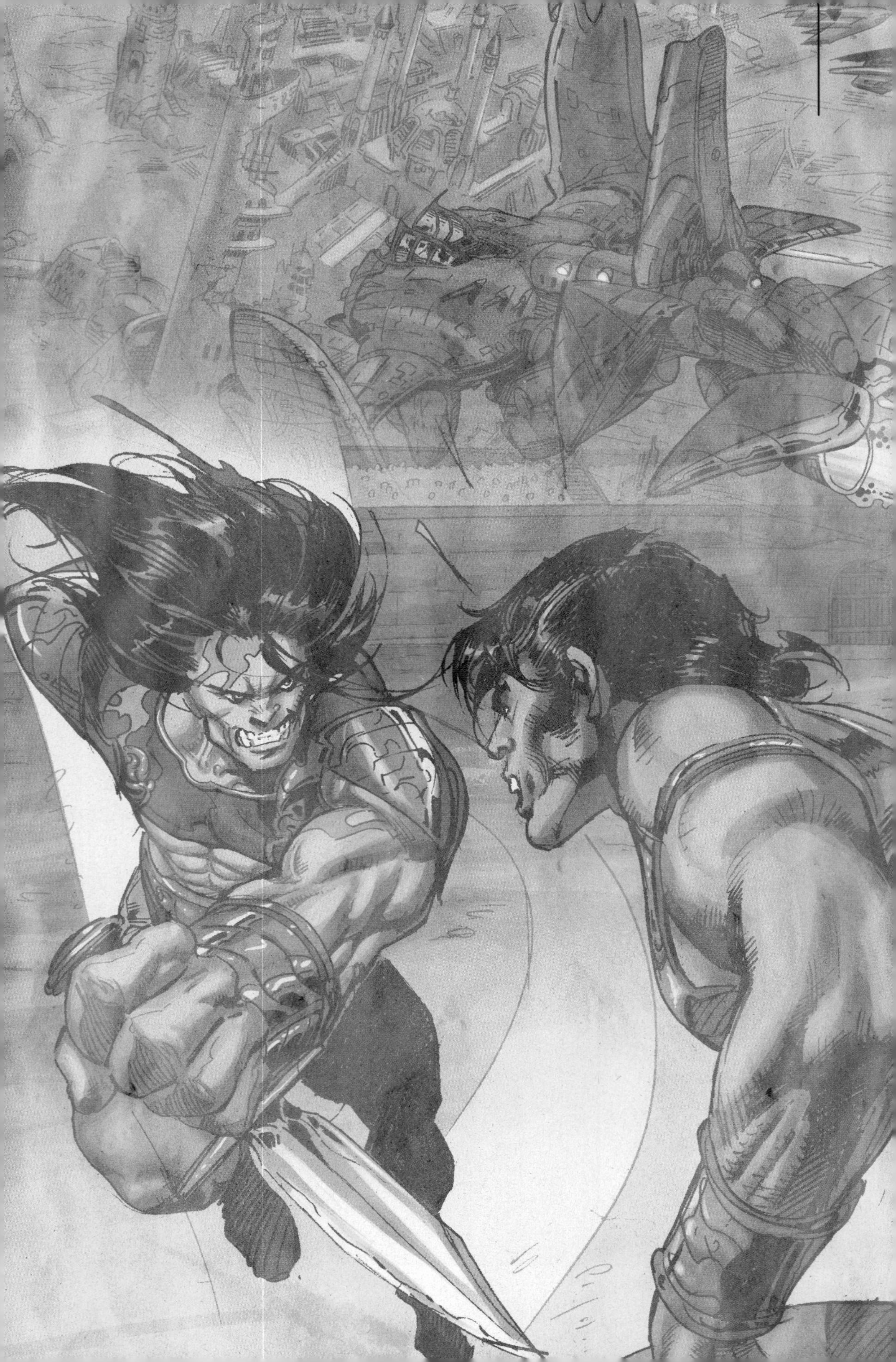

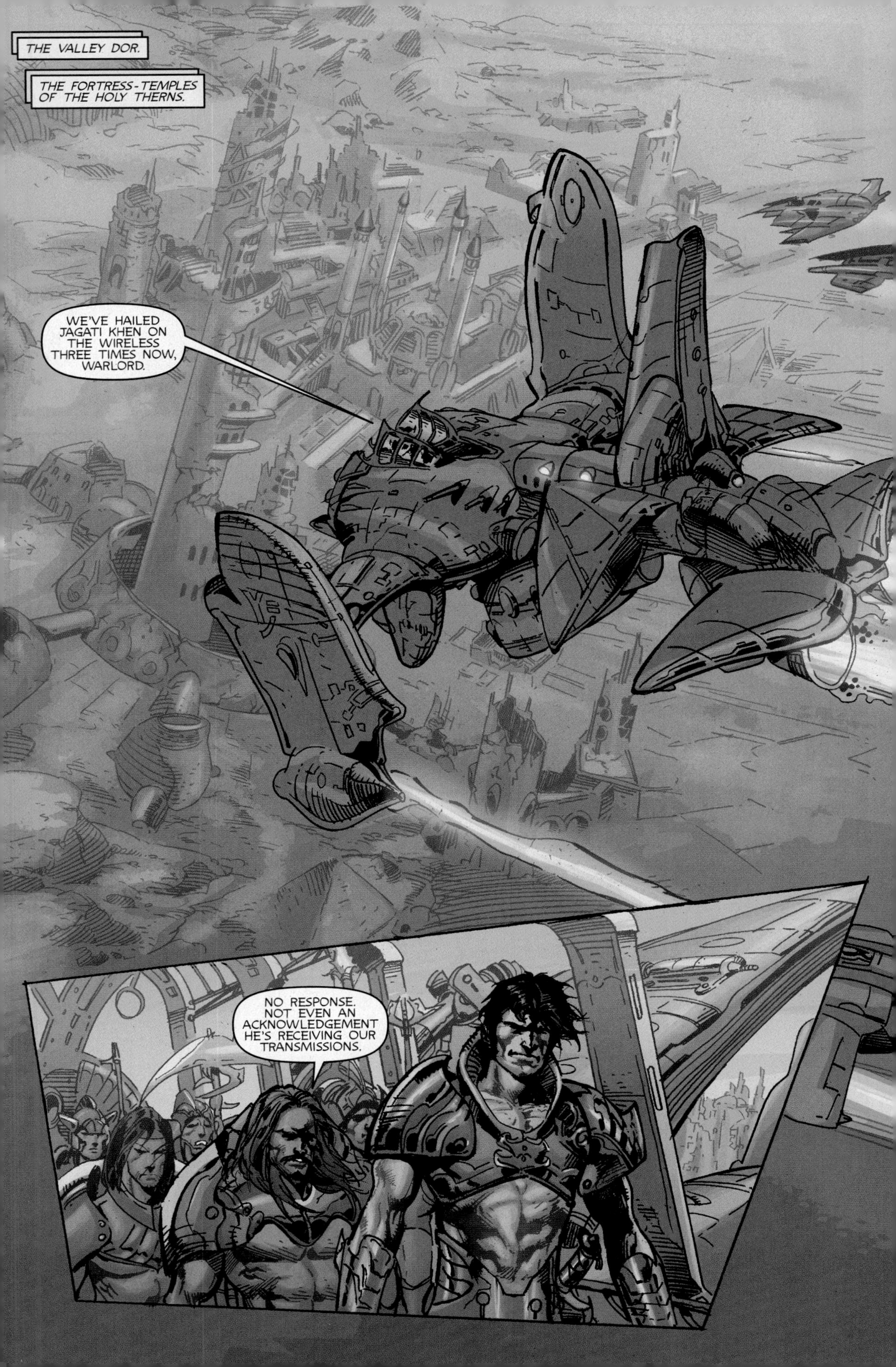
THE VALLEY DOR.
THE FORTRESS-TEMPLES OF THE HOLY THERNS.
WE'VE HAILED JAGATI KHEN ON THE WIRELESS THREE TIMES NOW, WARLORD.
NO RESPONSE. NOT EVEN AN ACKNOWLEDGEMENT HE'S RECEIVING OUR TRANSMISSIONS.

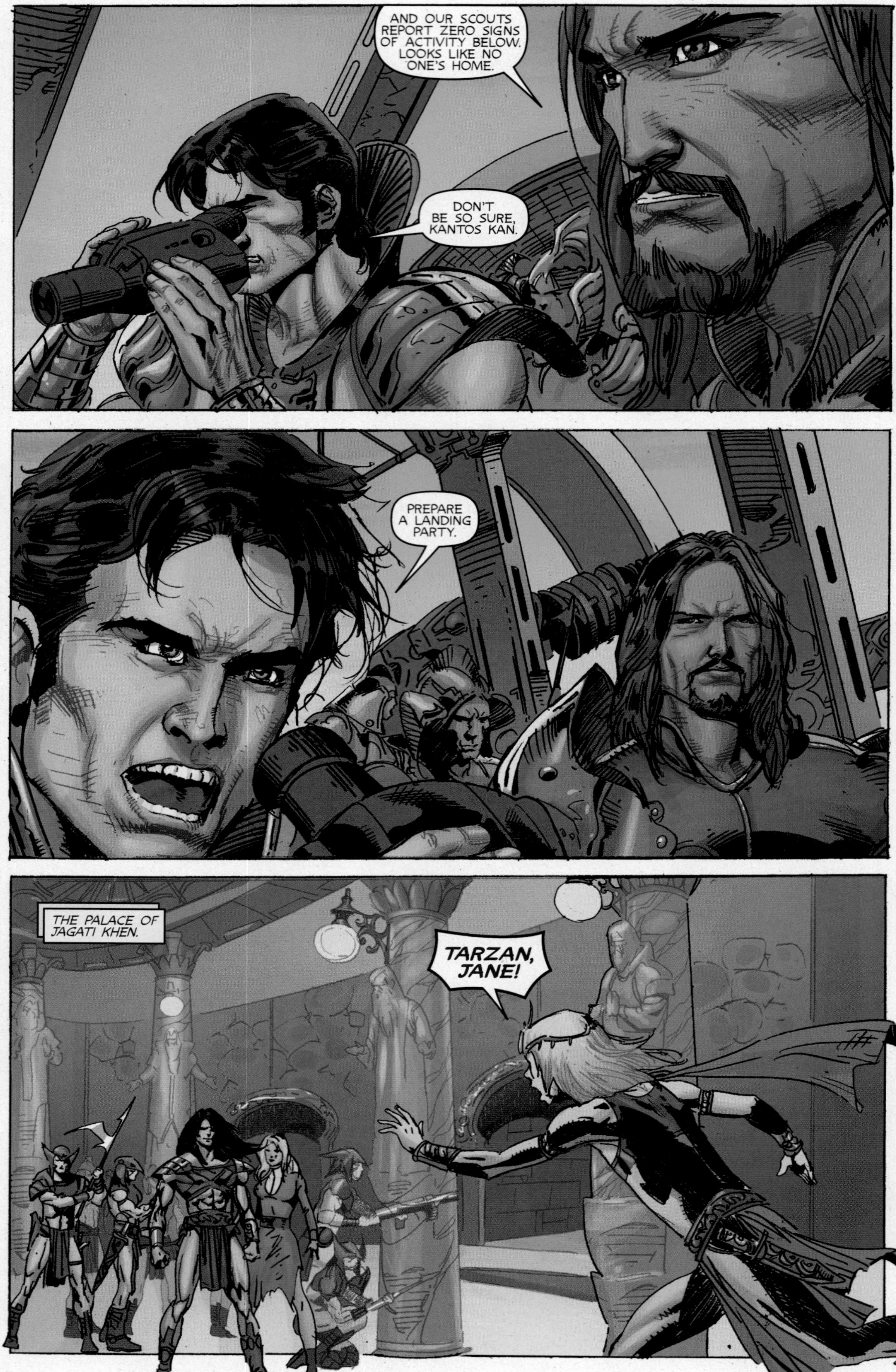
AND OUR SCOUTS REPORT ZERO SIGNS OF ACTIVITY BELOW. LOOKS LIKE NO ONE'S HOME.
DON'T BE SO SURE, KANTOS KAN.
PREPARE A LANDING PARTY.
THE PALACE OF JAGATI KHEN.
TARZAN, JANE!

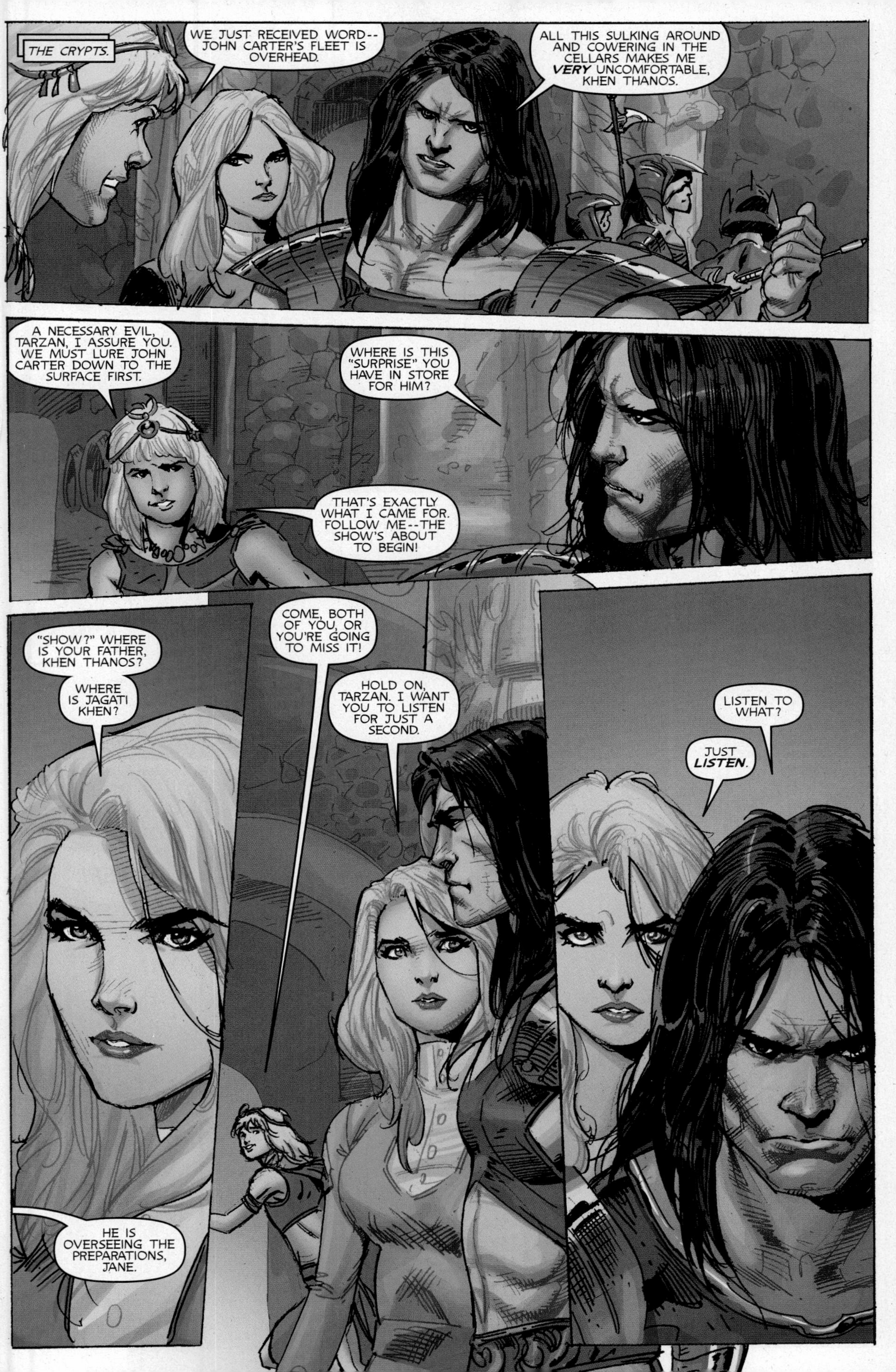
THE CRYPTS.
WE JUST RECEIVED WORD--JOHN CARTER'S FLEET IS OVERHEAD.
ALL THIS SULKING AROUND AND COWERING IN THE CELLARS MAKES ME VERY UNCOMFORTABLE, KHEN THANOS.
A NECESSARY EVIL, TARZAN, I ASSURE YOU. WE MUST LURE JOHN CARTER DOWN TO THE SURFACE FIRST.
WHERE IS THIS "SURPRISE" YOU HAVE IN STORE FOR HIM?
THAT'S EXACTLY WHAT I CAME FOR. FOLLOW ME--THE SHOW'S ABOUT TO BEGIN!
"SHOW?" WHERE IS YOUR FATHER, KHEN THANOS?
WHERE IS JAGATI KHEN?
HE IS OVERSEEING THE PREPARATIONS, JANE.
COME, BOTH OF YOU, OR YOU'RE GOING TO MISS IT!
HOLD ON, TARZAN. I WANT YOU TO LISTEN FOR JUST A SECOND.
LISTEN TO WHAT?
JUST LISTEN.

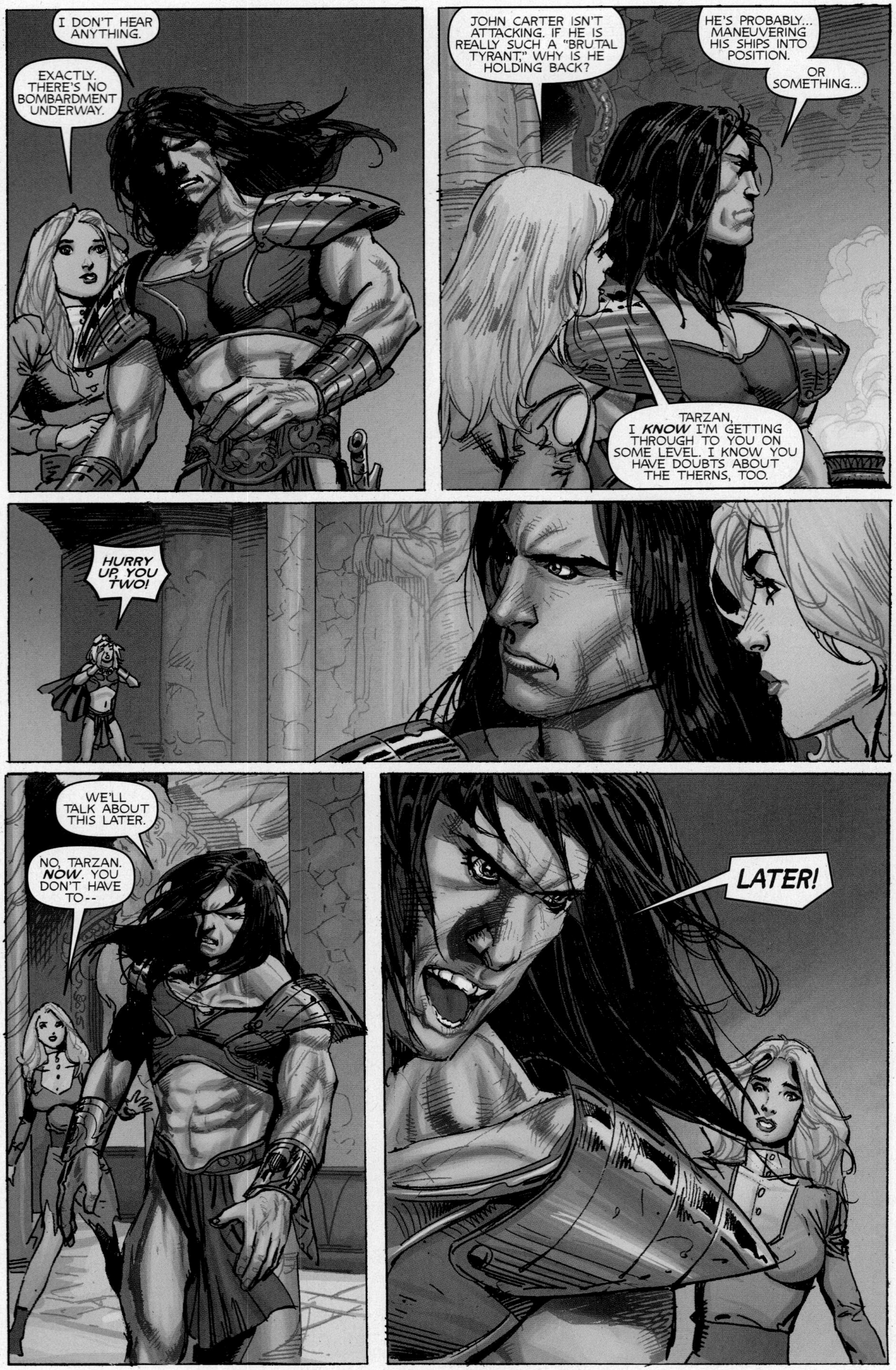
I DON'T HEAR ANYTHING.
EXACTLY. THERE'S NO BOMBARDMENT UNDERWAY.
JOHN CARTER ISN'T ATTACKING. IF HE IS REALLY SUCH A "BRUTAL TYRANT," WHY IS HE HOLDING BACK?
HE'S PROBABLY... MANEUVERING HIS SHIPS INTO POSITION.
OR SOMETHING...
TARZAN, I *KNOW* I'M GETTING THROUGH TO YOU ON SOME LEVEL. I KNOW YOU HAVE DOUBTS ABOUT THE THERNS, TOO.
HURRY UP, YOU TWO!
WE'LL TALK ABOUT THIS LATER.
NO, TARZAN. *NOW*. YOU DON'T HAVE TO--
LATER!

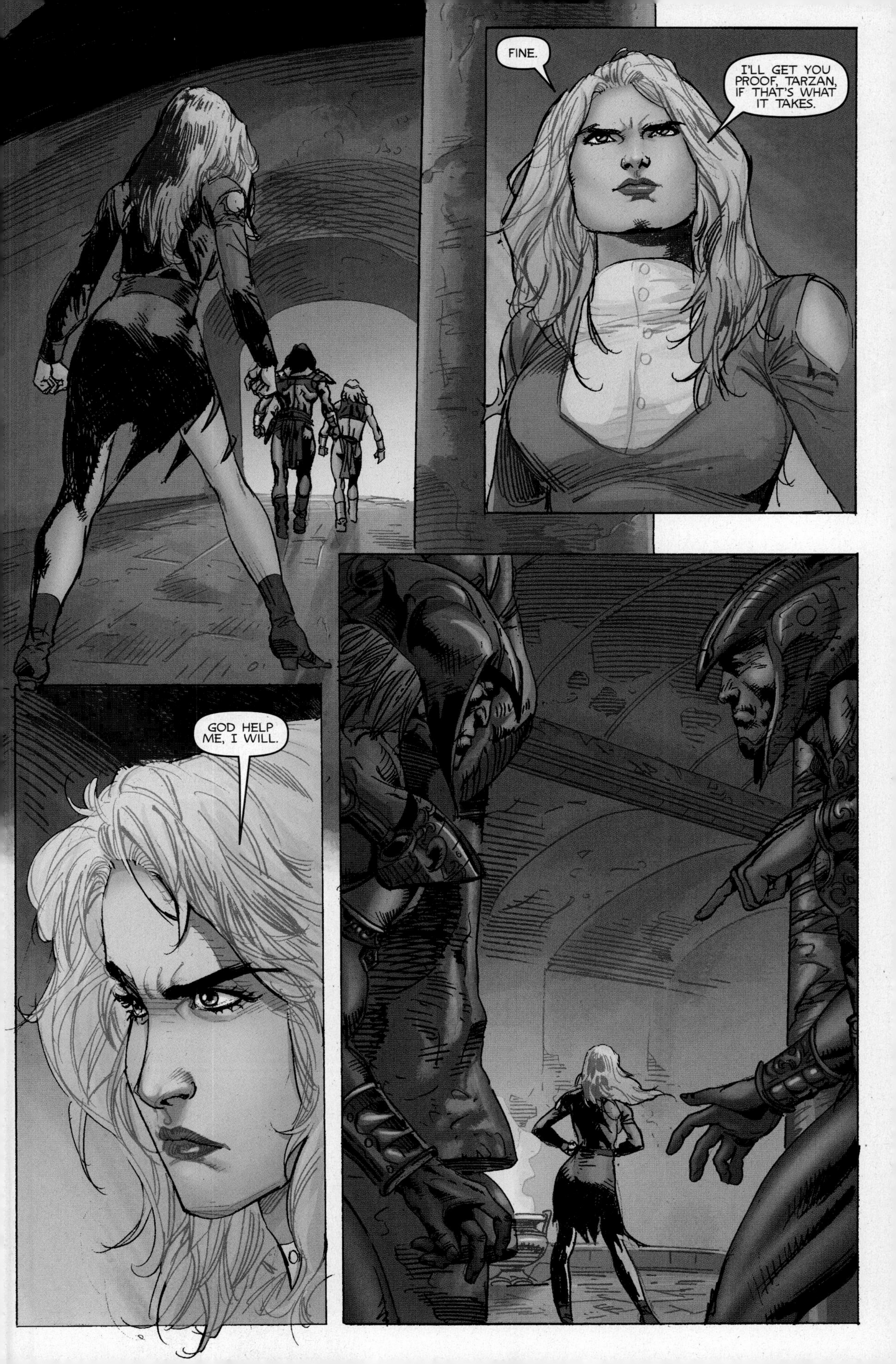
FINE.
I'LL GET YOU PROOF, TARZAN, IF THAT'S WHAT IT TAKES.
GOD HELP ME, I WILL.

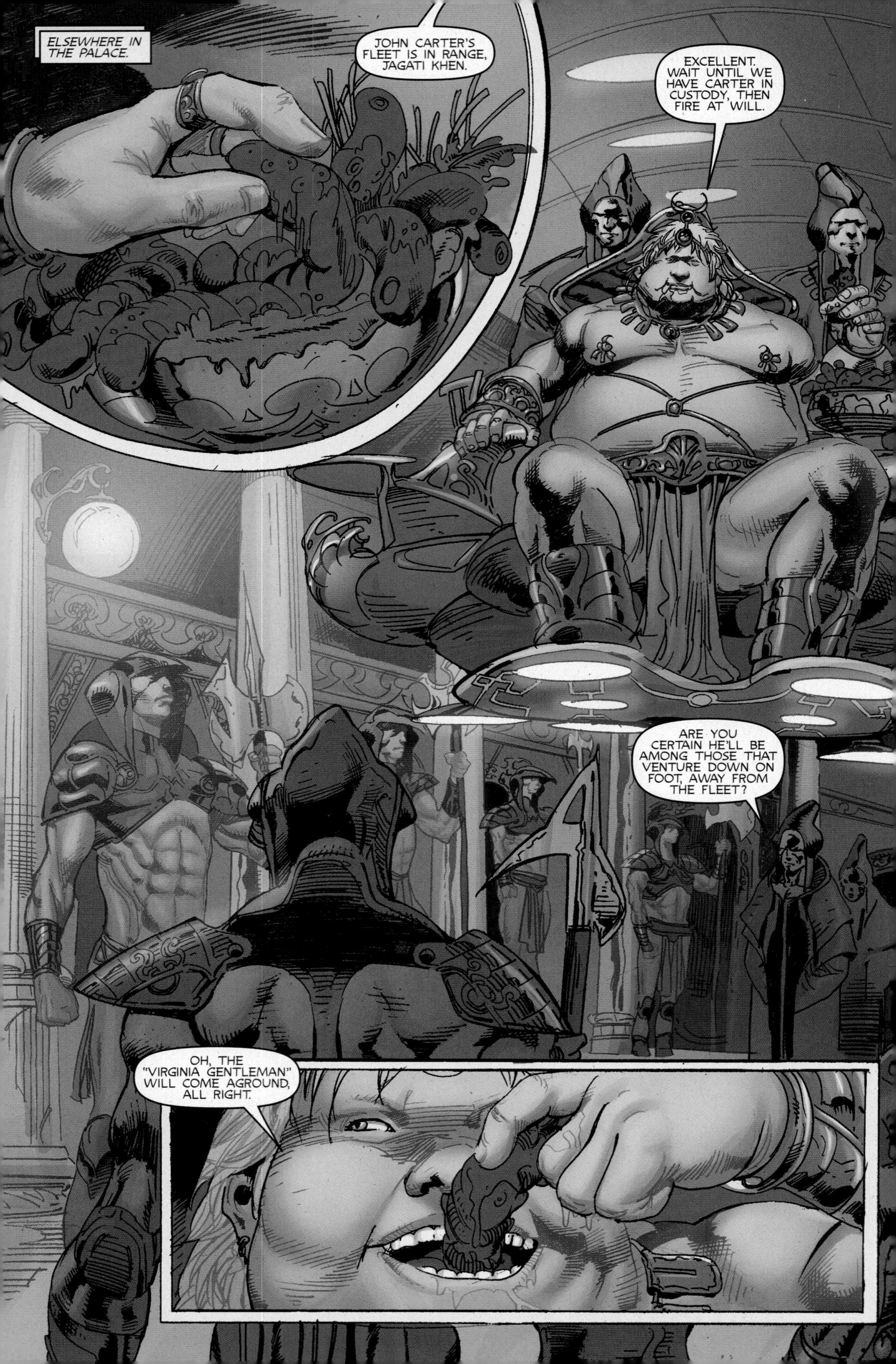
ELSEWHERE IN THE PALACE.
JOHN CARTER'S FLEET IS IN RANGE, JAGATI KHEN.
EXCELLENT. WAIT UNTIL WE HAVE CARTER IN CUSTODY, THEN FIRE AT WILL.
ARE YOU CERTAIN HE'LL BE AMONG THOSE THAT VENTURE DOWN ON FOOT, AWAY FROM THE FLEET?
OH, THE "VIRGINIA GENTLEMAN" WILL COME AGROUND, ALL RIGHT.

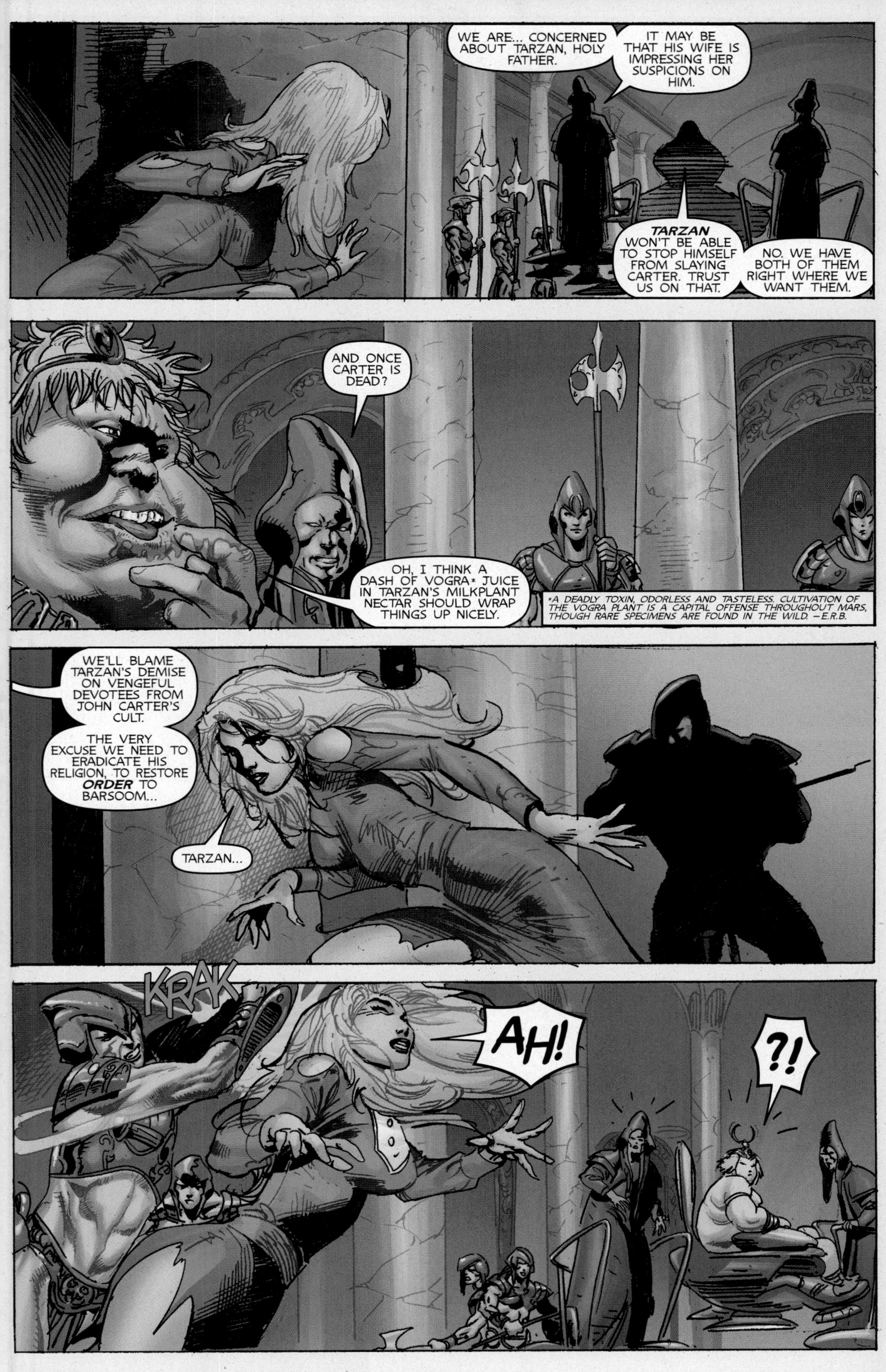
WE ARE... CONCERNED ABOUT TARZAN, HOLY FATHER.
IT MAY BE THAT HIS WIFE IS IMPRESSING HER SUSPICIONS ON HIM.
TARZAN WON'T BE ABLE TO STOP HIMSELF FROM SLAYING CARTER. TRUST US ON THAT.
NO. WE HAVE BOTH OF THEM RIGHT WHERE WE WANT THEM.
AND ONCE CARTER IS DEAD?
OH, I THINK A DASH OF VOGRA* JUICE IN TARZAN'S MILKPLANT NECTAR SHOULD WRAP THINGS UP NICELY.
*A DEADLY TOXIN, ODORLESS AND TASTELESS. CULTIVATION OF THE VOGRA PLANT IS A CAPITAL OFFENSE THROUGHOUT MARS, THOUGH RARE SPECIMENS ARE FOUND IN THE WILD. —E.R.B.
WE'LL BLAME TARZAN'S DEMISE ON VENGEFUL DEVOTEES FROM JOHN CARTER'S CULT.
THE VERY EXCUSE WE NEED TO ERADICATE HIS RELIGION, TO RESTORE ORDER TO BARSOOM...
TARZAN...
KRAK
AH!
?!

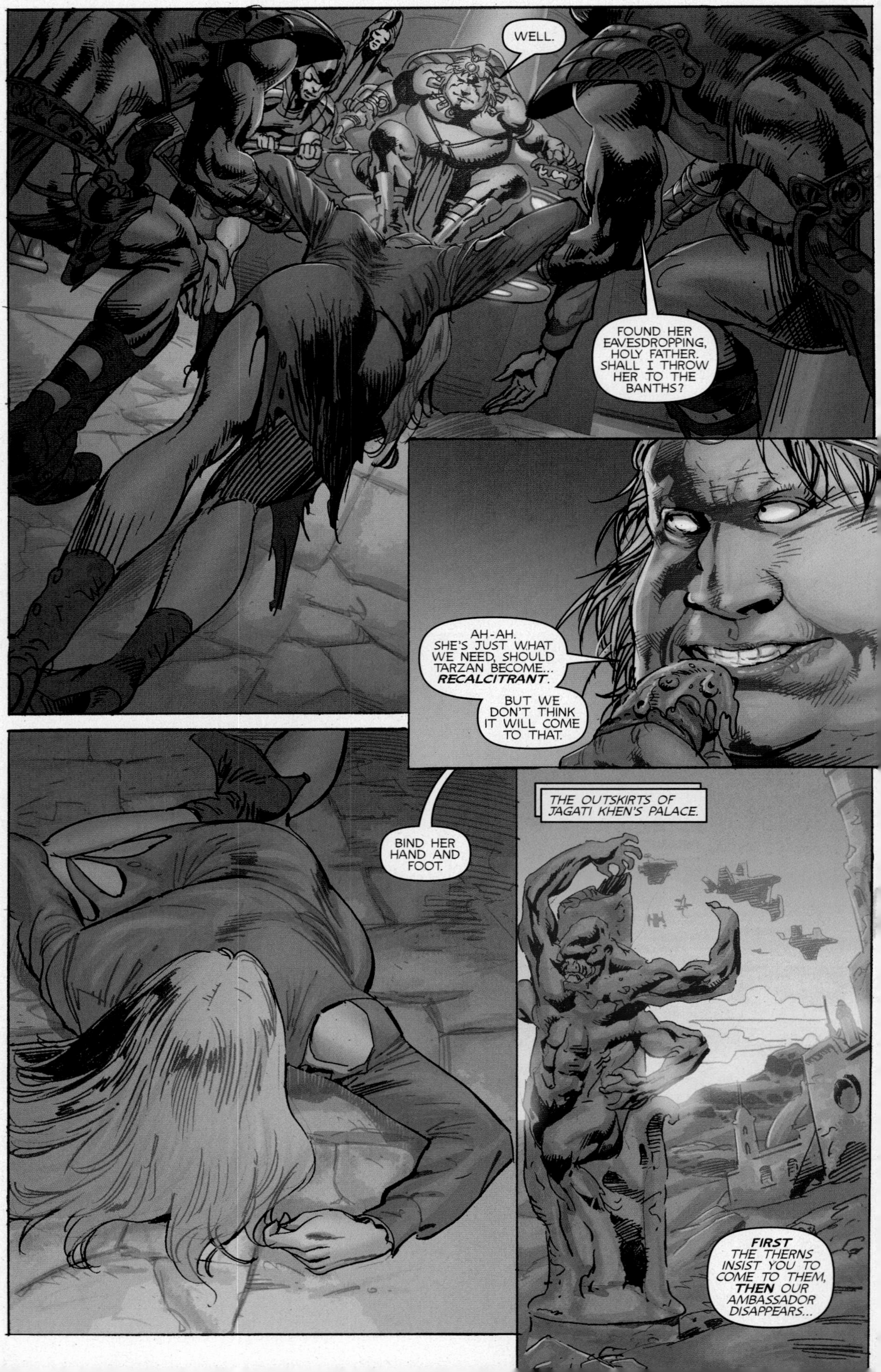
WELL.
FOUND HER EAVESDROPPING, HOLY FATHER. SHALL I THROW HER TO THE BANTHS?
AH-AH. SHE'S JUST WHAT WE NEED, SHOULD TARZAN BECOME... ***RECALCITRANT***.
BUT WE DON'T THINK IT WILL COME TO THAT.
BIND HER HAND AND FOOT.
THE OUTSKIRTS OF JAGATI KHEN'S PALACE.
FIRST THE THERNS INSIST YOU TO COME TO THEM, ***THEN*** OUR AMBASSADOR DISAPPEARS...

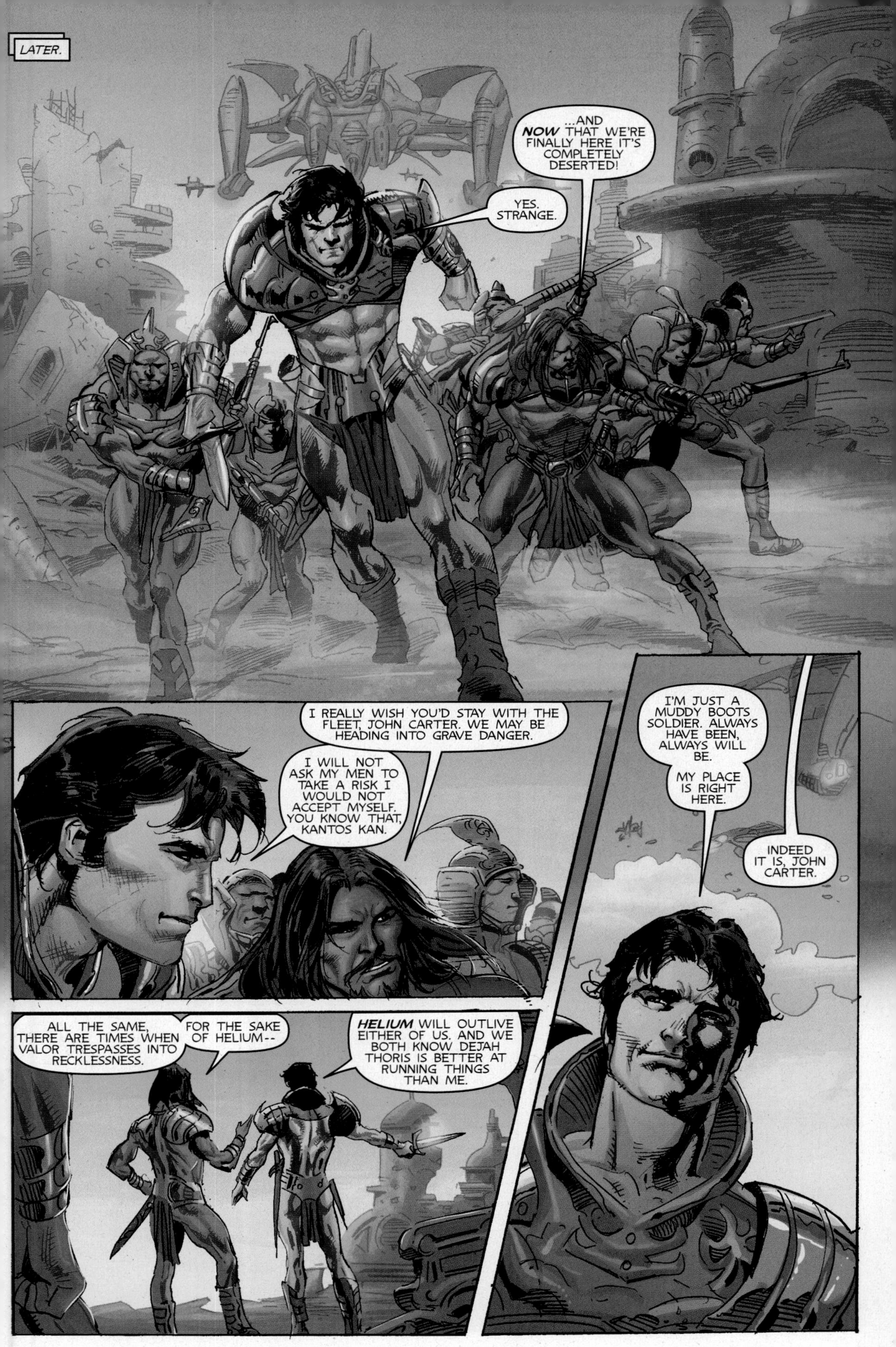

LATER.
...AND NOW THAT WE'RE FINALLY HERE IT'S COMPLETELY DESERTED!
YES. STRANGE.
I REALLY WISH YOU'D STAY WITH THE FLEET, JOHN CARTER. WE MAY BE HEADING INTO GRAVE DANGER.
I WILL NOT ASK MY MEN TO TAKE A RISK I WOULD NOT ACCEPT MYSELF. YOU KNOW THAT, KANTOS KAN.
I'M JUST A MUDDY BOOTS SOLDIER. ALWAYS HAVE BEEN, ALWAYS WILL BE.
MY PLACE IS RIGHT HERE.
INDEED IT IS, JOHN CARTER.
ALL THE SAME, THERE ARE TIMES WHEN VALOR TRESPASSES INTO RECKLESSNESS.
FOR THE SAKE OF HELIUM--
HELIUM WILL OUTLIVE EITHER OF US. AND WE BOTH KNOW DEJAH THORIS IS BETTER AT RUNNING THINGS THAN ME.

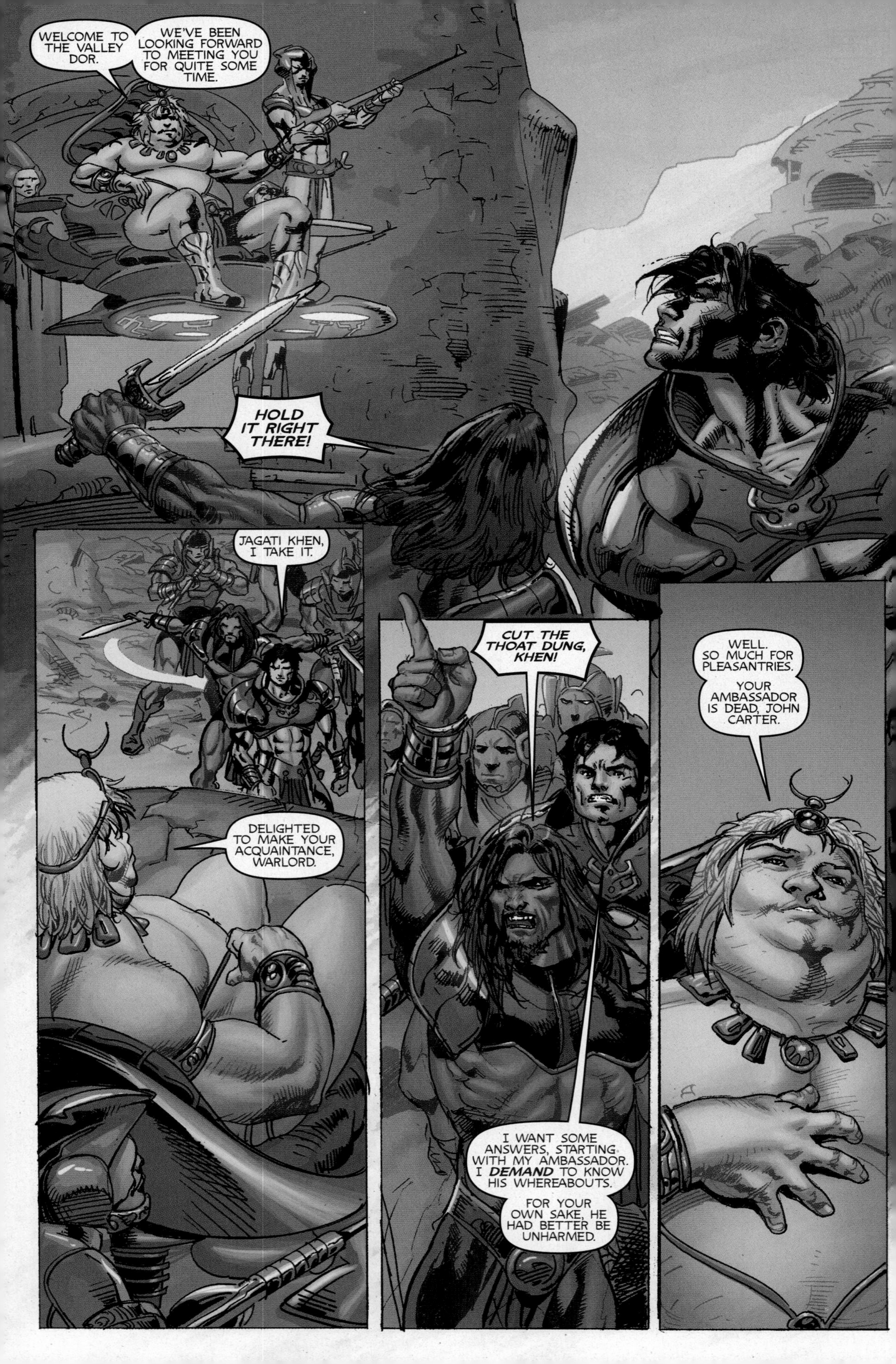
WELCOME TO THE VALLEY DOR.
WE'VE BEEN LOOKING FORWARD TO MEETING YOU FOR QUITE SOME TIME.
HOLD IT RIGHT THERE!
JAGATI KHEN, I TAKE IT.
DELIGHTED TO MAKE YOUR ACQUAINTANCE, WARLORD.
CUT THE THOAT DUNG, KHEN!
I WANT SOME ANSWERS, STARTING WITH MY AMBASSADOR. I DEMAND TO KNOW HIS WHEREABOUTS.
FOR YOUR OWN SAKE, HE HAD BETTER BE UNHARMED.
WELL. SO MUCH FOR PLEASANTRIES.
YOUR AMBASSADOR IS DEAD, JOHN CARTER.

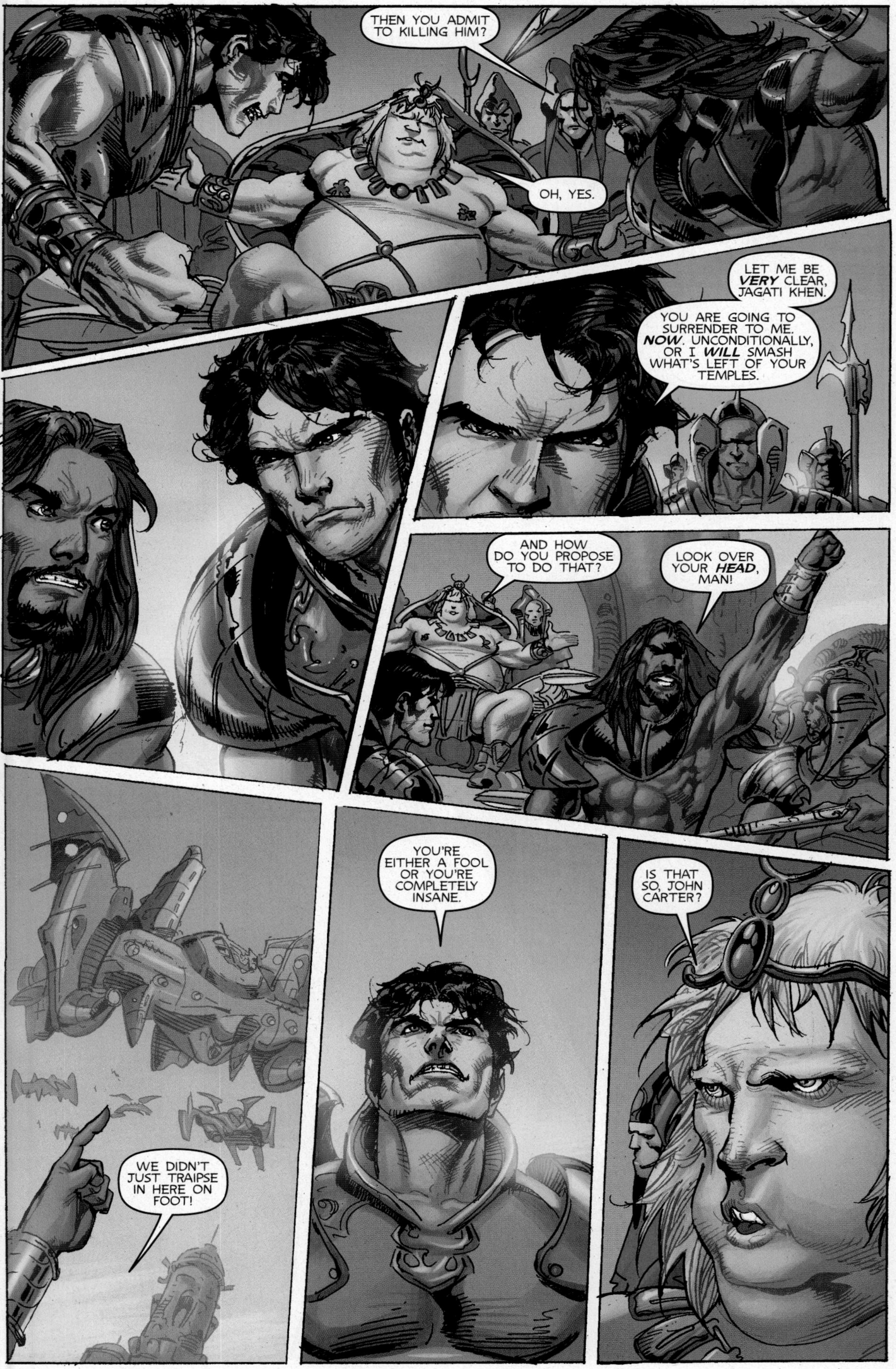
THEN YOU ADMIT TO KILLING HIM?
OH, YES.
LET ME BE **VERY** CLEAR, JAGATI KHEN.
YOU ARE GOING TO SURRENDER TO ME. **NOW**. UNCONDITIONALLY, OR I **WILL** SMASH WHAT'S LEFT OF YOUR TEMPLES.
AND HOW DO YOU PROPOSE TO DO THAT?
LOOK OVER YOUR **HEAD**, MAN!
WE DIDN'T JUST TRAIPSE IN HERE ON FOOT!
YOU'RE EITHER A FOOL OR YOU'RE COMPLETELY INSANE.
IS THAT SO, JOHN CARTER?

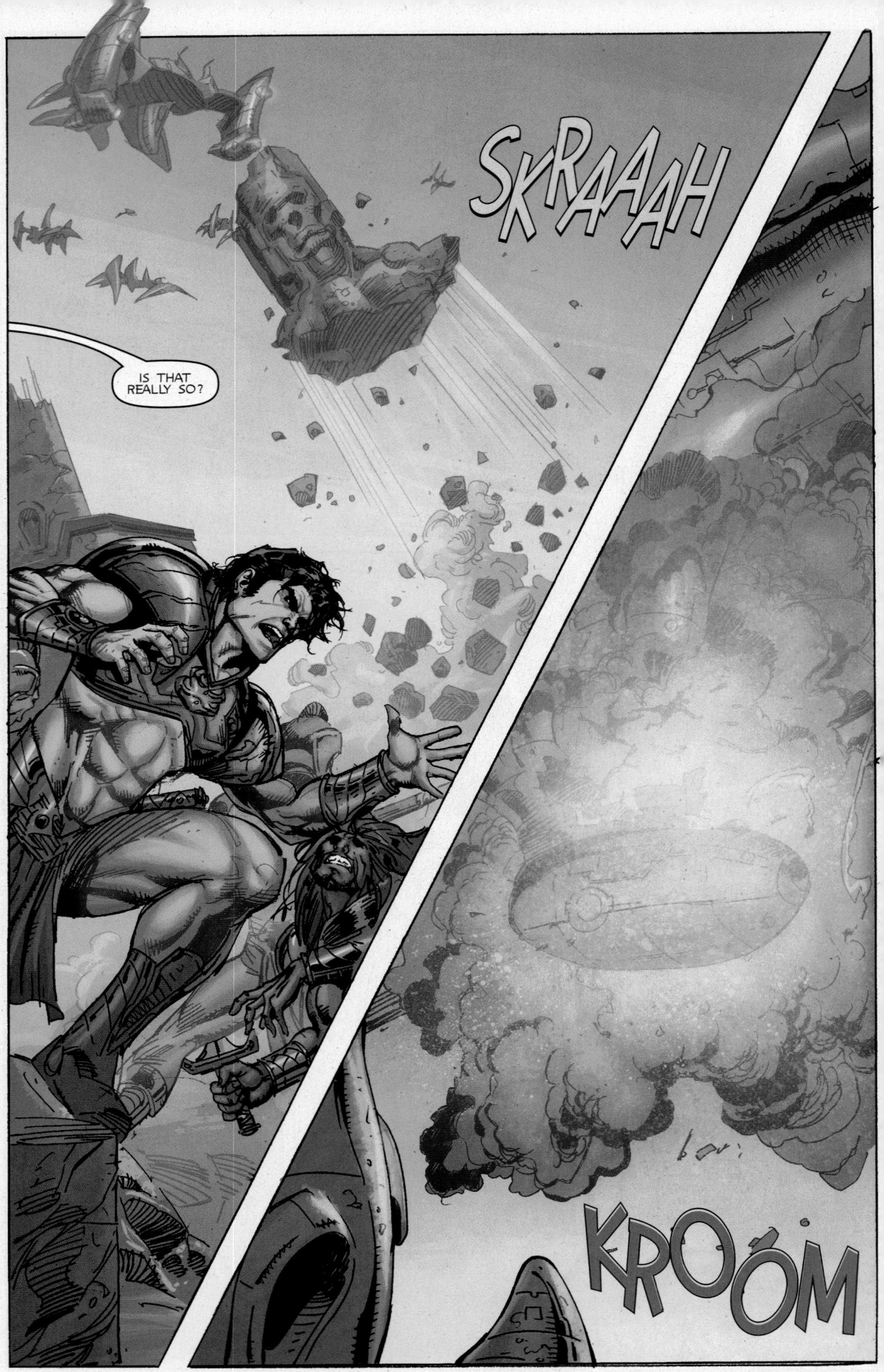
SKRAAAH
IS THAT REALLY SO?
KROOOM

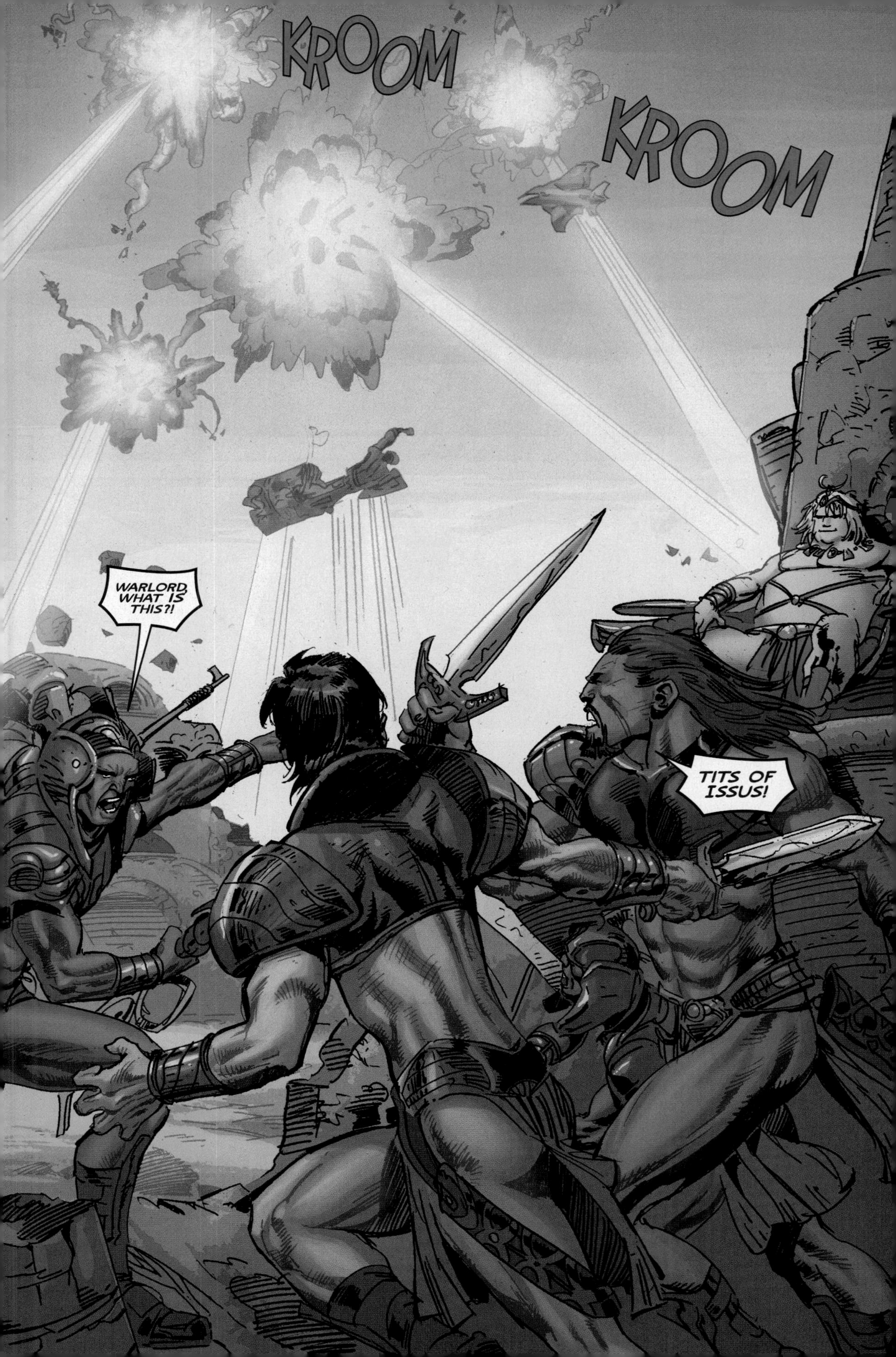
KROOM
KROOM
WARLORD, WHAT IS THIS?!
TITS OF ISSUS!

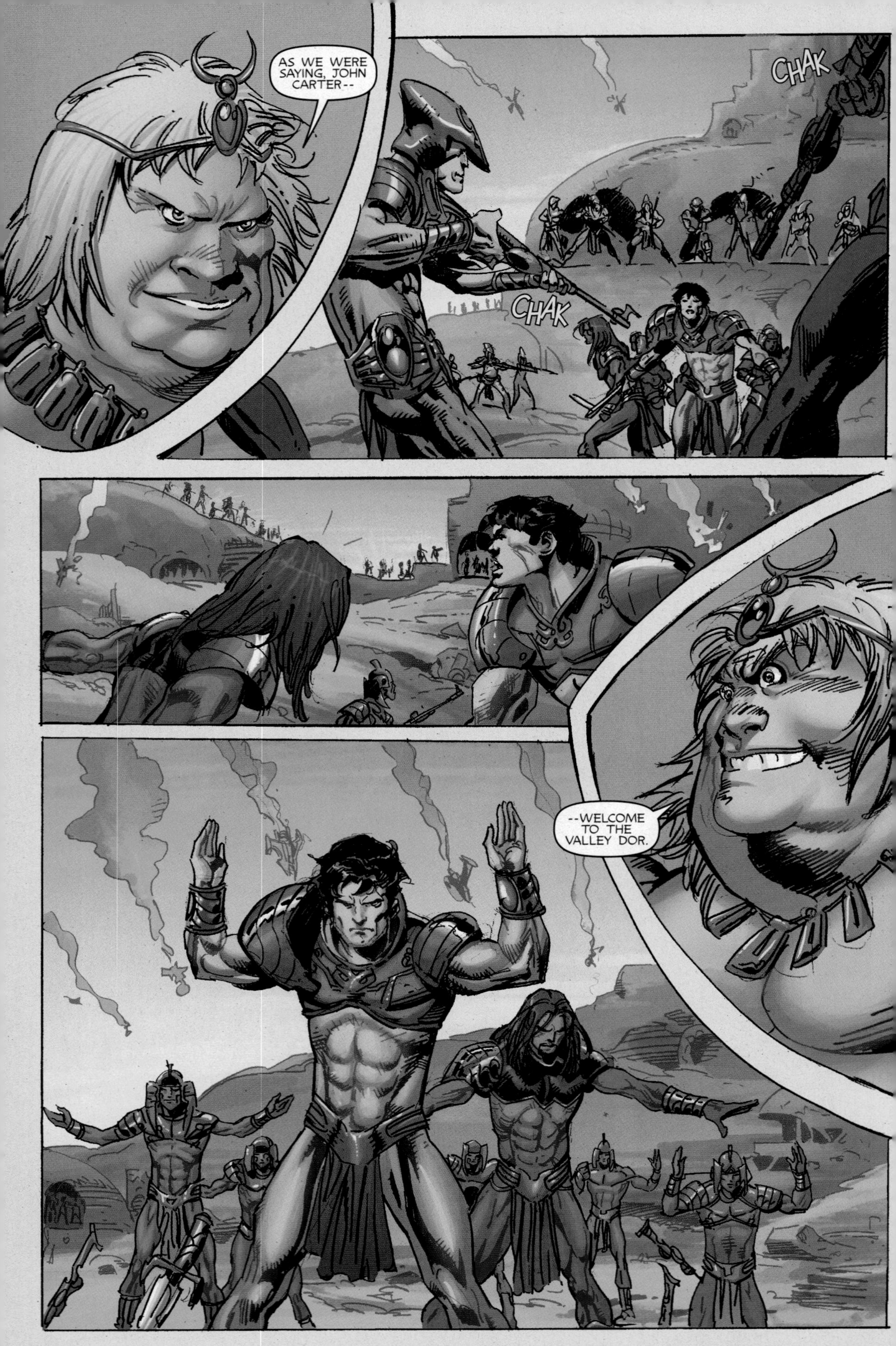
AS WE WERE SAYING, JOHN CARTER--
CHAK
CHAK
--WELCOME TO THE VALLEY DOR.

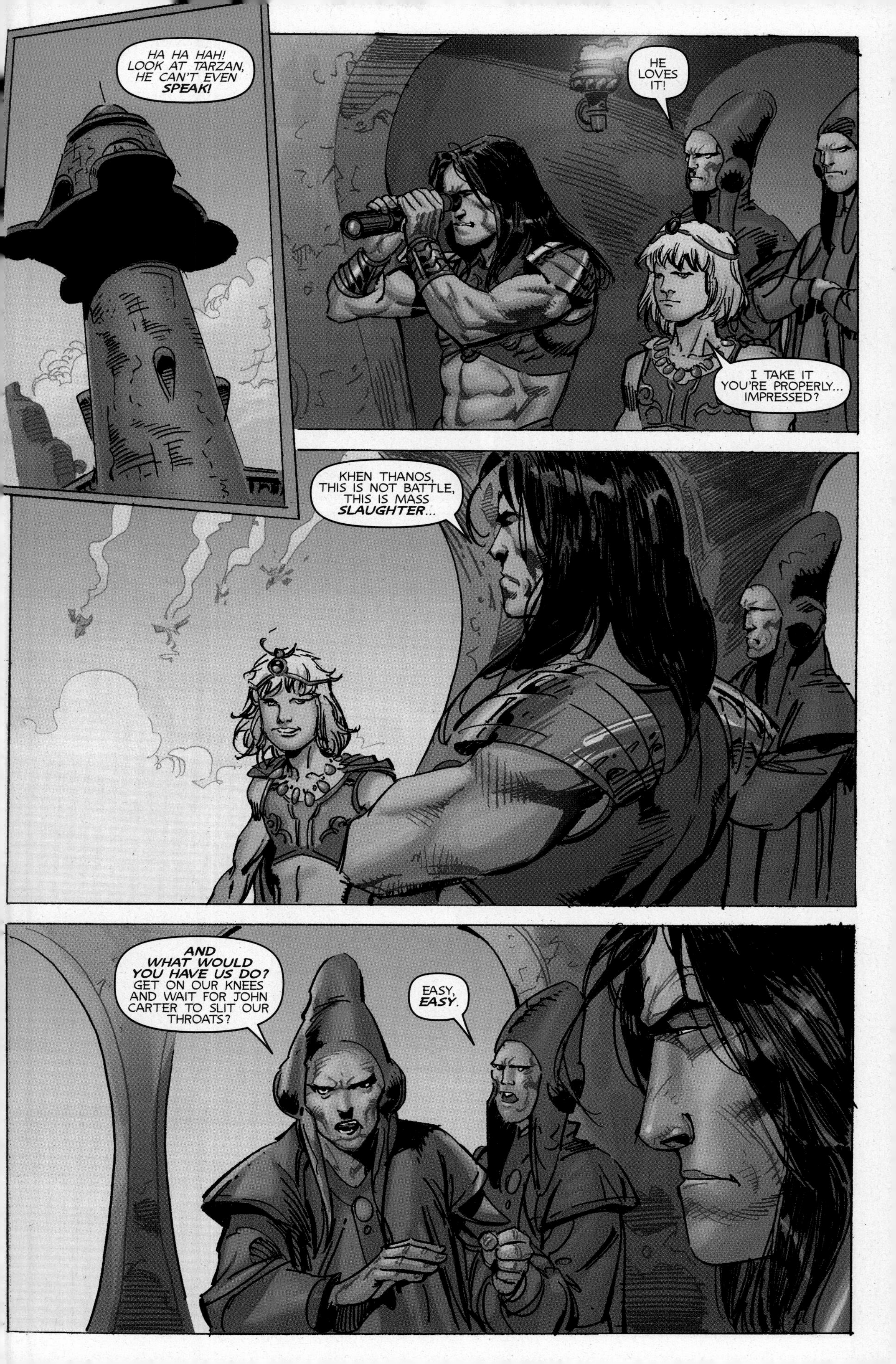
HA HA HAH! LOOK AT TARZAN, HE CAN'T EVEN SPEAK!
HE LOVES IT!
I TAKE IT YOU'RE PROPERLY... IMPRESSED?
KHEN THANOS, THIS IS NOT BATTLE, THIS IS MASS SLAUGHTER...
AND WHAT WOULD YOU HAVE US DO? GET ON OUR KNEES AND WAIT FOR JOHN CARTER TO SLIT OUR THROATS?
EASY, EASY.

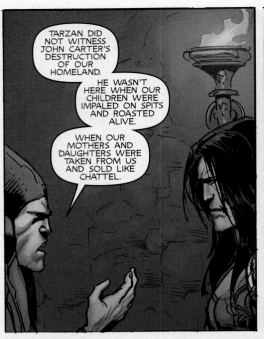

TARZAN DID NOT WITNESS JOHN CARTER'S DESTRUCTION OF OUR HOMELAND.

HE WASN'T HERE WHEN OUR CHILDREN WERE IMPALED ON SPITS AND ROASTED ALIVE.

WHEN OUR MOTHERS AND DAUGHTERS WERE TAKEN FROM US AND SOLD LIKE CHATTEL.

HOW DID YOU ACCOMPLISH THE DESTRUCTION OF CARTER'S FLEET?

DOWN THERE. LOOK.

THAT BOWL-SHAPED DEVICE IS CALLED A *MASS REPULSOR*.

WE THERNS HAVE DISCOVERED A MEANS OF REDIRECTING THE ENERGY OF THE "EIGHTH RAY" THAT POWERS BARSOOMIAN AIRSHIPS.

BY TRIANGULATING TWO OR MORE OF THESE DISHES, IT IS POSSIBLE TO IMPART THE LEVITATING IMPULSE REMOTELY, EVEN ONTO OBJECTS OF VERY GREAT SIZE.

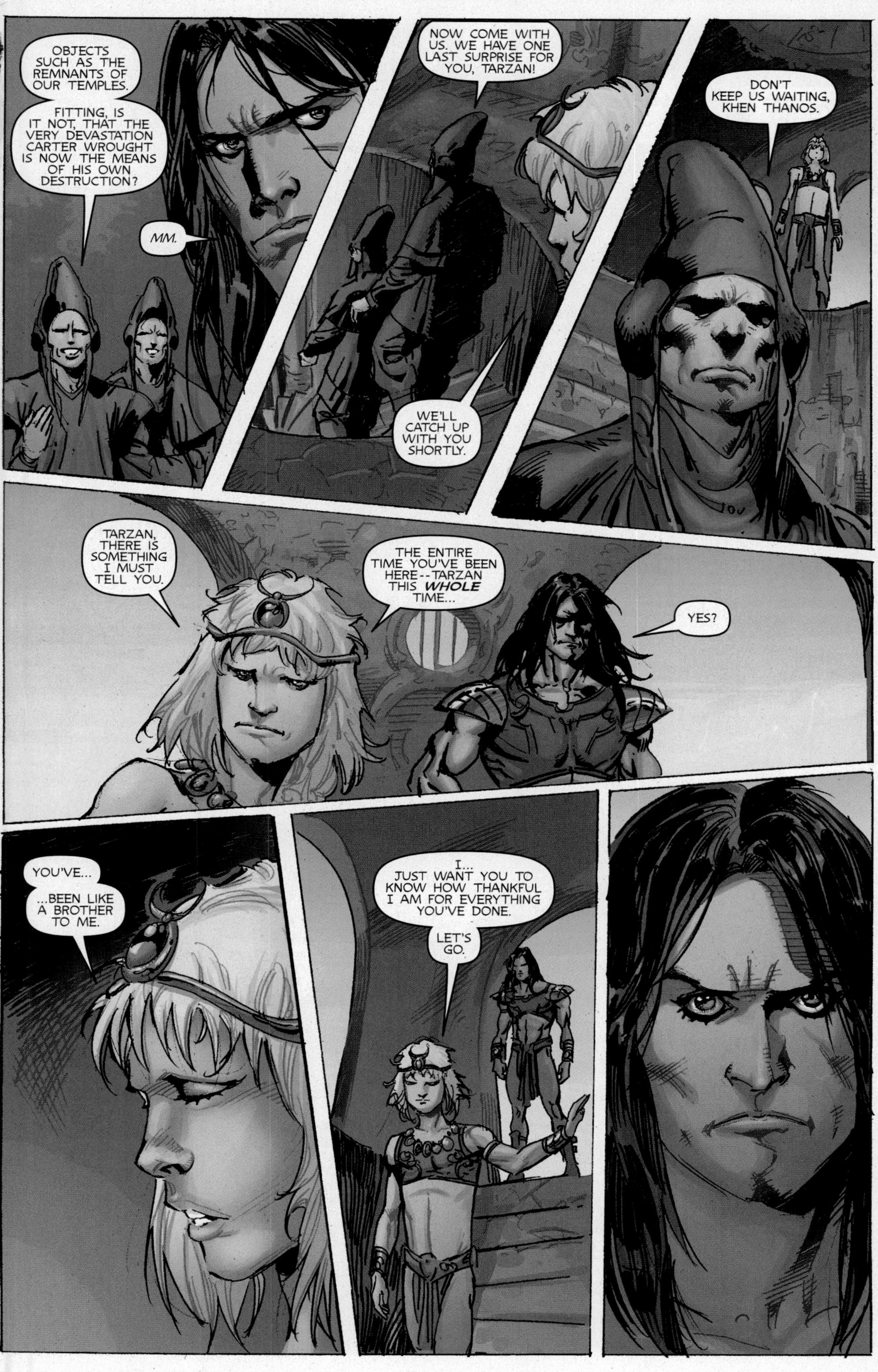
OBJECTS SUCH AS THE REMNANTS OF OUR TEMPLES.
FITTING, IS IT NOT, THAT THE VERY DEVASTATION CARTER WROUGHT IS NOW THE MEANS OF HIS OWN DESTRUCTION?
MM.
NOW COME WITH US. WE HAVE ONE LAST SURPRISE FOR YOU, TARZAN!
WE'LL CATCH UP WITH YOU SHORTLY.
DON'T KEEP US WAITING, KHEN THANOS.
TARZAN, THERE IS SOMETHING I MUST TELL YOU.
THE ENTIRE TIME YOU'VE BEEN HERE--TARZAN THIS *WHOLE* TIME...
YES?
YOU'VE...
...BEEN LIKE A BROTHER TO ME.
I... JUST WANT YOU TO KNOW HOW THANKFUL I AM FOR EVERYTHING YOU'VE DONE.
LET'S GO.

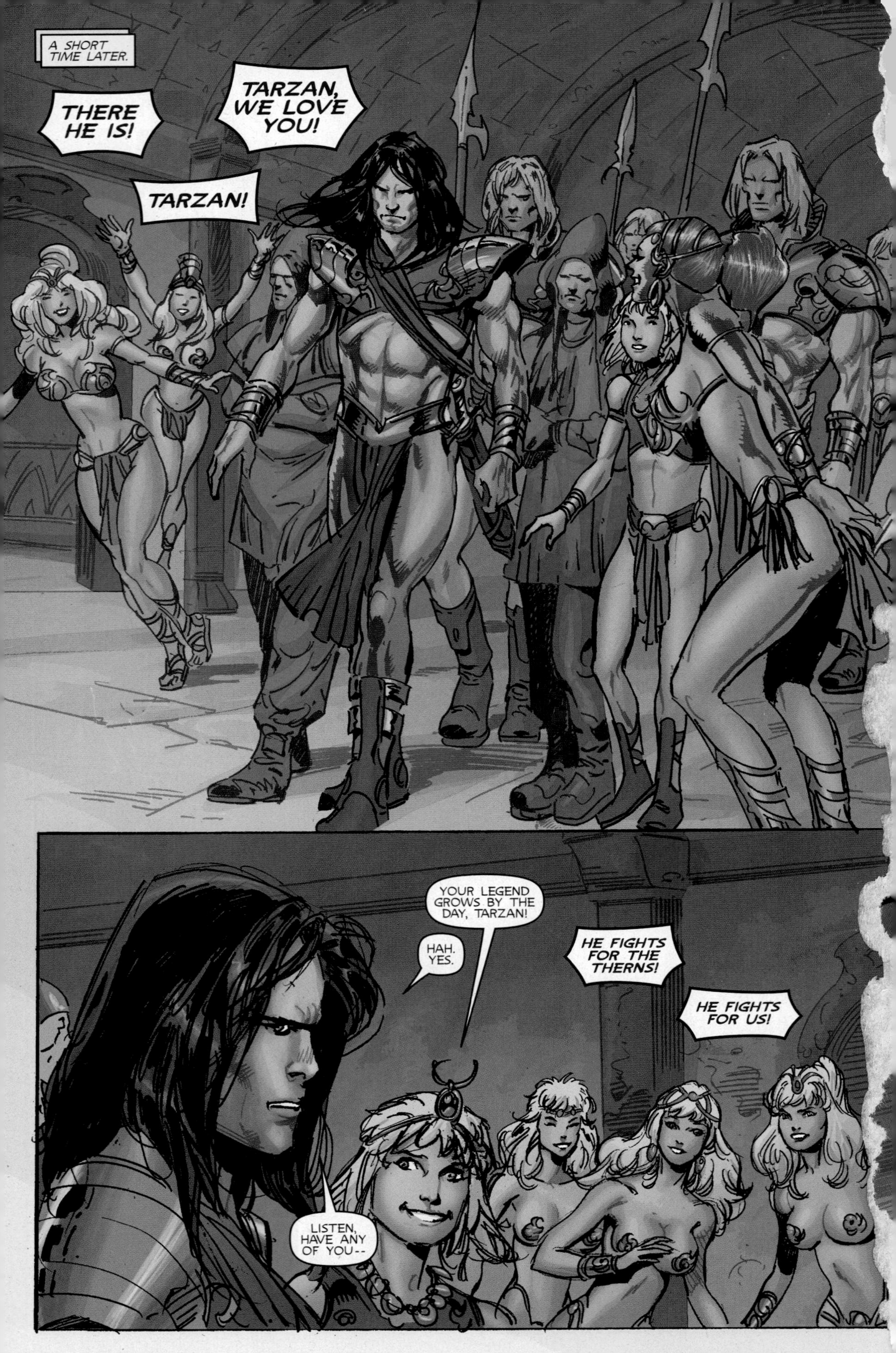
A SHORT TIME LATER.
THERE HE IS!
TARZAN, WE LOVE YOU!
TARZAN!
YOUR LEGEND GROWS BY THE DAY, TARZAN!
HAH. YES.
HE FIGHTS FOR THE THERNS!
HE FIGHTS FOR US!
LISTEN, HAVE ANY OF YOU--

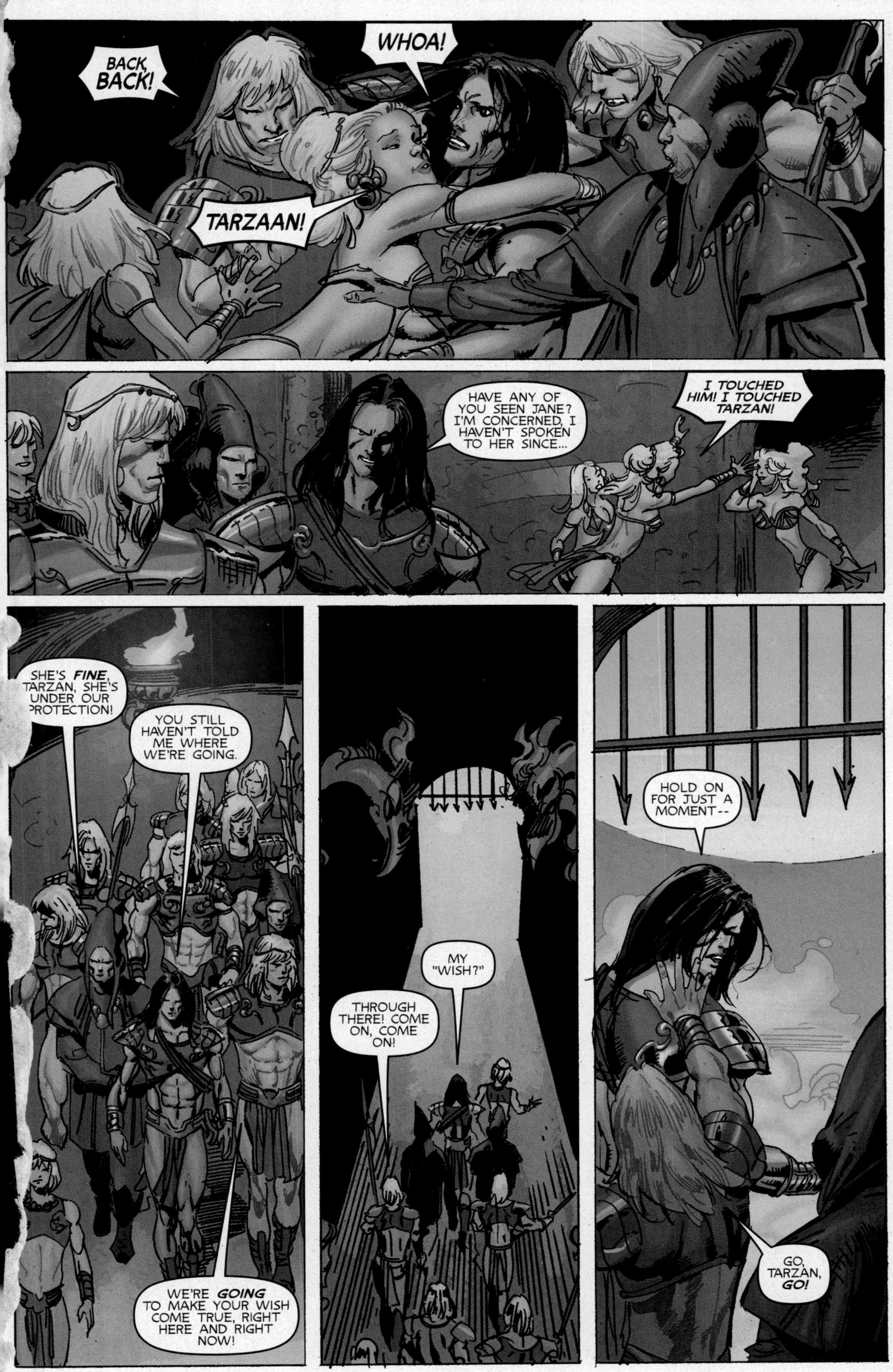
BACK, BACK!
WHOA!
TARZAAN!
HAVE ANY OF YOU SEEN JANE? I'M CONCERNED, I HAVEN'T SPOKEN TO HER SINCE...
I TOUCHED HIM! I TOUCHED TARZAN!
SHE'S FINE, TARZAN, SHE'S UNDER OUR PROTECTION!
YOU STILL HAVEN'T TOLD ME WHERE WE'RE GOING.
WE'RE GOING TO MAKE YOUR WISH COME TRUE, RIGHT HERE AND RIGHT NOW!
MY "WISH?"
THROUGH THERE! COME ON, COME ON!
HOLD ON FOR JUST A MOMENT--
GO, TARZAN, GO!

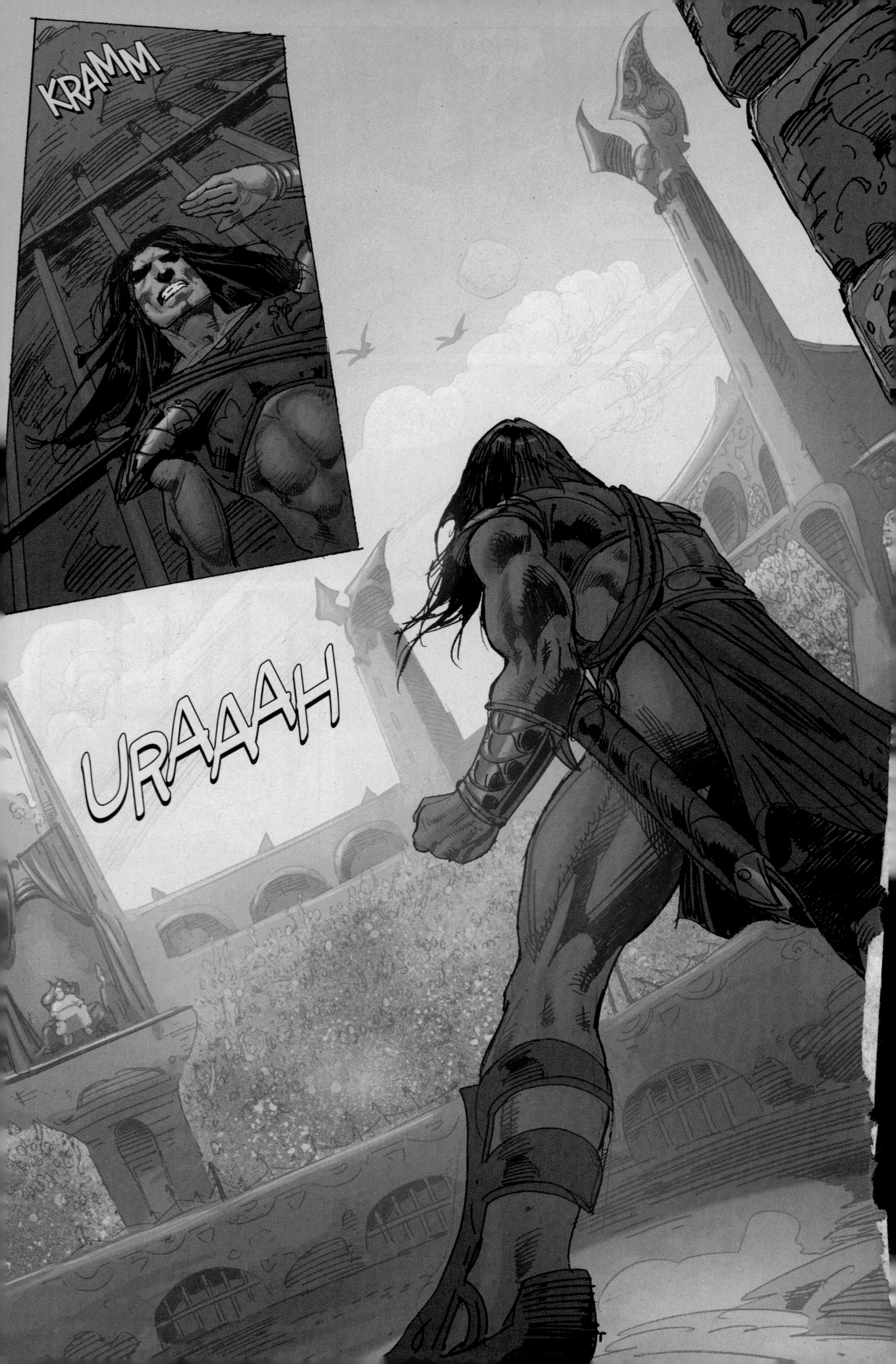
KRAMM
URAAAH

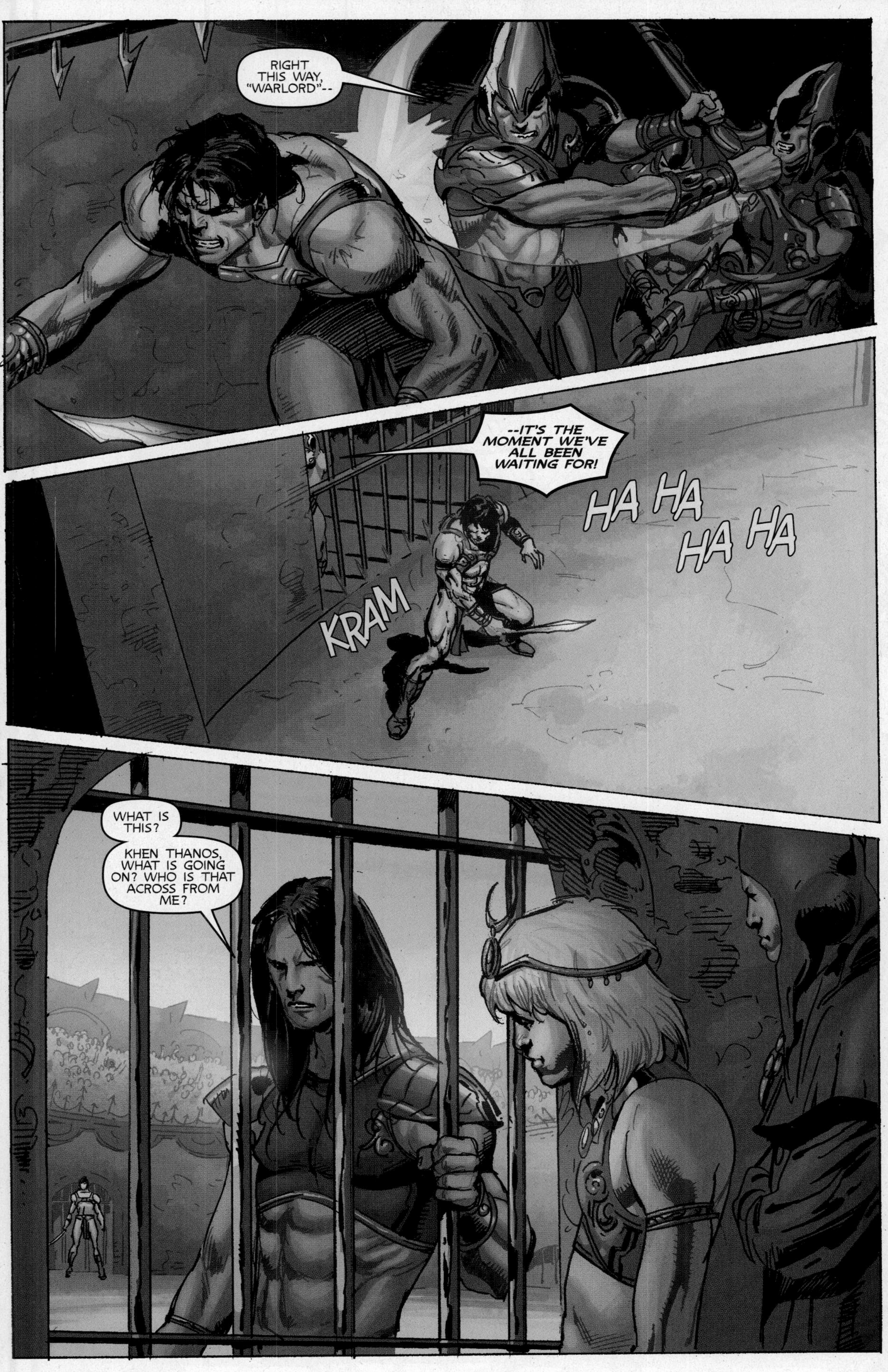
RIGHT THIS WAY, "WARLORD"--
--IT'S THE MOMENT WE'VE ALL BEEN WAITING FOR!
HA HA
HA HA
KRAM
WHAT IS THIS?
KHEN THANOS, WHAT IS GOING ON? WHO IS THAT ACROSS FROM ME?

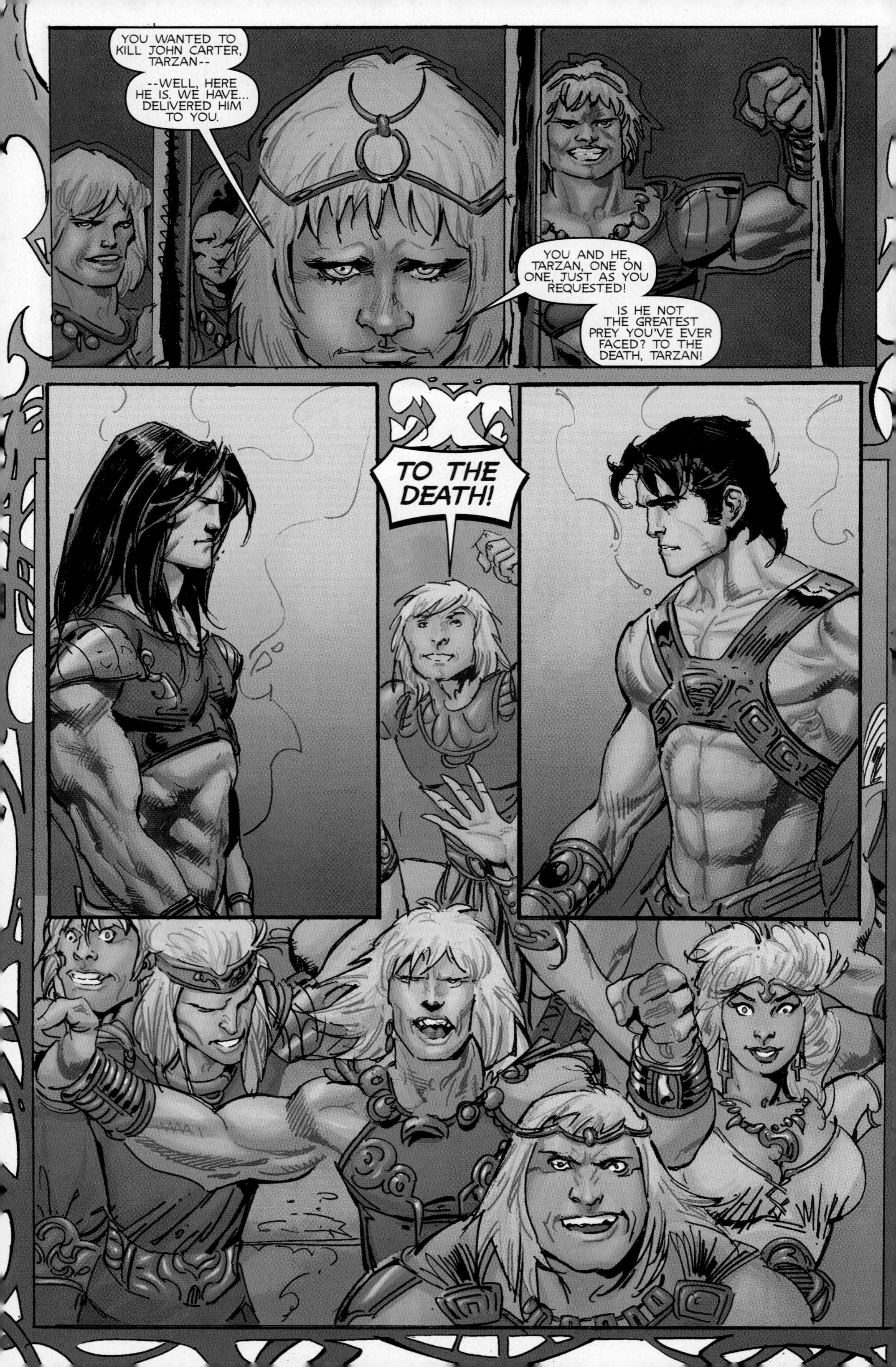
YOU WANTED TO KILL JOHN CARTER, TARZAN--
--WELL, HERE HE IS. WE HAVE... DELIVERED HIM TO YOU.
YOU AND HE, TARZAN, ONE ON ONE, JUST AS YOU REQUESTED!
IS HE NOT THE GREATEST PREY YOU'VE EVER FACED? TO THE DEATH, TARZAN!
TO THE DEATH!

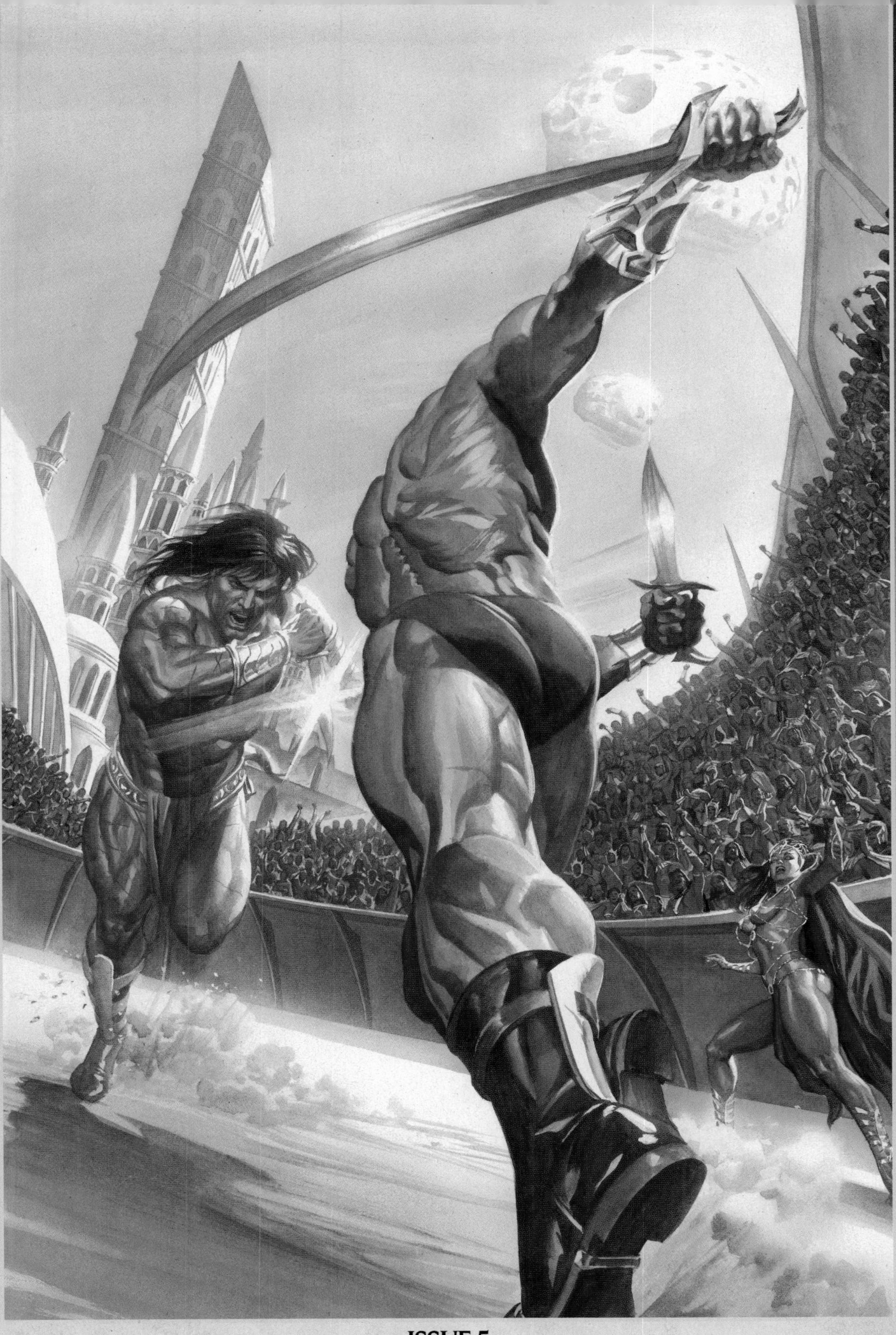

ISSUE 5
WORLDS COLLIDE

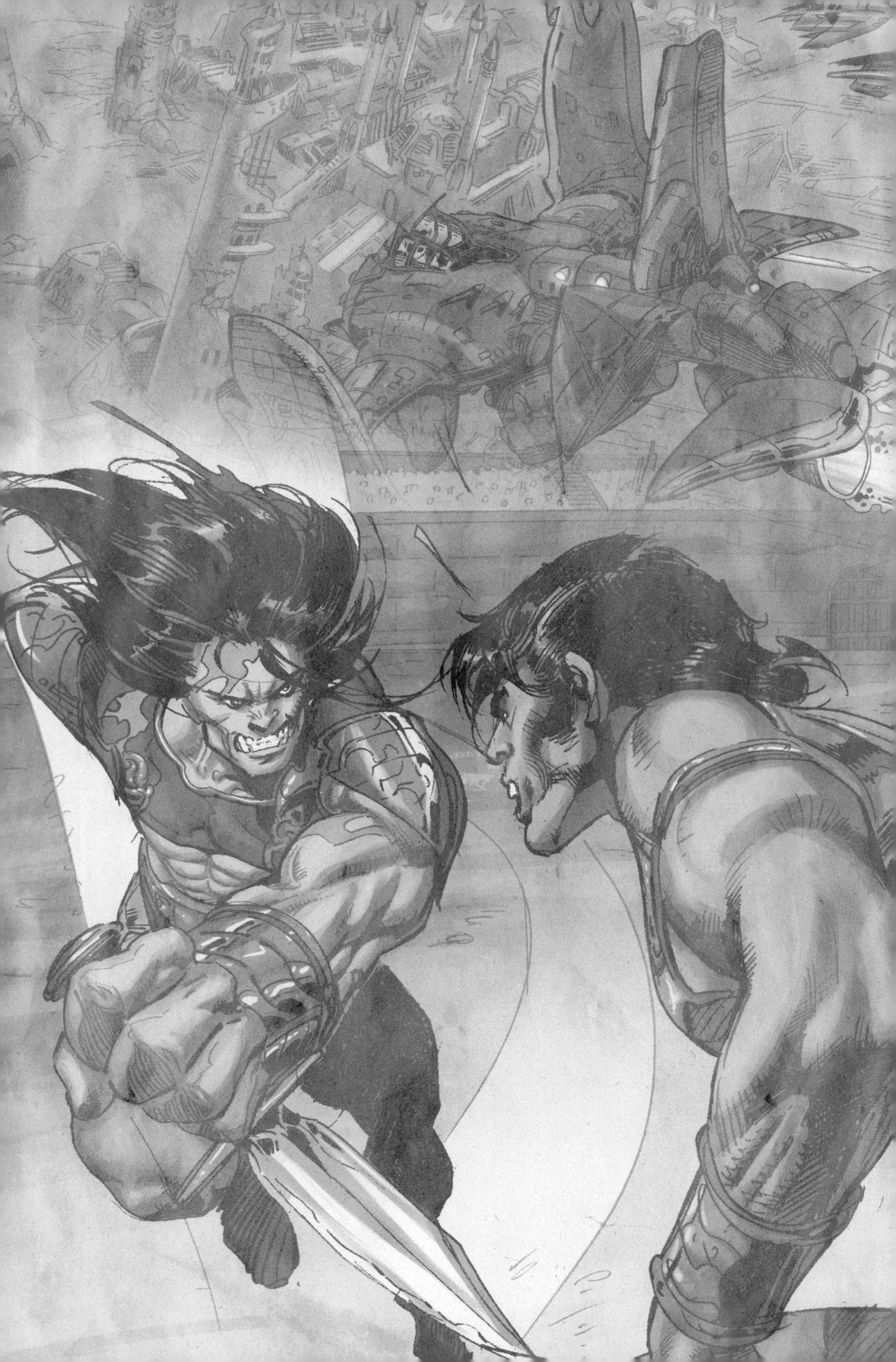

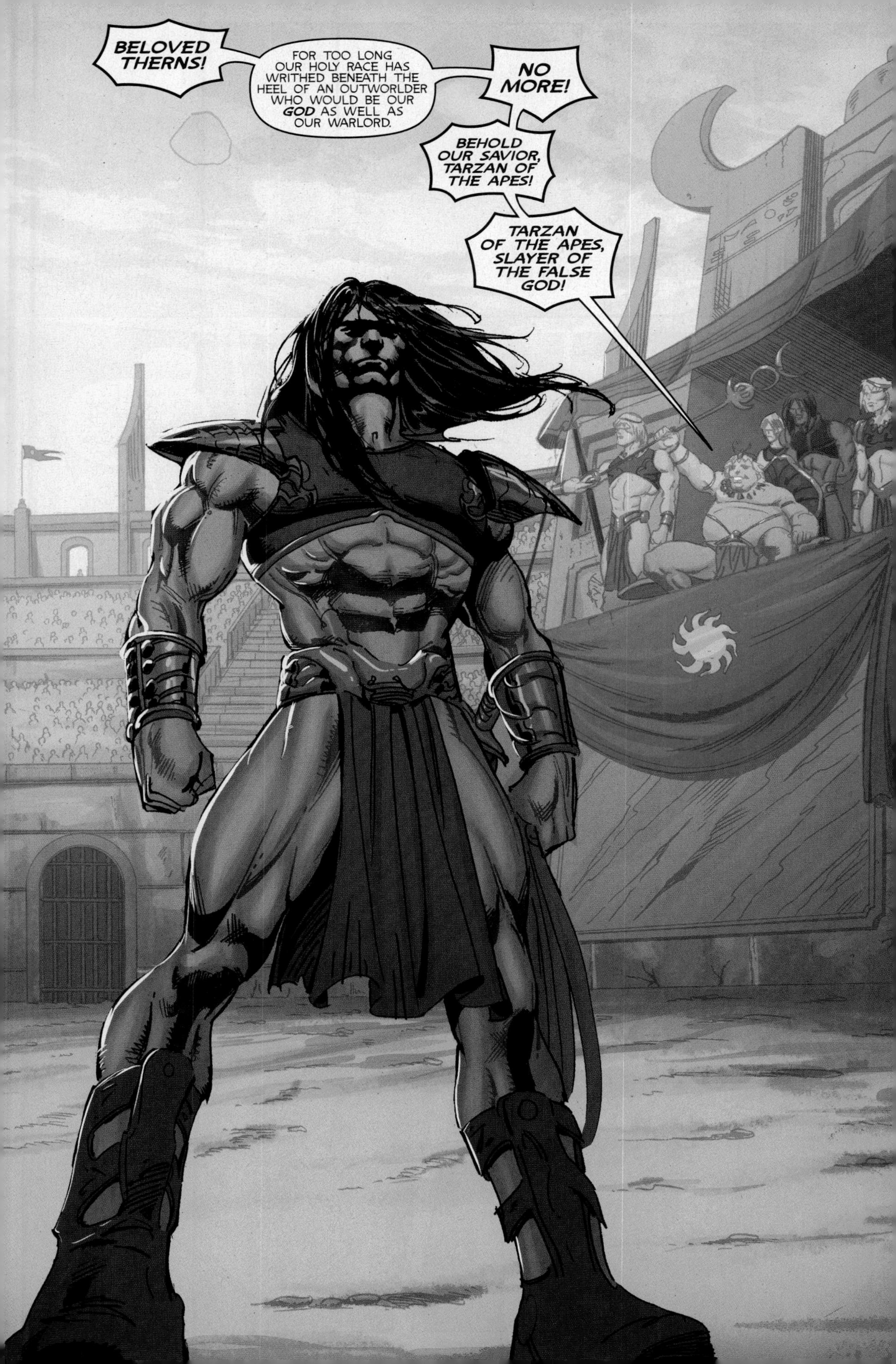
BELOVED THERNS!
FOR TOO LONG OUR HOLY RACE HAS WRITHED BENEATH THE HEEL OF AN OUTWORLDER WHO WOULD BE OUR GOD AS WELL AS OUR WARLORD.
NO MORE!
BEHOLD OUR SAVIOR, TARZAN OF THE APES!
TARZAN OF THE APES, SLAYER OF THE FALSE GOD!

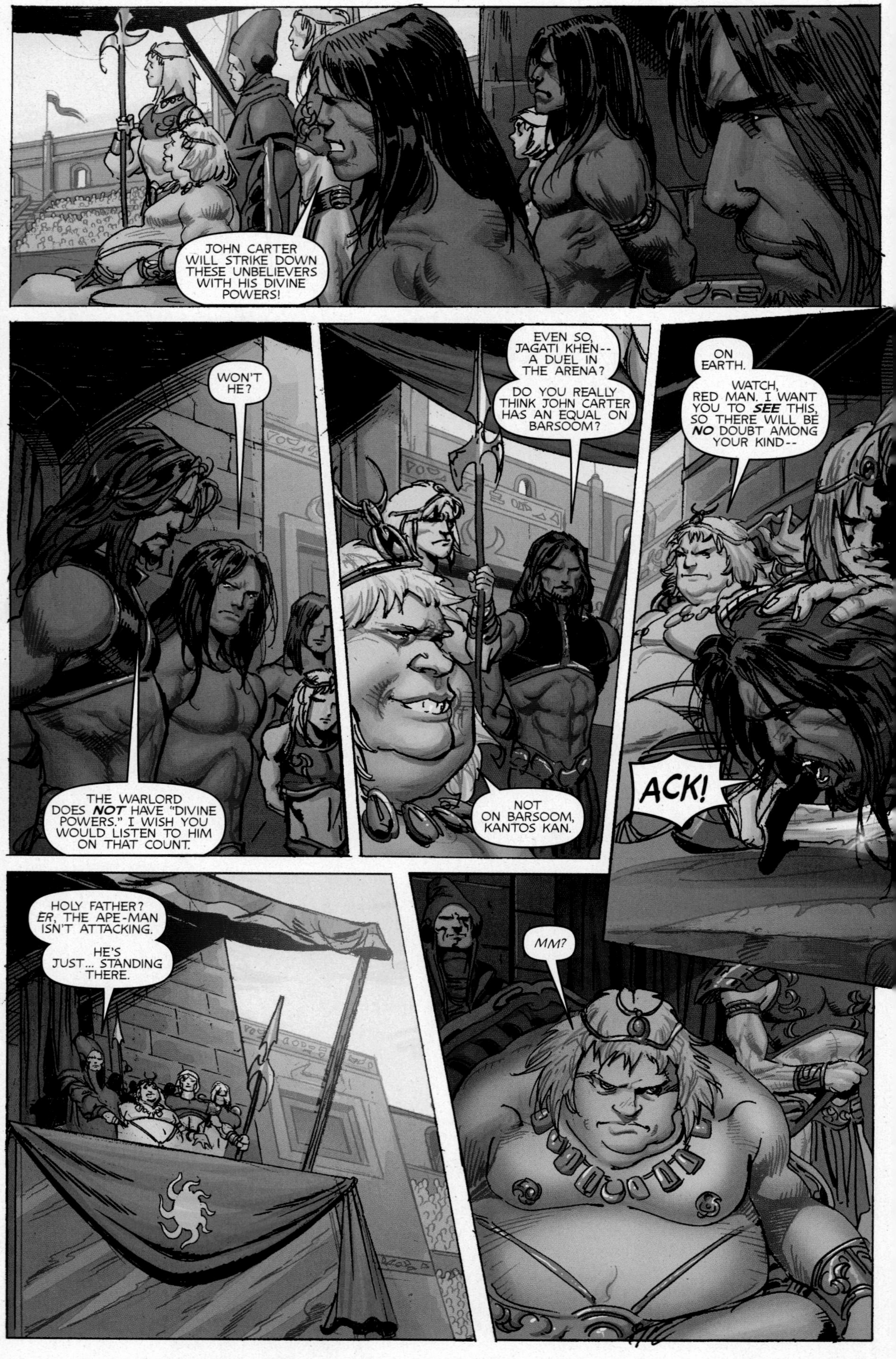
JOHN CARTER WILL STRIKE DOWN THESE UNBELIEVERS WITH HIS DIVINE POWERS!
WON'T HE?
THE WARLORD DOES **NOT** HAVE "DIVINE POWERS." I WISH YOU WOULD LISTEN TO HIM ON THAT COUNT.
EVEN SO, JAGATI KHEN-- A DUEL IN THE ARENA?
DO YOU REALLY THINK JOHN CARTER HAS AN EQUAL ON BARSOOM?
NOT ON BARSOOM, KANTOS KAN.
ON EARTH.
WATCH, RED MAN. I WANT YOU TO ***SEE*** THIS, SO THERE WILL BE ***NO*** DOUBT AMONG YOUR KIND--
ACK!
HOLY FATHER? *ER*, THE APE-MAN ISN'T ATTACKING.
HE'S JUST... STANDING THERE.
MM?

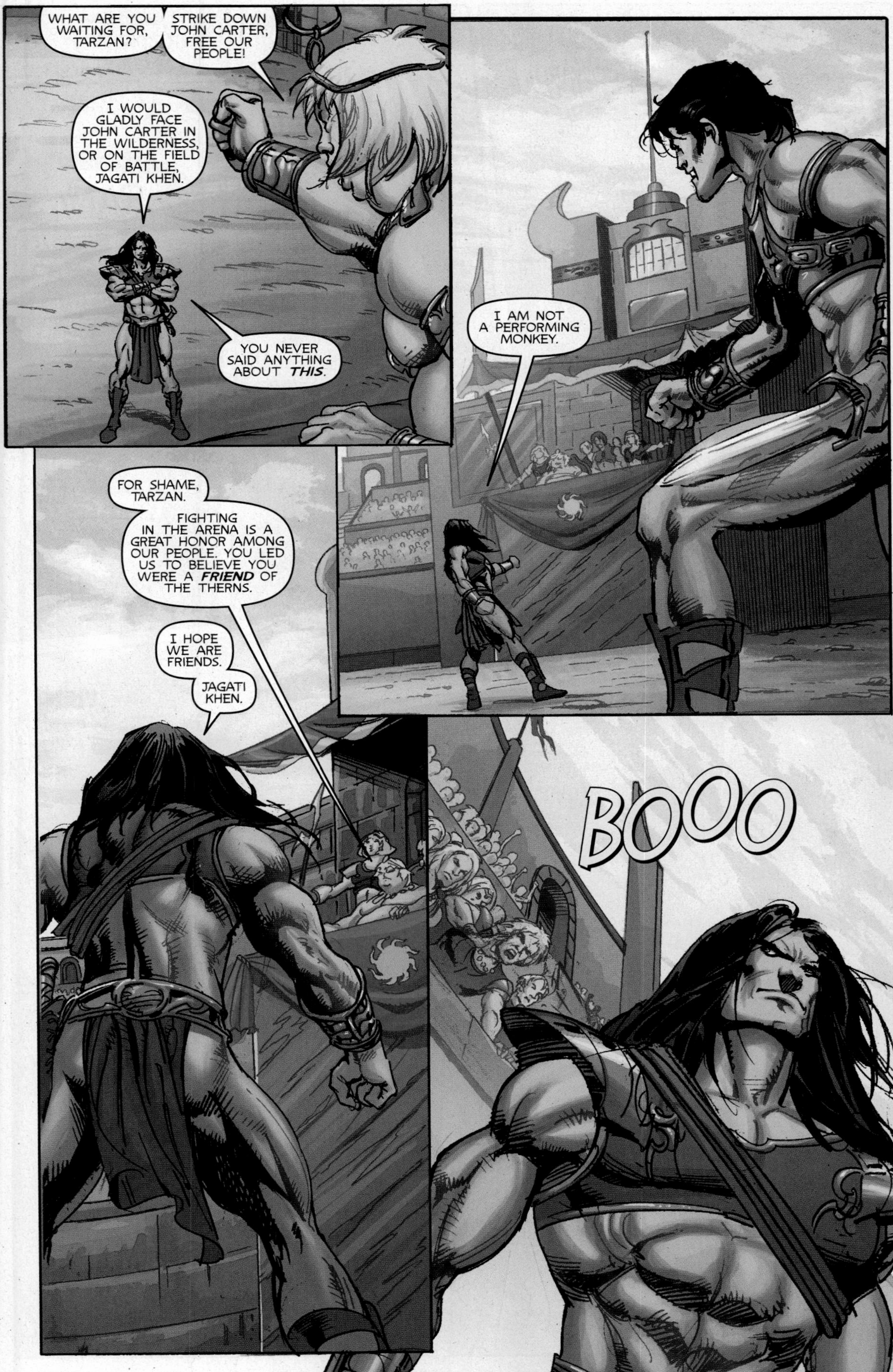

WHAT ARE YOU WAITING FOR, TARZAN?
STRIKE DOWN JOHN CARTER, FREE OUR PEOPLE!
I WOULD GLADLY FACE JOHN CARTER IN THE WILDERNESS, OR ON THE FIELD OF BATTLE, JAGATI KHEN.
YOU NEVER SAID ANYTHING ABOUT *THIS*.
I AM NOT A PERFORMING MONKEY.
FOR SHAME, TARZAN.
FIGHTING IN THE ARENA IS A GREAT HONOR AMONG OUR PEOPLE. YOU LED US TO BELIEVE YOU WERE A *FRIEND* OF THE THERNS.
I HOPE WE ARE FRIENDS.
JAGATI KHEN.
BOOO

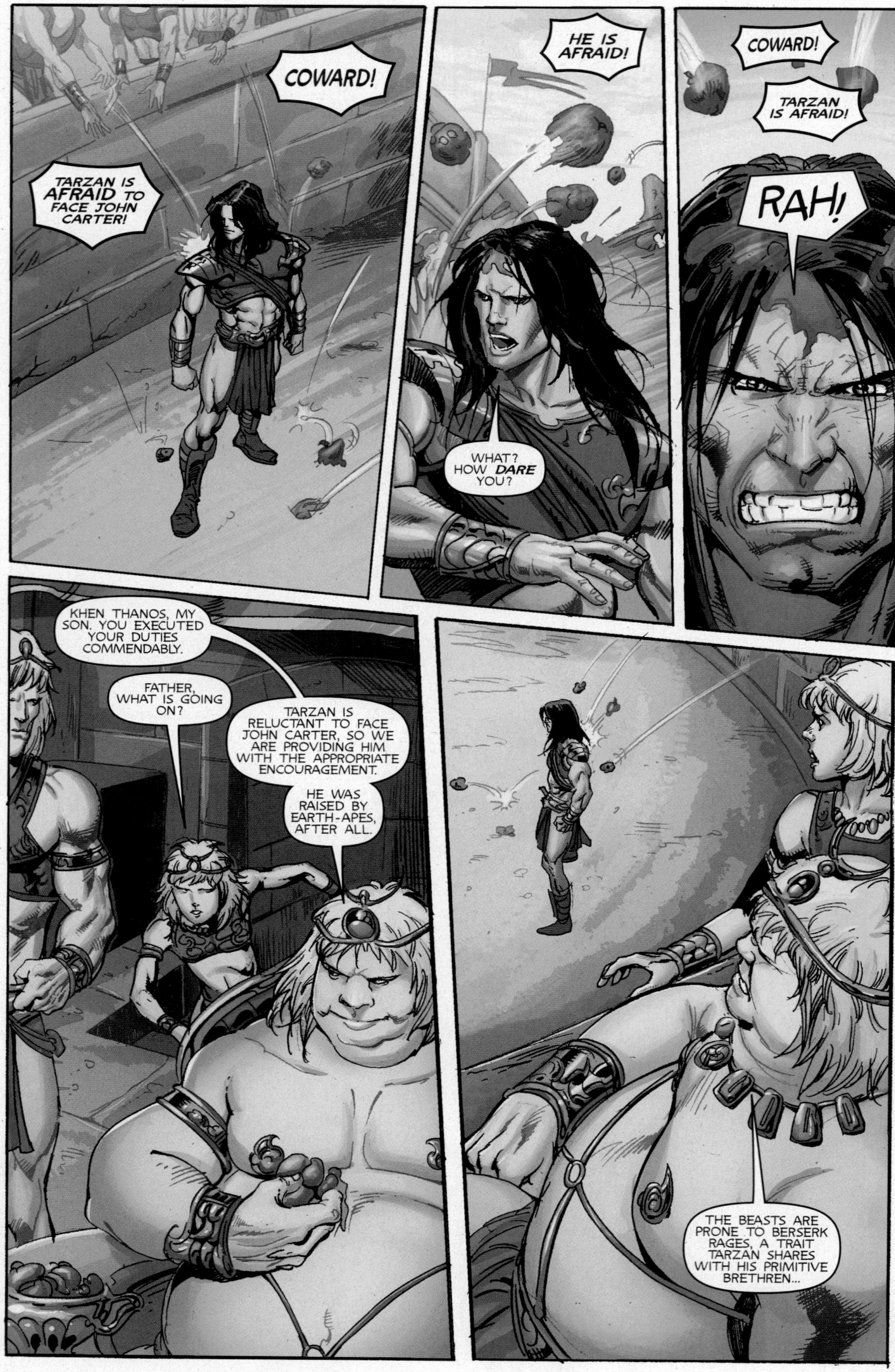

COWARD!
TARZAN IS AFRAID TO FACE JOHN CARTER!
HE IS AFRAID!
WHAT? HOW DARE YOU?
COWARD!
TARZAN IS AFRAID!
RAH!
KHEN THANOS, MY SON. YOU EXECUTED YOUR DUTIES COMMENDABLY.
FATHER, WHAT IS GOING ON?
TARZAN IS RELUCTANT TO FACE JOHN CARTER, SO WE ARE PROVIDING HIM WITH THE APPROPRIATE ENCOURAGEMENT.
HE WAS RAISED BY EARTH-APES, AFTER ALL.
THE BEASTS ARE PRONE TO BERSERK RAGES, A TRAIT TARZAN SHARES WITH HIS PRIMITIVE BRETHREN...

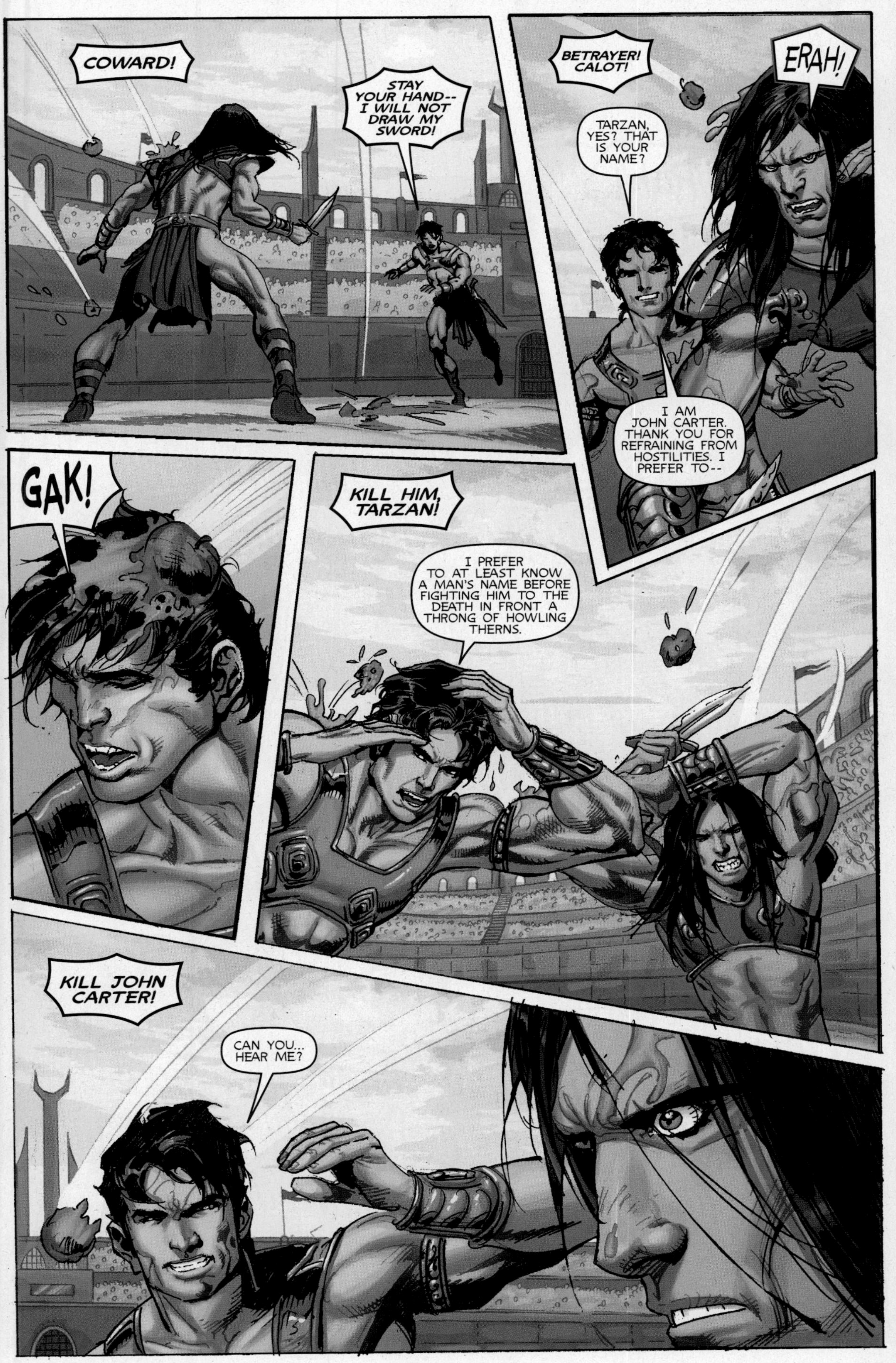
COWARD!
STAY YOUR HAND-- I WILL NOT DRAW MY SWORD!
BETRAYER! CALOT!
ERAH!
TARZAN, YES? THAT IS YOUR NAME?
I AM JOHN CARTER. THANK YOU FOR REFRAINING FROM HOSTILITIES. I PREFER TO--
GAK!
KILL HIM, TARZAN!
I PREFER TO AT LEAST KNOW A MAN'S NAME BEFORE FIGHTING HIM TO THE DEATH IN FRONT A THRONG OF HOWLING THERNS.
KILL JOHN CARTER!
CAN YOU... HEAR ME?

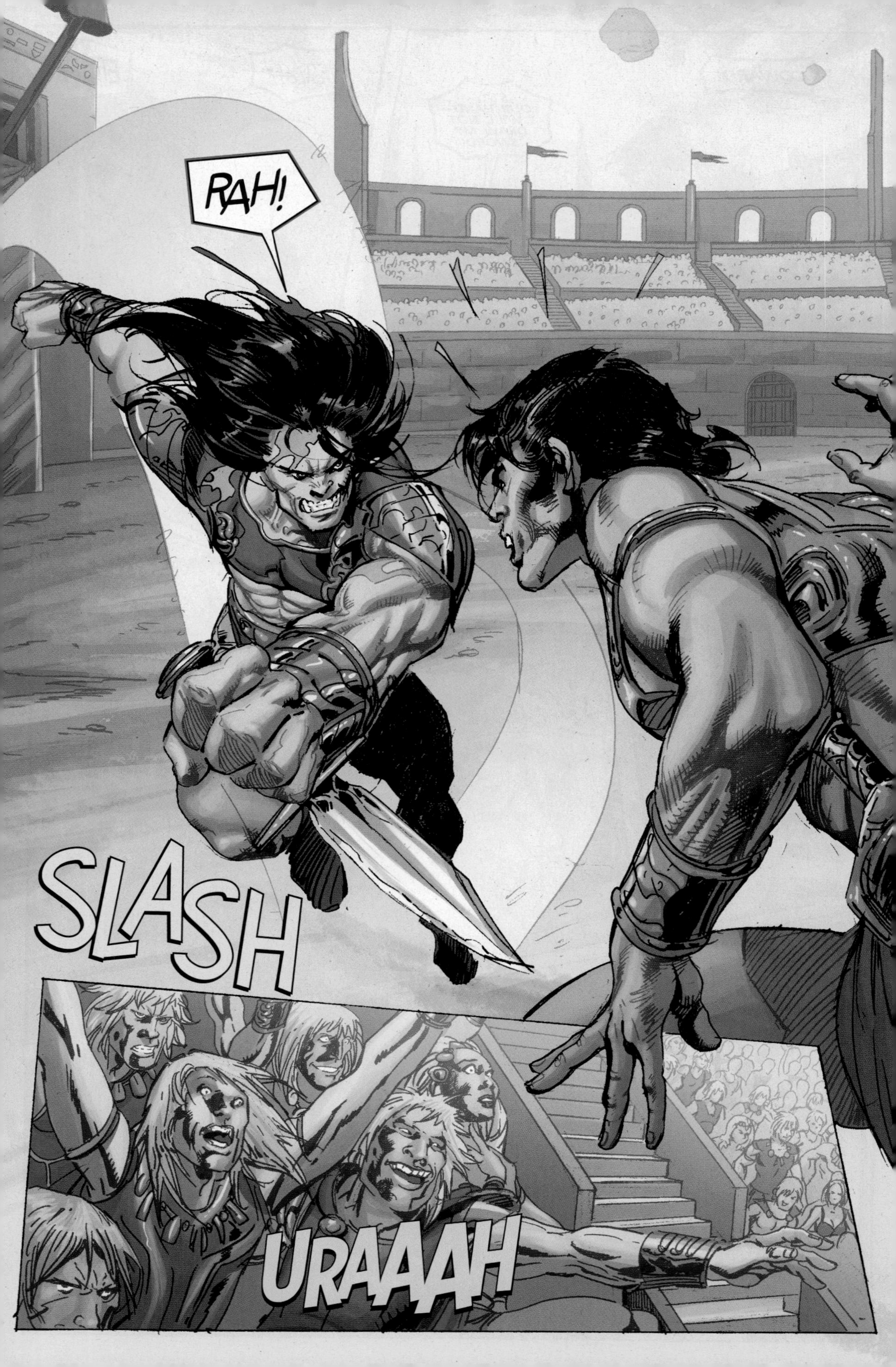
RAH!
SLASH
URAAAH

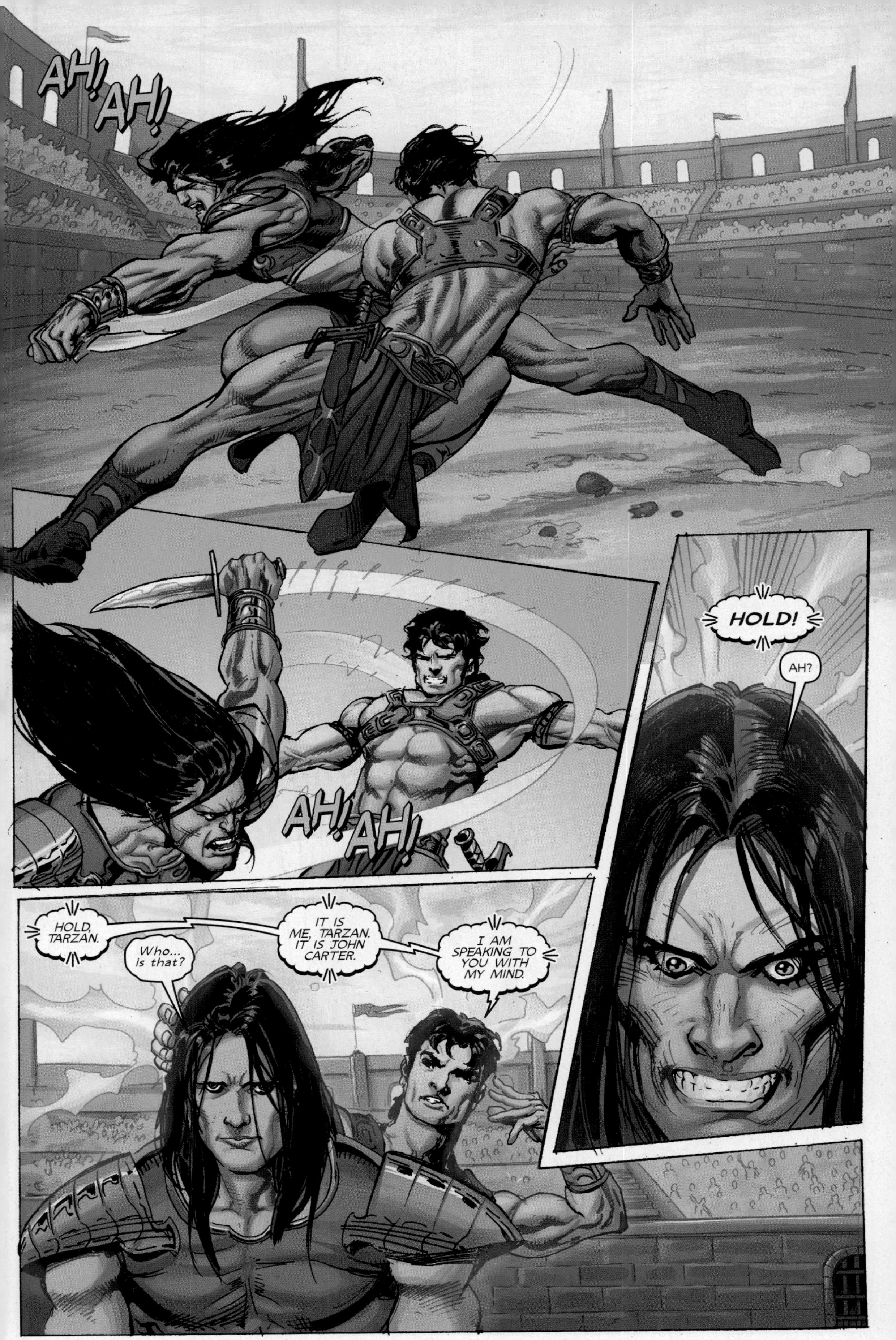
AH! AH!
AH! AH!
HOLD!
AH?
HOLD, TARZAN.
Who... is that?
IT IS ME, TARZAN. IT IS JOHN CARTER.
I AM SPEAKING TO YOU WITH MY MIND.

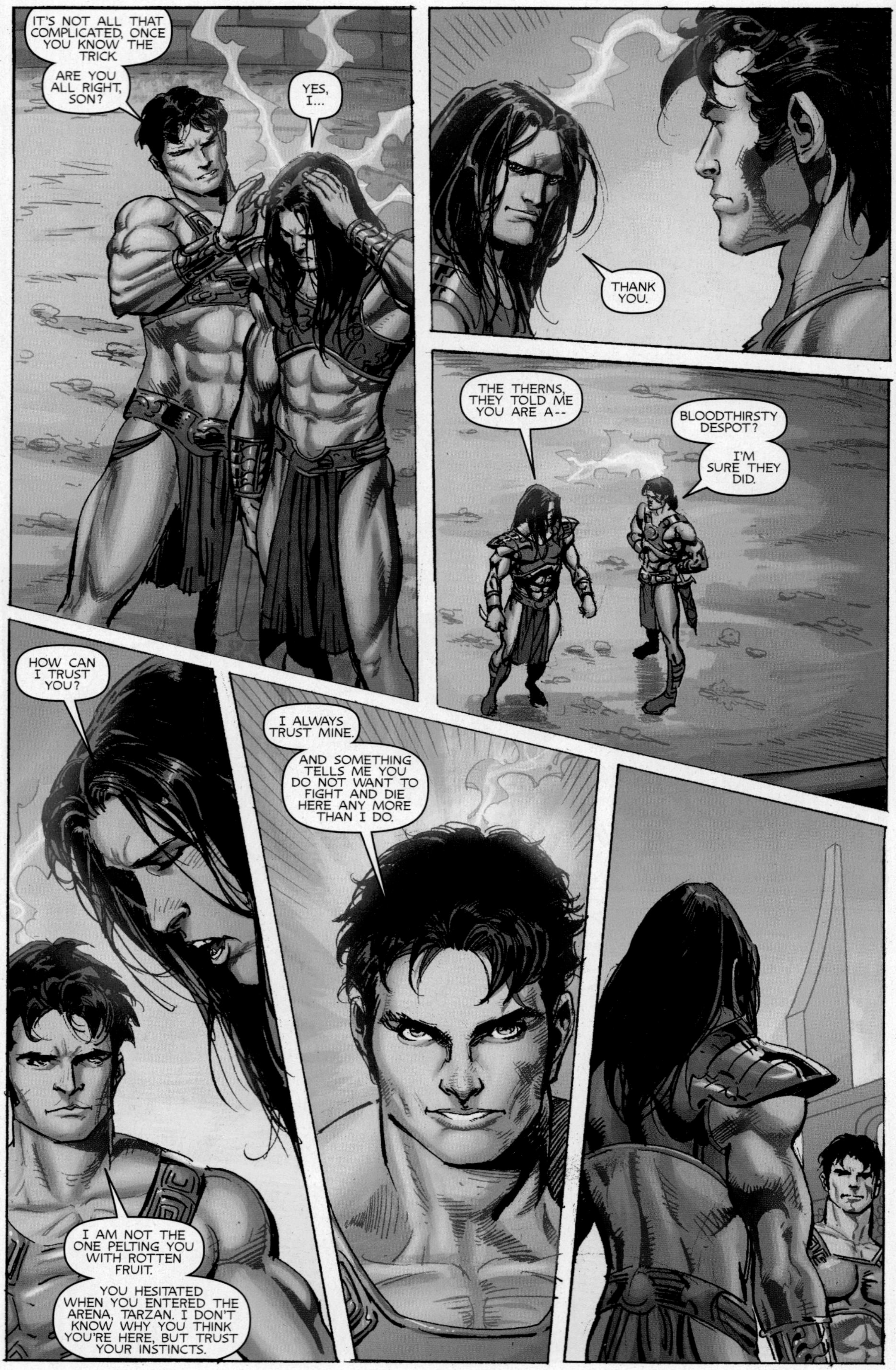

IT'S NOT ALL THAT COMPLICATED, ONCE YOU KNOW THE TRICK.
ARE YOU ALL RIGHT, SON?
YES, I...
THANK YOU.
THE THERNS, THEY TOLD ME YOU ARE A--
BLOODTHIRSTY DESPOT?
I'M SURE THEY DID.
HOW CAN I TRUST YOU?
I AM NOT THE ONE PELTING YOU WITH ROTTEN FRUIT.
YOU HESITATED WHEN YOU ENTERED THE ARENA, TARZAN. I DON'T KNOW WHY YOU THINK YOU'RE HERE, BUT TRUST YOUR INSTINCTS.
I ALWAYS TRUST MINE.
AND SOMETHING TELLS ME YOU DO NOT WANT TO FIGHT AND DIE HERE ANY MORE THAN I DO.

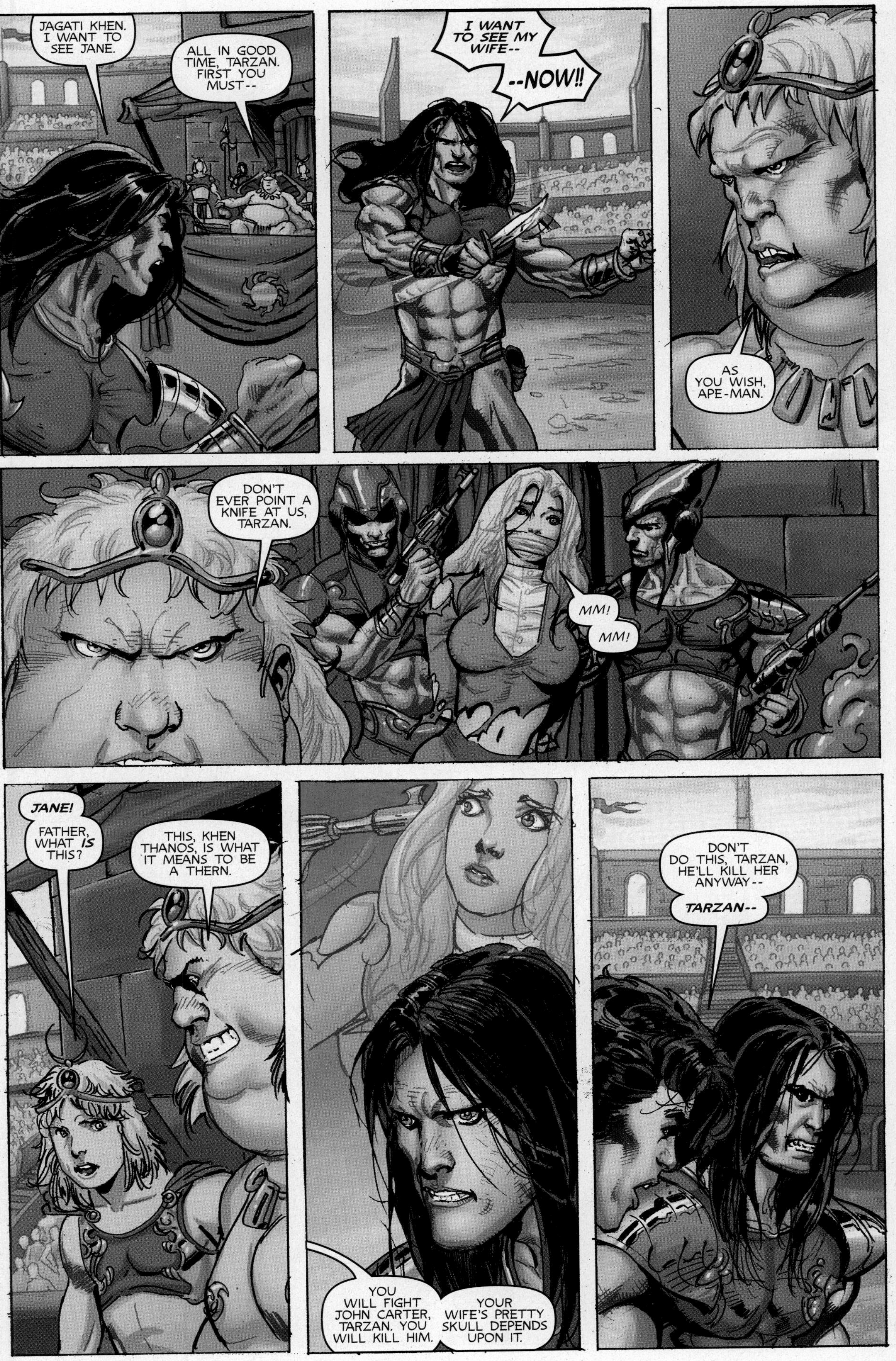
JAGATI KHEN. I WANT TO SEE JANE.
ALL IN GOOD TIME, TARZAN. FIRST YOU MUST--
I WANT TO SEE MY WIFE--
--NOW!!
AS YOU WISH, APE-MAN.
DON'T EVER POINT A KNIFE AT US, TARZAN.
MM!
MM!
JANE!
FATHER, WHAT IS THIS?
THIS, KHEN THANOS, IS WHAT IT MEANS TO BE A THERN.
YOU WILL FIGHT JOHN CARTER, TARZAN. YOU WILL KILL HIM.
YOUR WIFE'S PRETTY SKULL DEPENDS UPON IT.
DON'T DO THIS, TARZAN, HE'LL KILL HER ANYWAY--
TARZAN--

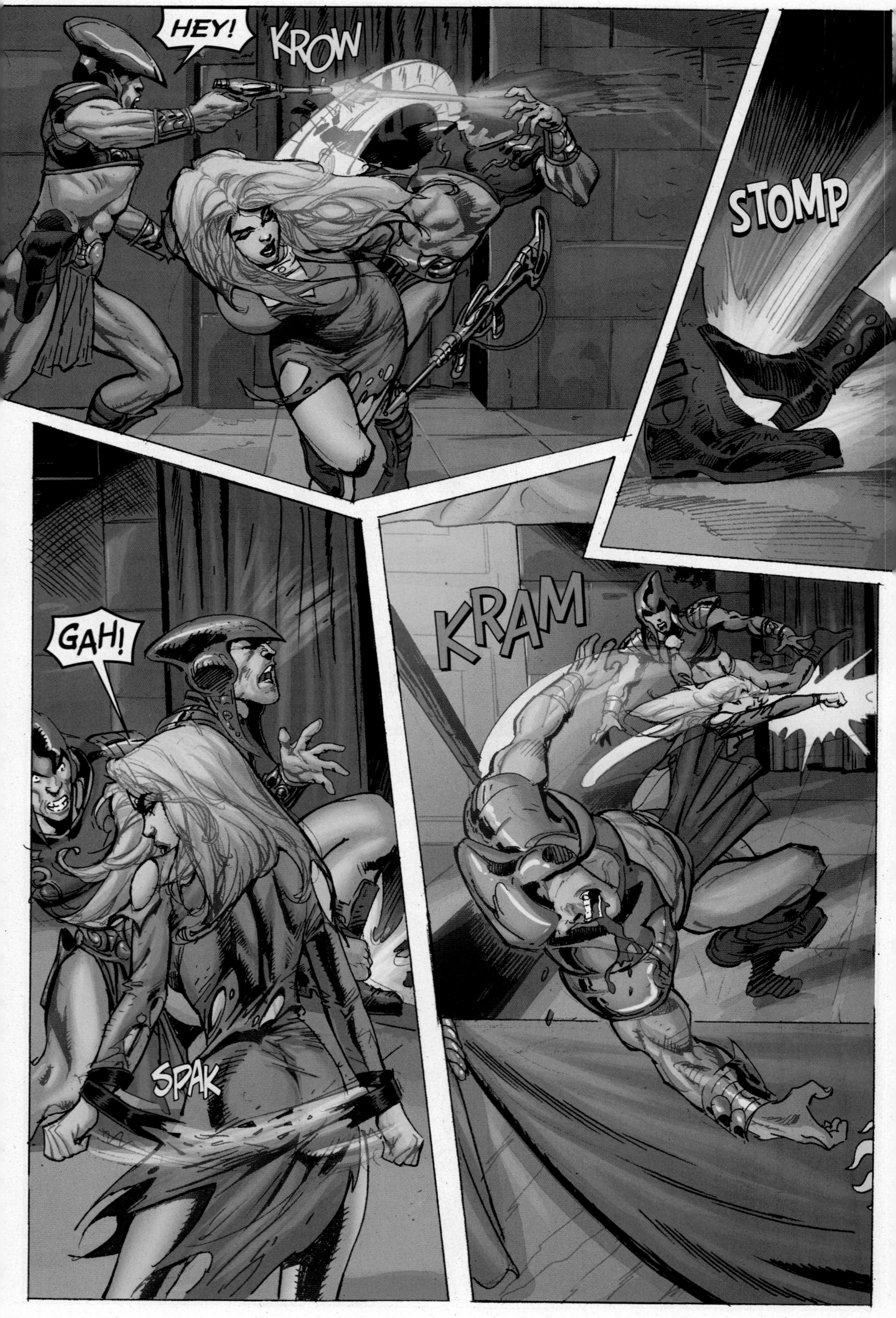
HEY!
KROW
STOMP
GAH!
SPAK
KRAM

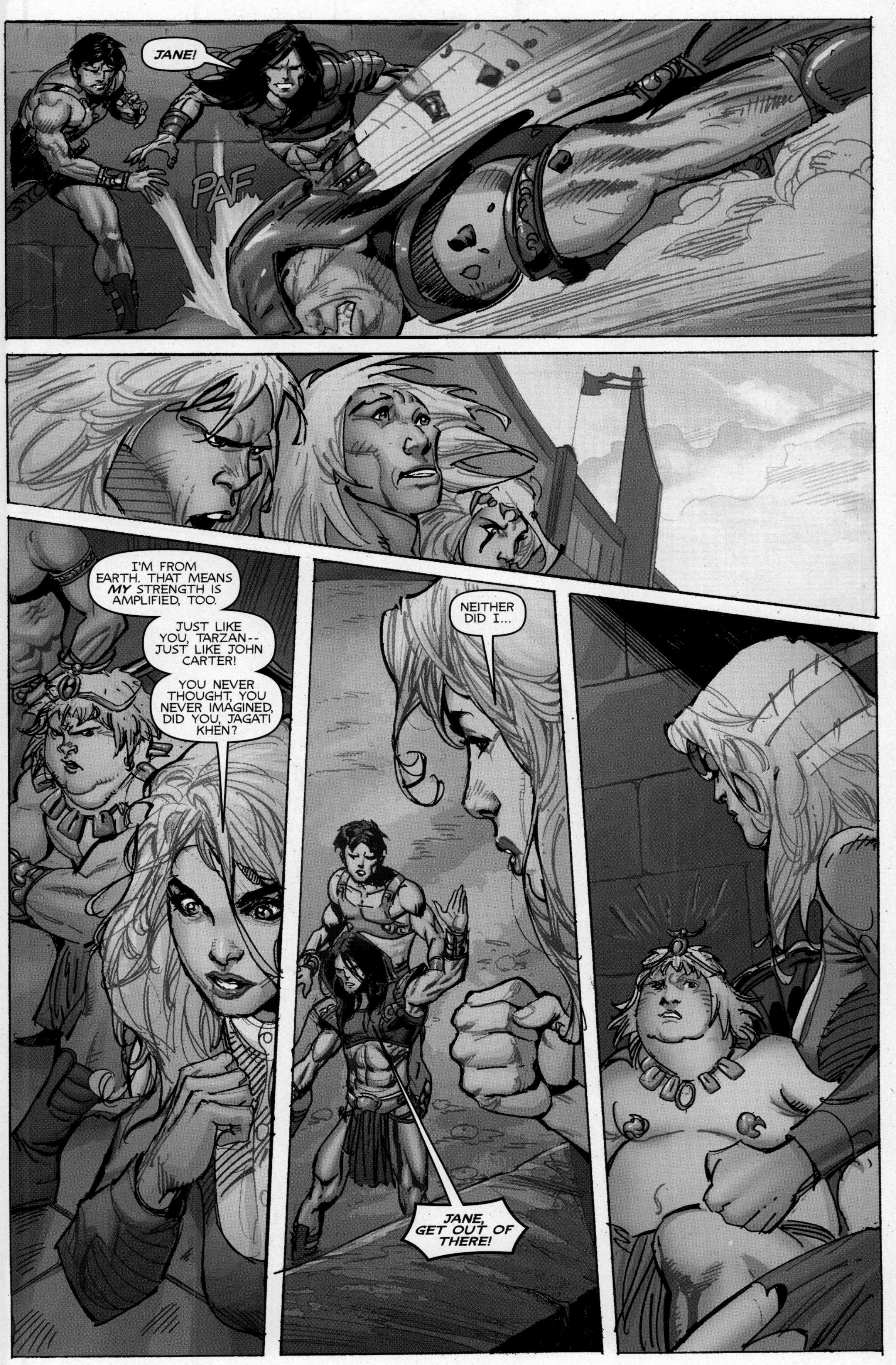

JANE!
PAF
I'M FROM EARTH. THAT MEANS MY STRENGTH IS AMPLIFIED, TOO.
JUST LIKE YOU, TARZAN-- JUST LIKE JOHN CARTER!
YOU NEVER THOUGHT, YOU NEVER IMAGINED, DID YOU, JAGATI KHEN?
NEITHER DID I...
JANE, GET OUT OF THERE!

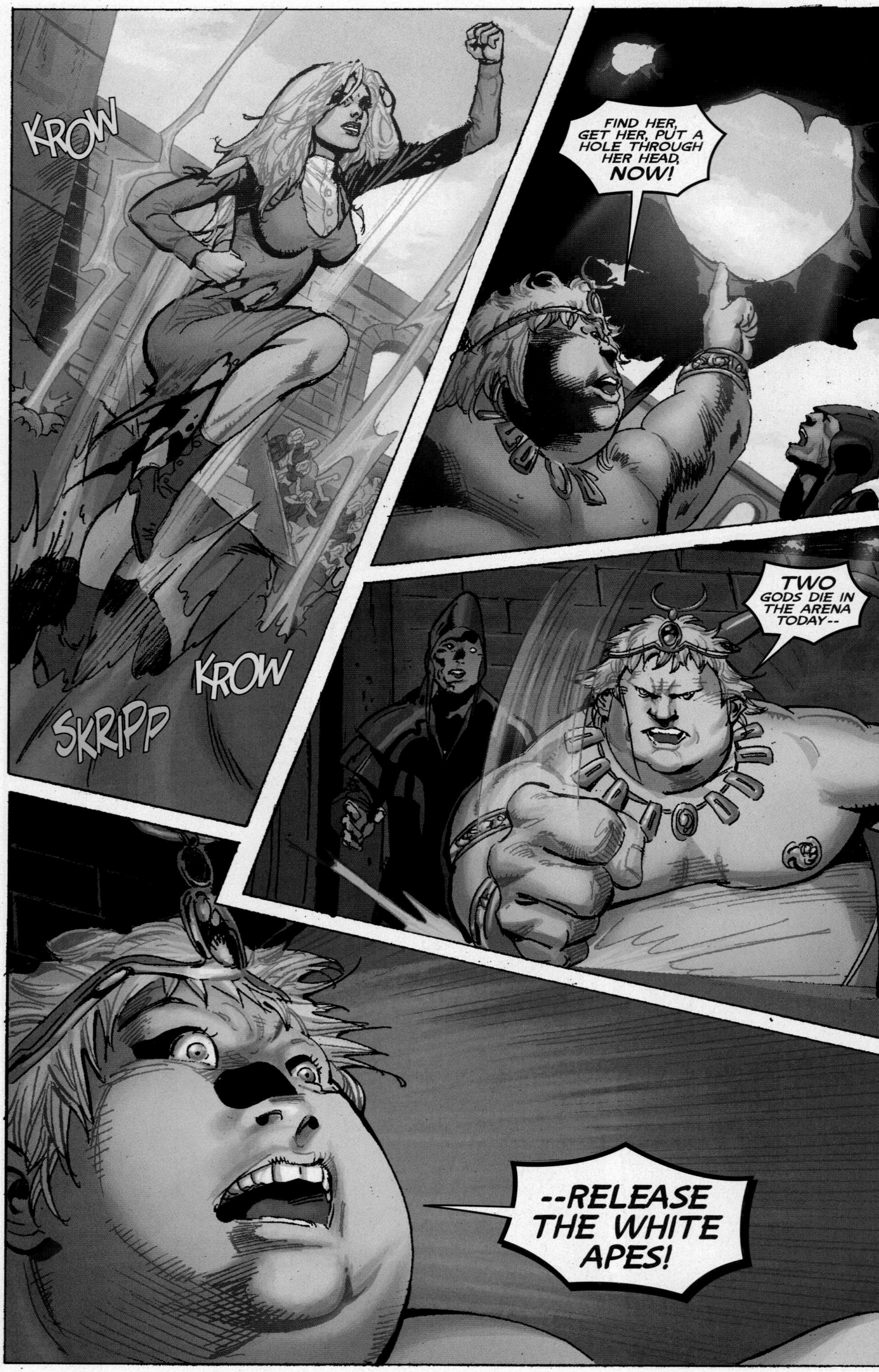
KROW
FIND HER, GET HER, PUT A HOLE THROUGH HER HEAD, NOW!
KROW
SKRIPP
TWO GODS DIE IN THE ARENA TODAY--
--RELEASE THE WHITE APES!

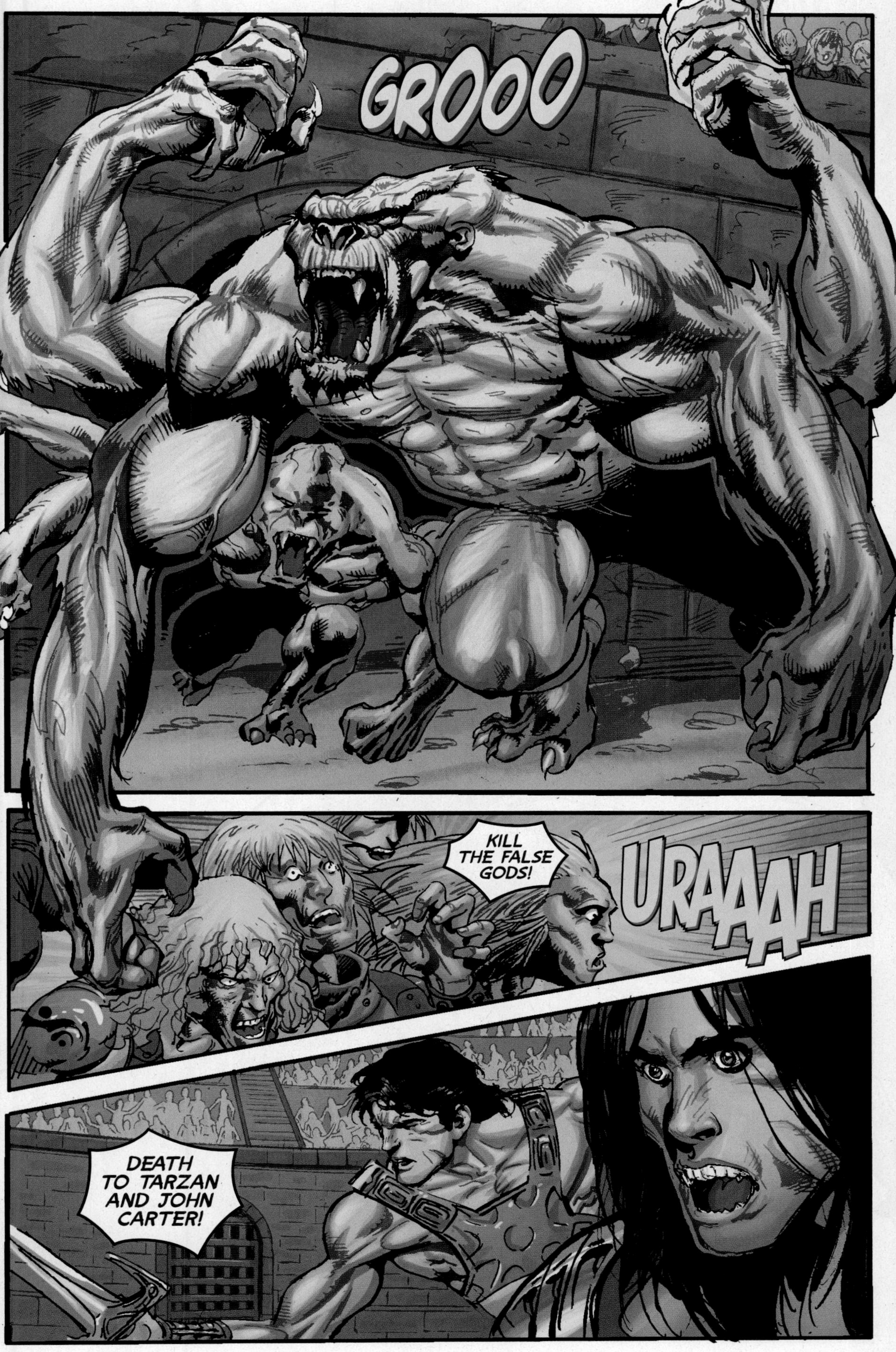
GROOO
KILL THE FALSE GODS!
URAAAH
DEATH TO TARZAN AND JOHN CARTER!

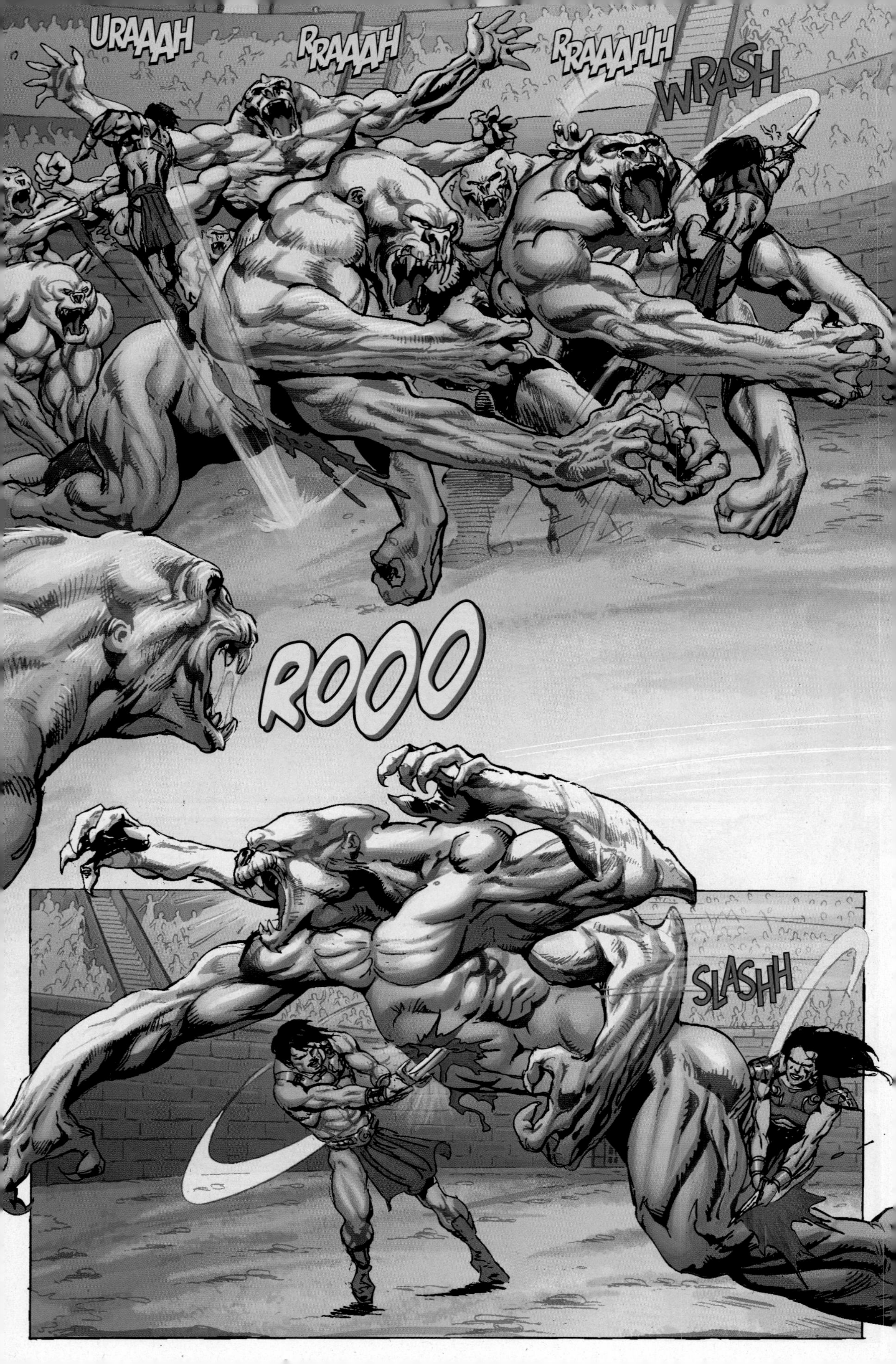
URAAAH
RRAAAH
RRAAAHH
WRASH
ROOO
SLASHH

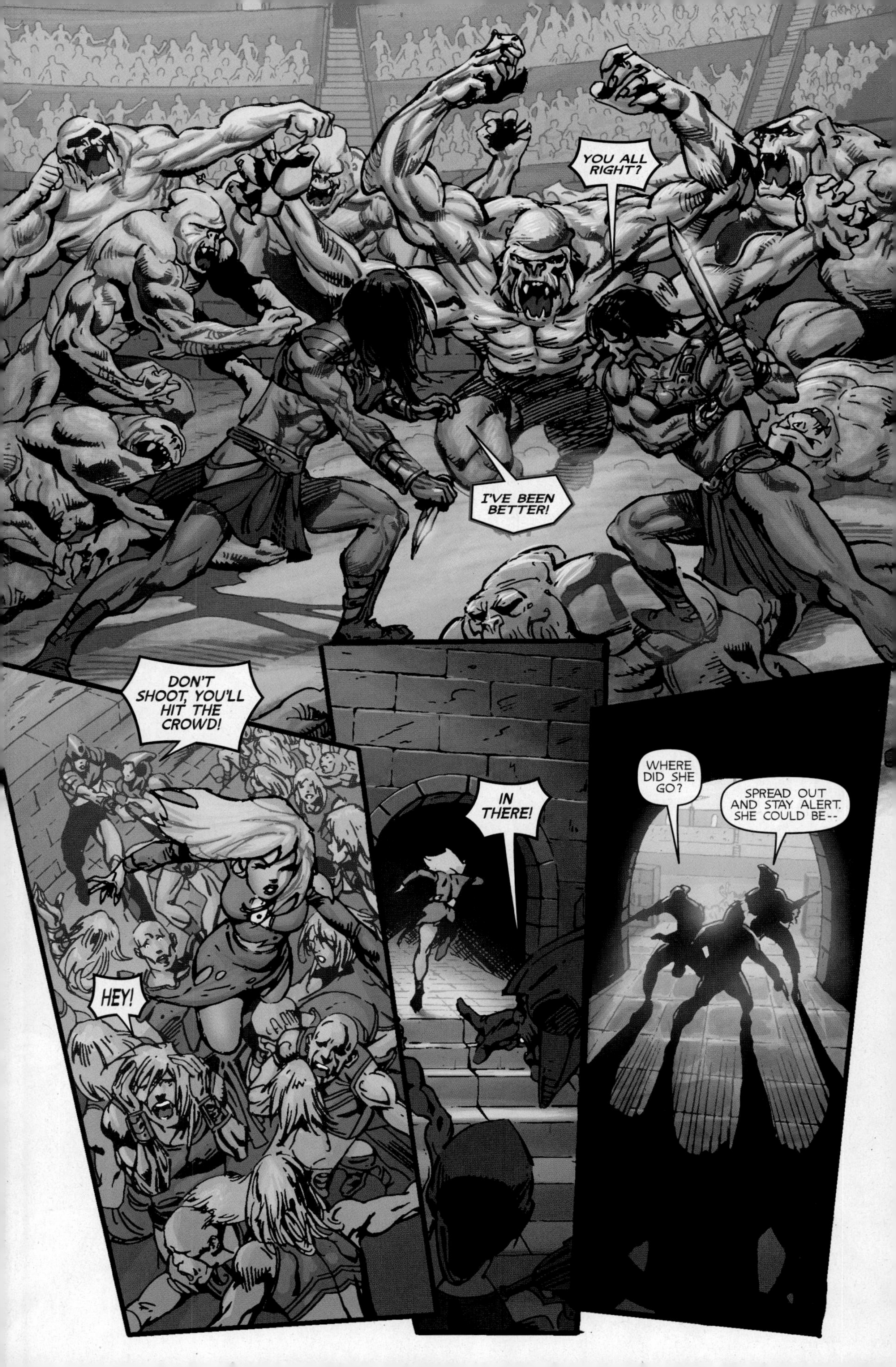
YOU ALL RIGHT?
I'VE BEEN BETTER!
DON'T SHOOT, YOU'LL HIT THE CROWD!
HEY!
IN THERE!
WHERE DID SHE GO?
SPREAD OUT AND STAY ALERT. SHE COULD BE--

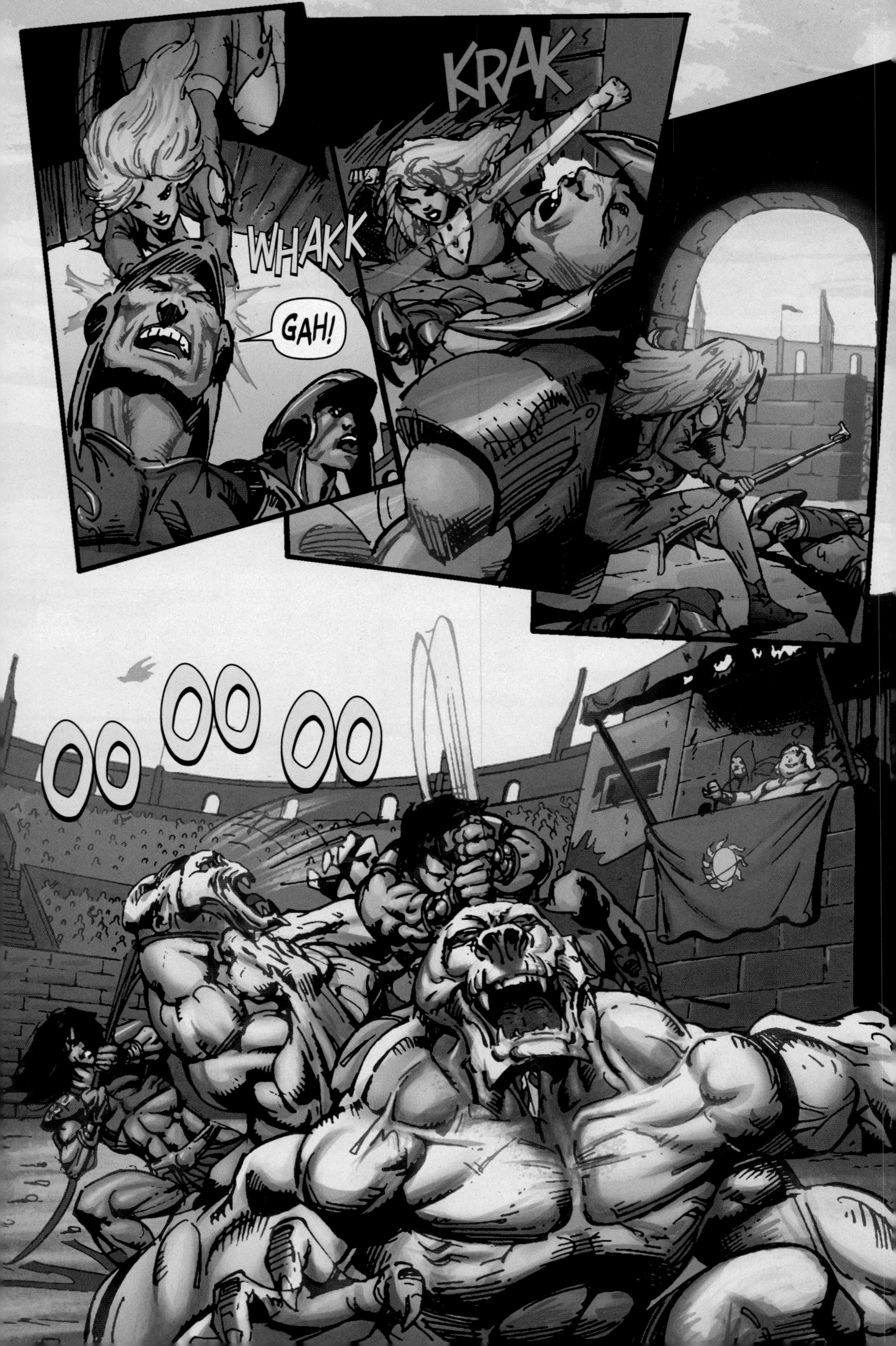
WHAKK
GAH!
KRAK
OO OO OO

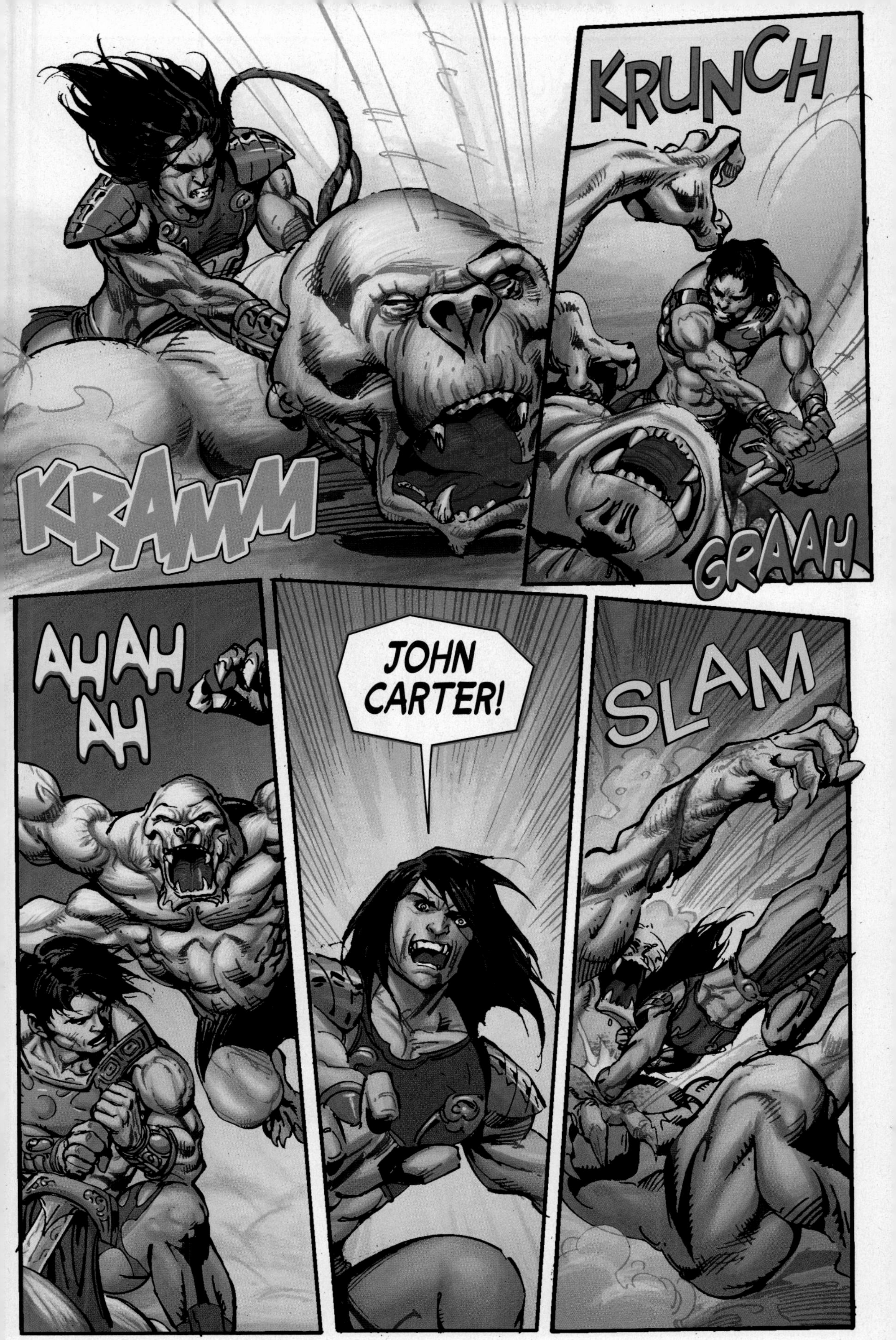
KRAMMM
KRUNCH
GRAAH
AHAH AH
JOHN CARTER!
SLAM

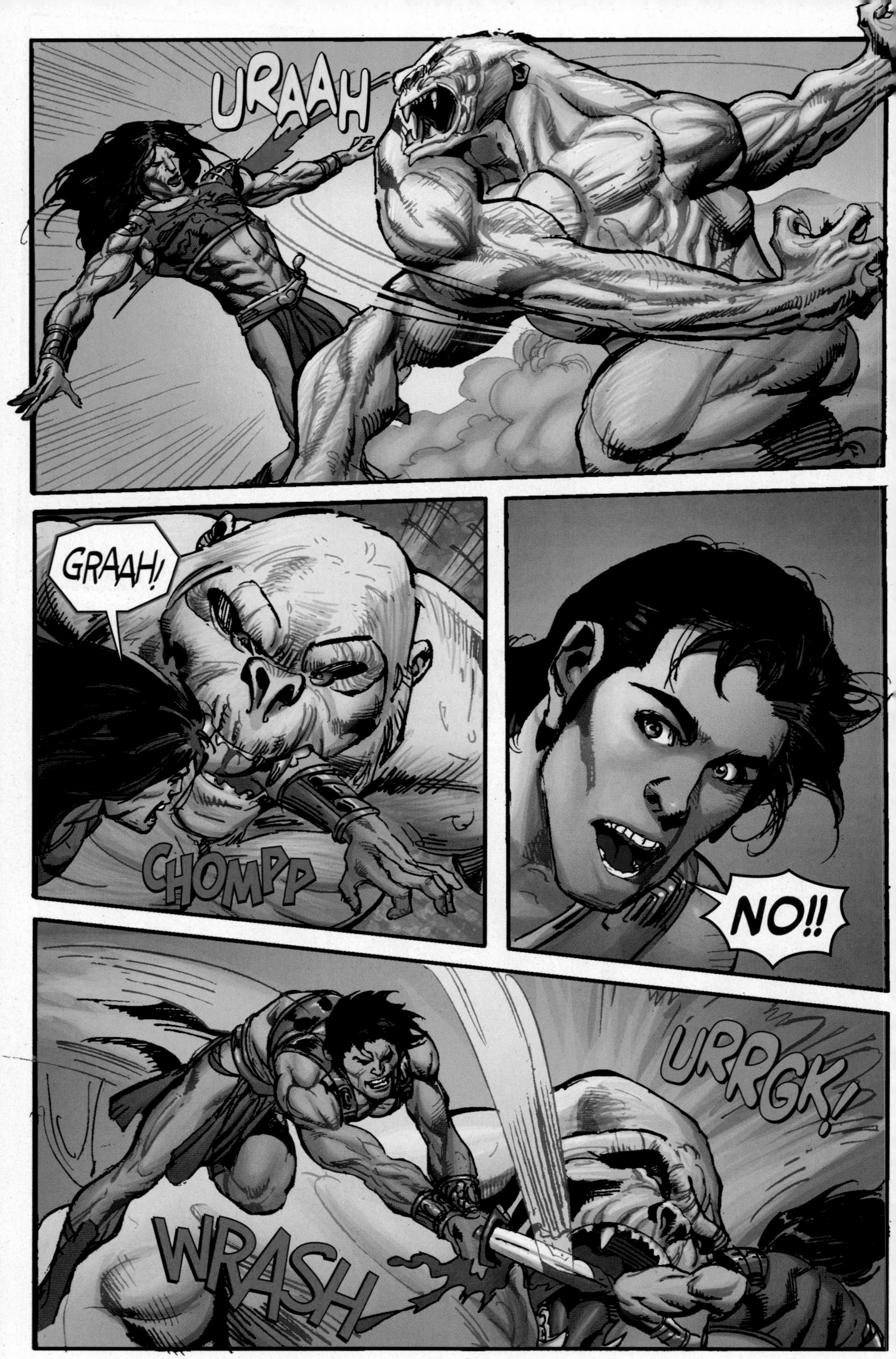
URAAH
GRAAH!
CHOMPP
NO!!
URRGK!
WRASH

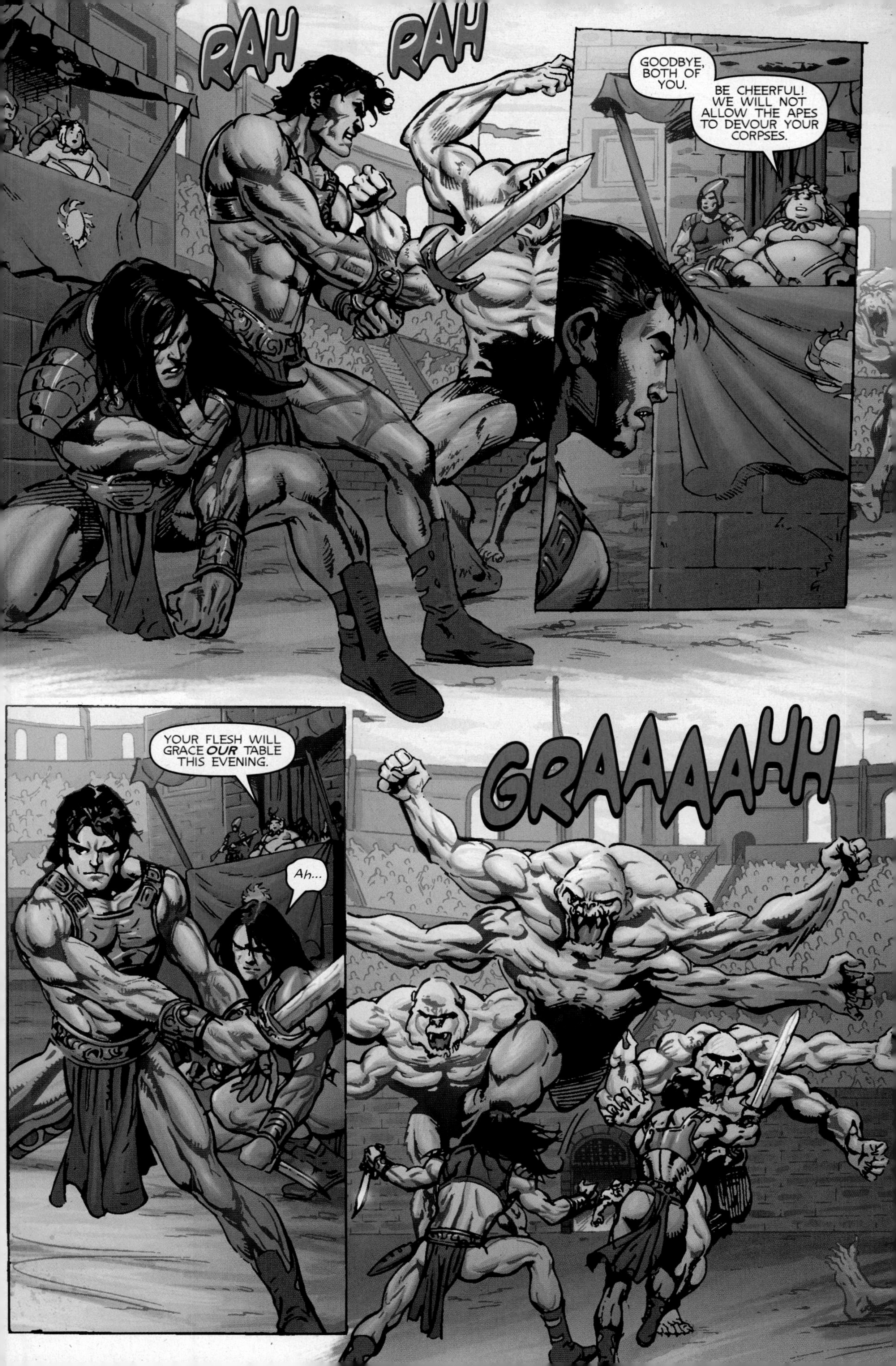
RAH RAH
GOODBYE, BOTH OF YOU.
BE CHEERFUL! WE WILL NOT ALLOW THE APES TO DEVOUR YOUR CORPSES.
YOUR FLESH WILL GRACE *OUR* TABLE THIS EVENING.
Ah...
GRAAAAHH

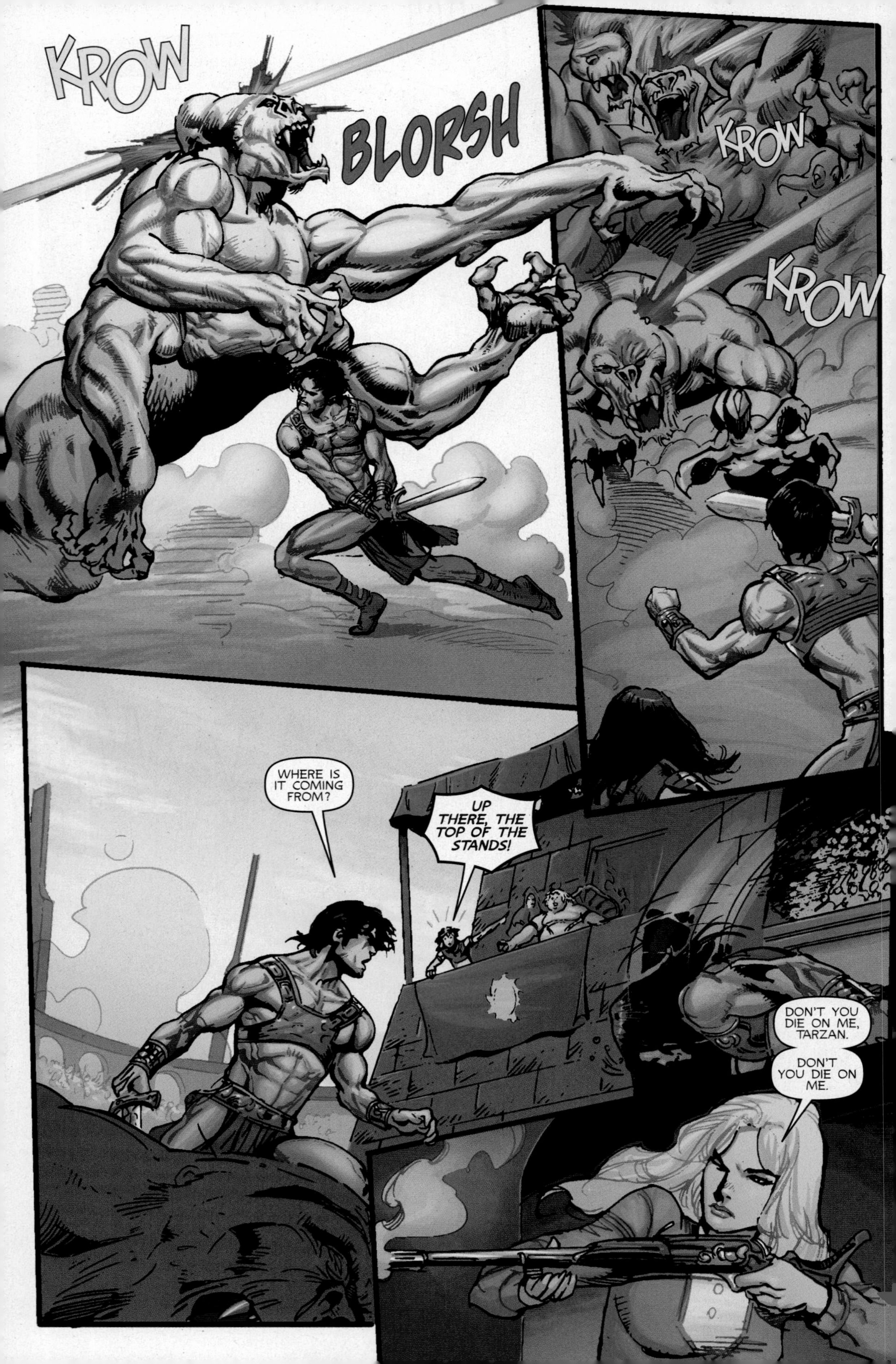
KROW
BLORSH
KROW
KROW
WHERE IS IT COMING FROM?
UP THERE, THE TOP OF THE STANDS!
DON'T YOU DIE ON ME, TARZAN.
DON'T YOU DIE ON ME.

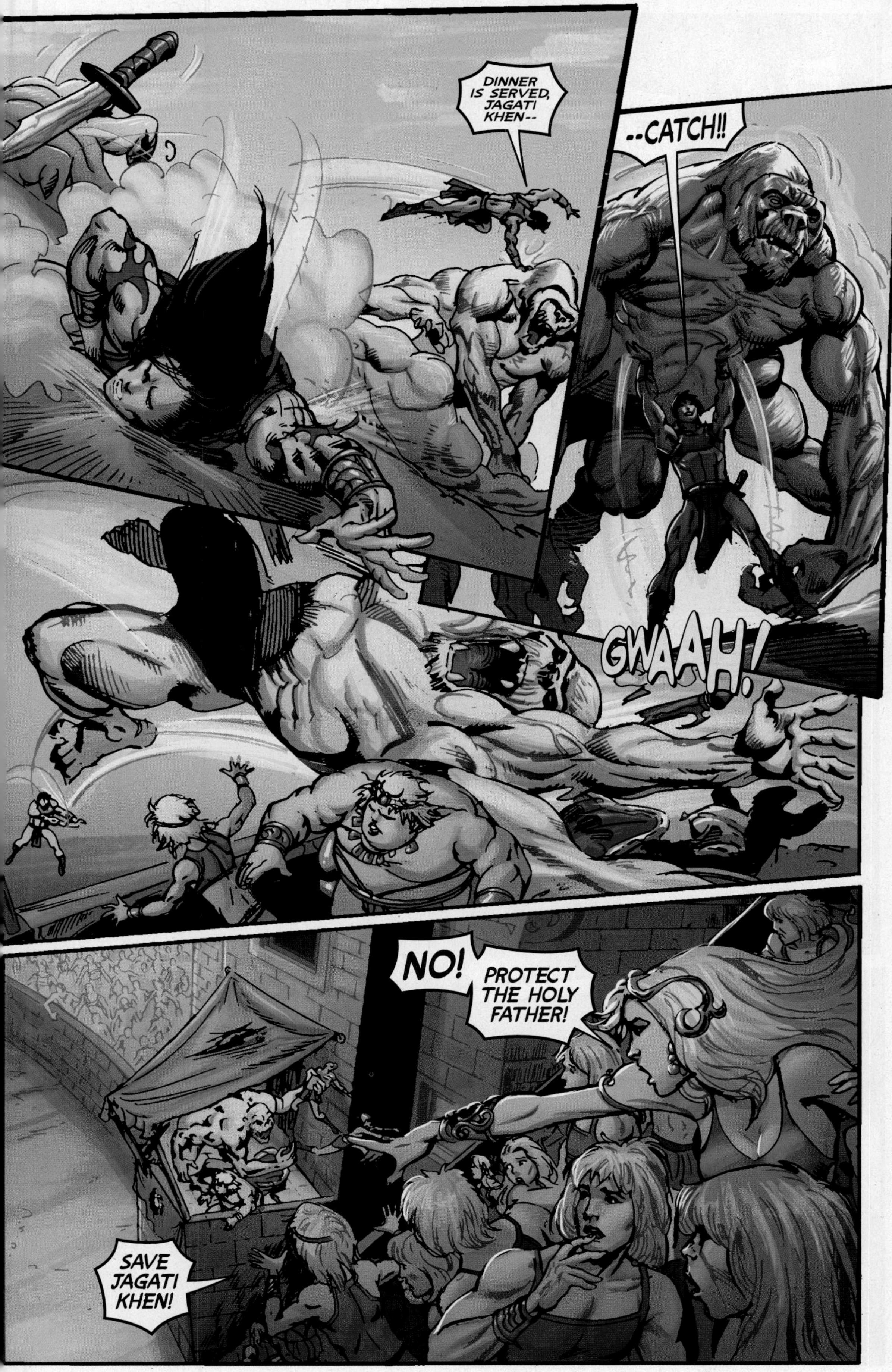
DINNER IS SERVED, JAGATI KHEN--
--CATCH!!
GWAAH!
NO!
PROTECT THE HOLY FATHER!
SAVE JAGATI KHEN!

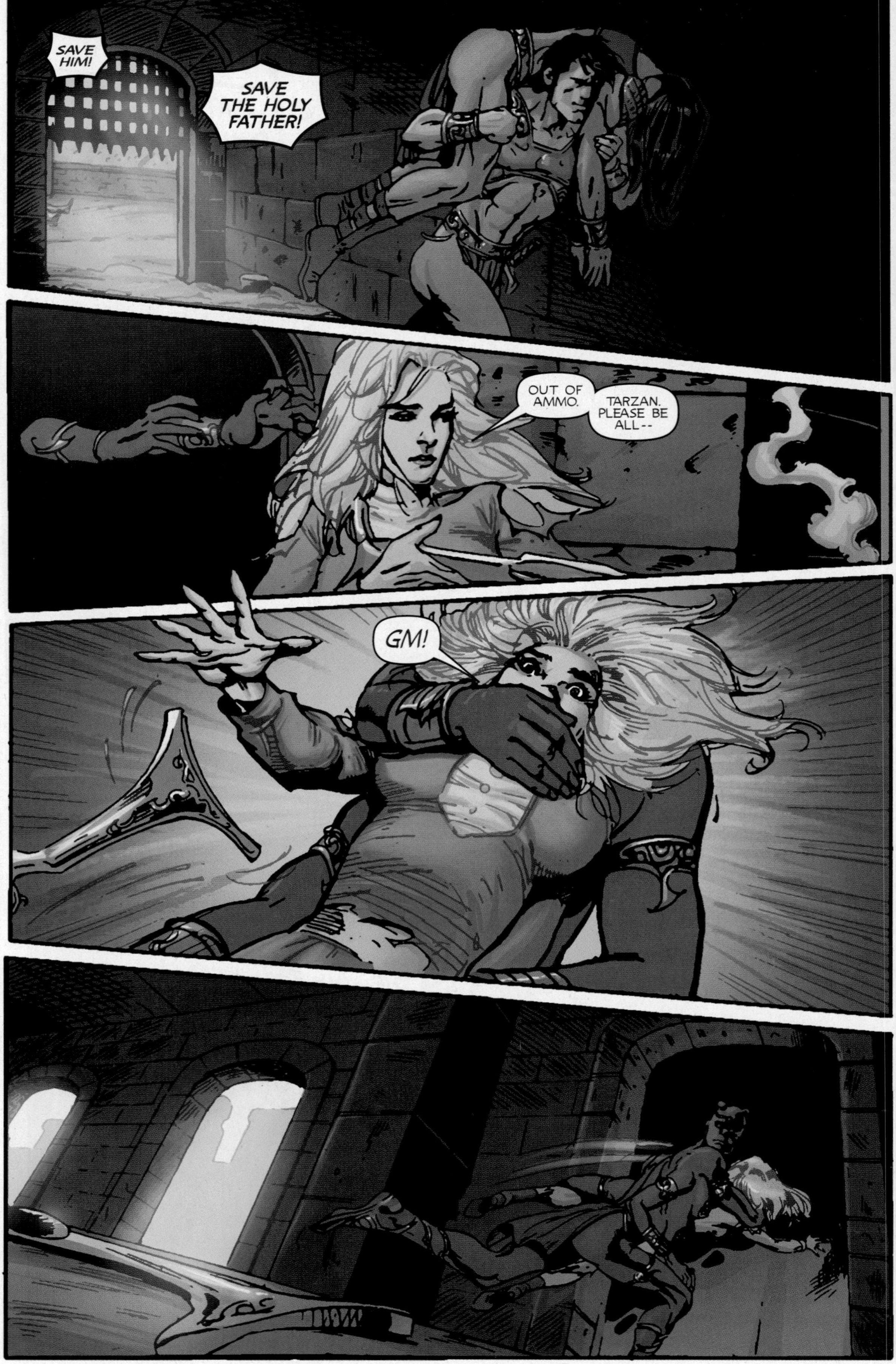
SAVE HIM!
SAVE THE HOLY FATHER!
OUT OF AMMO.
TARZAN. PLEASE BE ALL--
GM!

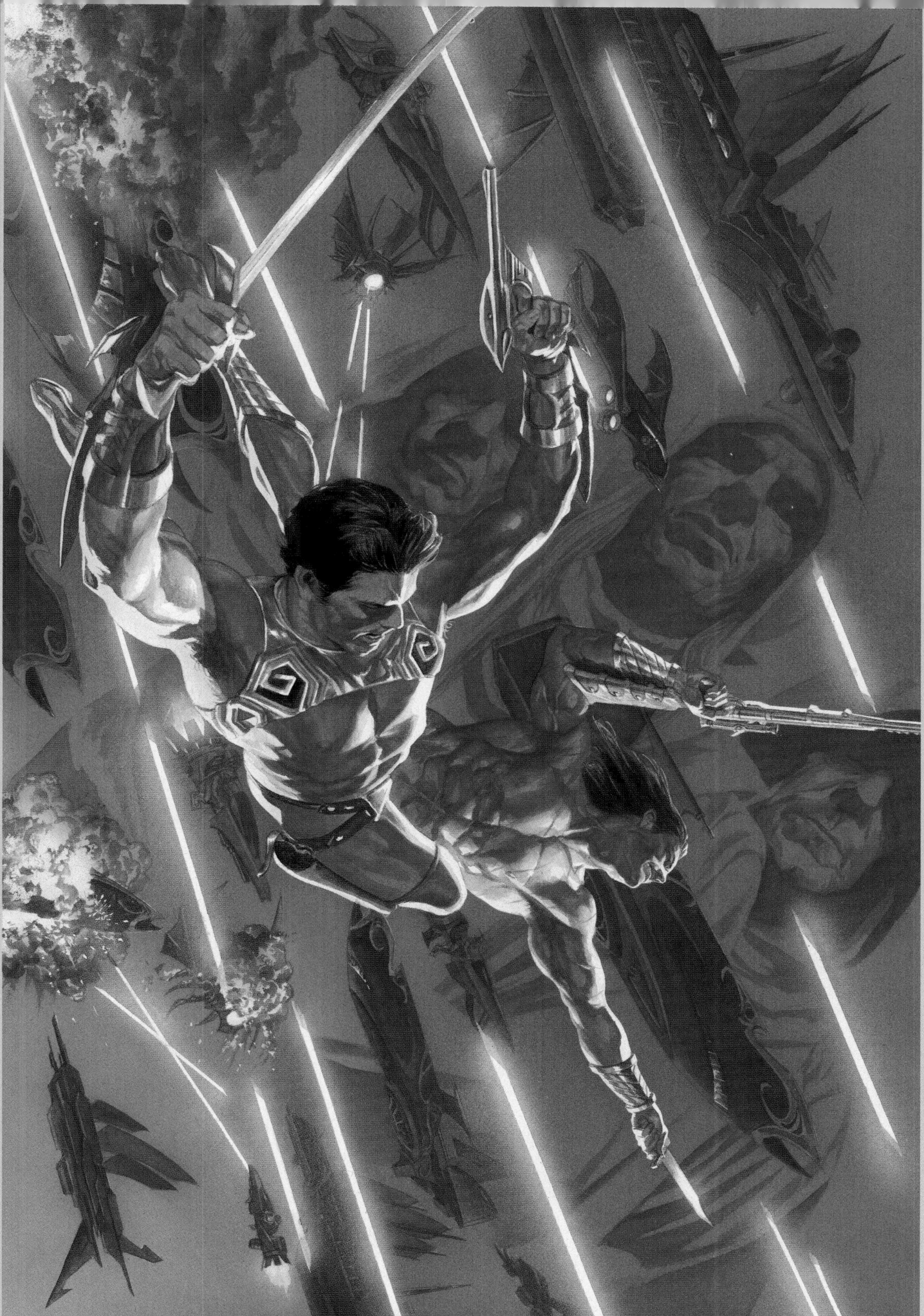

ISSUE 6

THE EYE OF THE GODDESS

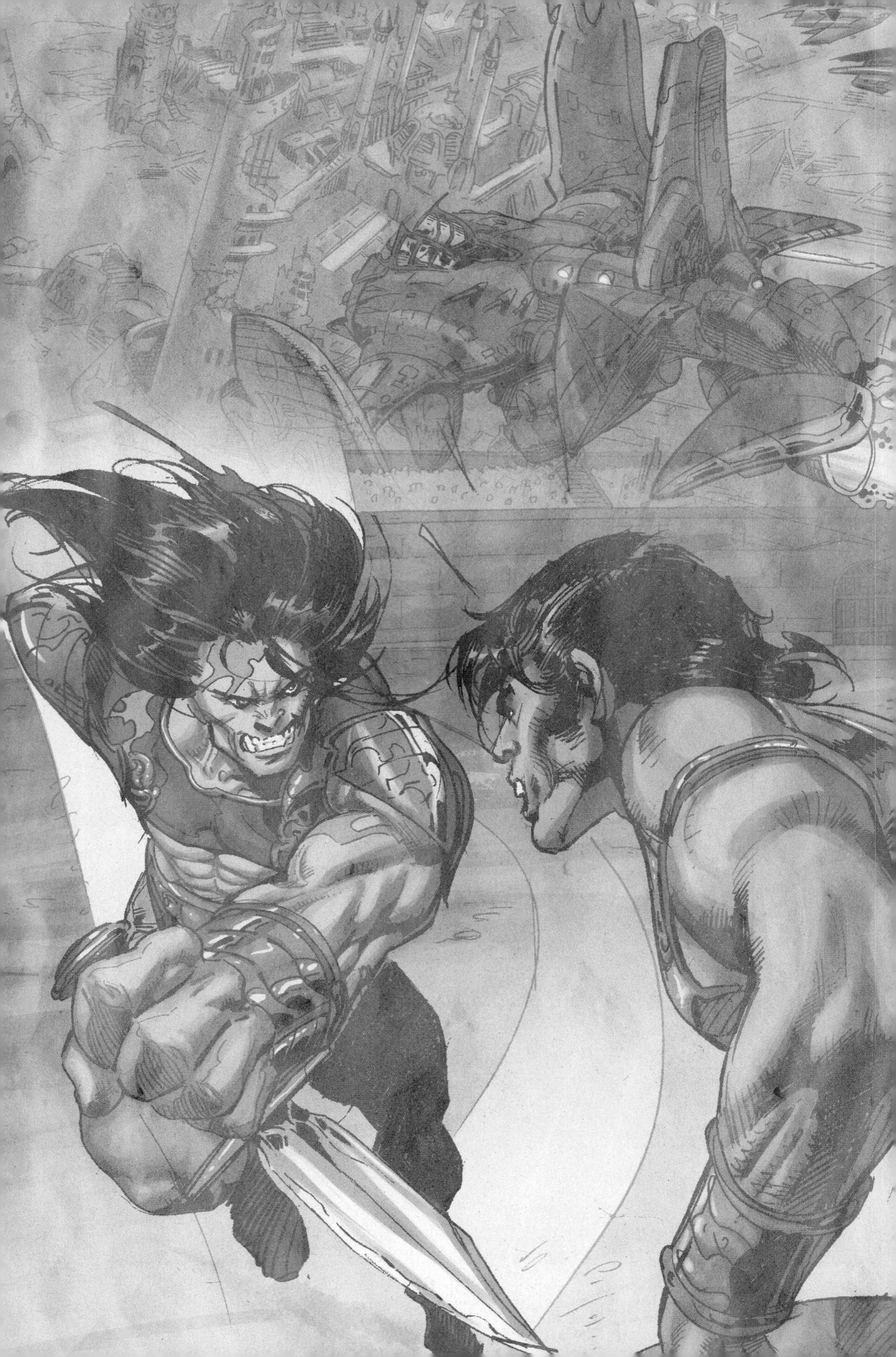

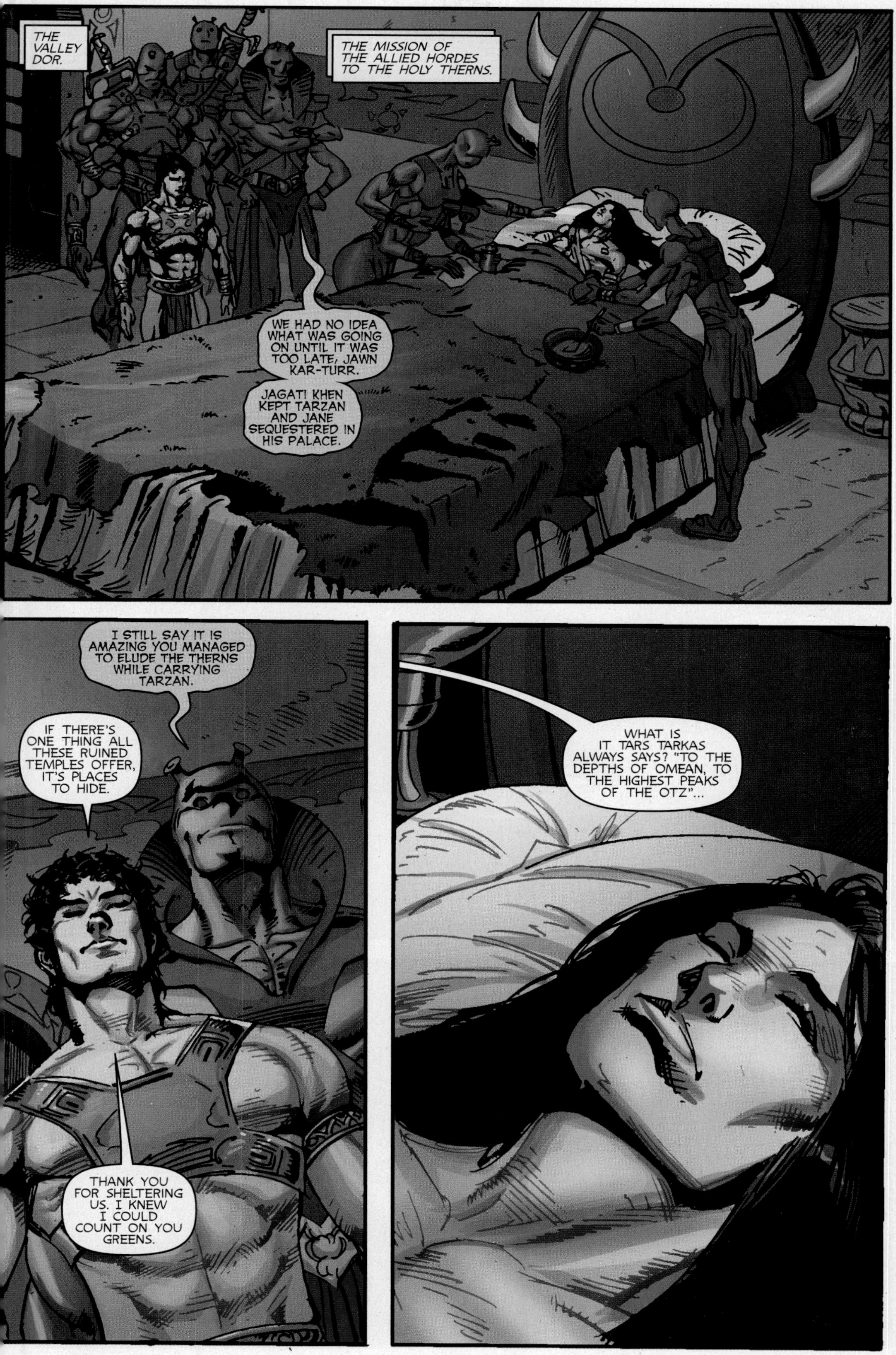

THE VALLEY DOR.
THE MISSION OF THE ALLIED HORDES TO THE HOLY THERNS.
WE HAD NO IDEA WHAT WAS GOING ON UNTIL IT WAS TOO LATE, JAWN KAR-TURR.
JAGATI KHEN KEPT TARZAN AND JANE SEQUESTERED IN HIS PALACE.
I STILL SAY IT IS AMAZING YOU MANAGED TO ELUDE THE THERNS WHILE CARRYING TARZAN.
IF THERE'S ONE THING ALL THESE RUINED TEMPLES OFFER, IT'S PLACES TO HIDE.
THANK YOU FOR SHELTERING US. I KNEW I COULD COUNT ON YOU GREENS.
WHAT IS IT TARS TARKAS ALWAYS SAYS? "TO THE DEPTHS OF OMEAN, TO THE HIGHEST PEAKS OF THE OTZ"...

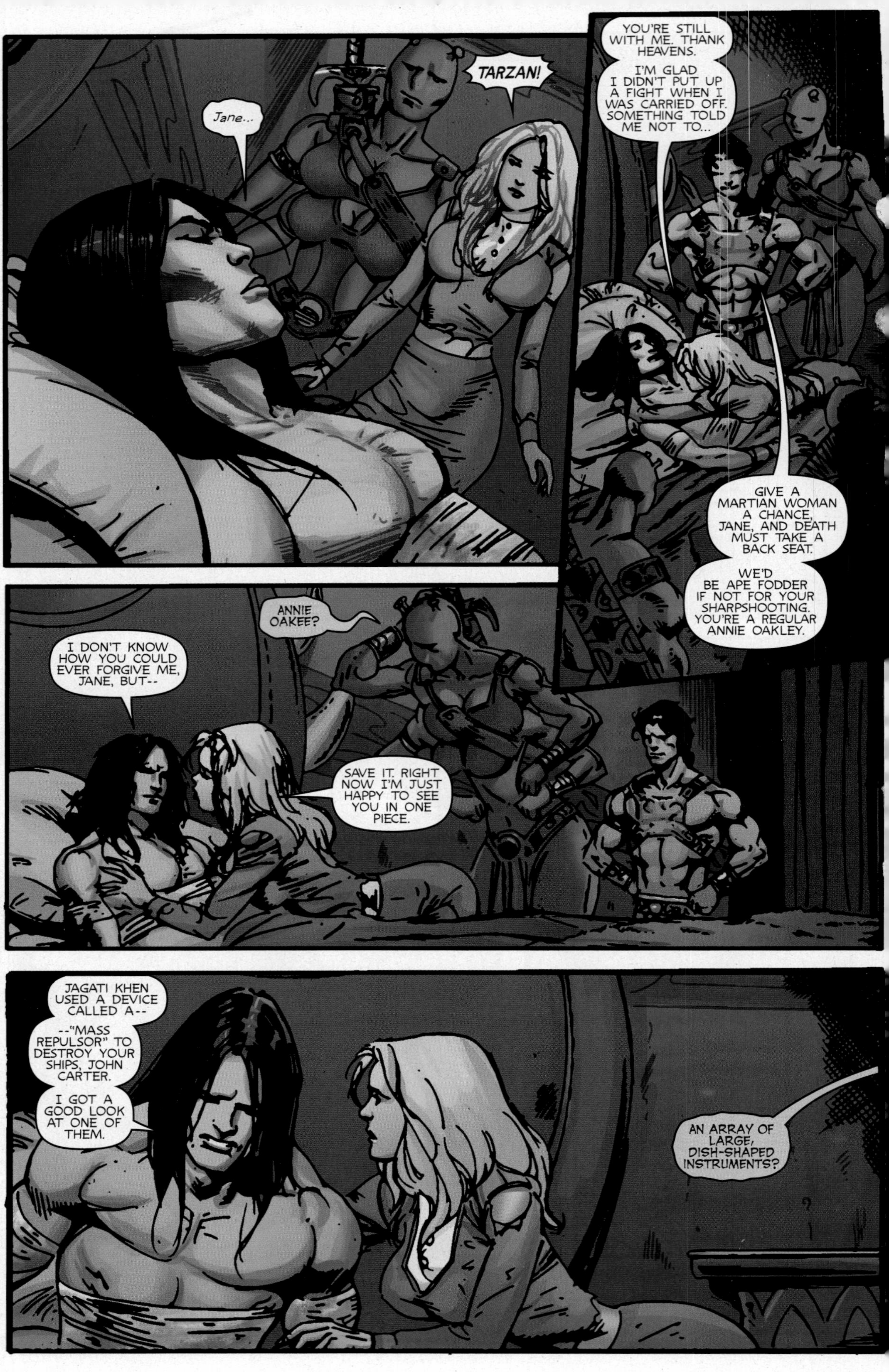
Jane...
TARZAN!
YOU'RE STILL WITH ME. THANK HEAVENS.
I'M GLAD I DIDN'T PUT UP A FIGHT WHEN I WAS CARRIED OFF. SOMETHING TOLD ME NOT TO...
GIVE A MARTIAN WOMAN A CHANCE, JANE, AND DEATH MUST TAKE A BACK SEAT.
WE'D BE APE FODDER IF NOT FOR YOUR SHARPSHOOTING. YOU'RE A REGULAR ANNIE OAKLEY.
ANNIE OAKEE?
I DON'T KNOW HOW YOU COULD EVER FORGIVE ME, JANE, BUT--
SAVE IT. RIGHT NOW I'M JUST HAPPY TO SEE YOU IN ONE PIECE.
JAGATI KHEN USED A DEVICE CALLED A--
--"MASS REPULSOR" TO DESTROY YOUR SHIPS, JOHN CARTER.
I GOT A GOOD LOOK AT ONE OF THEM.
AN ARRAY OF LARGE, DISH-SHAPED INSTRUMENTS?

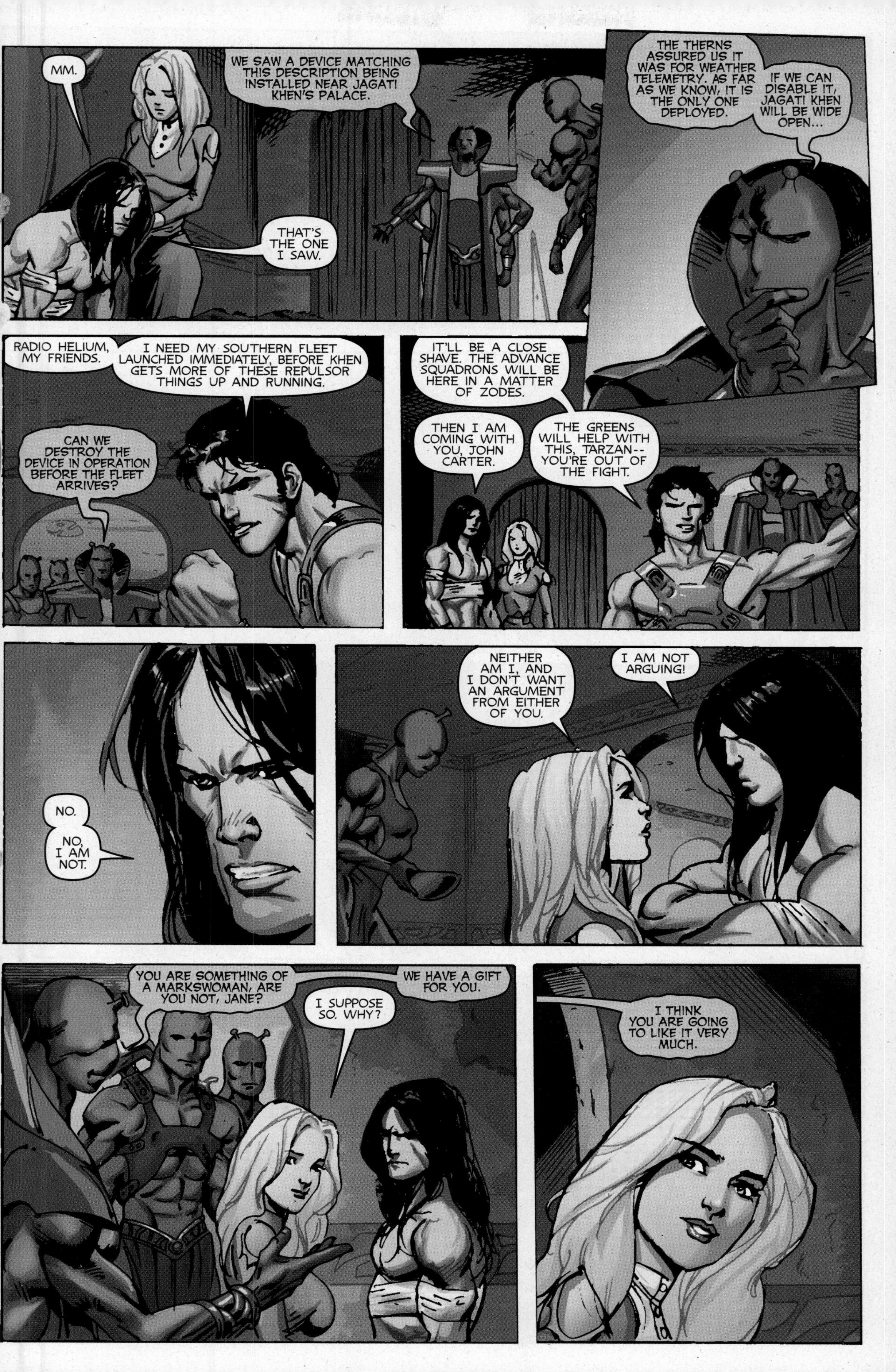
MM.
WE SAW A DEVICE MATCHING THIS DESCRIPTION BEING INSTALLED NEAR JAGATI KHEN'S PALACE.
THAT'S THE ONE I SAW.
THE THERNS ASSURED US IT WAS FOR WEATHER TELEMETRY. AS FAR AS WE KNOW, IT IS THE ONLY ONE DEPLOYED.
IF WE CAN DISABLE IT, JAGATI KHEN WILL BE WIDE OPEN...
RADIO HELIUM, MY FRIENDS.
I NEED MY SOUTHERN FLEET LAUNCHED IMMEDIATELY, BEFORE KHEN GETS MORE OF THESE REPULSOR THINGS UP AND RUNNING.
CAN WE DESTROY THE DEVICE IN OPERATION BEFORE THE FLEET ARRIVES?
IT'LL BE A CLOSE SHAVE. THE ADVANCE SQUADRONS WILL BE HERE IN A MATTER OF ZODES.
THEN I AM COMING WITH YOU, JOHN CARTER.
THE GREENS WILL HELP WITH THIS, TARZAN-- YOU'RE OUT OF THE FIGHT.
NO.
NO, I AM NOT.
NEITHER AM I, AND I DON'T WANT AN ARGUMENT FROM EITHER OF YOU.
I AM NOT ARGUING!
YOU ARE SOMETHING OF A MARKSWOMAN, ARE YOU NOT, JANE?
I SUPPOSE SO. WHY?
WE HAVE A GIFT FOR YOU.
I THINK YOU ARE GOING TO LIKE IT VERY MUCH.

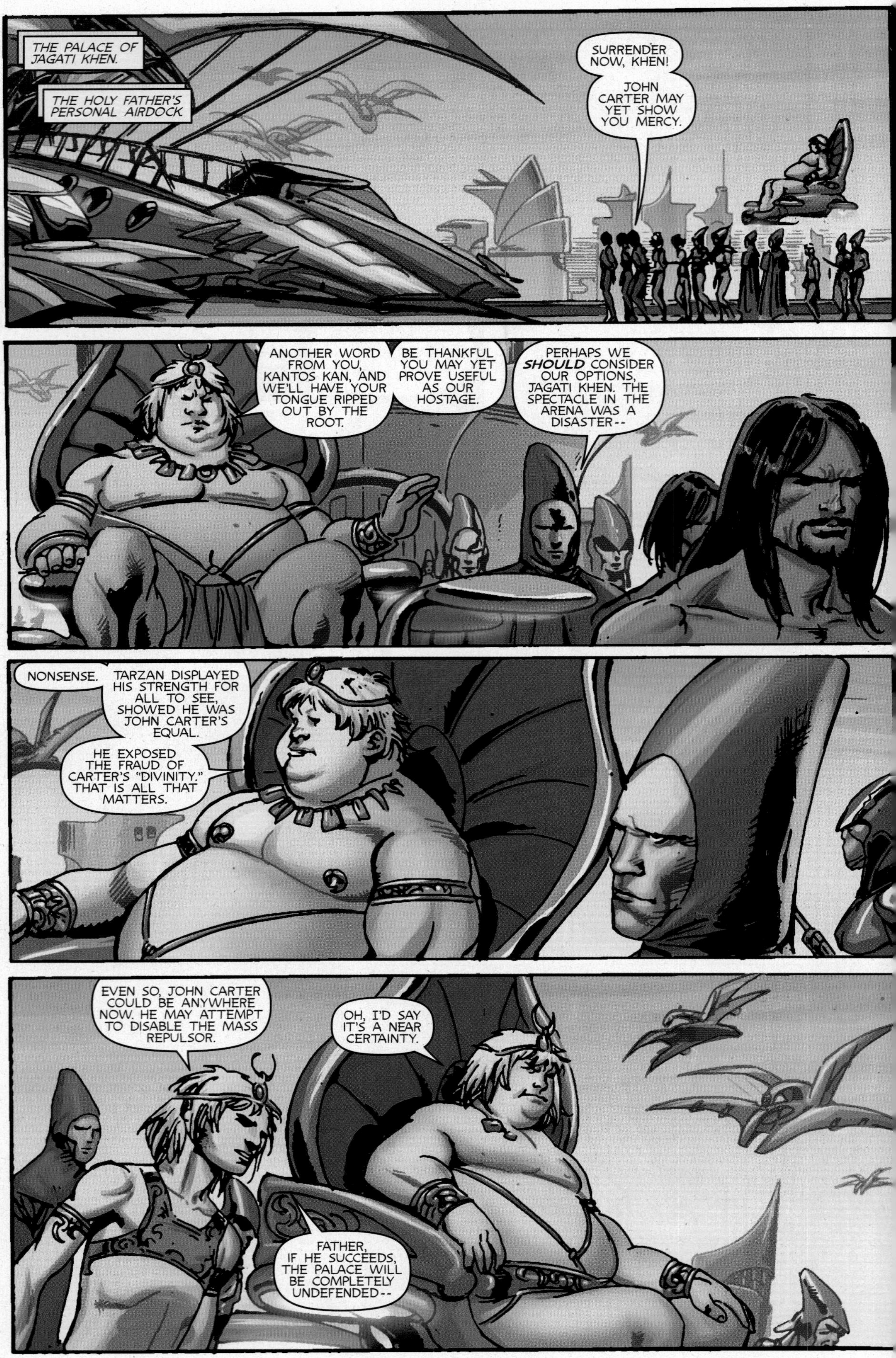
THE PALACE OF JAGATI KHEN.
THE HOLY FATHER'S PERSONAL AIRDOCK.
SURRENDER NOW, KHEN!
JOHN CARTER MAY YET SHOW YOU MERCY.
ANOTHER WORD FROM YOU, KANTOS KAN, AND WE'LL HAVE YOUR TONGUE RIPPED OUT BY THE ROOT.
BE THANKFUL YOU MAY YET PROVE USEFUL AS OUR HOSTAGE.
PERHAPS WE SHOULD CONSIDER OUR OPTIONS, JAGATI KHEN. THE SPECTACLE IN THE ARENA WAS A DISASTER--
NONSENSE.
TARZAN DISPLAYED HIS STRENGTH FOR ALL TO SEE, SHOWED HE WAS JOHN CARTER'S EQUAL.
HE EXPOSED THE FRAUD OF CARTER'S "DIVINITY." THAT IS ALL THAT MATTERS.
EVEN SO, JOHN CARTER COULD BE ANYWHERE NOW. HE MAY ATTEMPT TO DISABLE THE MASS REPULSOR.
OH, I'D SAY IT'S A NEAR CERTAINTY.
FATHER, IF HE SUCCEEDS, THE PALACE WILL BE COMPLETELY UNDEFENDED--

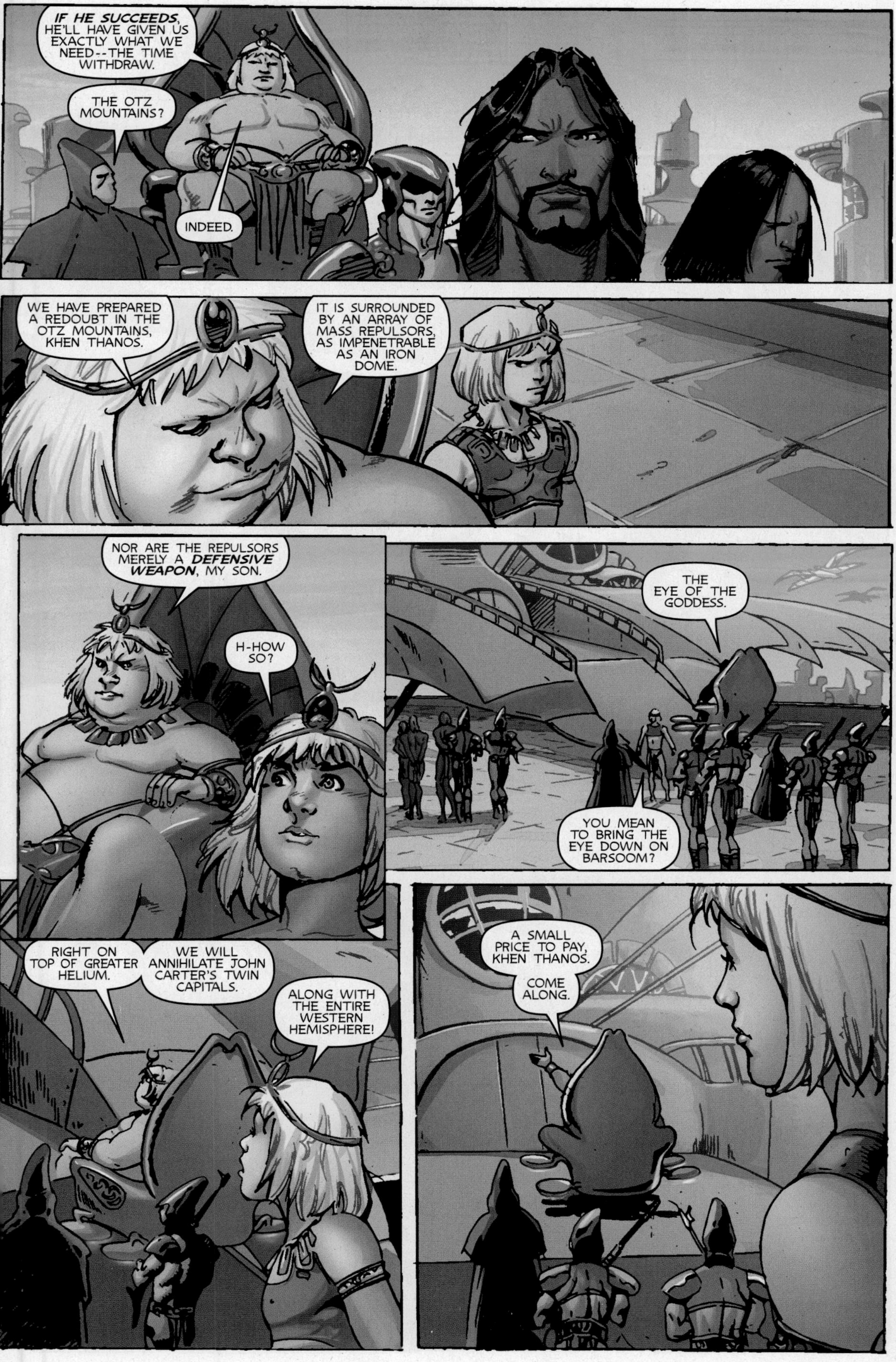

IF HE SUCCEEDS, HE'LL HAVE GIVEN US EXACTLY WHAT WE NEED--THE TIME WITHDRAW.
THE OTZ MOUNTAINS?
INDEED.
WE HAVE PREPARED A REDOUBT IN THE OTZ MOUNTAINS, KHEN THANOS.
IT IS SURROUNDED BY AN ARRAY OF MASS REPULSORS, AS IMPENETRABLE AS AN IRON DOME.
NOR ARE THE REPULSORS MERELY A *DEFENSIVE WEAPON*, MY SON.
H-HOW SO?
THE EYE OF THE GODDESS.
YOU MEAN TO BRING THE EYE DOWN ON BARSOOM?
RIGHT ON TOP OF GREATER HELIUM.
WE WILL ANNIHILATE JOHN CARTER'S TWIN CAPITALS.
ALONG WITH THE ENTIRE WESTERN HEMISPHERE!
A SMALL PRICE TO PAY, KHEN THANOS.
COME ALONG.

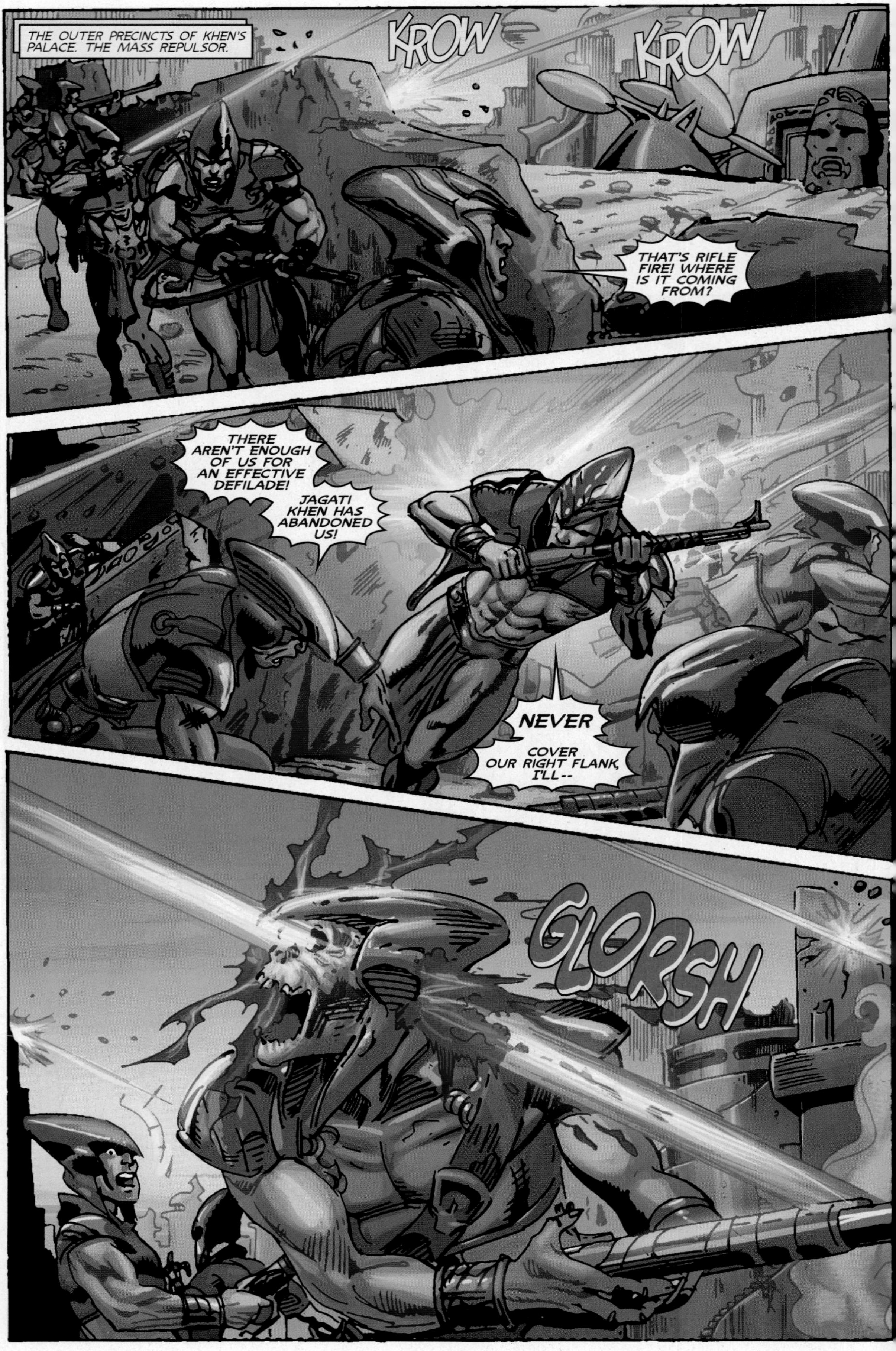
THE OUTER PRECINCTS OF KHEN'S PALACE. THE MASS REPULSOR.
KROW
KROW
THAT'S RIFLE FIRE! WHERE IS IT COMING FROM?
THERE AREN'T ENOUGH OF US FOR AN EFFECTIVE DEFILADE!
JAGATI KHEN HAS ABANDONED US!
NEVER
COVER OUR RIGHT FLANK, I'LL--
GLORSH

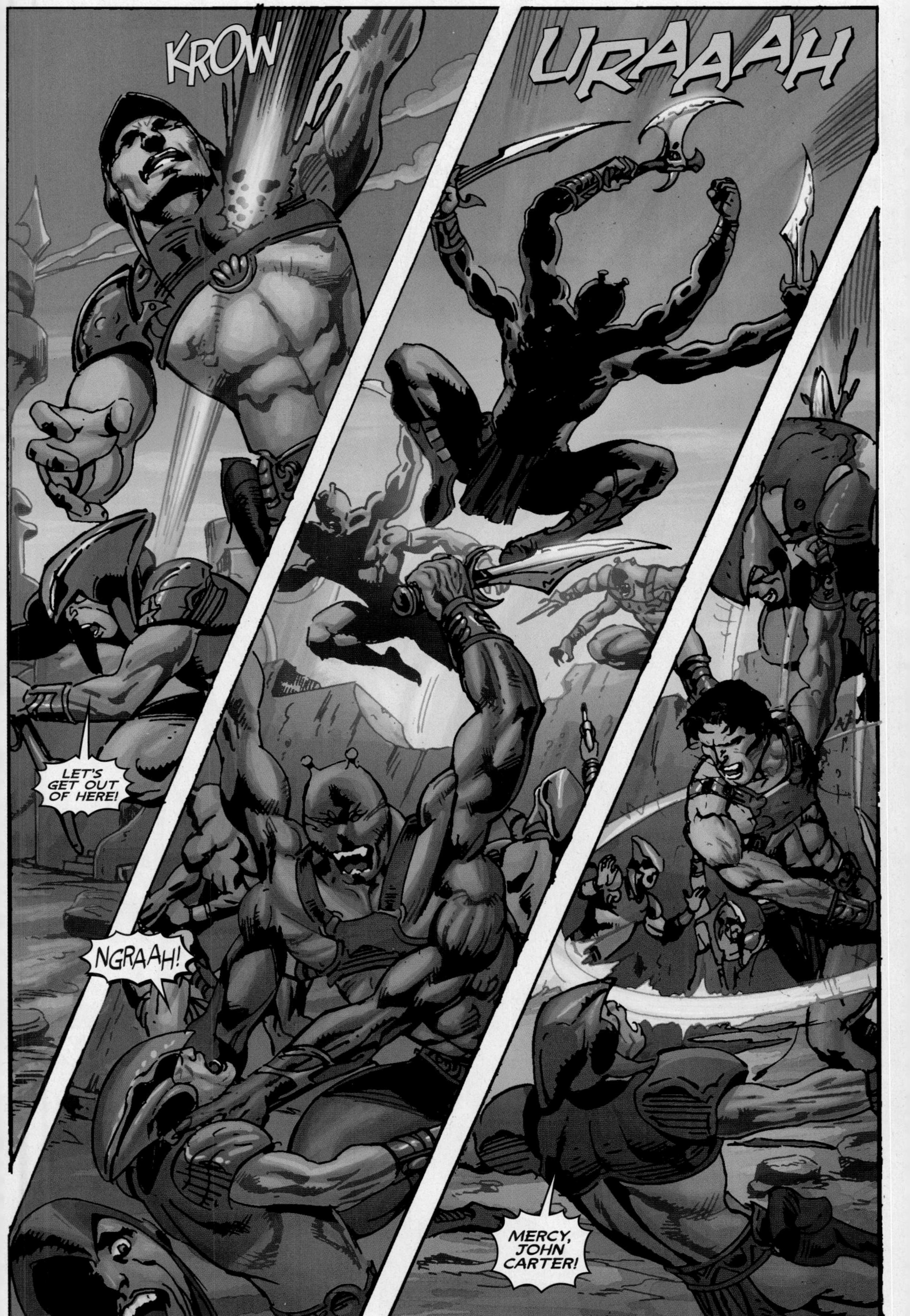
KROW
LET'S GET OUT OF HERE!
NGRAAH!
URAAAH
MERCY, JOHN CARTER!

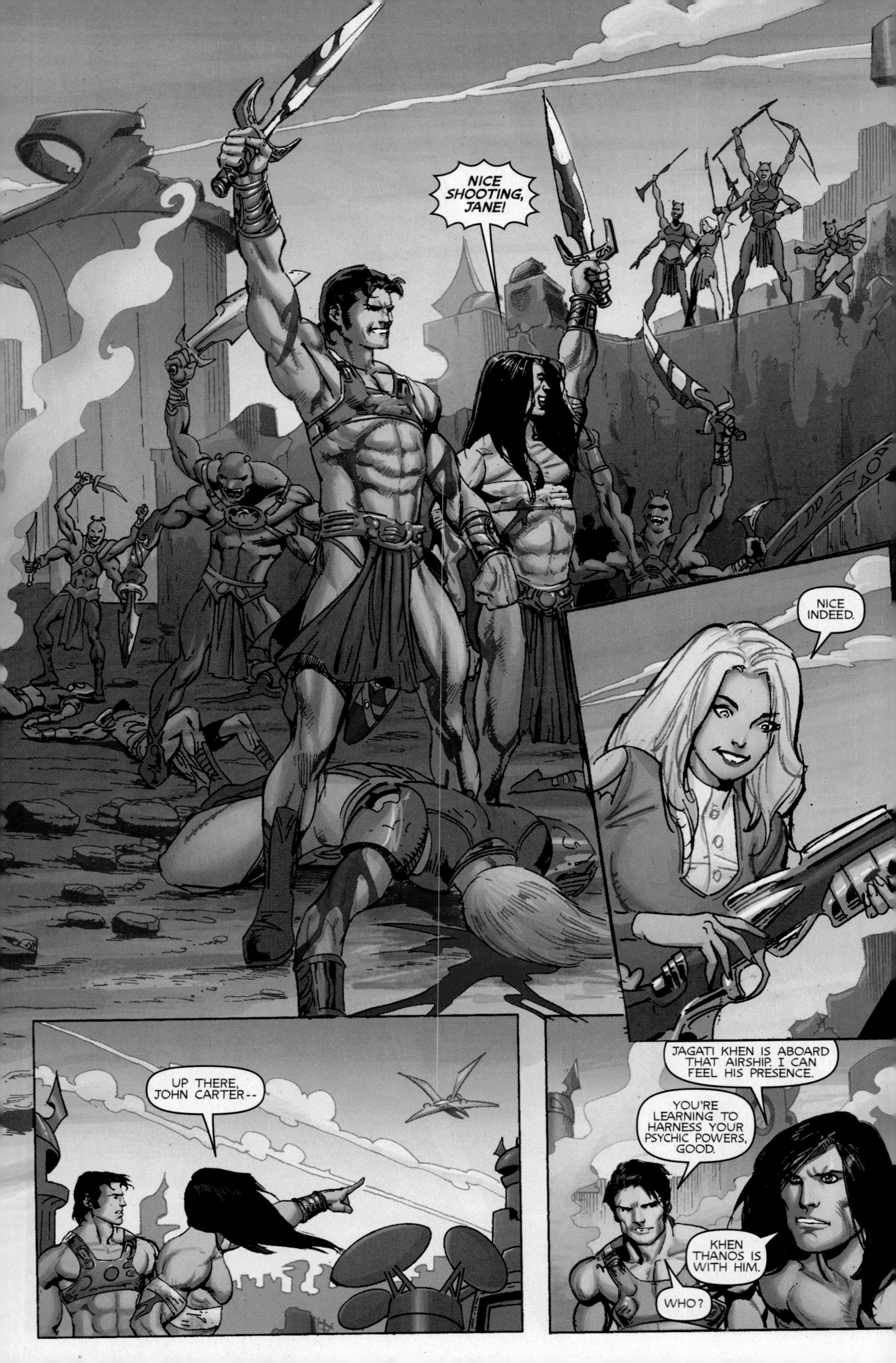
NICE SHOOTING, JANE!
NICE INDEED.
UP THERE, JOHN CARTER--
JAGATI KHEN IS ABOARD THAT AIRSHIP. I CAN FEEL HIS PRESENCE.
YOU'RE LEARNING TO HARNESS YOUR PSYCHIC POWERS. GOOD.
KHEN THANOS IS WITH HIM.
WHO?

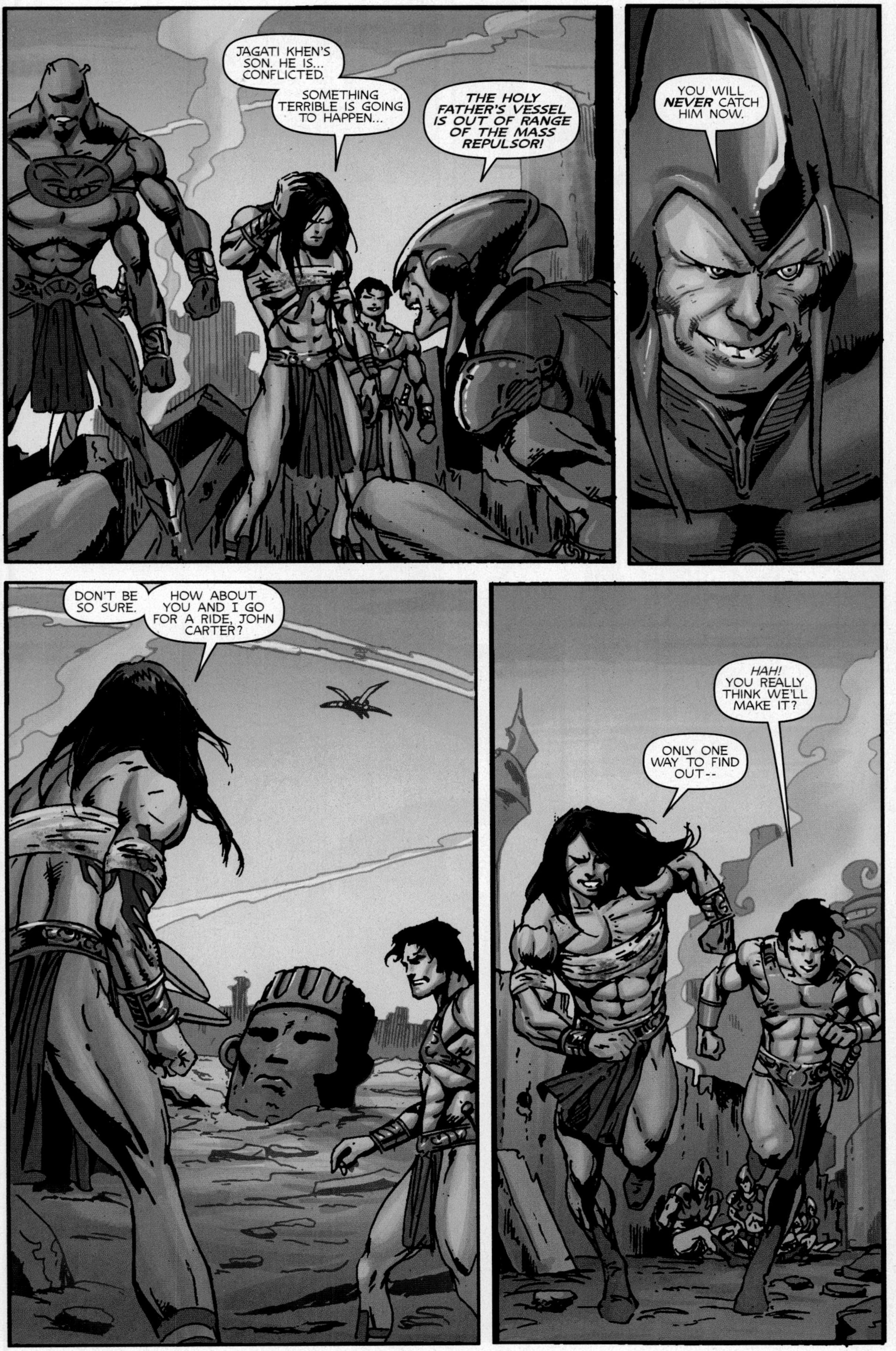
JAGATI KHEN'S SON. HE IS... CONFLICTED.
SOMETHING TERRIBLE IS GOING TO HAPPEN...
THE HOLY FATHER'S VESSEL IS OUT OF RANGE OF THE MASS REPULSOR!
YOU WILL ***NEVER*** CATCH HIM NOW.
DON'T BE SO SURE.
HOW ABOUT YOU AND I GO FOR A RIDE, JOHN CARTER?
HAH! YOU REALLY THINK WE'LL MAKE IT?
ONLY ONE WAY TO FIND OUT--

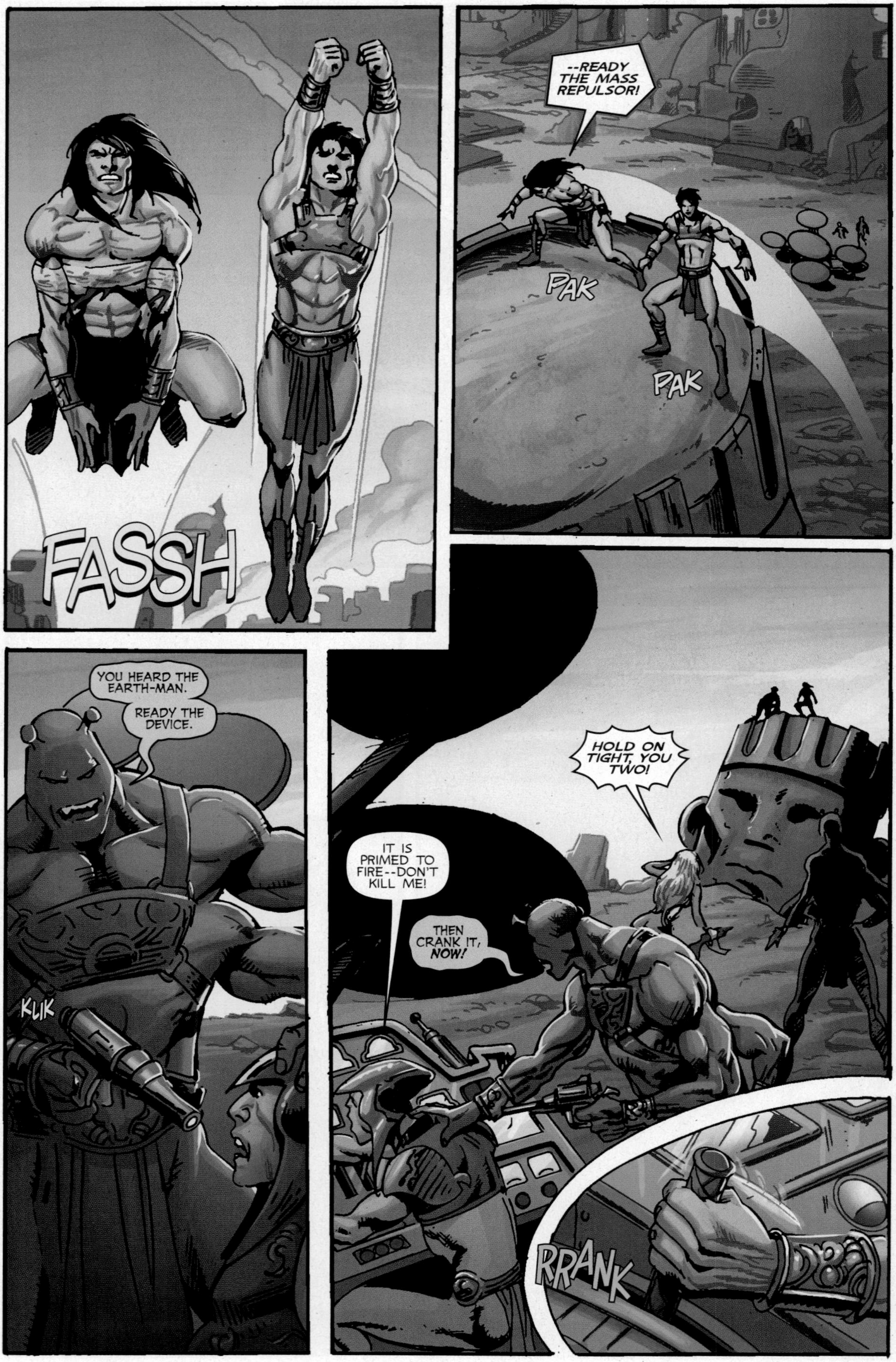
FASSH
--READY THE MASS REPULSOR!
PAK
PAK
YOU HEARD THE EARTH-MAN.
READY THE DEVICE.
KLIK
HOLD ON TIGHT, YOU TWO!
IT IS PRIMED TO FIRE--DON'T KILL ME!
THEN CRANK IT, NOW!
RRANK

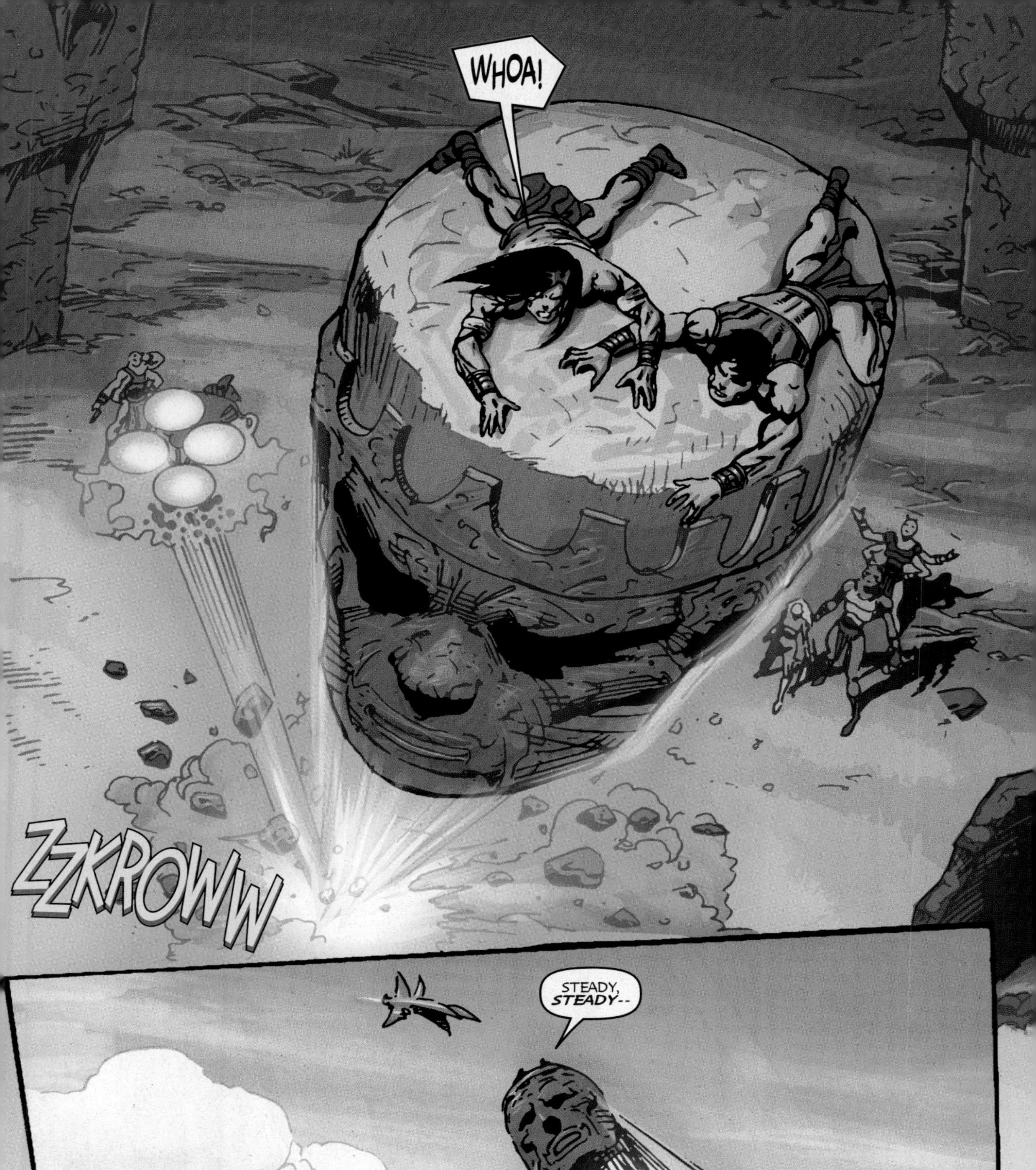
WHOA!
ZZKROWW
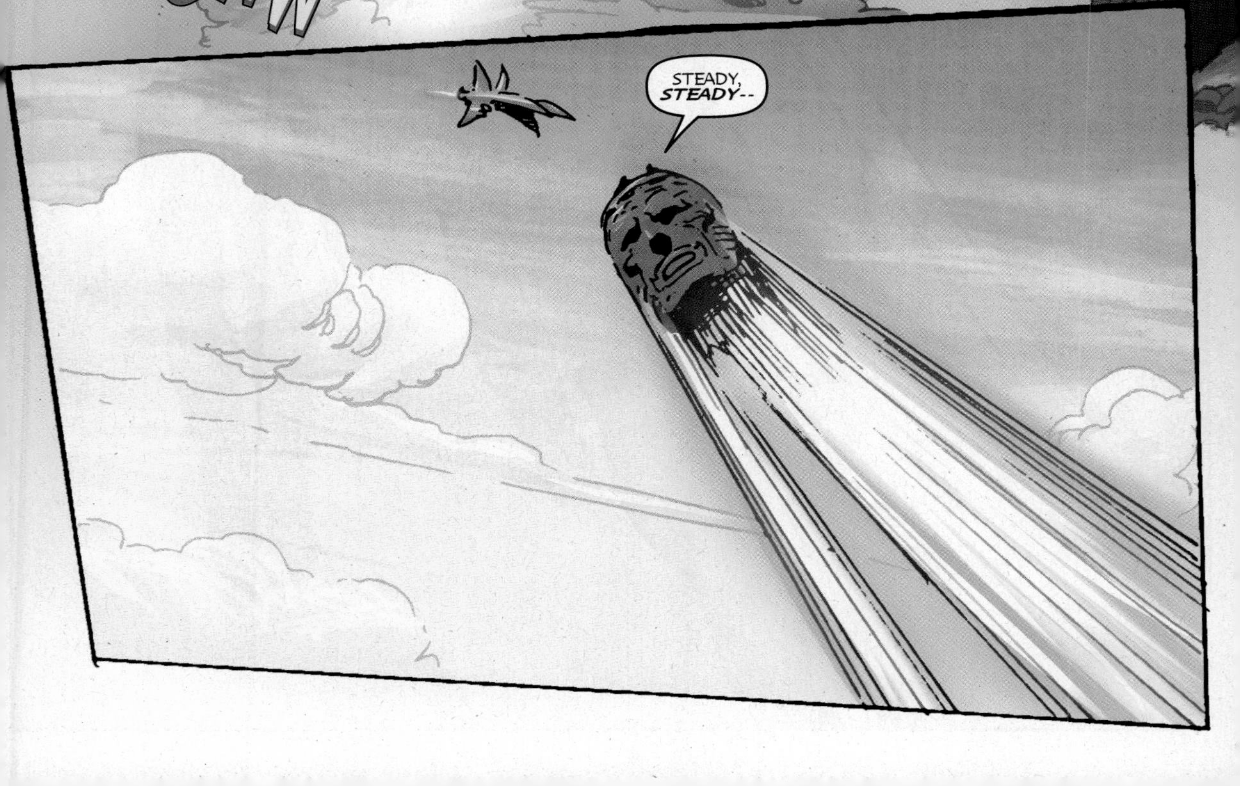
STEADY,
STEADY--

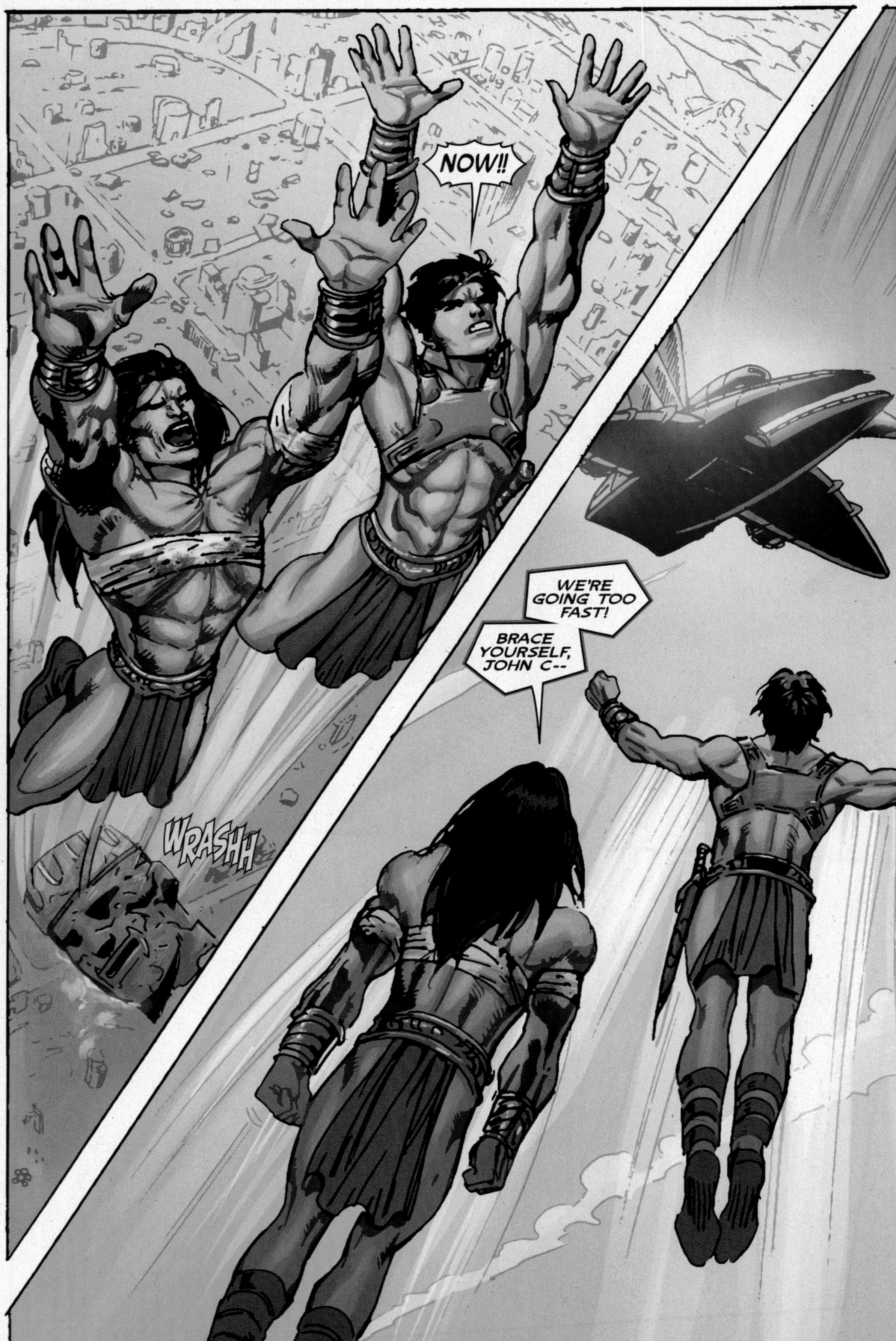
NOW!!
WRASHH
WE'RE GOING TOO FAST!
BRACE YOURSELF, JOHN C--

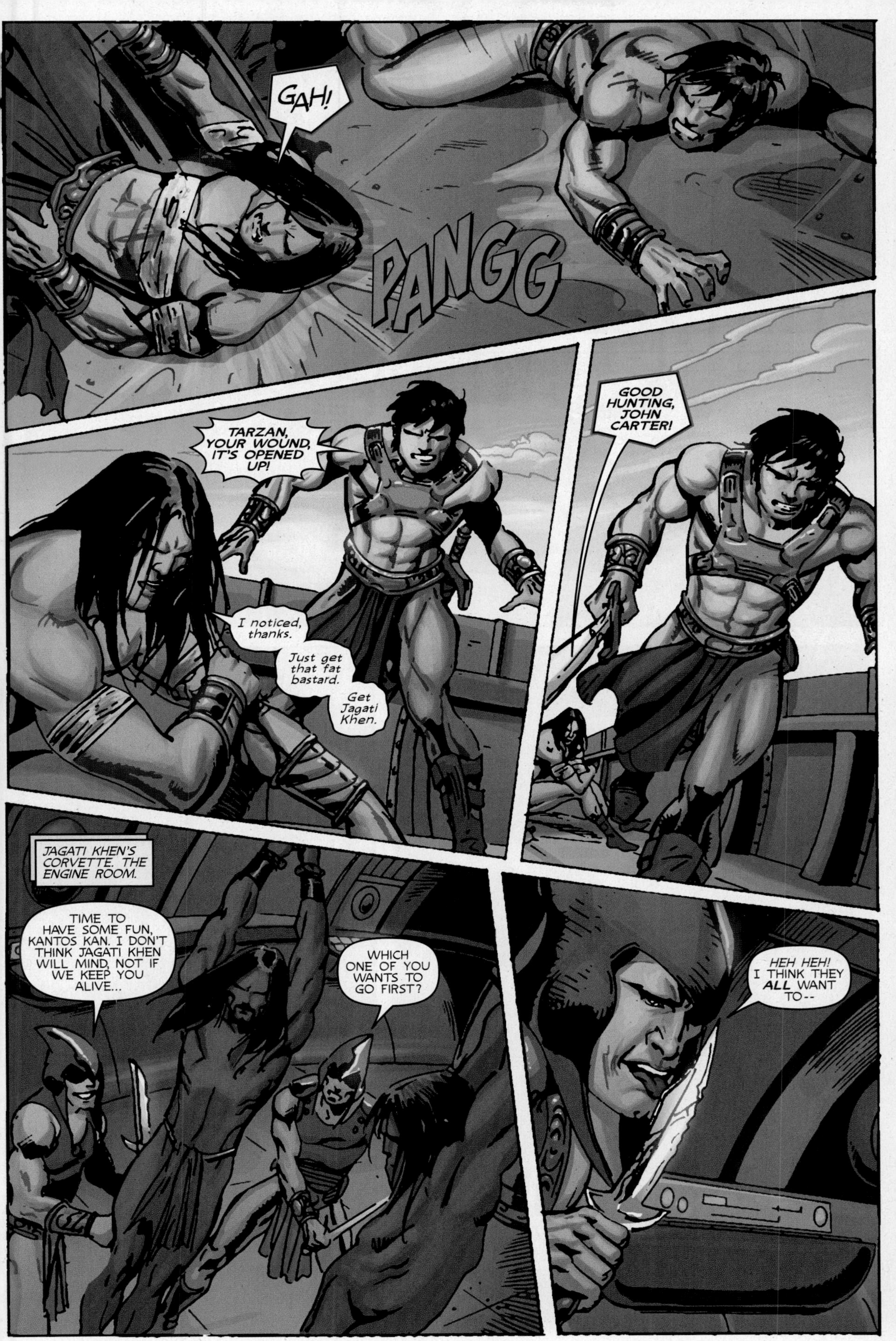
GAH!
PANGG
TARZAN, YOUR WOUND, IT'S OPENED UP!
I noticed, thanks.
Just get that fat bastard.
Get Jagati Khen.
GOOD HUNTING, JOHN CARTER!
JAGATI KHEN'S CORVETTE. THE ENGINE ROOM.
TIME TO HAVE SOME FUN, KANTOS KAN. I DON'T THINK JAGATI KHEN WILL MIND, NOT IF WE KEEP YOU ALIVE...
WHICH ONE OF YOU WANTS TO GO FIRST?
HEH HEH! I THINK THEY ALL WANT TO--

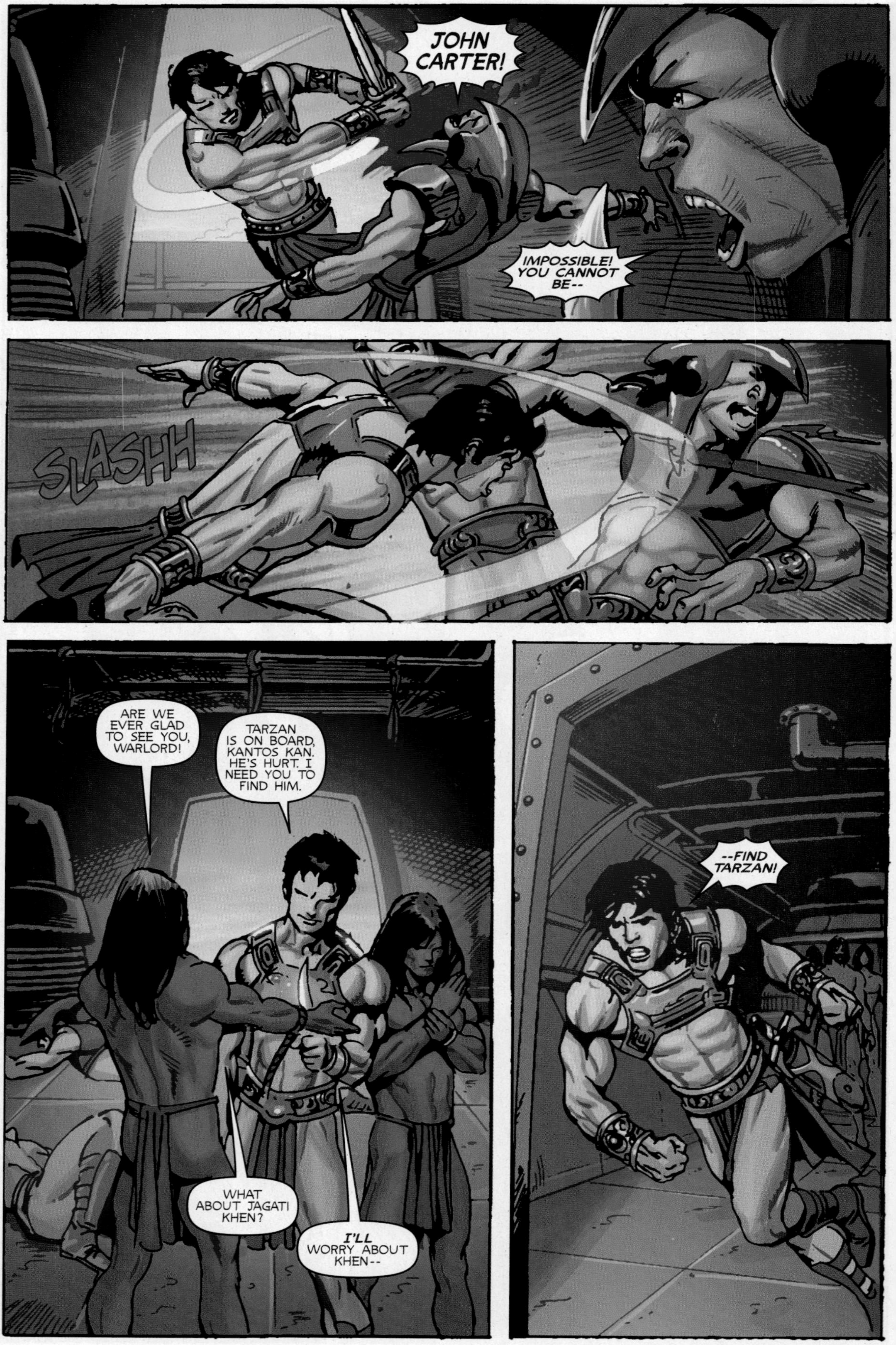
JOHN CARTER!
IMPOSSIBLE! YOU CANNOT BE--
SLASHH
ARE WE EVER GLAD TO SEE YOU, WARLORD!
TARZAN IS ON BOARD, KANTOS KAN. HE'S HURT. I NEED YOU TO FIND HIM.
WHAT ABOUT JAGATI KHEN?
I'LL WORRY ABOUT KHEN--
--FIND TARZAN!

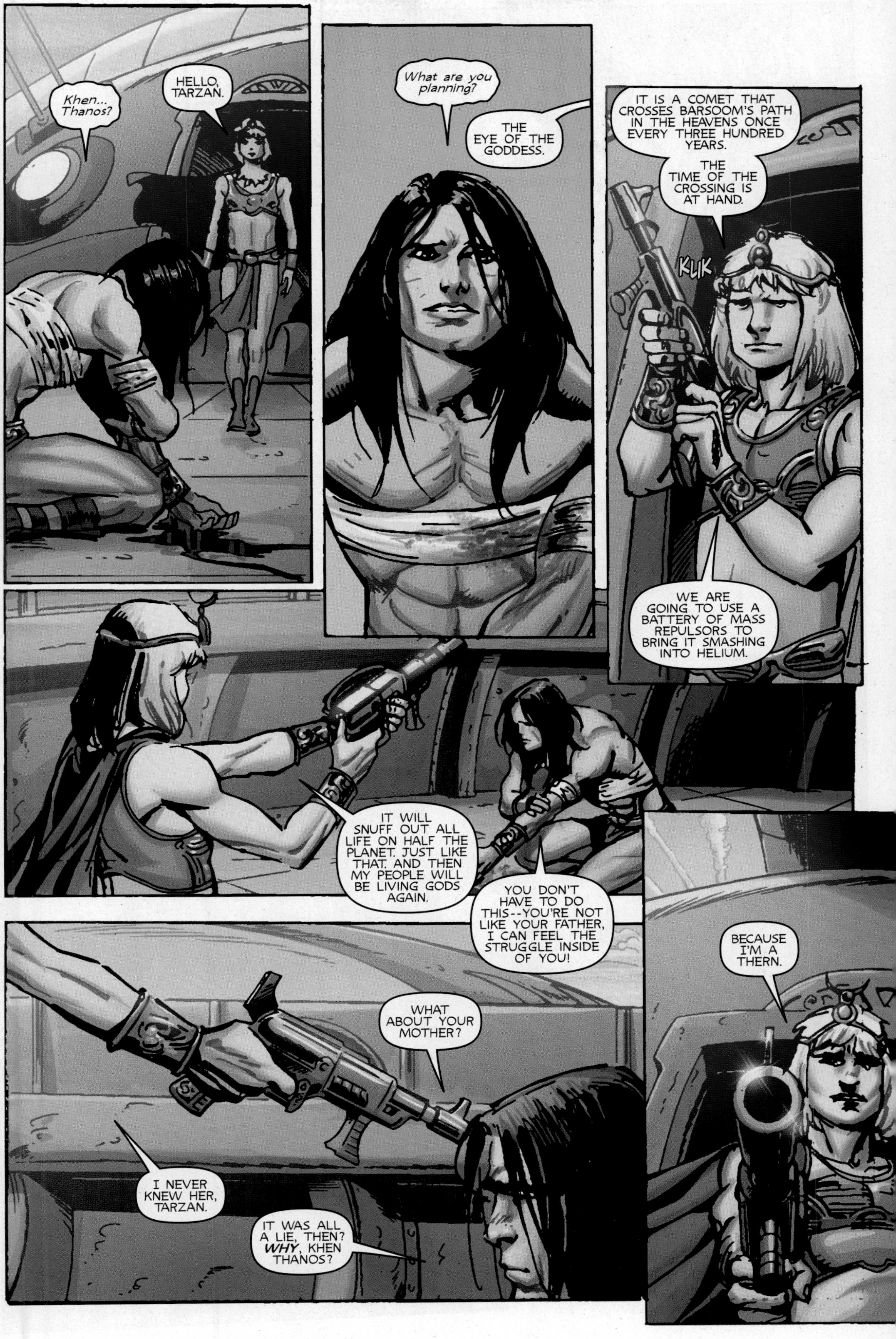
Khen... Thanos?
HELLO, TARZAN.
What are you planning?
THE EYE OF THE GODDESS.
IT IS A COMET THAT CROSSES BARSOOM'S PATH IN THE HEAVENS ONCE EVERY THREE HUNDRED YEARS.
THE TIME OF THE CROSSING IS AT HAND.
KLIK
WE ARE GOING TO USE A BATTERY OF MASS REPULSORS TO BRING IT SMASHING INTO HELIUM.
IT WILL SNUFF OUT ALL LIFE ON HALF THE PLANET. JUST LIKE THAT. AND THEN MY PEOPLE WILL BE LIVING GODS AGAIN.
YOU DON'T HAVE TO DO THIS--YOU'RE NOT LIKE YOUR FATHER, I CAN FEEL THE STRUGGLE INSIDE OF YOU!
WHAT ABOUT YOUR MOTHER?
I NEVER KNEW HER, TARZAN.
IT WAS ALL A LIE, THEN? *WHY*, KHEN THANOS?
BECAUSE I'M A THERN.

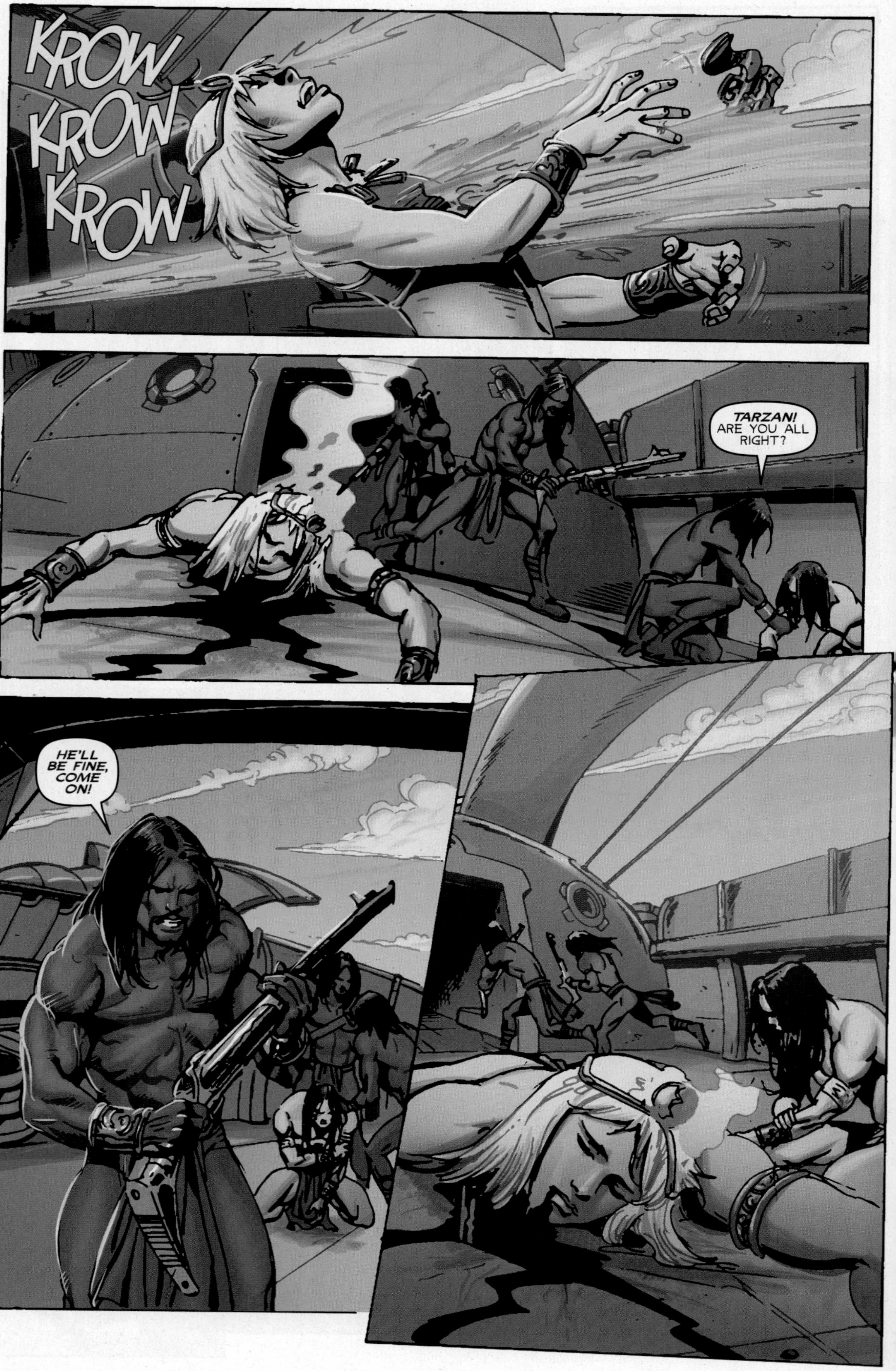
KROW
KROW
KROW
TARZAN! ARE YOU ALL RIGHT?
HE'LL BE FINE, COME ON!

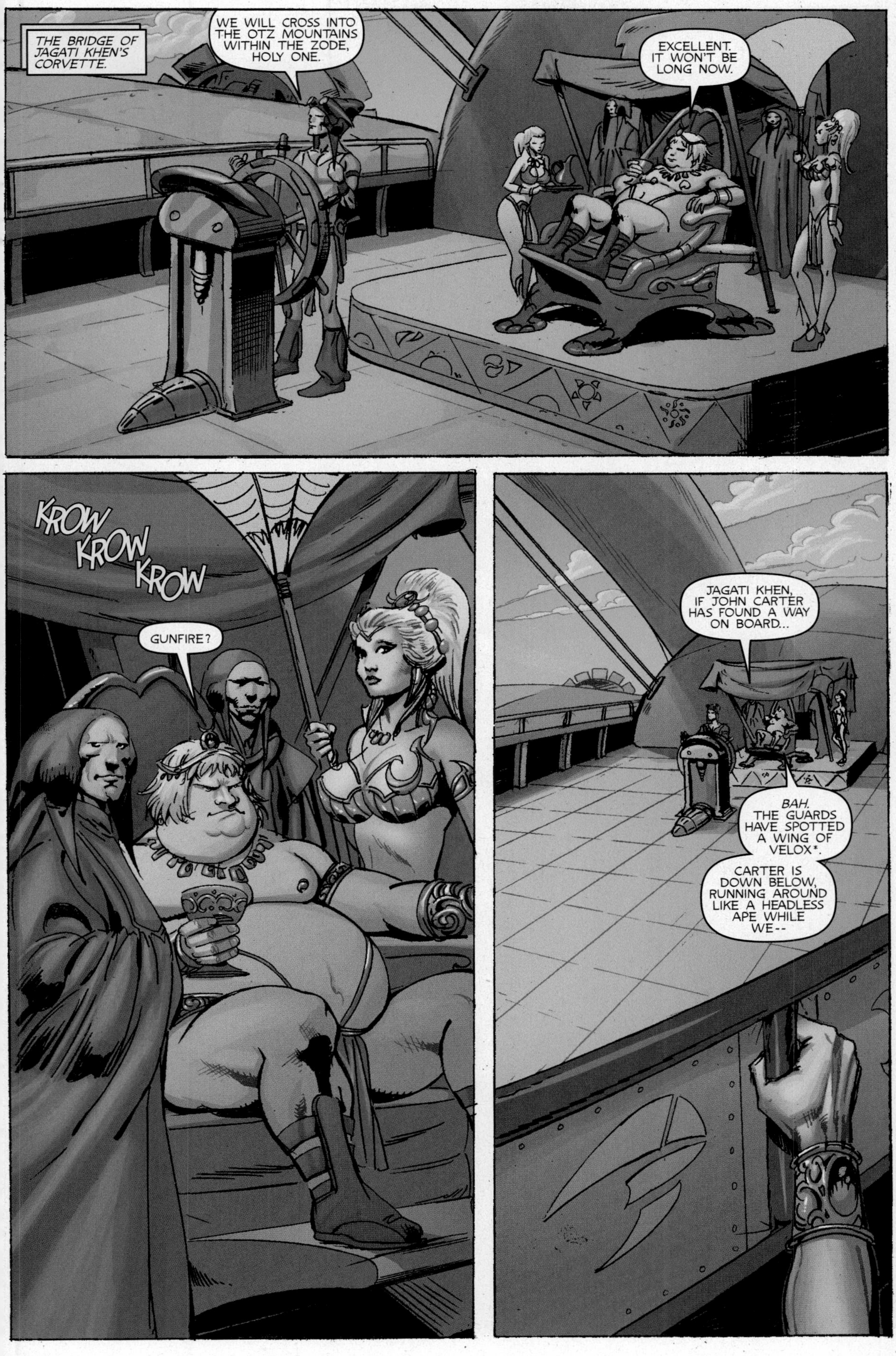
THE BRIDGE OF JAGATI KHEN'S CORVETTE.
WE WILL CROSS INTO THE OTZ MOUNTAINS WITHIN THE ZODE, HOLY ONE.
EXCELLENT. IT WON'T BE LONG NOW.
KROW KROW KROW
GUNFIRE?
JAGATI KHEN, IF JOHN CARTER HAS FOUND A WAY ON BOARD...
BAH. THE GUARDS HAVE SPOTTED A WING OF VELOX*.
CARTER IS DOWN BELOW, RUNNING AROUND LIKE A HEADLESS APE WHILE WE--

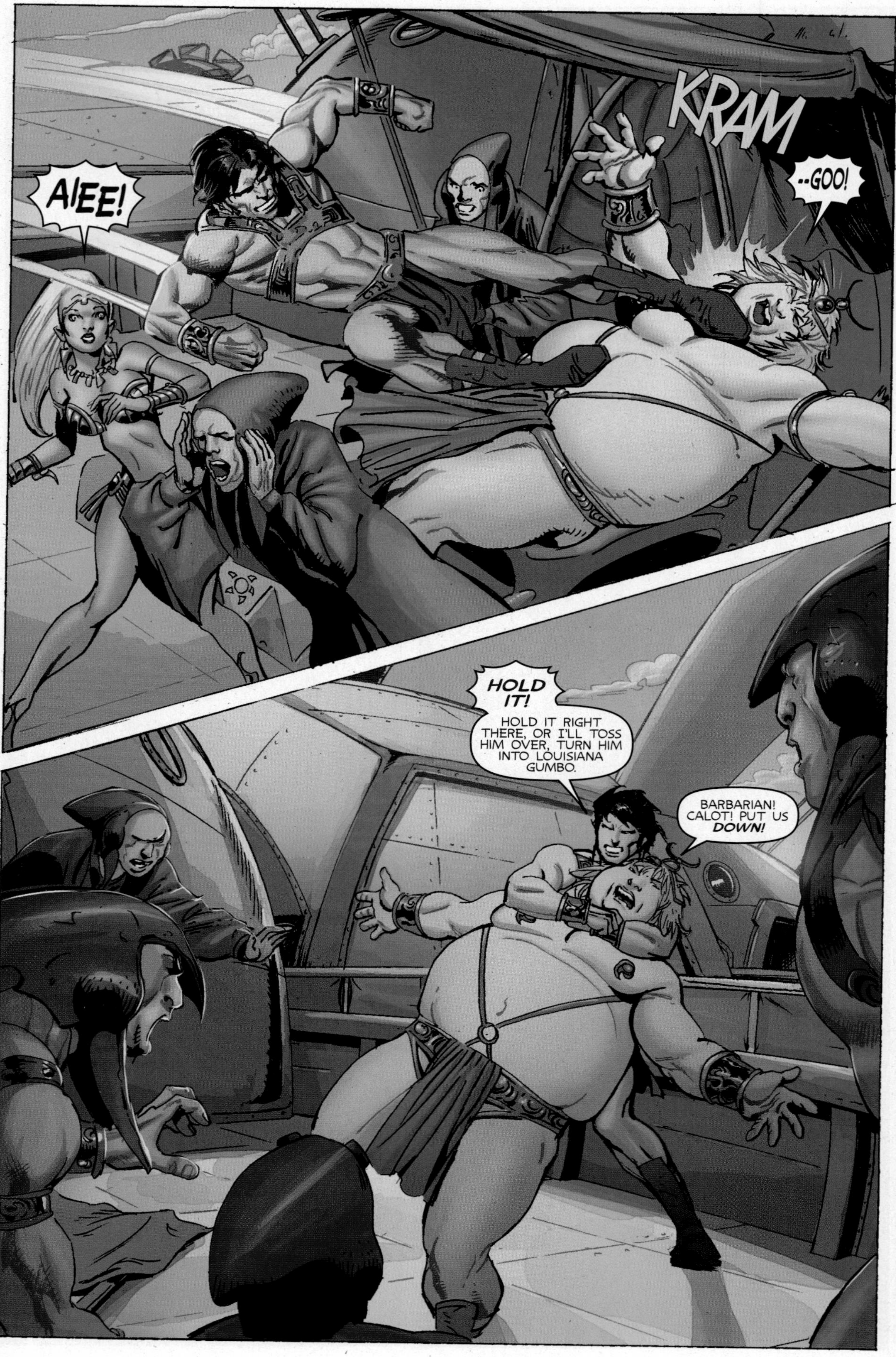
KRAM
AIEE!
--GOO!
HOLD IT!
HOLD IT RIGHT THERE, OR I'LL TOSS HIM OVER, TURN HIM INTO LOUISIANA GUMBO.
BARBARIAN! CALOT! PUT US DOWN!

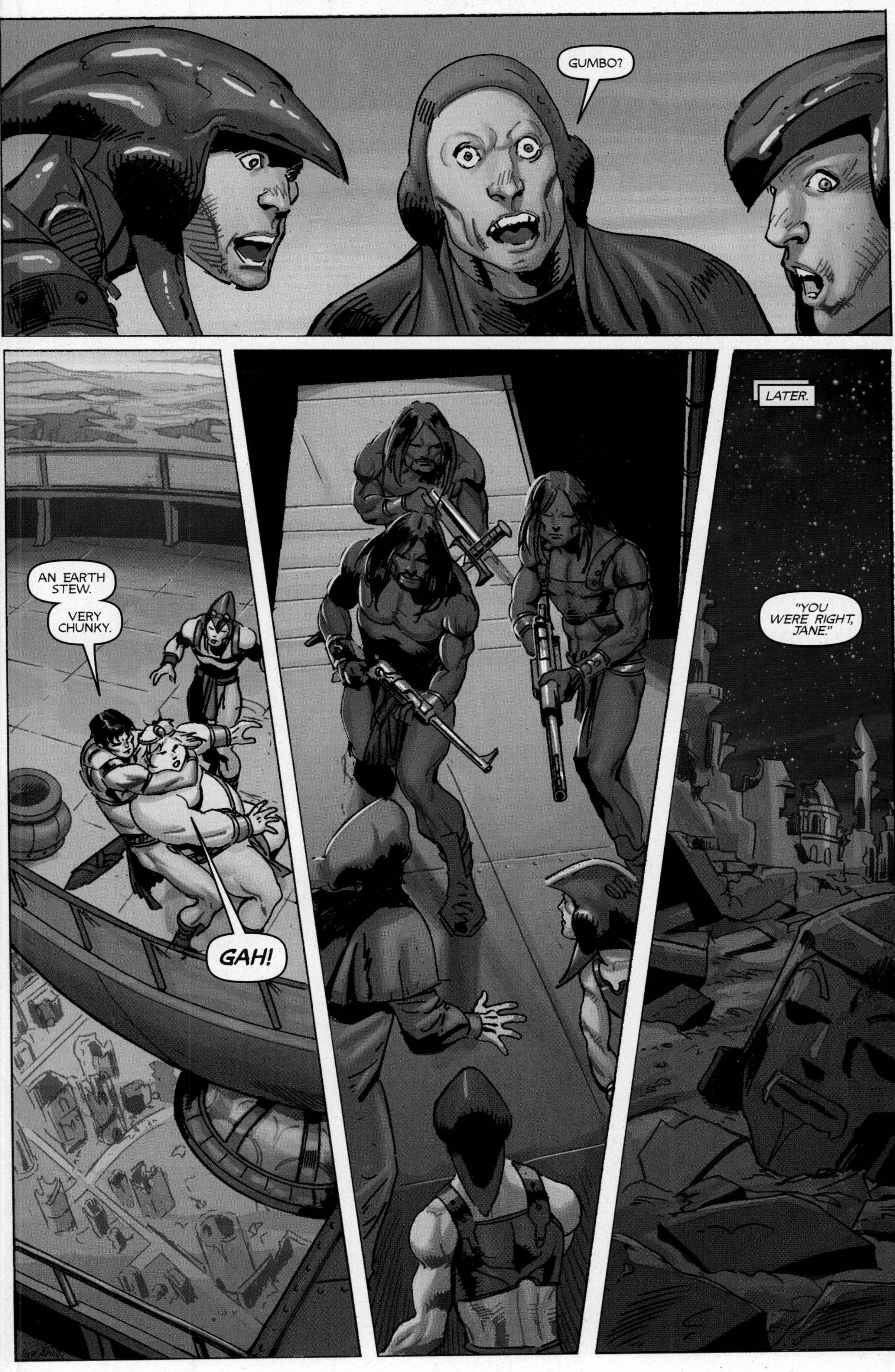
GUMBO?
AN EARTH STEW.
VERY CHUNKY.
GAH!
LATER.
"YOU WERE RIGHT, JANE."

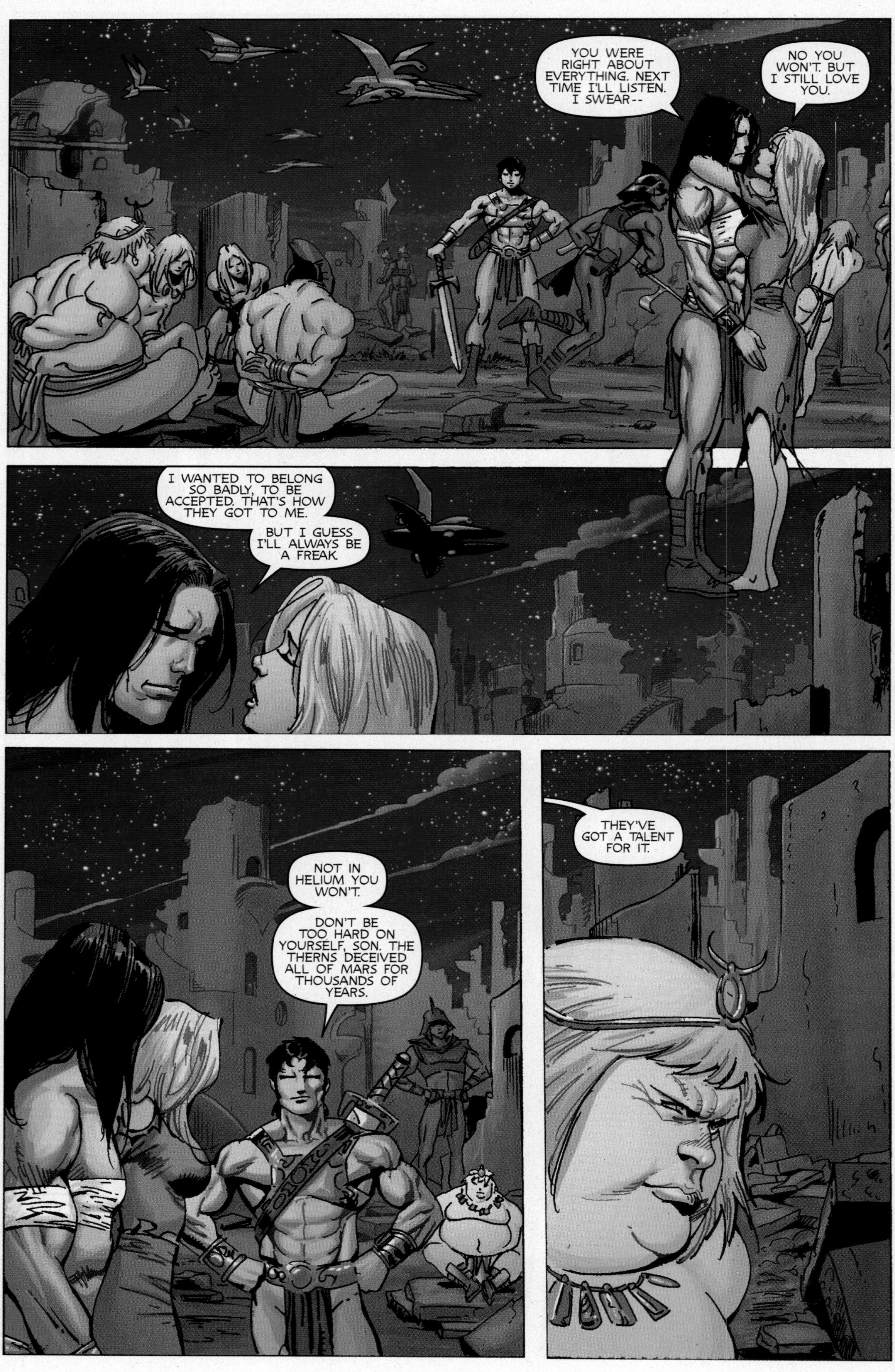
YOU WERE RIGHT ABOUT EVERYTHING. NEXT TIME I'LL LISTEN. I SWEAR--
NO YOU WON'T. BUT I STILL LOVE YOU.
I WANTED TO BELONG SO BADLY, TO BE ACCEPTED. THAT'S HOW THEY GOT TO ME.
BUT I GUESS I'LL ALWAYS BE A FREAK.
NOT IN HELIUM YOU WON'T.
DON'T BE TOO HARD ON YOURSELF, SON. THE THERNS DECEIVED ALL OF MARS FOR THOUSANDS OF YEARS.
THEY'VE GOT A TALENT FOR IT.

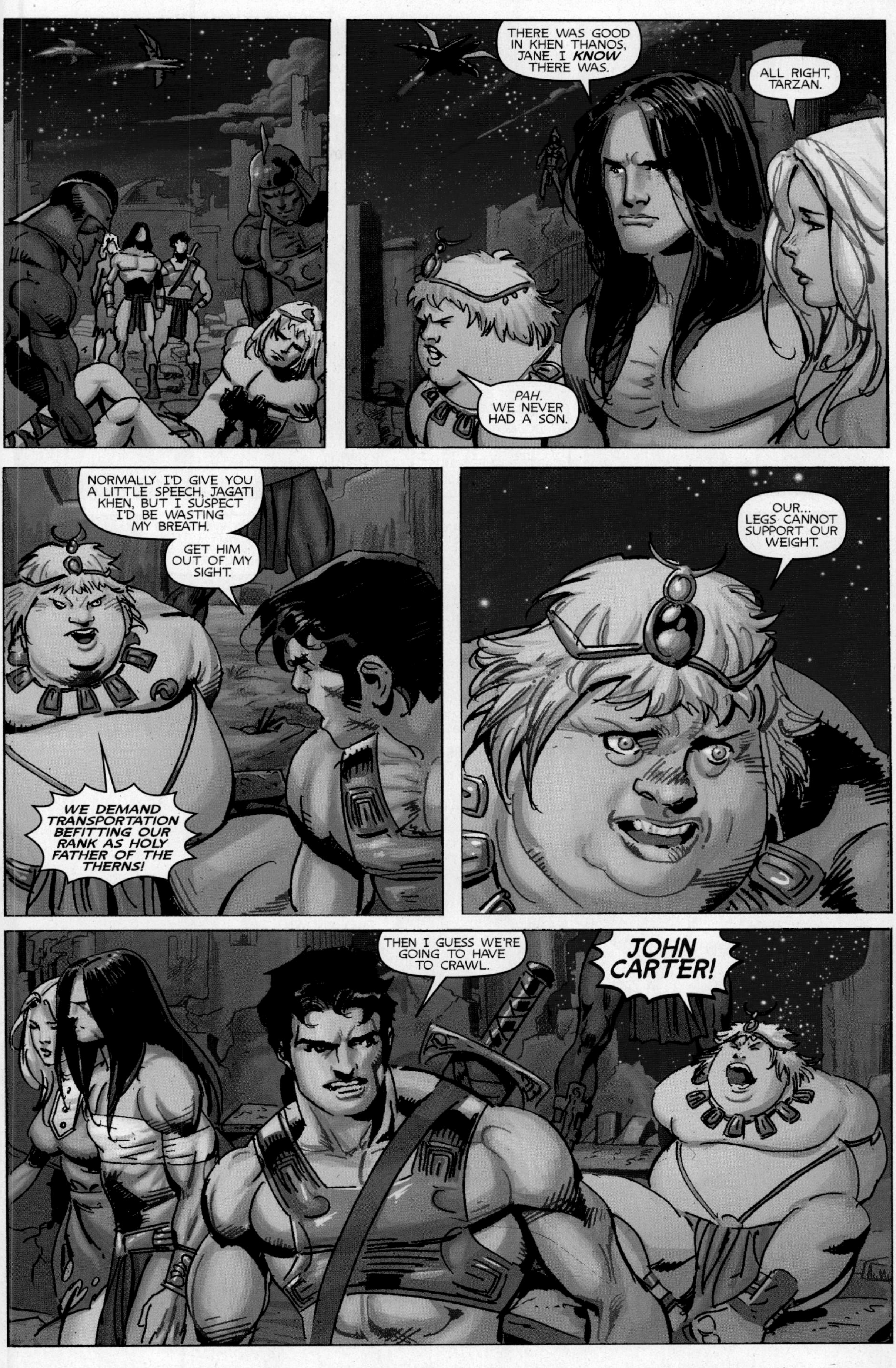
THERE WAS GOOD IN KHEN THANOS, JANE. I *KNOW* THERE WAS.
ALL RIGHT, TARZAN.
PAH. WE NEVER HAD A SON.
NORMALLY I'D GIVE YOU A LITTLE SPEECH, JAGATI KHEN, BUT I SUSPECT I'D BE WASTING MY BREATH.
GET HIM OUT OF MY SIGHT.
WE DEMAND TRANSPORTATION BEFITTING OUR RANK AS HOLY FATHER OF THE THERNS!
OUR... LEGS CANNOT SUPPORT OUR WEIGHT.
THEN I GUESS WE'RE GOING TO HAVE TO CRAWL.
JOHN CARTER!

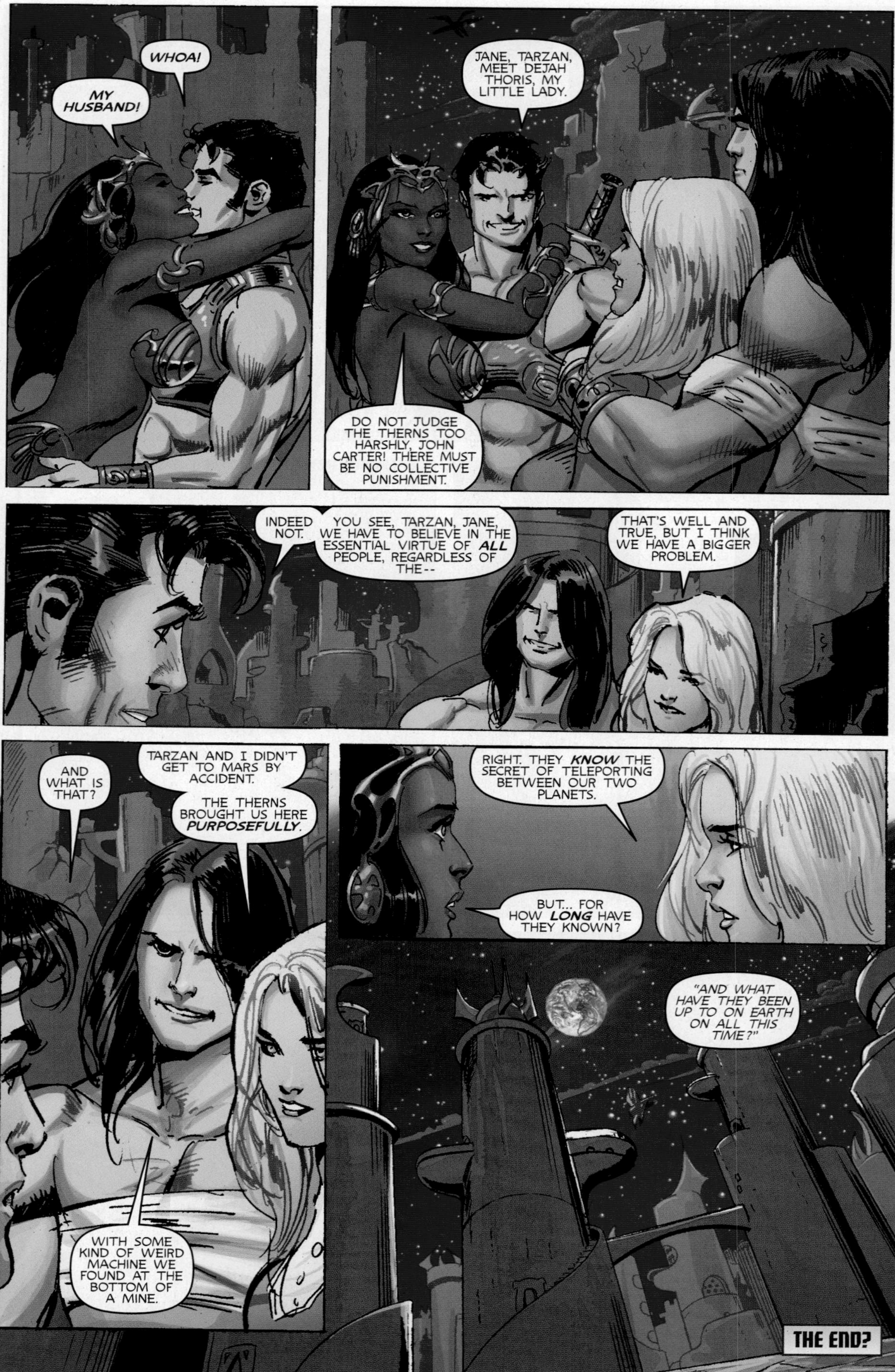
WHOA!
MY HUSBAND!
JANE, TARZAN, MEET DEJAH THORIS, MY LITTLE LADY.
DO NOT JUDGE THE THERNS TOO HARSHLY, JOHN CARTER! THERE MUST BE NO COLLECTIVE PUNISHMENT.
INDEED NOT.
YOU SEE, TARZAN, JANE, WE HAVE TO BELIEVE IN THE ESSENTIAL VIRTUE OF ALL PEOPLE, REGARDLESS OF THE--
THAT'S WELL AND TRUE, BUT I THINK WE HAVE A BIGGER PROBLEM.
AND WHAT IS THAT?
TARZAN AND I DIDN'T GET TO MARS BY ACCIDENT.
THE THERNS BROUGHT US HERE PURPOSEFULLY.
WITH SOME KIND OF WEIRD MACHINE WE FOUND AT THE BOTTOM OF A MINE.
RIGHT. THEY KNOW THE SECRET OF TELEPORTING BETWEEN OUR TWO PLANETS.
BUT... FOR HOW LONG HAVE THEY KNOWN?
"AND WHAT HAVE THEY BEEN UP TO ON EARTH ON ALL THIS TIME?"
THE END?

BONUS MATERIAL

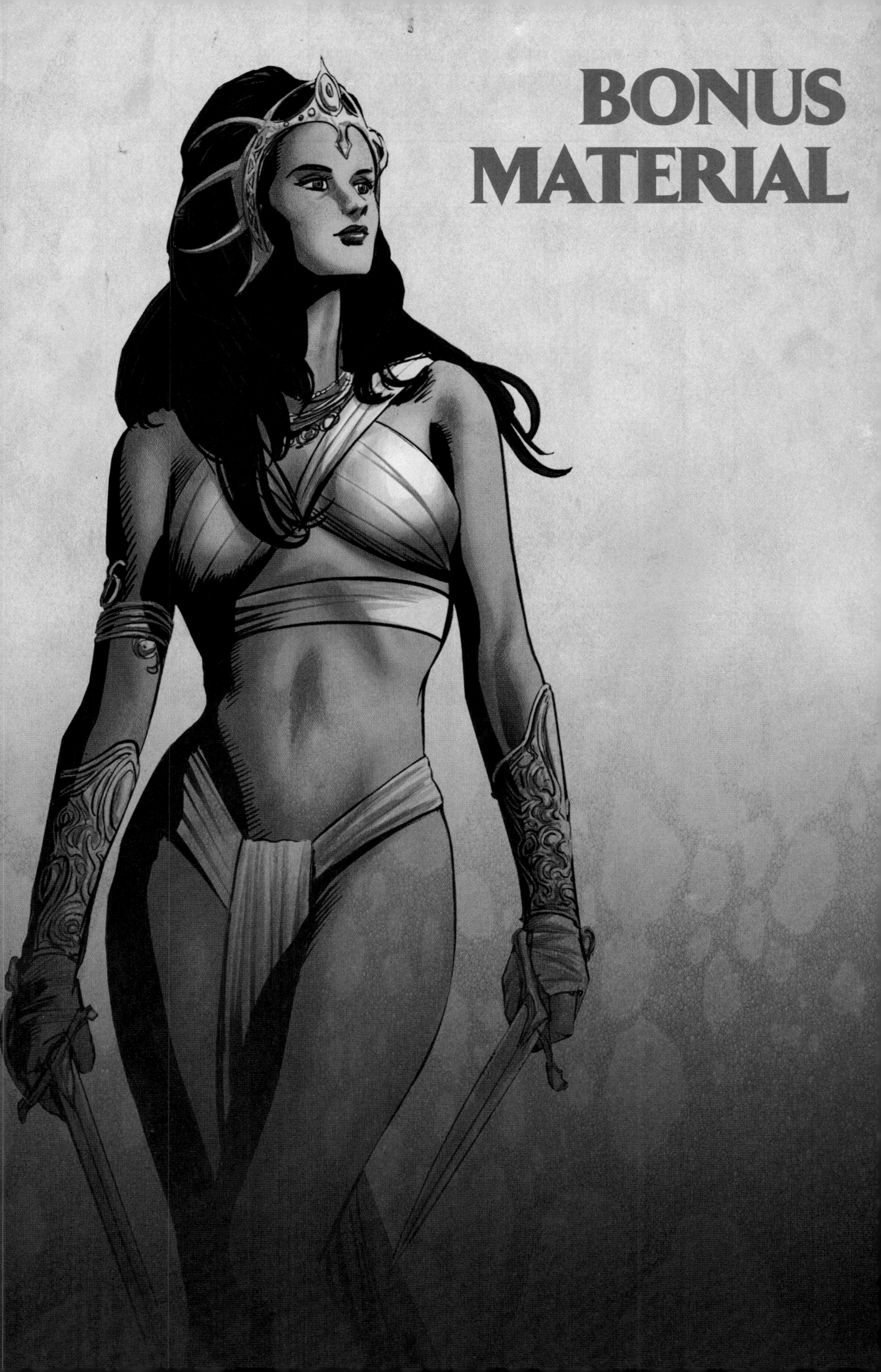

LORDS OF MARS #1: THE HUNTING PARTY
THE EYE OF THE GODDESS PART 1 OF 6
script by Arvid Nelson

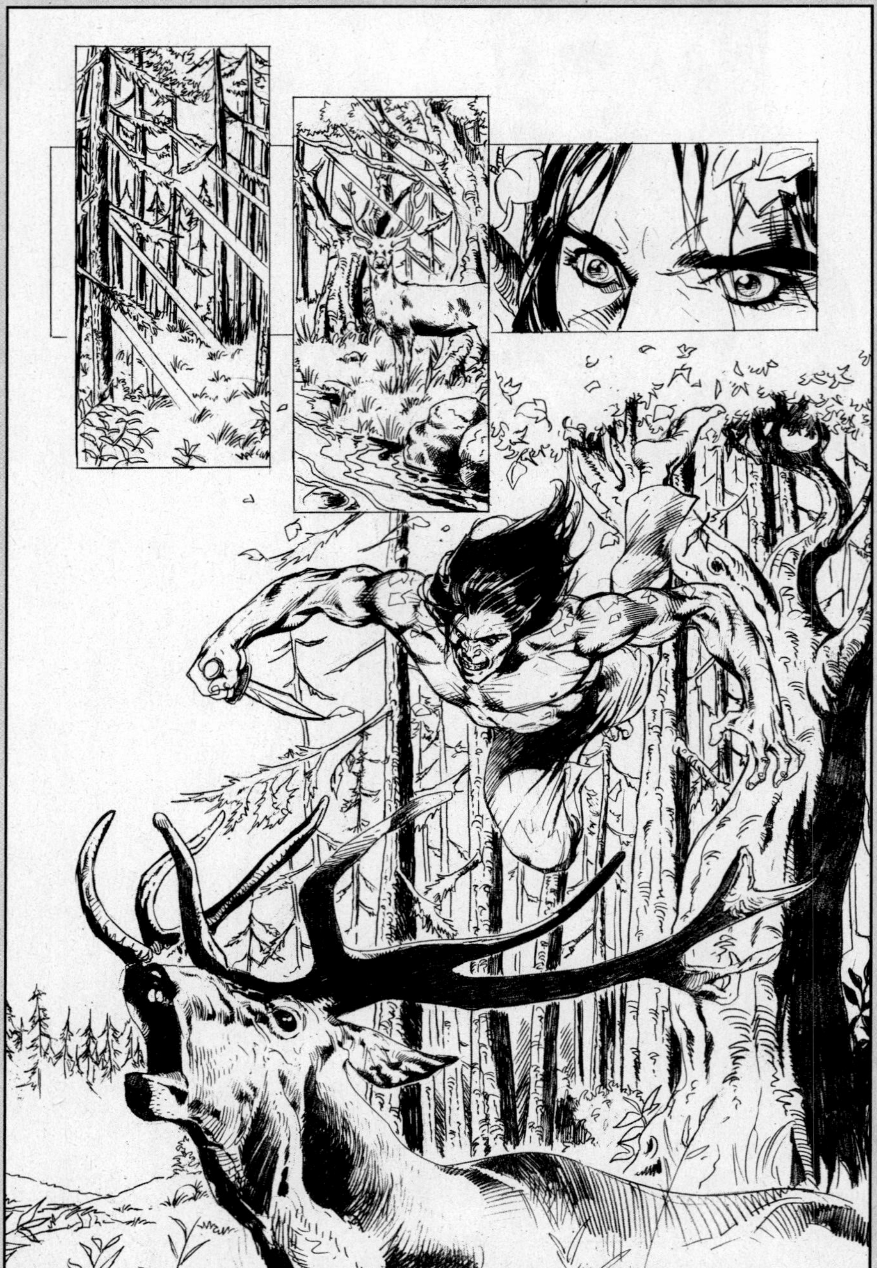

Welcome to Mars, Dear Artist!

PAGE 1

Splash. A small, clear stream winds through the bottom of a forested valley in Northerumberland, England. It's a sunny, beautiful Fall morning. Fingers of sunlight pierce the canopy of evergreens and broadleaf trees blazing in every shade of red, yellow and orange -- note, **Dear Colorist**.
A stag, a male deer, with antlers, is standing beside the stream.

All would be peaceful and idyllic, were it not for the fact that Tarzan is pouncing on the stag from the tree branches above, like a panther. He plunges a knife into the stag's next, killing it instantly in a spray of red.

Tarzan is stripped to the waist. He is wearing pants, regular, western-style woolen pants, but no shoes. Aside from the knife, he is unarmed. A big, dynamic action panel of our hero! And please note Tarzan is not in his "jungle" costume. He's not wearing his copper bracers or a loincloth, but his hair is still long.

Please leave room in the lower right hand corner for the titles, Dear Artist.

1. CAPTION (narration): Northumberland, England. 1910.
2. CAPTION (narration): The Viscountcy of Greystoke.
3. TARZAN (burst):   *HA!*
4. SFX: THAKK
5. CAPTION (title):   LORDS OF MARS #1
6. CAPTION (title):   THE EYE OF THE GODDESS, PART 1 OF 6:
7. CAPTION (title):   "THE HUNTING PARTY"

PAGE 2

Panel 1
Tarzan is in the foreground, wading through the underbrush with the deer slung over his shoulders in a fireman's carry (see reference). The blood from the carcass is dribbling down his chest, but he does not notice. He is sweating and straining, but he's happy. He's in his element. Tarzan is in a medium long or medium shot -- cut off at the waist or knees.

1. TARZAN (wavy, jumbled):   *Heff... heff...*

Panel 2
Reverse angle. Tarzan is in an extreme long shot now, facing away from the reader. He's still wading off into the woods with the stag slung over his back.

Unbeknownst to him, two men in black ulsters are spying on him. The two spies are in the foreground, their backs facing the reader. One of them is observing Tarzan with a pair of binoculars -- see the reference file for an example of binoculars from Tarzan's era.

An "ulster" is a type of overcoat men wore in Tarzan's day. See the reference file for an example.

The coats must be black, Dear Artist and **Dear Colorist**. The two guys spying on Tarzan are "bad guys", and we need to get that across visually. They are wearing black, woolen scarves wrapped around their necks and lower face, concealing their necks and mouths, making them look even more mysterious.

The two spies also happen to be *therns*, a race of evil, white-skinned people from Mars. Therns know the secret of teleporting from Mars to Earth -- more on that later. Here's what you need to know right now, Dear Artist:

1.   All therns are bald. Completely bald, with no fringe of hair around the edge of the scalp. The two men spying on Tarzan are bald. They are not wearing hats.

2.   Therns have very pale, Caucasian-looking skin -- please note, **Dear Colorist**. Not so pale as to be alarming, but it's noticeable. Like the Helgast from the Killzone video games.

Panel 3
Reverse angle, looking at the two thern spies in a medium shot or medium close-up -- cut off at the waist or shoulders. We can see the therns clearly now, in full detail. They are exchanging a sidelong glance that is more mysterious than evil. The one holding the binoculars has lowered them so he can look at his partner. The black of the scarves and the ulsters exaggerates the paleness of their skin. The eyes of both men are a pale, icy blue -- note, **Dear Colorist**.

Dear Artist, please don't let this panel or the one above get lost on the page. I know there's no dialog, but these two panels are critical for establishing the mystery of this story.

PAGE 3

Panel 1
Tarzan has emerged from the woods into a broad of expanse of lawns, the lawns of Greystoke Manor, his family's ancestral home. Greystoke Manor rears up in the background, regal, majestic and stately. See the **brideshead** series of images in the reference folder, Dear Artist, for an example of what the manor house looks like. This is Castle Howard, in England, if you want to search for more images, but it's not an important setting for this story.

Tarzan is in the foreground, with the stag still slung over his back. Jane, his wife, is calling and waving to Tarzan in the background. She is standing in a **topiary** garden (see the topiary series in the reference folder) on a terrace attached to the manor house. Tarzan is smiling.

Jane has blonde hair and blue eyes. There's a reference image of her in the file for this issue.

1. JANE (burst):   *Tarzan!*

Panel 2
Tarzan is now standing with Jane in the topiary garden. White gravel walkways wind through the geometrically shaped shrubs. Tarzan is shrugging the stag off of his shoulders and onto the gravel. Half his torso and one of his arms is covered in the stag's blood, but he doesn't notice. Jane just smiles dreamily at Tarzan, her husband, her hero.

2. TARZAN: Dinner is served, Jane.
3. SFX: SPLAK

Panel 3
Closer on Tarzan and Jane. They are close to each other now. Jane is cradling Tarzan's chin in one of her hands. She is smiling dreamily at him, and he is smiling dreamily at her. They are happy.

This could be a romance novel front cover.

4. JANE: Looks... delicious.

Panel 4
Tarzan's butler, a fussy, older man in an Edwardian tuxedo (see **butler.jpg** in the reference folder) emerges from the manor house in the background. Jane and Tarzan turn to look at him.

5. BUTLER: Lady Jane! Lord Greystoke, sir, I--

PAGE 4

Panel 1
Inset into panel 2, upper left-hand corner. Close on the butler's face. His eyes are wide with shock as he does a double-take at Tarzan's appearance. This is Edwardian England. He's not used to seeing long-haired men stripped to the waist and covered with blood.

Panel 2
Angle on Tarzan. He's covered with blood, and the dead stag is lying at his feet. He's holding up his hands in a gesture that reads "what did I do?" It's critical Tarzan look scary and wild in this panel, Dear Artist. We're not telling the reader "THE BUTLER IS SHOCKED AT TARZAN'S APPEARANCE" with words, so it has to be instantly clear from the art and the art alone. A little comic beat.

1. TARZAN: Is something wrong?

Panel 3
The butler has recovered from his shock and returned to his dignified aloofness. He's a professional. He purses his lips and turns his nose up slightly.

2. BUTLER: No. No indeed. Your Lordship.
3. BUTLER: I... have an invitation from Lord Marchmain, sir, an old acquaintance of your family.
4. BUTLER: He has organized a hunting party on his estates to welcome you to your ancestral home. Several local families of note will be in attendance.

Panel 4
Tarzan has dropped to his haunches. He is plunging his knife into the stag's belly, beginning the process of gutting and skinning the carcass. Jane looks on to one side. The butler is holding up a hand to Tarzan, motioning "hold on a moment!", but neither Jane nor Tarzan are looking at him. Another little comic beat.

5. TARZAN: Tell him I accept.
6. SFX: THAK
7. BUTLER: I... beg your pardon, sir, but has Your Lordship ever handled a firearm before?

Panel 5
Close on Tarzan, still squatting above the stag. He is sawing open its belly with his knife. Tarzan is grinning slyly at the fussy, overwrought butler over his shoulder. The butler is in the background, looking slightly perplexed. We can see Jane's feet and legs in the midground, but she's not important in this panel.

8. TARZAN: Hah! I've killed lions and crocodiles with nothing more than a rope and a knife...

PAGE 5

Panel 1
A pheasant (see reference) flaps into the sky in a nervous explosion of feathers. A rifle round flies past the bird, missing it completely. Please note, Dear Artist and **Dear Colorist** -- the sky is grey in this scene. We're cutting in time and place with this panel, and the grey sky will be a subtle way of hinting the shift to the reader.

1. CAPTION (voice):   "...what difficulty could I possibly have with a gun?"
2. SFX: KRAK
3. CAPTION (narration):   One week later.

Panel 2
A hunting party of English gentlemen, among them Tarzan and Jane, is assembled in a broad expanse of semi-wild meadows on the edge of a pine forest.

All the men, including Tarzan, are wearing standard hunting costumes worn by English gentlemen in the 1910s. See the **hunting party** series in the reference folder. The suits are all standard, drab English colors -- grey, brown, houndstooth, tweed. Please note that Tarzan is *not* wearing a hat. His hair is pulled back in a pony tail.

Jane is wearing a navy blue cloak with a hood that perfectly accents her blonde hair. Tarzan is holding a smoking rifle and looking up from the barrel -- he fired the shot in the previous panel. He is snarling with irritation.

Lord Marchmain, the guy hosting this hunting party, is standing right next to Tarzan. Marchmain is actually a thern. As such, he is completely bald, and his skin and eyes are exactly like that of the therns on page 2 of this issue -- take note, **Dear Colorist**. Marchmain is an older man, with a white, handlebar moustache.

Three other gentlemen complete the hunting party. They are younger men, about Tarzan's age. All have smart, short-clipped facial hair of varying styles. And they are all laughing at Tarzan, Lord Marchmain included. Tarzan's fellow aristocrats don't have any respect for him, and they're using his poor marksmanship as an excuse to ridicule him. That has to come across in every panel in this scene, Dear Artist -- Tarzan is not accepted by the English lords.

The three other gentlemen are also therns, like Marchmain, but they are wearing wigs that make their hair look completely normal. The men all have Marchmain's piercing blue thern eyes -- note, **Dear Colorist**.

The men are all using Winchester 1873 rifles -- see the reference folder. Jane is the only person without a gun.

| 4. TARZAN: | ***Damn.*** |
| 5. SFX: | HA Ha hA hA |

Panel 3
Closer on Marchmain and Tarzan. Marchmain is slapping Tarzan condescendingly on the back. Tarzan looks surly and irritated. He's clearing the spent casing from his Winchester '73 -- a lever-action rifle, see youtube.com/watch?v=kJ_nsfj8wfM for an example of how the chambering mechanism works (fast forward to about 2 minutes).

But Tarzan is no gun expert. He's unwisely grabbing the hot barrel in the process of clearing the spent round. The rest of the hunters are snickering at him behind his back. Jane looks on sympathetically.

| 6. MARCHMAIN: | I say, Greystoke. I find it rather hard to believe you really are a legendary big game hunter. |
| 7. TARZAN: | Give me a knife, give me a rock, anything but this blasted-- |

PAGE 6

Panel 1
Tarzan draws his hand back from the hot rifle barrel with sudden shock. Marchmain condescendingly chides him. The rest of the hunters snicker in the background.

| 1. TARZAN (burst): | ***Dah!*** |
| 2. MARCHMAIN: | Careful! The barrel gets quite hot, you know. |

Panel 2
Lord Marchmain turns to Jane and offers her his rifle. He grins mischievously at her -- he's trying to drive a wedge between Tarzan and Jane, but Jane refuses to take the bait. She holds up her hands as if to say "no thanks".

3. MARCHMAIN:	Why don't ***you*** show him how it's done, Jane.
4. JANE:	I think I'll pass, Lord Marchmain.
5. MARCHMAIN:	Come now. I'm told you Americans love your guns.

Panel 3
Close on Jane's beautiful face. She's frowning. She wishes neither she nor Tarzan had come on the hunting party.

| 6. JANE: | Not this American. |

Panel 4
One of other English lords, other than Marchmain, speaks up ("LORD #1" in the dialog below). Another of the lords, "LORD #2" in the dialog below, is standing near him, raising an eyebrow inquisitively. Tarzan glares at Lord #1 over his shoulder.

| 7. LORD #1: | I've got it! You just need the proper ***motivation***, Greystoke. |
| 8. LORD #2: | Oh? |

Panel 5
Lord #1 finishes his joke, and his peers, including Lord Marchmain, erupt with laughter.

9. LORD #1: I've got several tropical specimens growing in my hothouse. If you manage to hit one thing -- just one! -- I will **personally** give you a banana!
10. SFX: HAA HA h HA

Panel 6
Tarzan is infuriated. Remember, he was raised by apes, Dear Artist. His savage ape nature is always threatening to explode to the surface. A lot like The Incredible Hulk, in fact. Tarzan stabs a finger at Lord #1 and shouts at him.

Jane has to hold Tarzan back. She's the only one who can keep him from flying off the handle. She shouts at him like she's scolding a dog -- it's the only way to get through to him when he's angry.

Marchmain and the rest of the therns are laying a trap for Tarzan -- they're going to force him to lose control of himself, and then herd him into a cave, where he'll be teleported to Mars. Just for your information, Dear Artist. This will all become clear to the reader later.

11. TARZAN (burst): *I'll hit something all right!*
12. JANE: Tarzan!

PAGE 7

Panel 1
Jane and Tarzan glare at Lord #1. Lord #1 is pursing his lips and turning his nose up while smiling arrogantly at the two of them.

1. JANE: How dare you, sir?
2. LORD #1: Just having a bit of fun, Lady Jane. You and your husband really ought to be less touchy, or you're going to find life in England rather intolerable.

Panel 2
Jane and Tarzan continue to face off against Lord #1. We can clearly see the forest in the background. An older man, one of Marchmain's gamekeepers, is trotting out of the forest. The gamekeeper is dressed much like the gentlemen, but he's more shabby looking, and he's wearing a bowler hat. See the **gamekeeper.jpg** image in the reference folder. He's holding a shotgun in one hand, with a strap for slinging it over his back. The gamekeeper is in an extreme long shot.

The gamekeeper is completely bald, with piercing blue eyes -- **Dear Colorist**. You guessed it! He's another thern in disguise, part of the trap.

3. JANE: You are doing a **fine** job of making England intolerable **without** any help from us, thank you very much!
4. JANE: Let's go, Tarzan. We don't need to put up with--
5. GAMEKEEPER (burst): *Lord Marchmain!*

Panel 3
The gamekeeper is standing face-to-face with Lord Marchmain. He is out of breath, and now he is holding his hat meekly in one hand. Marchmain looks at the gamekeeper as if he were a slave. Jane and Tarzan aren't important in this panel, but if we can see them, they're just looking on inquisitively.

6. GAMEKEEPER: Lord Marchmain, sir.

7. MARCHMAIN: What is it, man?
8. GAMEKEEPER: Caught another one, Lordship.

Panel 4
Now we *do* see Jane and Tarzan. They are looking inquisitively at Marchmain and the gamekeeper. No one is paying attention to them or to what Jane is saying. The gamekeeper is pointing off into the woods with his shotgun with one hand and clutching his hat with the other.

9. JANE: Another what?
10. GAMEKEEPER: Right by the old mine, sir.

Panel 5
Lord Marchmain is grim-faced and pissed off. He is framed dead-on, striding right towards the reader as he clutches his rifle. His gamekeeper is by his side, pointing ahead. Tarzan, Jane and the rest of the hunters follow behind.

11. MARCHMAIN: Take me there *now*.

Panel 6
Close on Jane and Tarzan -- medium close-up of them, cutting them off at the shoulders. They exchange curious looks. What's going on? An end beat, transitioning to the second half of this scene.

PAGE 8

Panel 1
Big panel, the biggest on this page. A poacher (an illegal, trespassing hunter) is lying on a carpet of rust-colored pine needles in the middle of a pine forest. His right leg is caught in a mantrap -- a device a lot like a bear trap, but without serrated jaws. See the reference file for two examples of mantraps.

The poacher is wincing in pain and clutching his trapped leg. Beads of sweat appear on his brow. An old, beat-up shotgun lies on the ground beside him. He's dressed a lot like the gamekeeper, but even shabbier. His clothes are tatty and patched up. The poacher is not wearing a hat, and he's completely bald, with piercing blue eyes -- another thern, **Dear Colorist**.

This panel looks down on the poacher, as if from the point of view of someone standing over him.

He's a pitiful sight.

Dear Letterer: the off-panel voice is coming from the direction of the point of view of this panel.

1. POACHER (wavy, jumbled): *Ah*...
2. VOICE (off): A poacher!

Panel 2
The hunting party stands over the trapped man. Marchmain is in front, with Tarzan and Jane nearby and clearly visible. Tarzan and Jane are the only ones who look concerned. Everyone else is glowering down at the trapped poacher as if he were a rat. The gamekeeper is still with the party.

This panel looks up at the hunting party, as if from the point of view of the poacher. We do not need to see the poacher in this panel.

3. MARCHMAIN: The third this year.
4. MARCHMAIN: *<sigh...>*

Panel 3
Close on the poacher. His jaw is stubbly. There's pathetic fear on his face. The reader should feel sympathy for him.

5. POACHER: Lord Marchmain, I--I didn't mean any trouble I didn't!
6. POACHER: Me wife had another child, Lordship, and I was only trying to--

PAGE 9

Panel 1
Lord Marchmain stands over the poacher with look of mild disgust on his face. The poacher desperately pleads with Marchmain.

1. MARCHMAIN: A *likely* story.
2. POACHER: Please, Lordship, me leg, I think it's broke--

Panel 2
Angle on Jane, Marchmain, and Marchmain's gamekeeper. Of the three, the gamekeeper is the least important. He is holding up a large, iron key, so that the reader can see it. Jane looks at Marchmain with disapproval. Marchmain looks coldly down a the poacher, not visible in this panel.

3. JANE: I thought mantraps were *illegal*.
4. MARCHMAIN: So is poaching, my dear. Set him free.
5. GAMEKEEPER: Aye, Lord Marchmain.

Panel 3
The gamekeeper is squatting down beside the trapped poacher. He has inserted the key into the mantrap, and he's prying the jaws open. The poacher pulls his leg free, but he remains lying on the ground. He winces in pain.

6. SFX: SKEEK
7. POACHER: *Ah!*

Panel 4
Angle on the entire group. Tarzan looks at Marchmain, anger flashing on his face, but Marchmain remains cool and aloof. The poacher is lying on his side in the pine needles. He can't get up. He

looks desperately up at Lord Marchmain.

8. MARCHMAIN: Now. You are going to crawl back home.
9. TARZAN: *What?*
10. POACHER: Lord Marchmain, sir, it's *miles* to the nearest road!

Panel 5
Close on Lord Marchmain, losing his composure a little bit. Poachers really piss him off. Spittle flies from his mouth. Consider a stylized background, Dear Artist, to accentuate Marchmain's burst of anger.

11. MARCHMAIN: *YOU ARE GOING TO CRAWL BACK TO WHEREVER YOU CAME FROM!*

PAGE 10

Panel 1
Close on Tarzan and Marchmain. Tarzan looks pissed. Marchmain has regained his composure. He's back to his cool aloofness. He stares coldly down at the poacher, who is not visible in this panel.

1. MARCHMAIN: Let this be a lesson to you. If I catch you on my land again, I'll have you shot.
2. MARCHMAIN: Is that perfectly clear?
3. TARZAN: You can't be serious. This man needs a doctor--

Panel 2
One of the other members of the hunting party, "LORD #3", speaks up. He works the lever of his Winchester and grins rakishly. Time for a little fun! His friends -- everyone except for Jane and Tarzan -- look at him with inquisitive smiles. They're already thinking the same thing he is. We must clearly see Lord #3 cocking the rifle in this panel.

4. LORD #3:   Let's help this chap on his way, shall we? Have a little sport.
5. SFX: CHAK

Panel 3
Lord #3 takes aim and fires at the ground at the crippled poacher's feet. The bullet impacts in the dirt, kicking up a spray of pine needles. The bullet does not -- not -- hit the poacher, but it does cause him to cry out and crawl away from the hunting party in abject terror. Everyone except for Jane and Tarzan think what Lord #3 is doing is riotously funny. Jane and Tarzan are dumbstruck with horror. Everyone else is laughing heartily.

6. SFX: KRAK
7. POACHER (burst): *Ah!*
8. SFX: HA hA Ha HA

PAGE 11

Panel 1
Lord #2 takes a shot at the dirt at the poacher's feet, kicking up another spray of earth and pine needles, and forcing the poor poacher to keep crawling away from the hunting party. Again, he's not hitting the poacher, he's just forcing him to crawl away, like a villain in a Wild West movie forcing the wimpy bartender to "dance, boy" by firing his six-guns into the floorboards.

Again, everyone but Tarzan and Jane (and the poacher) are having a great time.

1. LORD #2:   Daresay we've found something you can hit, Greystoke!
2. SFX: KRAK
3. POACHER (burst):   ***N-no! Your Lordships--***

Panel 2
Two more of the hunters fire at the ground behind the poacher, who keeps crawling pathetically away. Tarzan is grabbing onto Lord #1 by his hunting jacket, forcing his shot to go wide. Again -- no one is actually hitting the poacher. Tarzan looks really upset. His fellow aristocrats are still having a great time.

4. LORD #1 (burst):   ***Teach the miscreant a lesson!***
5. LORD #3 (burst):   ***Crawl back under your rock, you!***
6. TARZAN: Stop this now. I'm *warning* you--
7. SFX: KRAKK KRAK

Panel 3
Lord #1 swats Tarzan's hand off of his jacket and snarls at Tarzan. Tarzan is losing control. The savage ape is coming out. His eyes flash with anger and disbelief -- how *dare* Lord #1 defy him?

8. LORD #1:   If you're not going to join in, Greystoke, then ***stay the bloody hell out of our way!***

Panel 4
Tarzan stands rigidly in place. He's snarling like an ape, losing control. Jane is desperately trying to calm him down, but he's too pissed off to listen to her. It's too late. In the background, the huntsmen continue merrily firing on the poor, helpless poacher.

9. JANE (burst):   Tarzan, no! You'll only make things--
10. TARZAN: Ah... ah... ah...

PAGE 12

Panel 1
Tarzan officially loses it. He's in savage ape-mode now, a predatory beast of the jungle. He forgets his rifle, throwing it aside like the useless stick it is, and lunges towards Lord #1, smashing him

across the face with a backhand swipe of one of his iron fists. Lord #1 doesn't even have time to bring his rifle to bear. His head whips back and he goes flying backwards, blood and spittle flying out of his mouth. His wig stays in place.

The other lords, including Marchmain and his gamekeeper, have swiveled around to face Tarzan. They are not pointing their rifles at Tarzan, they have not had time to react. The pitiful poacher is lying on the ground in front of them. He is looking over his shoulder at Tarzan.

Jane is prominent in this panel, throwing her hands up in front of her face. This is a disaster. You can see the fear in her face. She's not afraid for Tarzan, she's afraid of what he'll do to the others, and the consequences that must follow.

Big panel!

1. SFX (Tarzan):	RAAH!
2. SFX:	SKASHH
3. JANE (burst):	*No, Tarzan!*

Panel 2
Tarzan leaps onto Lord #2 and crumples him with a double-fisted downwards smash, right on the bridge of the man's nose. The man drops his rifle without even getting the chance to fire. In the background, Marchmain and the one remaining lord are finally reacting, bringing their rifles to bear.

The gamekeeper, if we can see him, is still dumbstruck. The crippled poacher observes wide-eyed, still sprawled on the ground, as he will be for the rest of this scene.

4. SFX (Tarzan):	RAH! RAH!
5. SFX:	KRASH
6. MARCHMAIN (burst):	*He's gone mad!*

PAGE 13

Panel 1
Tarzan smashes into Lord #3, shoulder-tackling him with all the fury of a freight train. Lord #3 has a chance to fire his rifle, but not to aim. The rifle harmlessly explodes behind Tarzan's head. Lord #3 winces in pain, his eyes screwed up tight.

1. SFX (Tarzan):	RAH! RAH!
2. SFX:	THWACK

Panel 2
Lord Marchmain has turned to flee, wisely. But Tarzan is bounding up to him on all fours, like a bull ape on a rampage. Tarzan's hunting suit is ripped and tattered by this point. There's fear on Marchmain's face and savage intent on Tarzan's.

3. MARCHMAIN (burst):	*Stay away from me! Madman! I'll--*
4. SFX (Tarzan):	RAH! RAH!

Panel 3
Tarzan has grabbed Marchmain by the collar of his jacket. He is forcing Marchmain's head into the pine needles, face-first. Fury on Tarzan's face. Marchmain loses his hunting cap, exposing his bald head.

5. MARCHMAIN (burst):   *Gah!*
6. SFX: KRUNCH

Panel 4
Tarzan is straddling Marchmain's back and raising up one of his fists to bring it smashing down on the back of Marchmain's head, like an MMA fighter. Marchmain cowers in terror, covering his face like a fighter who's given up and is waiting for the referee to pull the other guy off. He looks at Tarzan through his fingers, terror on his face. Tarzan screams with fury. He's gonna kill Marchmain. Consider a stylized background for this panel, Dear Artist, to highlight the intensity of the moment.

7. SFX (Tarzan):   URAAAH-AH!

PAGE 14

Panel 1
But no. Jane has fearlessly rushed up to Tarzan to stop him from killing Marchmain. She grabs onto his wrist with one of her hands and desperately pleads with him. Tarzan twists around to look at her. Just seeing Jane is enough to calm him down. There's a bewildered look on his face. He's still mounted on Marchmain's back.

Lords #1 – 3 are sprawled on the ground around Tarzan, clutching their bruised and battered bodies, but none of them are seriously injured. Some of their wigs have come partly loose. The gamekeeper and the poacher look on, still dumbstruck.

1. JANE (burst):   *No!*

Panel 2
Closer on Tarzan and Jane. Tarzan looks confused and afraid, like an ape. He's a little disoriented, but he's coming back to his senses and he knows something bad happened. Jane is still trying to soothe him, very gently.

2. TARZAN (wavy, jumbled):   *Jane?*
3. JANE: No, Tarzan.

Panel 3
The battered lords are picking themselves off the ground and coming to their senses. They are pointing accusingly at Tarzan, their eyes wide with fear. The gamekeeper is readying his shotgun.

Jane is still beside Tarzan, who is still on top of Marchmain. Jane pleading with the hunters, holding up her hands in a "let's just calm down" gesture. Both she and Tarzan are looking at the hunters.

4. LORD #2 (burst): *Greystoke's a madman! He was going to kill Lord Marchmain--we all saw him!*
5. JANE: H-hold on, let's all just calm down--

Panel 4
But the lords aren't listening to Jane. They pick up their rifles and take aim at Jane and Tarzan. Very important: none of the lords are actually hitting Tarzan or Jane. They are missing on purpose, trying to scare Tarzan into running away.

And they're succeeding. Tarzan is back in savage ape-mode. He snatches up Jane in one of his arms, as effortlessly as if she were a teddy bear, and bounds away from the rifles on his free hand as well as his feet, like a frightened ape. He is terrified, like a hunted animal. All he can think about is "RUN AWAY". Jane has lost control of him again. She shouts at him, but it has no effect.

Dear Letterer: the first two balloons in this panel, #6 and #7, can be tailless.

6. LORD #3 (burst): *Madman!*
7. LORD #2 (burst): *Raving brute!*
8. SFX: KRAK
9. JANE (burst): *Tarzan!*
10. SFX (Tarzan): AH! AH!

PAGE 15

Panel 1
The gamekeeper and the three English lords who accompanied Marchmain on the hunt are in the foreground, their backs facing the reader. They are chasing after and firing at Tarzan and Jane, who are fleeing into the background. Jane is slung over Tarzan's back, a lot like in **page 15 panel 1.png** in the reference folder. Tarzan and Jane are almost lost in the underbrush, but the reader can see them clearly.

Note that we do **not** see Marchmain or the poacher in this panel.

1. LORD #1 (burst): *Kill the monkey man!*
2. SFX: KRAK

Panel 2
Lord Marchmain and the poacher are in the foreground of this panel. Marchmain is offering the poacher a hand, helping him get to his feet. The poacher's leg definitely isn't broken. Strange.

In the background, we can see the gamekeeper and the three English gentlemen, disappearing into the underbrush and firing their rifles. Tarzan and Jane are nowhere to be seen.

Marchmain and the poacher are the "stars" of this panel, Dear Artist, even though they don't have any lines.

3. LORD #2 (burst): *Bloody savage, kill him!*
4. SFX: KRAK KRAKK

Panel 3

Closer on Marchmain and the poacher -- a medium shot of them, cutting them off at the waist. The poacher is standing, and both men are smiling mysteriously at each other. Marchmain is clapping the poacher on the shoulder. The trap is set.

This panel needs to be big, Dear Artist. We need to "hang a sign" on the strange behavior of Marchmain and the poacher. This panel should make the reader wonder "What's going on? I've got to find out more!!"

5. MARCHMAIN: Perfect.

PAGE 16

Panel 1

Cut to Tarzan and Jane. They have reached the entrance to an abandoned mine -- just a black hole in a shallow hillside, with old, rotting support timbers supporting the entrance. The mine has clearly been abandoned for a long time.

Tarzan is fleeing into the mine, with Jane still over his shoulder. In his animal terror, the mine represents safety to Tarzan. Jane, of course, realizes she and Tarzan will only be trapped in the mine. She's trying to reason with Tarzan, but she's not having any success.

A few rifle rounds from the hunters and gamekeeper -- none of whom are visible in this panel -- are screaming into the panel and burrowing into the support timbers of the mine.

1. JANE (burst):   *No! Tarzan, we'll be trapped if we--*
2. SFX: KRAK SPWANGG

Panel 2

Tarzan and Jane have entered the mine, but there's a sudden drop a few yards/meters after the entrance. Tarzan and Jane tumble into the abyss. There is terror on both of their faces. Who knows how far down the bottom is? Tarzan has let go of Jane.

3. JANE (burst):   *TARZAN!*

Panel 3

Fortunately for Tarzan and Jane, the landing is only about twelve feet (three and a half meters) below, and sandbags are piled up at the base of the drop off, cushioning Tarzan's and Jane's fall. Tarzan and Jane slam into the sandbags. Neither of them are hurt in any way, but it's okay to leave the reader guessing.

The interior of the mine is very gloomy, of course. There's a tunnel that continues at the base of the drop off, leading to who-knows-where. An old trolley-car track winds into the dark passage.

Check out **lords01page16.png** in the reference for a diagram of the cave, Dear Artist. It should make the layout of the mine crystal clear.

4. SFX: PAKK

PAGE 17

Panel 1

Cut to Mars, or "Barsoom". Before I go any further, Dear Artist, download the main reference file for Warlord of Mars at rexmundi.net/barsoomreference.zip. Most of your questions about the visuals will be answered in there.

John Carter and Kantos Kan are standing in the foreground, in a moss-covered plaza of Korad, one of the ancient, dead cities of Mars. John Carter is the hero of Warlord of Mars, of course. Kantos Kan is a red Martian, one of John Carter's first allies on Mars and now the commander of Carter's aerial navy. An image of Kantos Kan is included in the reference file for *this* issue (not the main reference for Warlord of Mars).

Carter and Kantos are grimly observing a pile of bloody, hacked-up white ape corpses sprawled on the moss in the foreground. In the background, a stream of battered, bandaged Helium warriors is limping by. Some of the men cannot walk on their own and are leaning on their comrades for support. The men look wearied and beaten.
Airships of all sizes patrol the air above the city.

Reference for the airships, the white apes and the red Martians is in the main file for Warlord of Mars. The plaza itself is a wide expanse of mossy turf, like a lawn. Huge, weird, skyscraper-like buildings rise into the sky all around the plaza. Burroughs never describes the dead cities of Mars in much detail, so use your imagination, Dear Artist. Just keep in mind Korad is deserted. Aside from the white apes, nothing lives there.

The symbol of Helium, John Carter's nation, is a yellow sunburst on a field of red. Everyone wears the Helium sunburst on their capes. The Helium sunburst flies from the decks of the airships above.

Dear Colorist -- we're in Mars now, so please adjust the color palette accordingly. The moss covering the ground is yellowish, but otherwise most Martian stone and soil is reddish to reddish-brown. The sky is orange. Also, note the capes the men are wearing are red, with yellow sunbursts.

1. CAPTION (narration):	*Mars.*
2. CAPTION (narration):	*The ancient ruins of Korad.*
3. CAPTION (narration):	*John Carter has begun a campaign to rid the Red Planet of the terrible white apes, but he is not off to an auspicious start...*
4. KAN:	We've cleared the southwestern district, Warlord, but casualties are high.

Panel 2
Closer on Kantos Kan and John Carter. The first panel of this page was about introducing the setting. This panel is about introducing the characters.

5. KAN:	I recommend we move to full-scale aerial bombardment. Wipe this place off the face of Barsoom and be *done* with it, John Carter.
6. CARTER:	Whatever it takes.

Panel 3
A messenger -- a Helium warrior -- has trotted up to Carter and Kantos Kan. He is saluting crisply at the two men. Carter and Kantos Kan are swiveling to face the messenger.

7. MESSENGER:	*Warlord!* An emissary from the Holy Therns has arrived. He said it is most urgent and requests an immediate audience.

Panel 4
Close on Carter and Kantos Kan. Kantos Kan is pumping his right fist into his left palm. He's pissed off. He doesn't like the therns. Carter is more patient -- he can't afford to be emotional. He's holding up a hand to Kantos Kan, in a friendly gesture reading "patience".

8. KAN: Of all the *arrogance...*
9. CARTER: Hold, Kantos Kan.

PAGE 18

Panel 1
Cut to the tops of one of the abandoned skyscrapers of Korad. A large landing platform projects
from the side of the skyscraper, like a mushroom growing off the side of an upright tree. The landing pad is lined with Helium warriors at strict attention. The spires of Korad and the Arizona-like
landscape of Mars spread out in the distance. the mighty battleships of Helium float majestically in
the sky.

A luxurious eight-man airship hovers at the far end of the landing platform, with a gangplank
extending from an open hatch and touching down on the surface. A long, purple carpet (**Dear
Colorist**) extends from the gangplank to the center of the landing pad, where John Carter and
Kantos Kan are meeting with a delegation of the therns.

I've already described the therns a little bit, but this is very important -- all therns on Mars wear
long, blond wigs. Therns never appear bald in public, it would be horribly embarrassing to them.
The therns in this scene share the pale skin and blue eyes of Lord Marchmain (**Dear Colorist**), but
the long blond hair is critically different. Therns all wear purple capes -- purple is their color.

The thern emissary and his half-dozen attendants are kowtowing in front of Carter and Kantos Kan
like praying Muslims -- see **prayer.jpg** in the reference file for this issue.

All the characters are in an extreme long shot. This is a big panel, Dear Artist, a "wow" panel,
showing off the otherworldly grandeur of Mars. Think of a big, splashy shot from The Empire
Strikes Back, of the Millennium Falcon docking at Cloud City. That's exactly what this panel is.

1. CAPTION (voice): "Let's hear what he has to say."
2. THERN EMISSARY: O wise and benevolent Warlord!

Panel 2
Closer on Carter, Kantos and the thern delegation. Carter looks half amused, half annoyed by the
over-the-top submissiveness of the therns. He knows the therns would slit his throat if they got the
chance. Kantos Kan is folding his arms over his chest. He does not look amused.

The thern emissary is a typical thern -- effeminate, devious and very pretty. He's clearly the leader of the delegation, as he's wearing the most jewelry, including a bejeweled golden circlet around his head.

3. THERN EMISSARY: Your glory exceeds that of the sun, and your power is unrivalled throughout all Barsoom.

4. THERN EMISSARY: Thank you for deigning to meet with me, your humble and loyal servant, on such short notice.

5. CARTER: All right, man. On your feet. What's this all about?

PAGE 19

Seven panel page, Dear Artist! Please make room for the words.

Panel 1
The thern emissary is on one knee now. So are all his men. He is calmly looking up at Carter.

1. THERN EMISSARY: The white apes, Warlord. According to our ancient faith, their bodies are vessels for the souls of slain therns.

2. THERN EMISSARY: You have conquered my people, and we therns acknowledge your mastery.

Panel 2
Close-up of the thern emissary. He his entourage are standing now, but all we see in this panel is the emissary's head. His facial expression suggests sadness, but he's making a veiled threat.

3. THERN EMISSARY: But this wholesale slaughter of the apes is deeply offensive to us. You must respect our beliefs, or there could be... unpleasant consequences.

Panel 3
Kantos Kan and Carter. Kantos Kan's arms are still folded over his chest. He is glowering at the therns. Carter is calmer.

4. KAN: Now that sounds like a threat to me. Those filthy apes are a men ace. The sooner they're gone, the better!

5. CARTER: What do you suggest I do?

Panel 4
Kantos, Carter and the thern emissary.

6. THERN EMISSARY: Ah. Our new leader, Jagati Khen, has formally assumed his title of Holy Father of the Therns.

7. THERN EMISSARY: Khen's *first* act as Holy Father was to swear allegiance to you, Warlord. Of course.

8. KAN: Of course.

Panel 5
Angle on the therns. The emissary is steepling his hands and making a little mini bow -- a gesture of false humility and deference.

9. THERN EMISSARY: But our religion precludes the Holy Father from leaving his home in the Valley Dor.

10. THERN EMISSARY: He therefore humbly requests you travel there to discuss this matter with him in person.

Panel 6

Angle on Carter and Kantos Kan. Kantos Kan is smiling for the first time. Carter is smiling, too.

11. KAN:	Hah! Let *him* come to the Warlord if he's so anxious to talk.
12. CARTER:	I'll consider it, thern.

Panel 7

The thern emissary is pleading with Carter, a little bit like Tarzan's butler from the beginning of this issue. Carter looks annoyed. He's done talking. He's waving the therns away, "shoo, shoo".

13. THERN EMISSARY:	Mighty Warlord, Jagati Khen would be most grateful if you could extend him the favor of a definite--
14. CARTER:	*I'll consider it.*
15. CARTER:	Now I must take my leave. Good day.

PAGE 20

Panel 1

The thern emissary and his entourage are in the foreground, walking towards the reader. They are all exchanging cryptic smiles, like Lord Marchmain and the poacher on the last panel of page 15. Although the therns don't speak in this panel, they are the "stars". The reader must clearly understand they are up to no good, even though we're not saying "THEY'RE UP TO SOMETHING" with dialog.

Carter and Kantos Kan are in the background, looking at the backs of the therns. Please try to make it clear the therns can't hear Carter and Kantos, Dear Artist. But even if they could hear, they wouldn't care.

1. KAN:	Well, they're not lacking for boldness. I'll give them that.

Panel 2

Carter and Kan are in the foreground, walking off the landing platform. Two old comrades talking business. Kantos Kan looks at Carter with concern.

2. CARTER:	I might as well go. The therns are defanged, after all. They clearly want some thing from us, and it's not the apes--maybe we can give it to them and avoid a pointless rebellion.

3. KAN: How can we ensure your safety, Warlord?

Panel 3
Carter is grinning at Kantos Kan and throwing an arm around his shoulder. With his other arm he's pointing at something off panel, something to his side. Kantos Kan smiles inquisitively.

4. CARTER: We've got ways. Several thousand ways, actually.
5. KAN: Where?
6. CARTER: Right out there, Kantos Kan! Right out there.

Panel 4
Carter's pointing arm and hand are in the foreground, pointing into the background. Now we can see what Carter was pointing to -- Helium's invincible air navy. A mighty battleship is drifting by. Two or three one-man scout bikes are zipping past it like jet fighters screaming past a blimp. The sunburst of Helium snaps proudly from the battleship. More Helium warships are visible in the distance.

Big panel! The biggest on this page, the last we'll see of Mars for this issue.

7. CARTER (off):   The fleet.

PAGE 21

Panel 1
Back on Earth, in the abandoned mine where Tarzan and Jane are trapped. Tarzan is sitting up in the sandbags and clutching his head. The fall snapped him out of his apish panic. He's back to being a human again. He winces like he has a hangover, like Bruce Banner recovering from a Hulk episode.

1. CAPTION (narration):   *Earth.*
2. TARZAN (wavy, jumbled):   *Ahh...*

Panel 2
Tarzan realizes that Jane is nearby, and that she might be hurt. He rushes over to her, concern on his face. Jane is still lying in the sandbags. She's okay, but it's taking her longer to gather her senses.

3. TARZAN (burst):   **Jane!**

Panel 3
Tarzan is holding Jane in his arms, very gently. There's concern and love in his eyes. Jane is smiling weakly at Tarzan. This panel highlights Jane's and Tarzan's emotional connection.

4. TARZAN: Jane, are you all right?
5. JANE (wavy, jumbled):   *I... think so...*

Panel 4
Angle on Jane and Tarzan. Both of them are sitting up in the sandbags. Tarzan looks a little dejected now. He's not holding Jane anymore. Jane is smiling slyly at him.

6. TARZAN: I'm sorry I lost control again.
7. JANE: Some friends your family has.
8. TARZAN: You're not upset?

Panel 5
Close on Jane. Smiling slyly.

9. JANE: Part of me wishes I hadn't stopped you from smashing Marchmain to kingdom come. Believe me.

PAGE 22

Panel 1
Jane and Tarzan are getting to their feet, dusting themselves off, and looking up at the ledge above. Weak sunlight filters through the unseen entrance to the cave. Tarzan and Jane have puzzled looks on their faces.

1. JANE: You know, it's strange. For all their bragging about their marksmanship, they didn't hit us even once.
2. JANE: It's almost as if they were... I don't know, *herding* us into this cave.
3. JANE: But why would they do that?

Panel 2
Tarzan is taking Jane by the hand and leading her towards the darkened passage leading deeper into the abandoned mine. He's smiling confidently at her.

4. TARZAN: Well, we're not leaving the way we came, not while they're looking for us. Come on.

Panel 3
Close on Tarzan, peering into the darkened passage leading into the abandoned mine. His eyes are steely, and his facial expression betrays worry, just a little bit. He's in a medium close-up, cut off at the shoulders. Jane is in the background behind him.

This is the final panel of this issue, Dear Artist! Please make it feel like an end beat.

5. TARZAN: Let's see if we can find another way out.
6. CAPTION (narration):   *"A Voice in the Wilderness", next!*

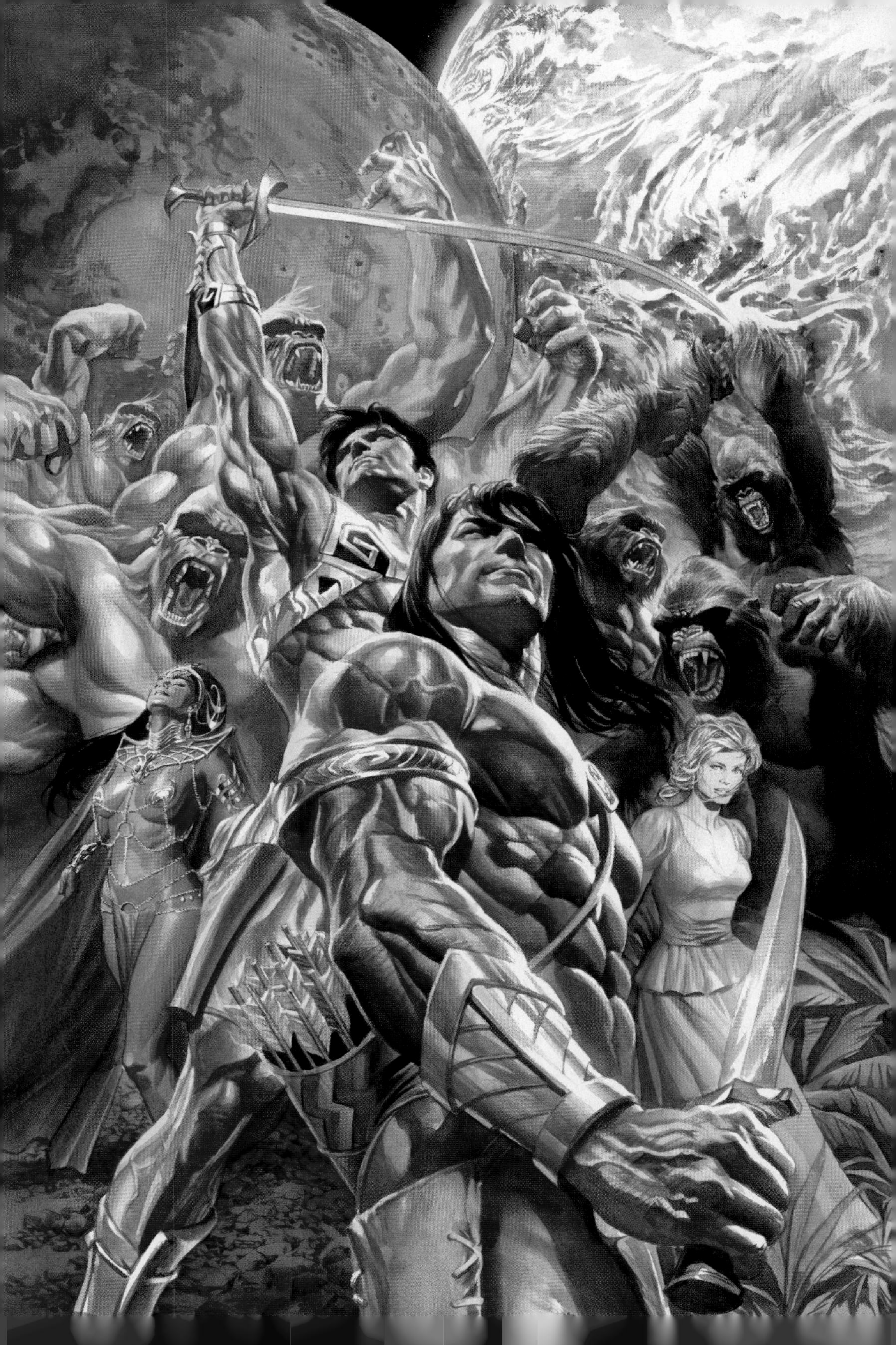

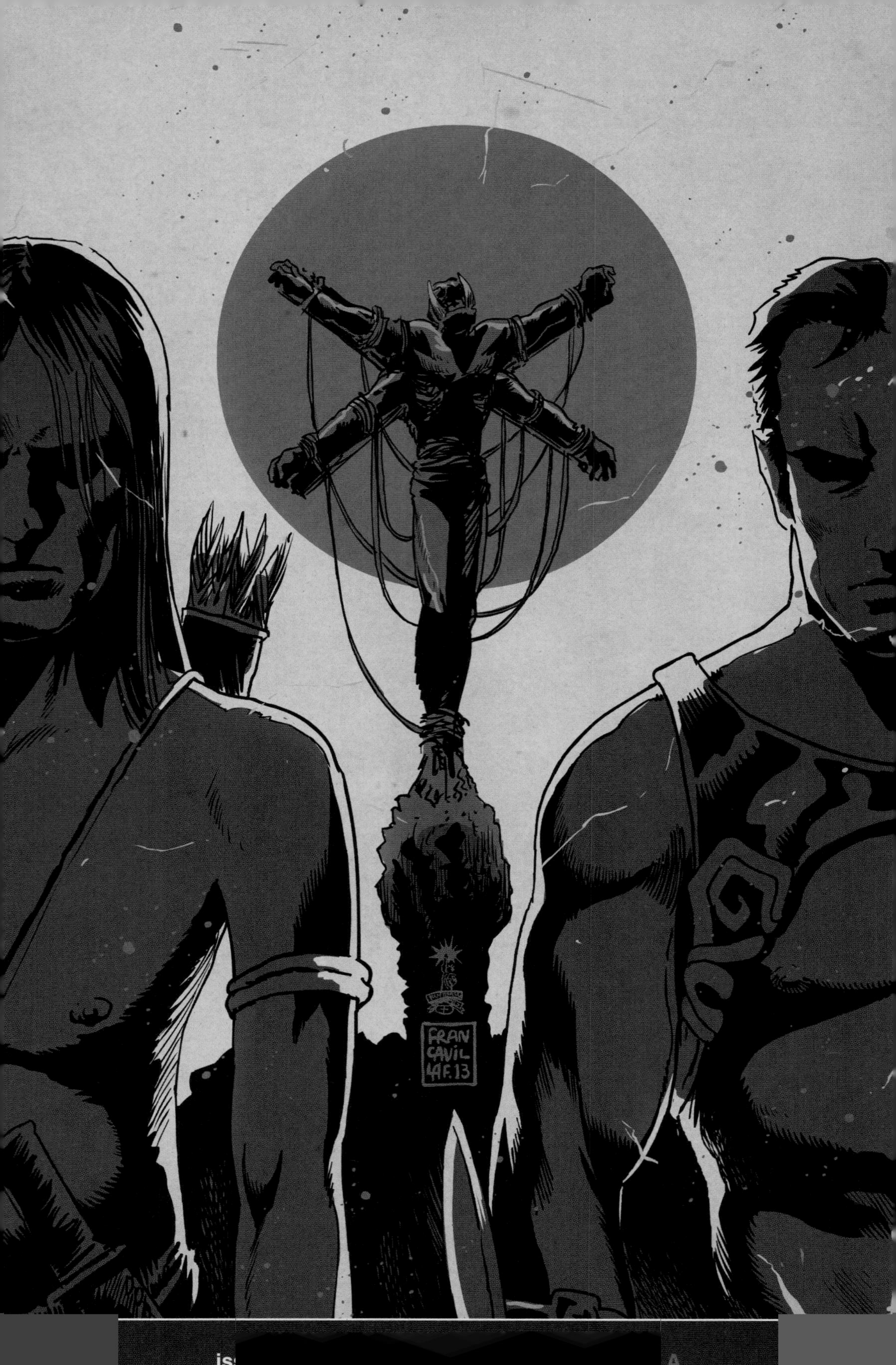
FRAN
CAVIL
LAF.13

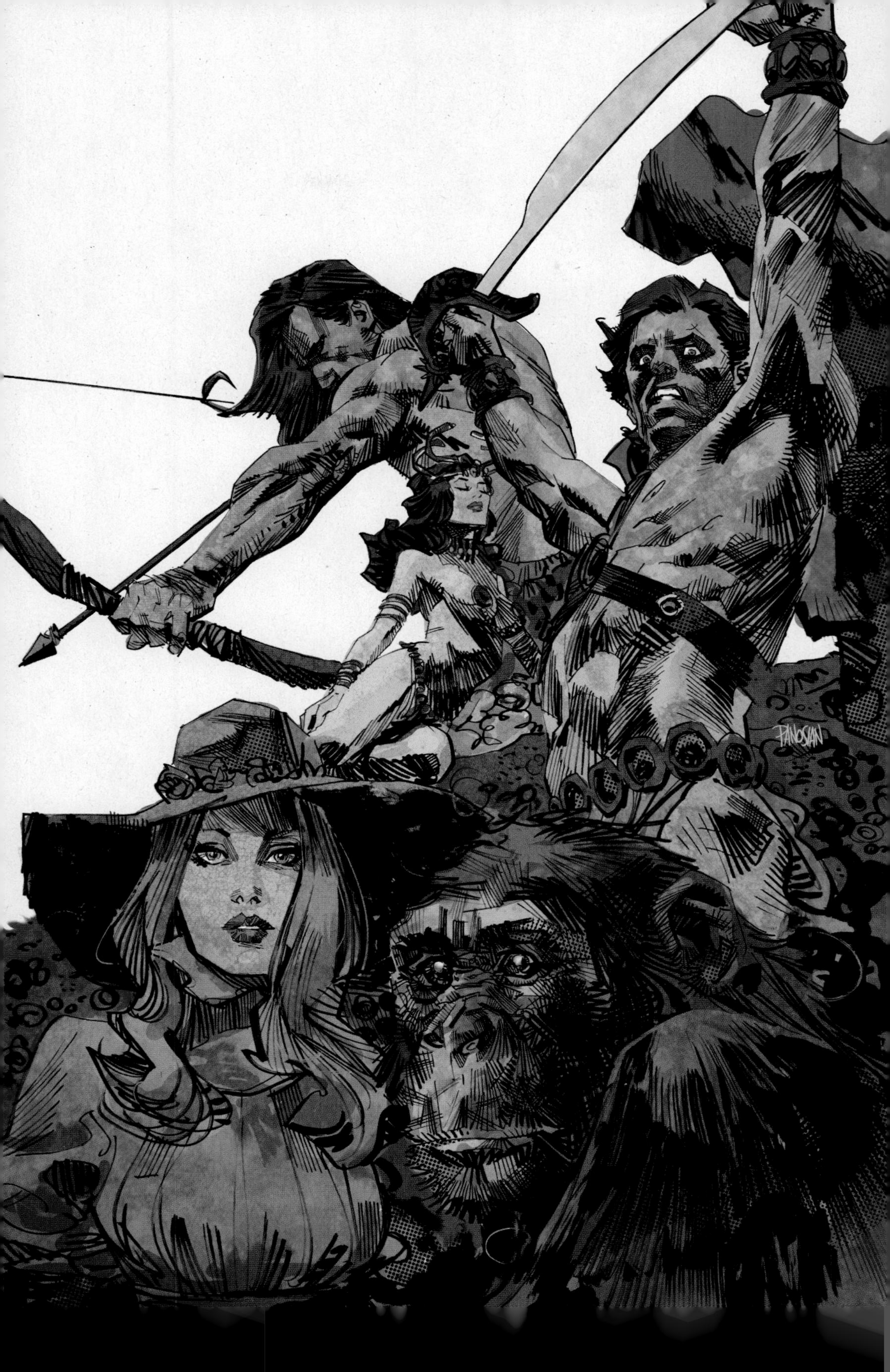
PANOSIAN

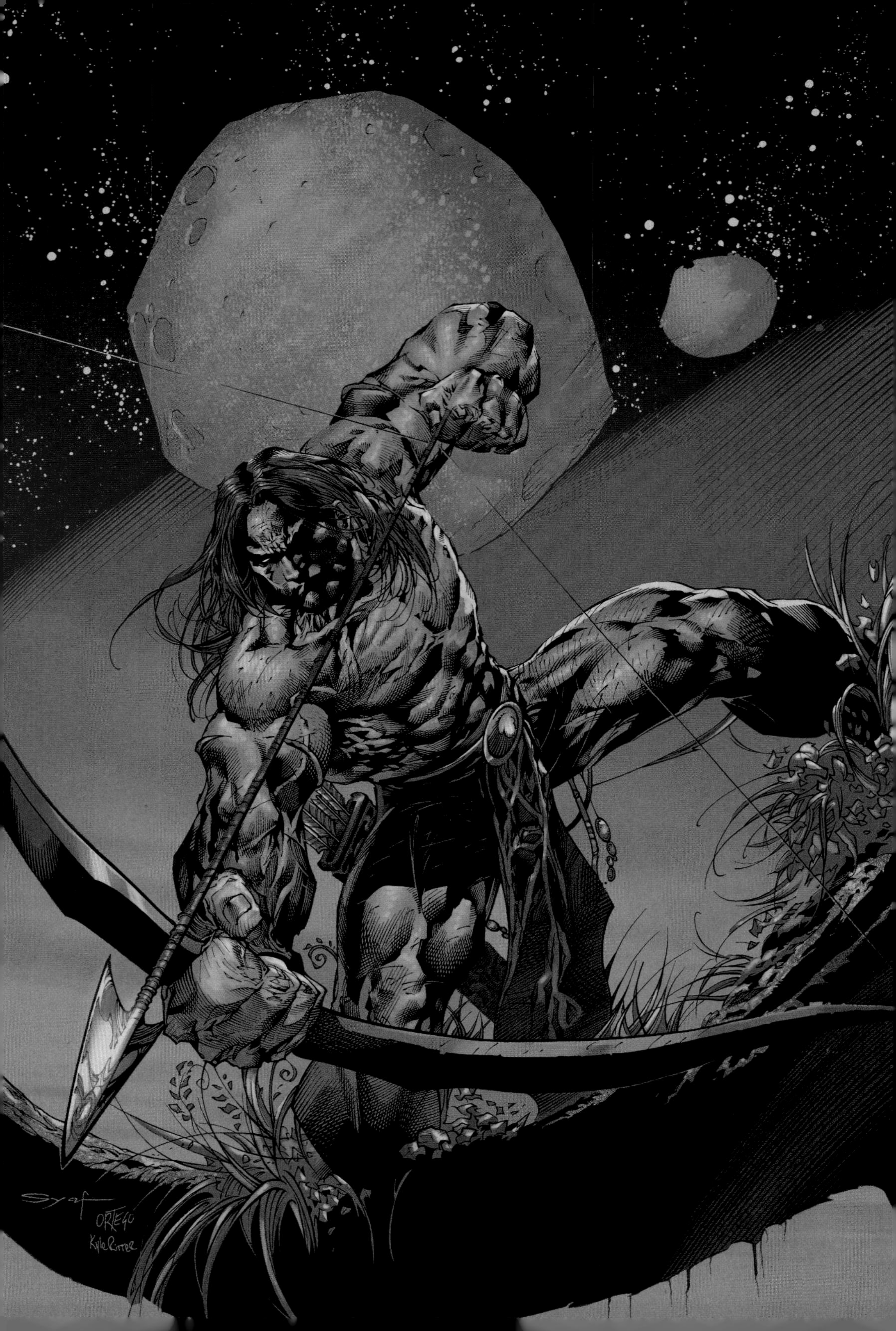
ORTEGO
Kyle Ritter

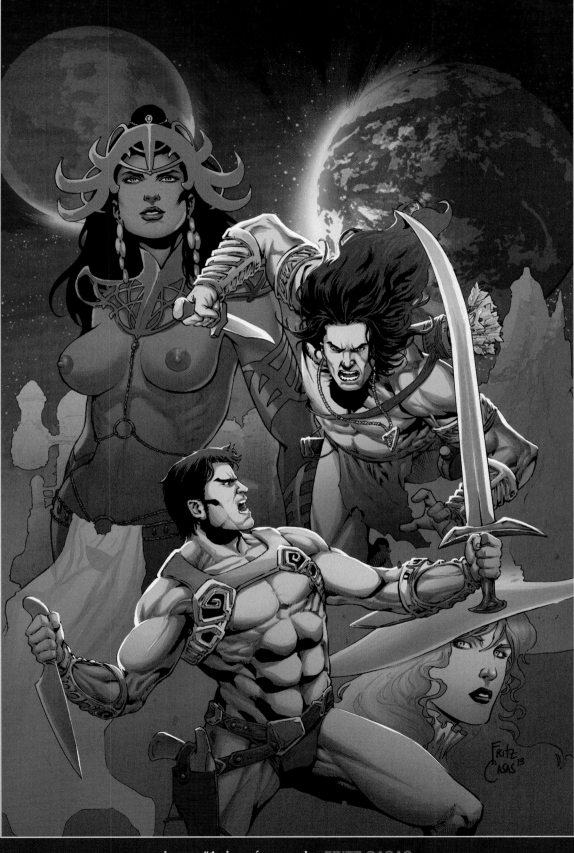

issue #1 risqué cover by **FRITZ CASAS**
colors by **ADRIANO LUCAS**

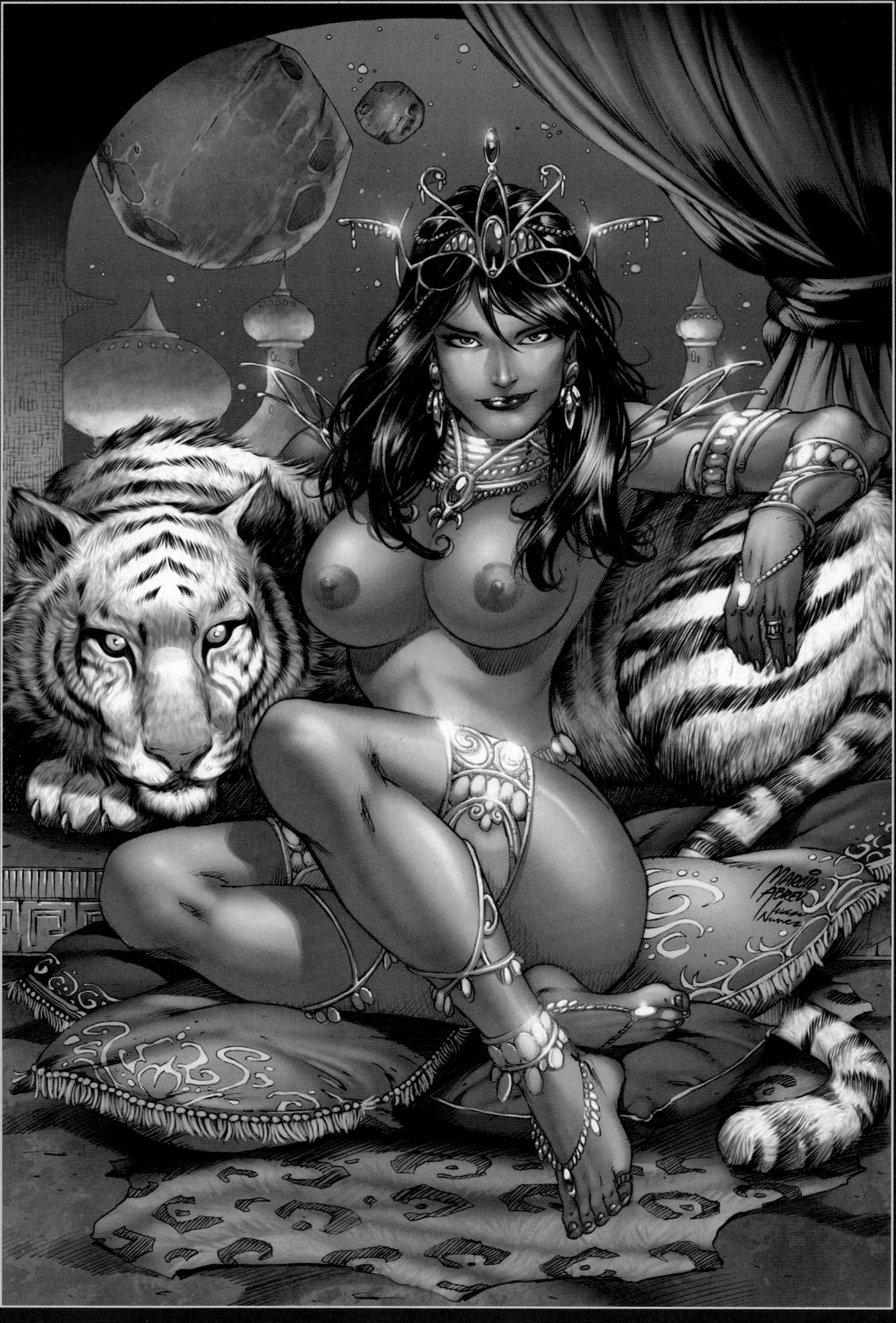
MARCIO ABREU
Ivan Nunes

issue #1 risqué cover by MARCIO ABREU
colors by IVAN NUNES

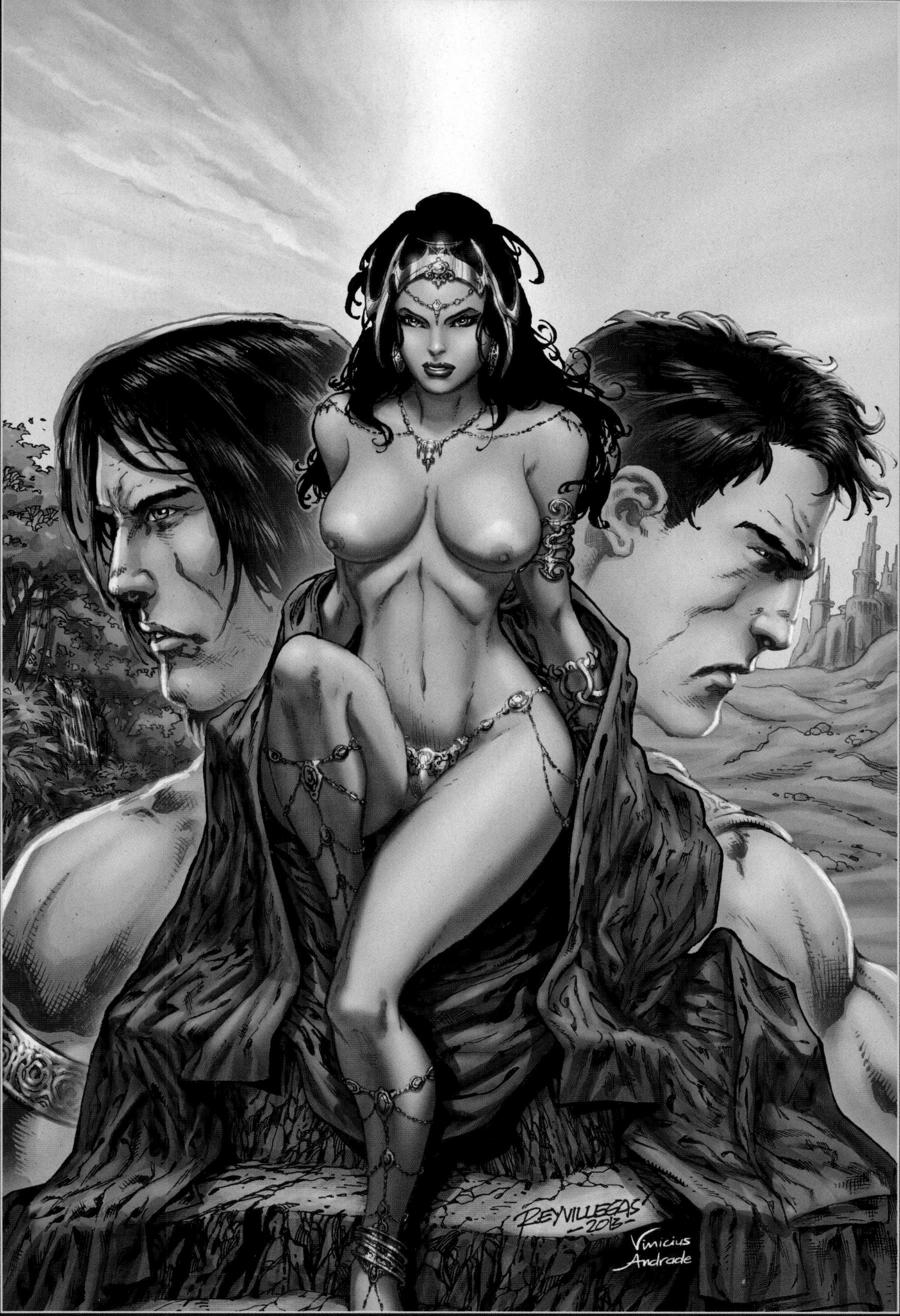
REYVILLEGAS
2013
Vinicius
Andrade

issue #1 risqué cover by REY VILLEGAS
colors by VINICIUS ANDRADE

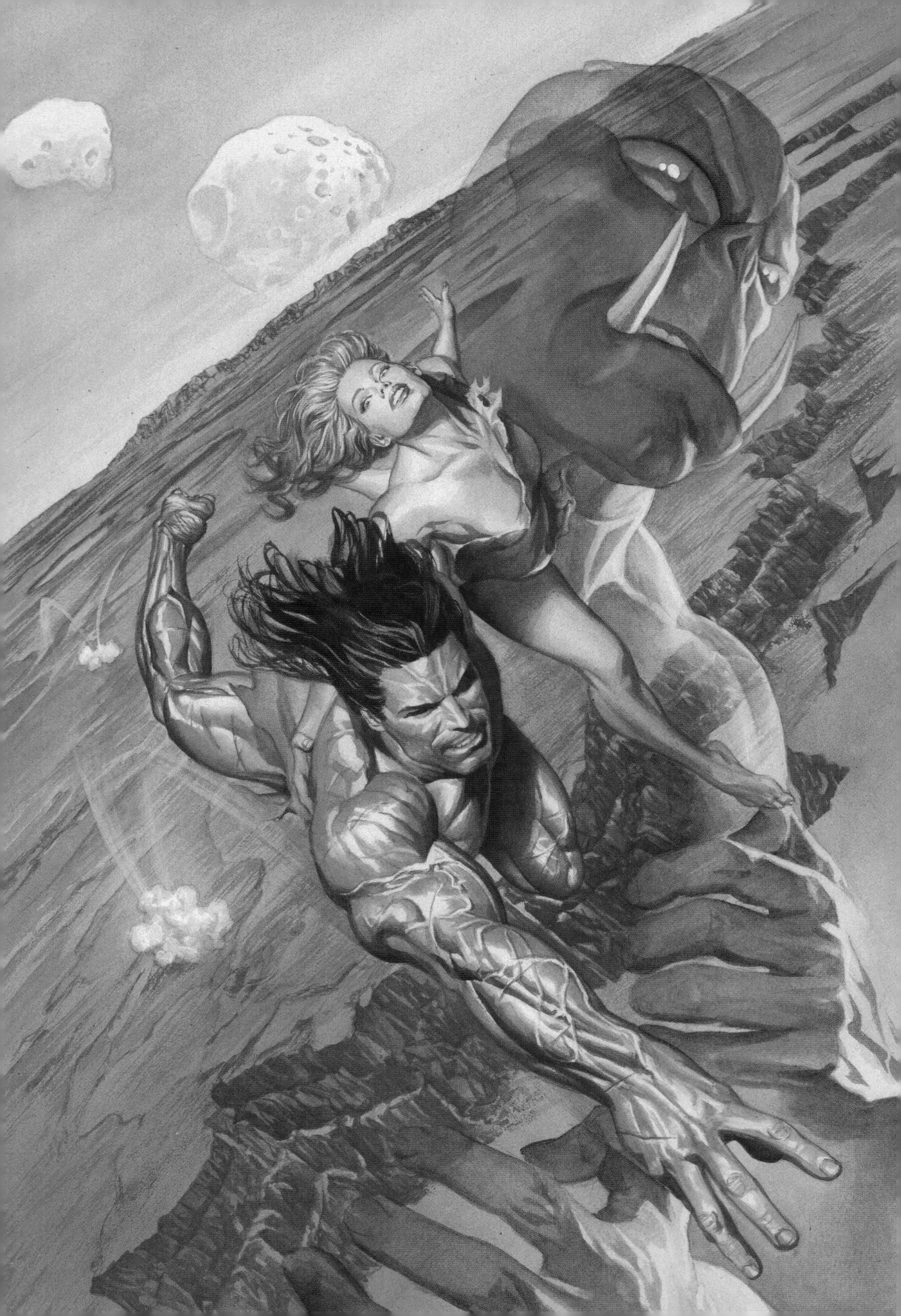

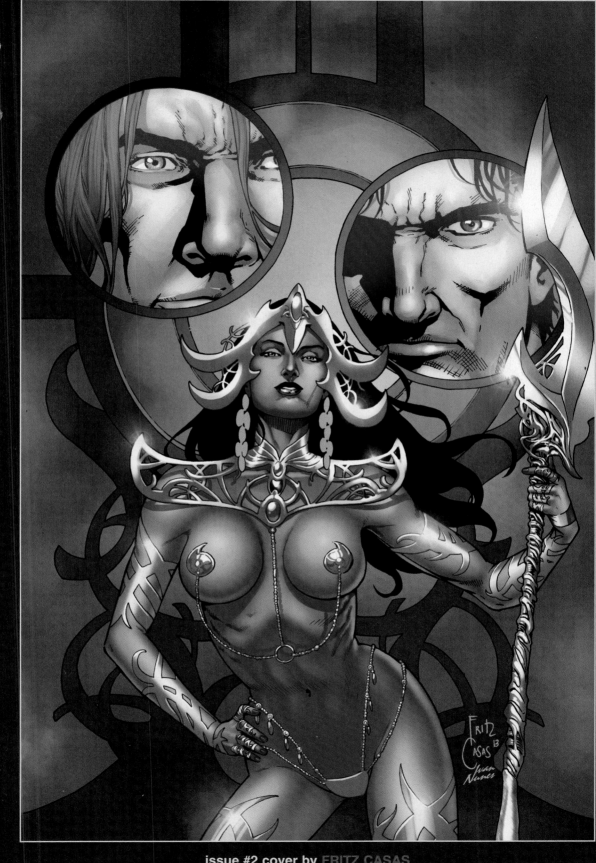

issue #2 cover by FRITZ CASAS
colors by IVAN NUNES

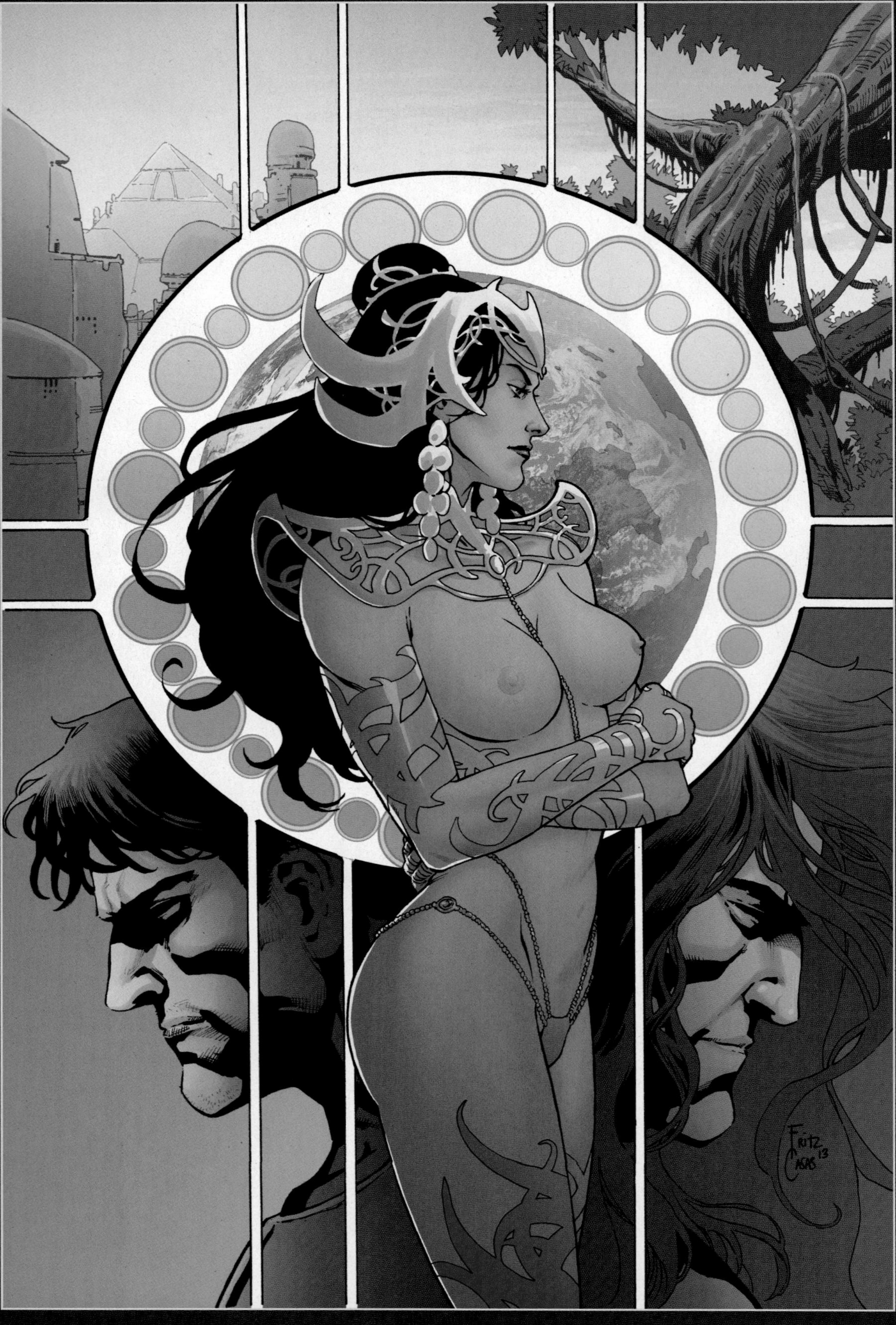

issue #2 risqué cover by FRITZ CASAS
colors by ADRIANO LUCAS

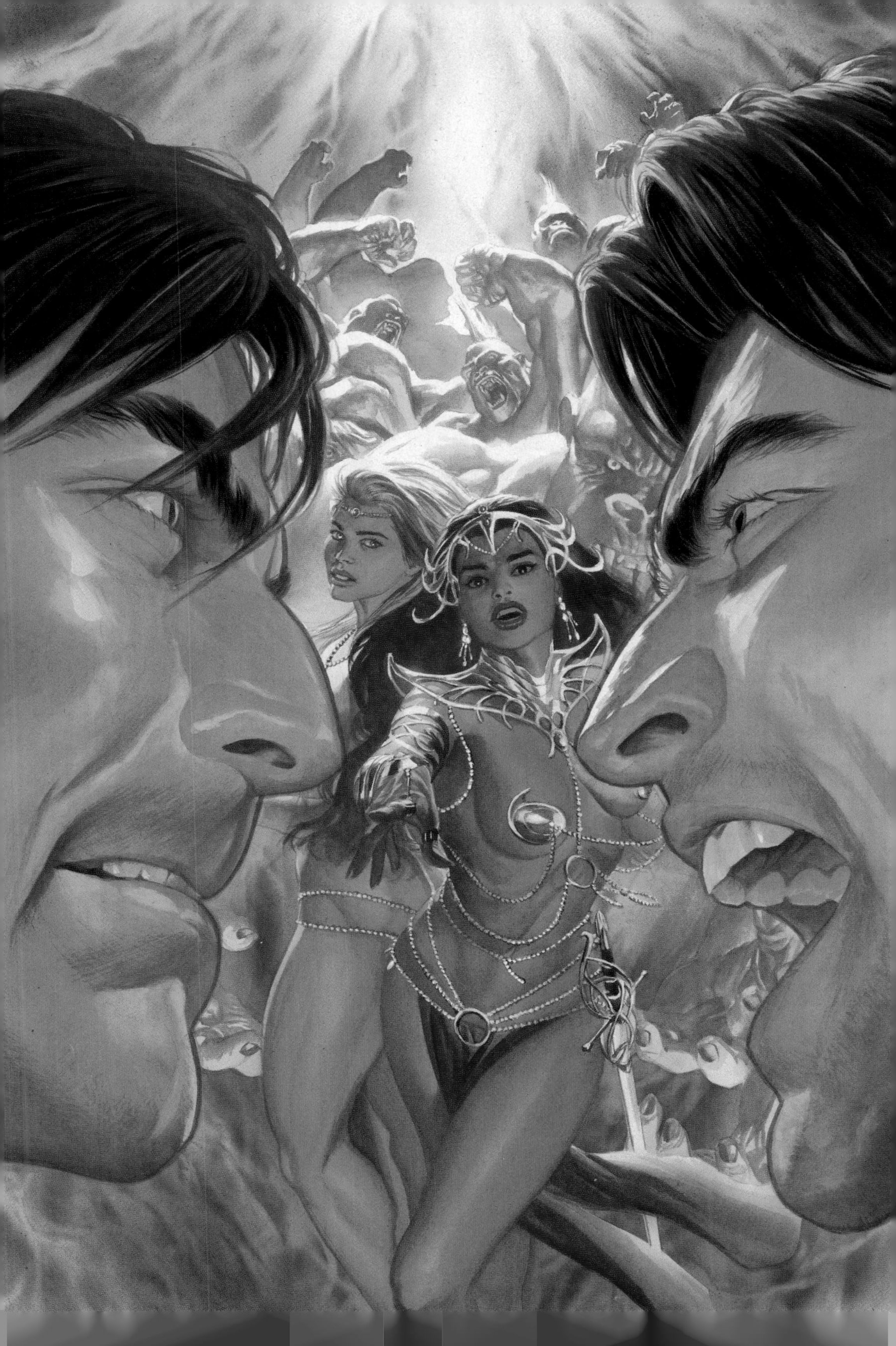

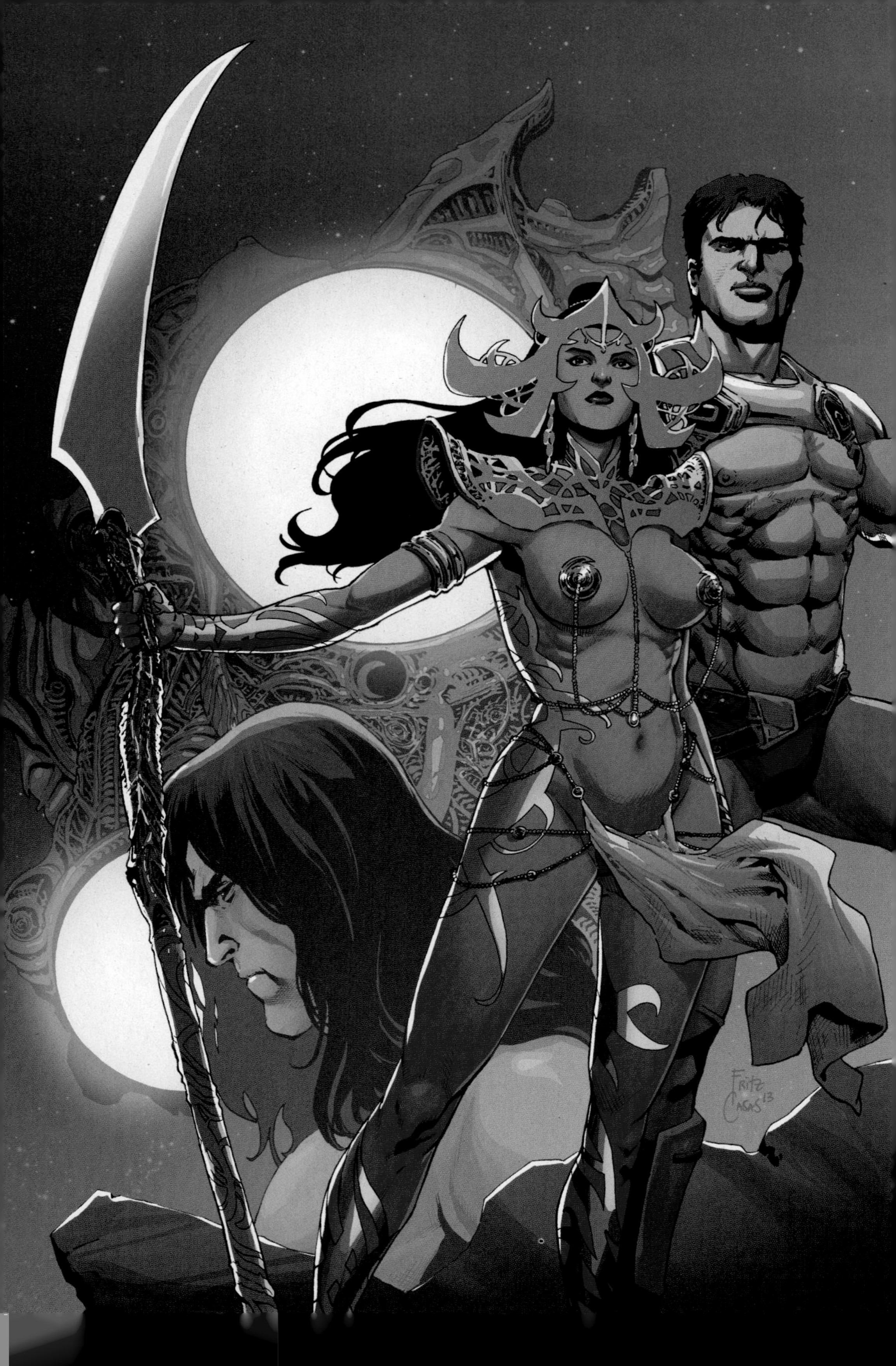
FRITZ CASAS '13

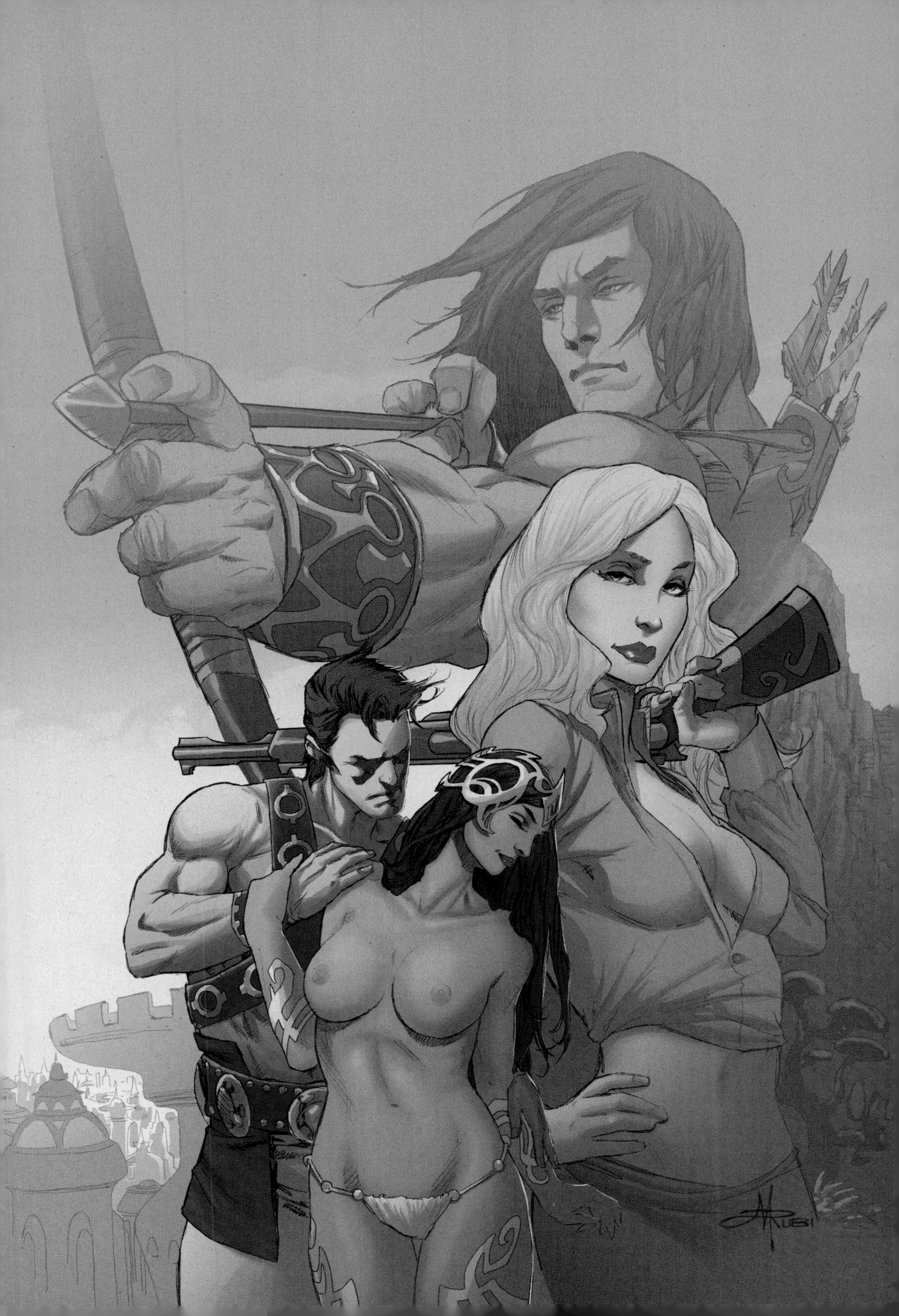

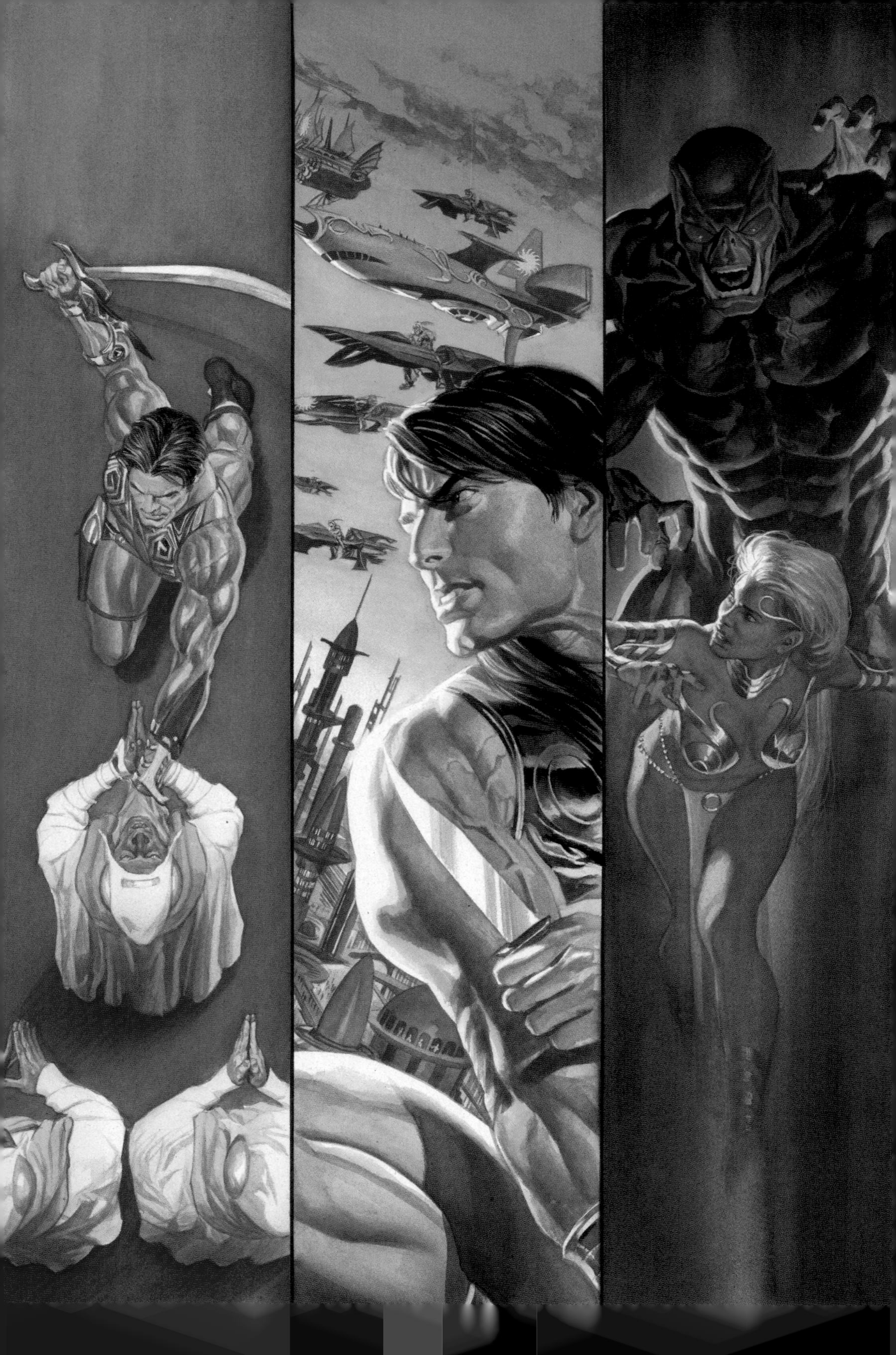

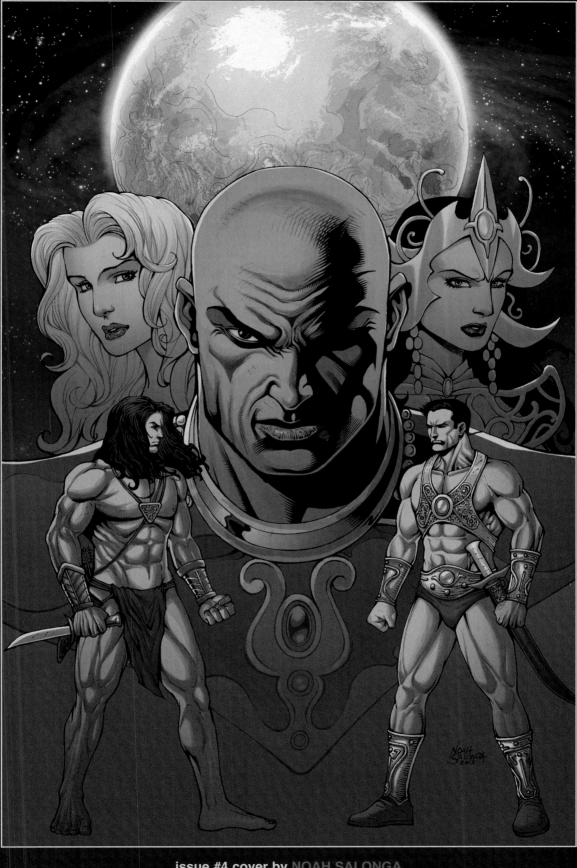

issue #4 cover by NOAH SALONGA
colors by ADRIANO LUCAS

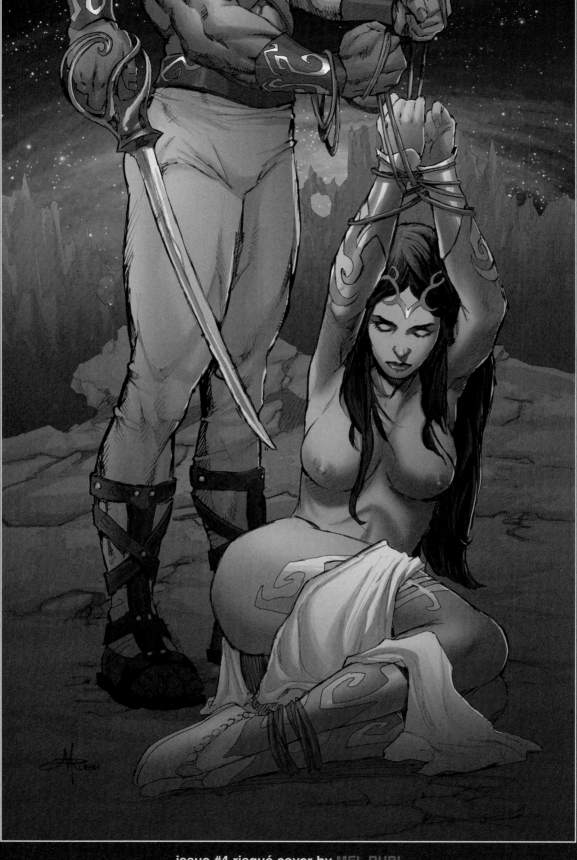

issue #4 risqué cover by MEL RUBI
colors by ADRIANO LUCAS

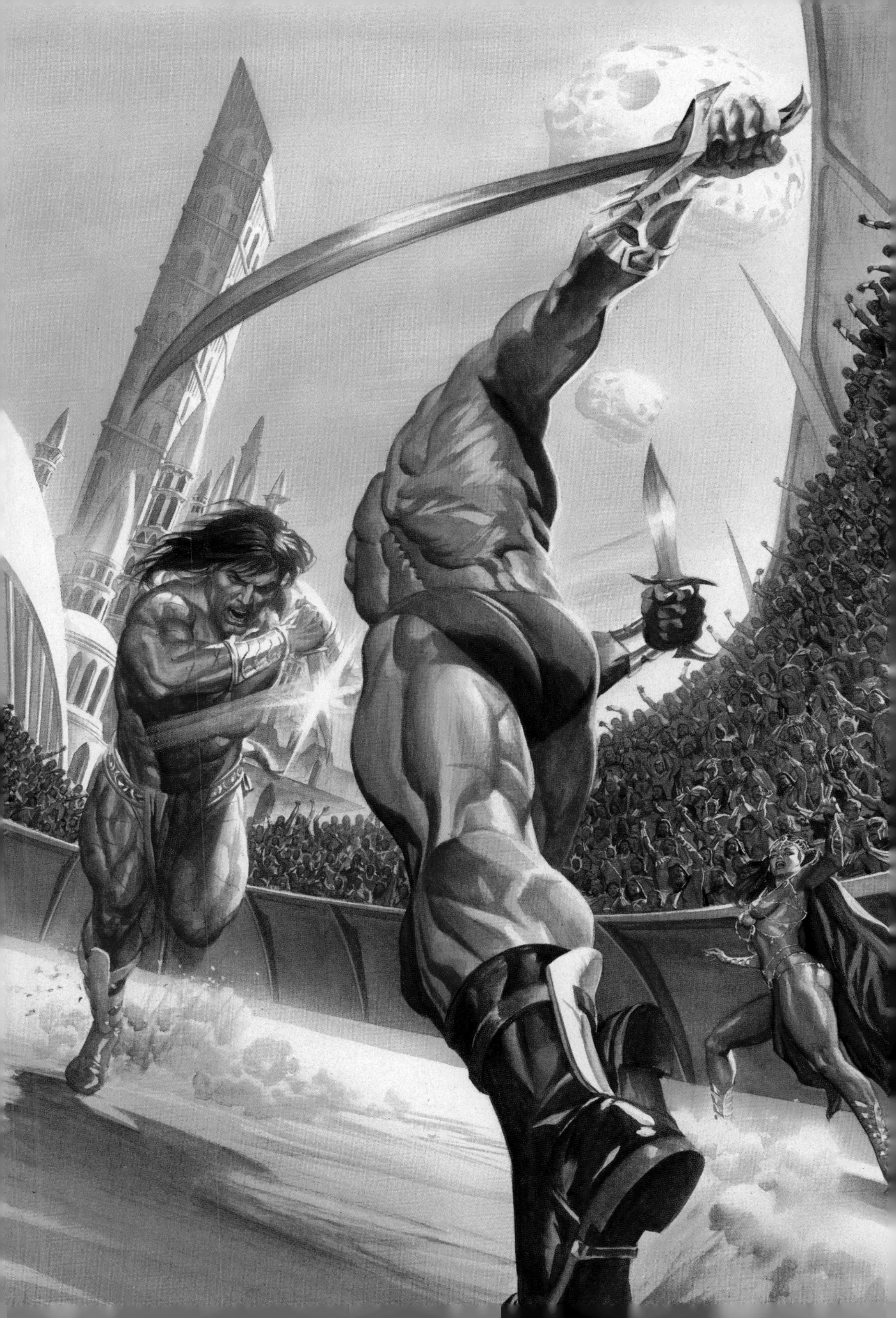

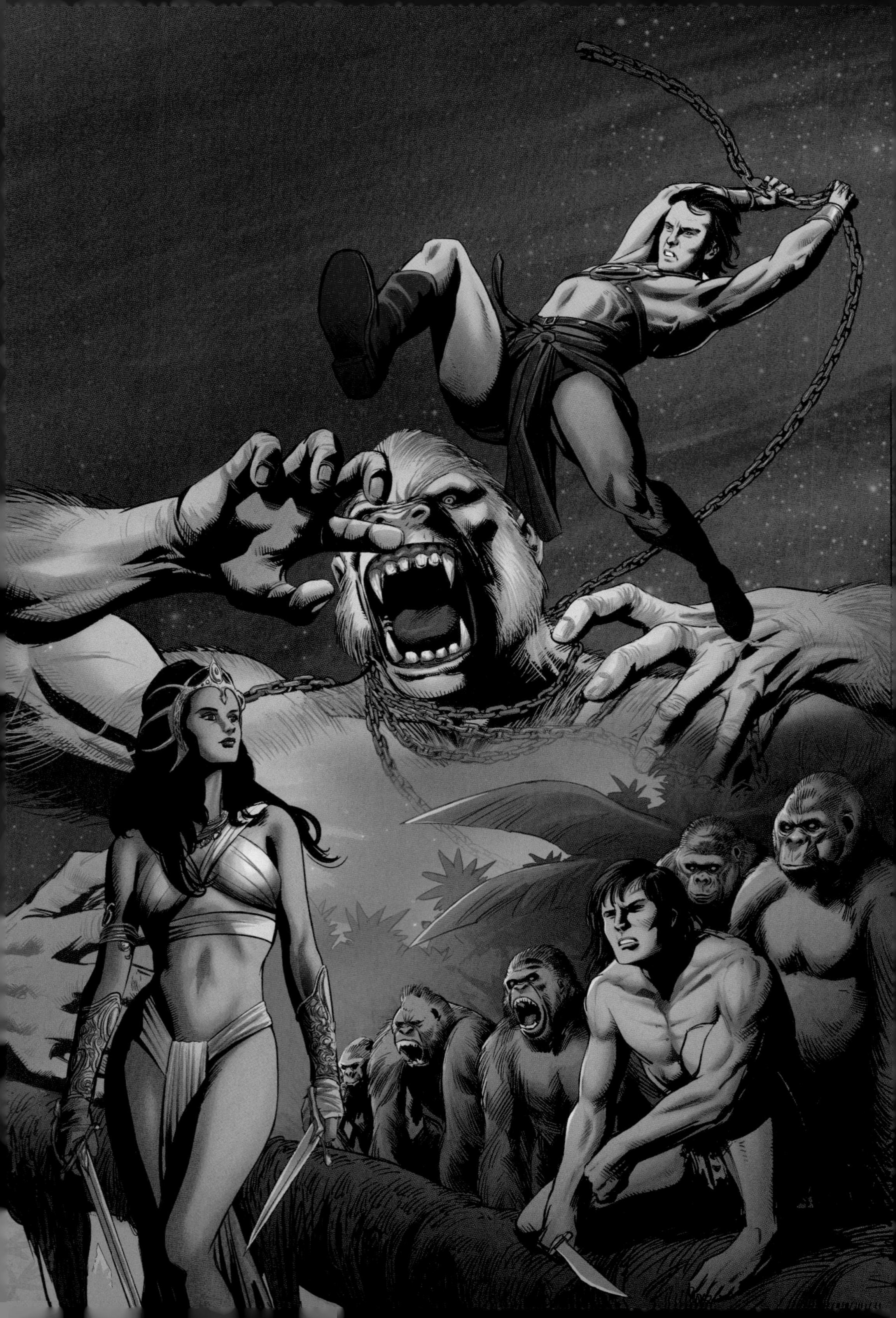

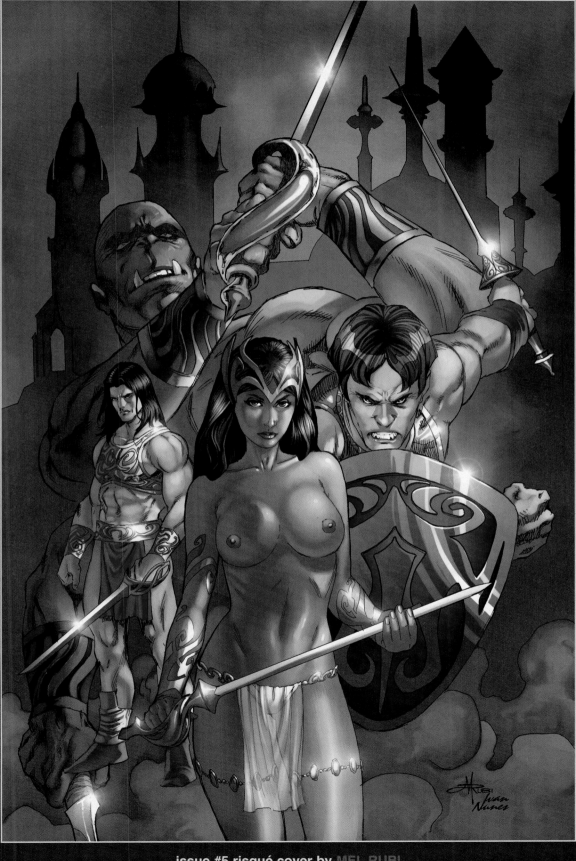

issue #5 risqué cover by MEL RUBI
colors by IVAN NUNES

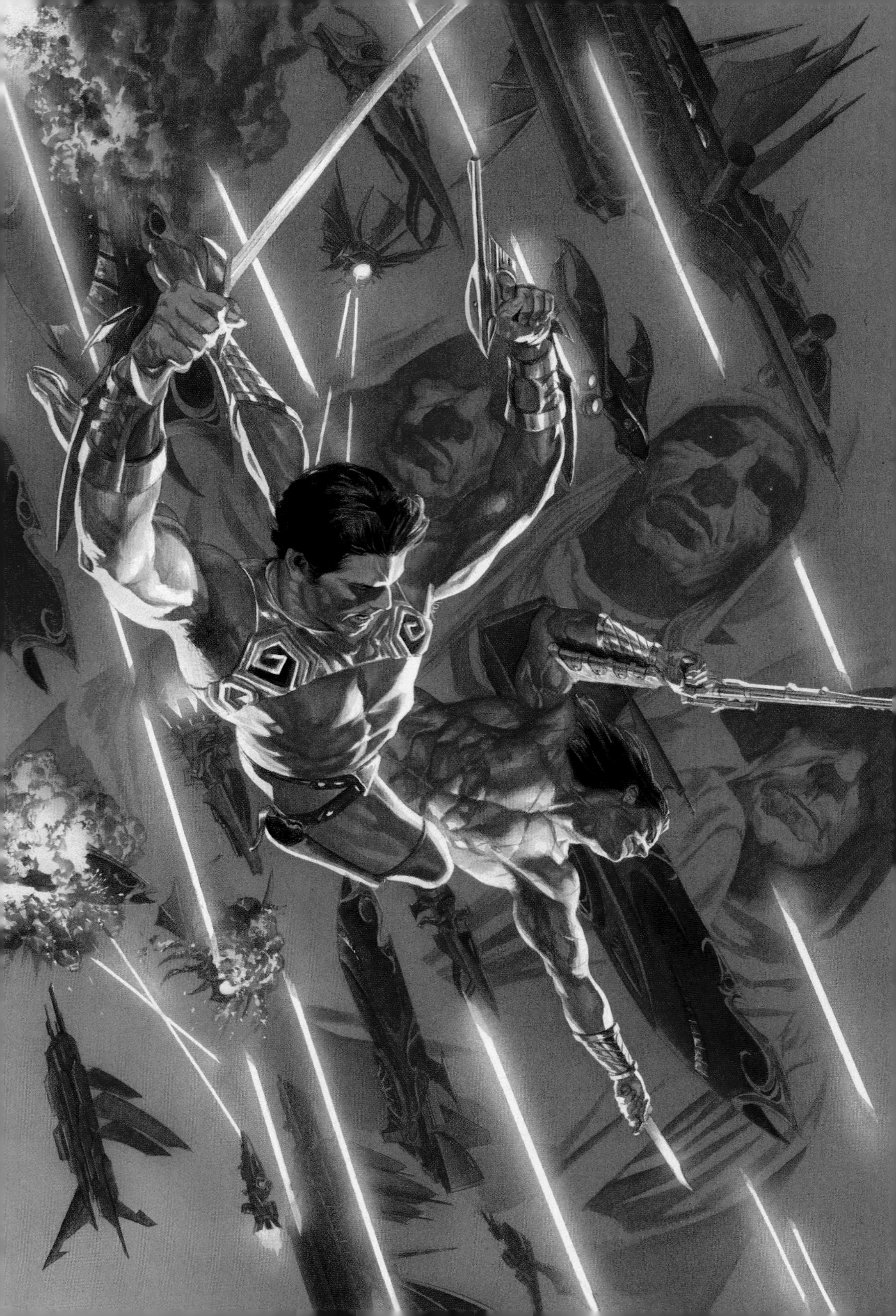

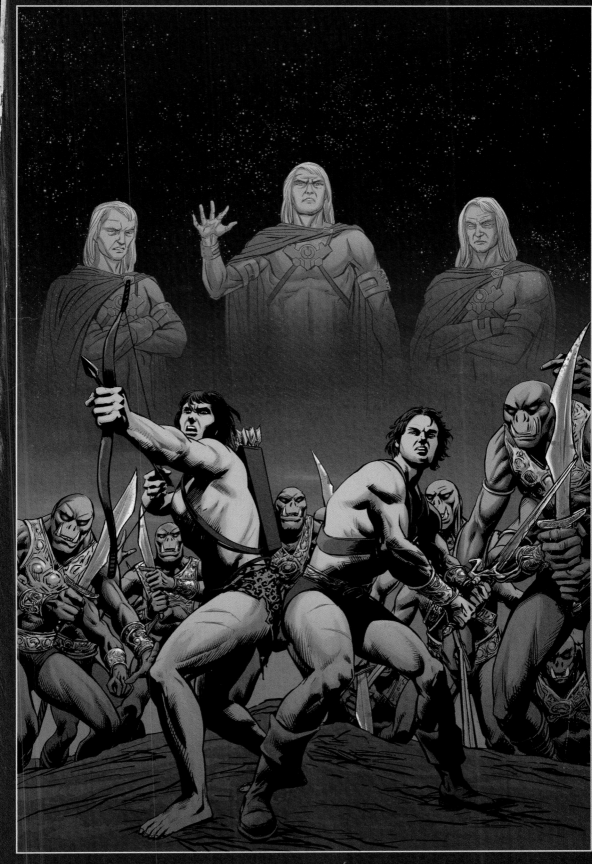

issue #6 cover by JOSÉ MALAGA
colors by ADRIANO LUCAS

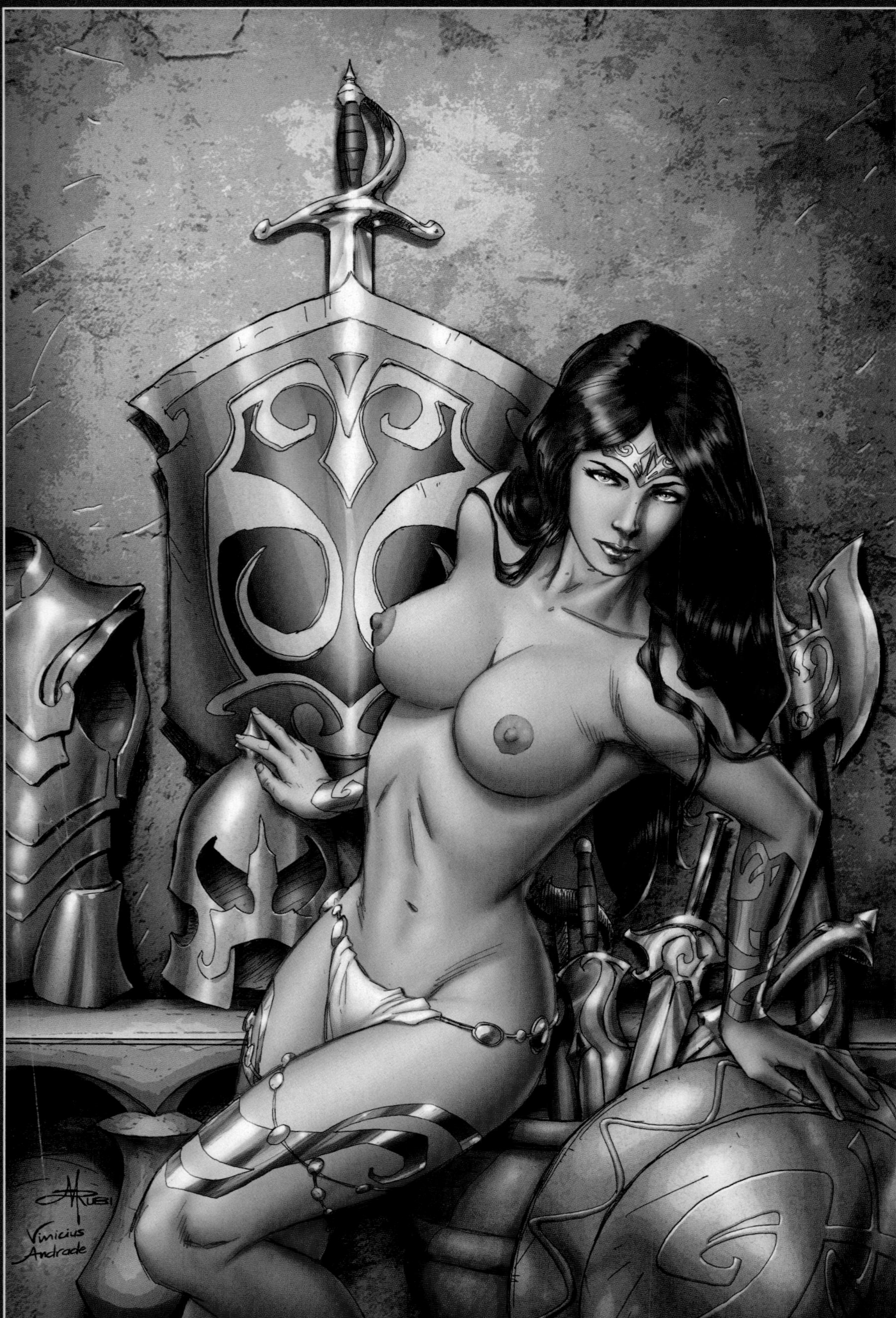
Vinicius
Andrade

issue #6 risqué cover by **MEL RUBI**
colors by VINICIUS ANDRADE